3D Printing in Healthcare

Scrivener Publishing
100 Cummings Center, Suite 541J
Beverly, MA 01915-6106

Publishers at Scrivener
Martin Scrivener (martin@scrivenerpublishing.com)
Phillip Carmical (pcarmical@scrivenerpublishing.com)

3D Printing in Healthcare

Novel Applications

Rishabha Malviya
Department of Pharmacy, School of Medical and Allied Sciences, Galgotias University

and

Rishav Sharma
Department of Pharmacy, School of Medical and Allied Sciences, Galgotias University

Scrivener Publishing

WILEY

This edition first published 2024 by John Wiley & Sons, Inc., 111 River Street, Hoboken, NJ 07030, USA and Scrivener Publishing LLC, 100 Cummings Center, Suite 541J, Beverly, MA 01915, USA

For more information about Scrivener publications please visit www.scrivenerpublishing.com.

Wiley Global Headquarters
111 River Street, Hoboken, NJ 07030, USA

For details of our global editorial offices, customer services, and more information about Wiley products visit us at www.wiley.com.

Library of Congress Cataloging-in-Publication Data

ISBN 978-1-394-23420-2

Cover image: Pixabay.Com
Cover design by Russell Richardson

Set in size of 11pt and Minion Pro by Manila Typesetting Company, Makati, Philippines

Printed in the USA

10 9 8 7 6 5 4 3 2 1

Contents

Foreword

It is a matter of great joy and satisfaction for me to introduce this unique book entitled *3D Printing in Healthcare: Novel Applications,* edited by Dr. Rishabha Malviya and his team. I am excited to explore this exhaustive resource that explains vividly the multidimensional potential of 3D printing technology and its integration into healthcare.

3D printing has transformed into an immense tool that is revolutionizing healthcare. In this book, Dr. Malviya and the co-authors have successfully explained the deep impact of 3D printing on ever-evolving medical research, pharmaceutical development, surgical planning, and personalized medicine.

The book begins with an insightful introduction that provides a historical background for the use of 3D printing in healthcare and illustrates the impressive development of the technology. The subsequent chapters explore various features of 3D printing, highlighting its numerous uses and the potential for transforming patient care and therapeutic approaches.

The chapters on the current advances in the incorporation of 3D printing in medical science provide readers with an exclusive overview of fascinating therapeutic applications, ranging from cardiovascular disease models to tumor simulations. The researchers also submit insightful knowledge about the potential and difficulties of the pharmaceutical industry to prepare them for further investigation.

The extensive discussion of the function of 3D printing in surgical planning is one of the strongest points of this compilation. The development of anatomical models, patient-specific prosthetics, implants, and surgical guidance are discussed in chapters 4 and 5. The authors have skillfully described the benefits, difficulties, and moral issues associated with the application of 3D printing in surgical practice.

The readers will receive a thorough understanding of the effects of 3D printing on medicine delivery systems in the later chapters. Furthermore, chapters 6 and 7 explain various 3D printing methods, along with their applications in medical devices and their regulatory concerns.

The adaptability of 3D printing methods across medical specialties is demonstrated well in chapter 8. The chapter provides an exhaustive account of the future of regenerative medicine by examining the development of organ models, long-lasting implants, and local scaffolds.

Chapters 9 through 14 add to our knowledge about how 3D printing has the potential to revolutionize fields such as hospital management, urology, ophthalmology, and plastic and reconstructive surgery. The book emphasizes aptly the diversity and limitless prospects provided by 3D printing for improving patient care and medical education.

The authors have adroitly organized this harmonious collection of information, masterfully compiling insights into a paragon that will certainly become an integral tool for professionals as well as academicians.

I wish that prospective readers will take advantage of the countless possibilities of 3D printing in healthcare as presented in this book and keep pushing forward into frontiers of knowledge and creativity to blaze a new, transformative path.

Prof. Ranjit Singh
Vice Chancellor
Shobhit University, Gangoh
Saharanpur, UP India

Preface

This book, *3D Printing in Healthcare: Novel Applications*, aims to enlighten readers about the rapidly developing field of 3D printing and its significant effects on the healthcare sector. 3D printing has emerged as an innovation with enormous potential to change how we approach healthcare as technology pushes the frontiers of invention.

In the fields of medicine, pharmaceuticals, surgical planning, and personalized medical treatment, the novel emergence of 3D printing technology has opened a wide range of potential. With personalized solutions that were previously impossible, 3D printing has opened up novel possibilities in patient care, from developing unique medications to manufacturing prosthetics and implants that are particular to each patient.

Chapter 1 introduces the subject and builds the groundwork for study. It delves into the evolution and background of 3D printing, charting its extraordinary path from its inauspicious origins to its current significance in the field of healthcare. Also discussed are the many kinds of 3D printers that are employed in additive manufacturing, as well as how they are modified for usage in medical settings.

Chapter 2 reviews current developments in medical science brought about by 3D printing technology, including the clinical uses of 3D printed models in different medical domains, ranging from cardiovascular illness to tumors, and congenital heart disease.

Chapter 3 explores personalized medicine and the creation of dosage forms utilizing 3D printing methods. It also discusses the benefits and drawbacks of various 3D printing technologies and the applications of these technologies in healthcare, including the creation of immediate-release tablets, capsules, and implants for a range of illnesses.

Chapter 4 explores the possibilities of 3D printed anatomical models for surgical planning, while chapter 5 explores the roles of 3D printing technologies that are used to produce surgical guides, knee implants, spinal implants, and other patient-specific applications.

In chapter 6, our researchers have examined the current developments in 3D printed medication delivery devices. This section also covers regulatory concerns and potential developments in this area.

Chapter 7 explores the field of personalized medicine using 3D printing, and chapter 8 discusses organ models for preoperative diagnostics, permanent non-bioactive implants, local bioactive and biodegradable scaffolds, and direct printing of tissues and organs.

Chapters 9 to 14 explore extensively the different specialized uses of 3D printing in the medical field, covering topics including hospital management and administration, surgical training for urological operations, ophthalmology, and preserving safety and efficacy in point-of-care. Throughout these chapters, readers will find insightful information about the potential of 3D printing to revolutionize each of these sectors.

3D Printing in Healthcare: Novel Applications will be a useful tool for researchers, healthcare professionals, and tech enthusiasts. We encourage researchers to experience the boundless possibilities of 3D printing in revolutionizing healthcare and defining a better future for patient care globally. We are deeply grateful to everyone who helped with this book and greatly appreciate the dedicated support and valuable assistance rendered by Martin Scrivener and the Scrivener Publishing team during its publication.

The Editors

1

Introduction to 3D Printing in Healthcare

Abstract

In this technologically advanced decade, many cutting-edge hybrid applications, innovations, and smart utilities are being developed and implemented all over the world to improve and streamline everyday life. India's young population is a huge draw for these ventures. The healthcare system is increasingly incorporating these technologies into its central operating model. The primary application of 3D printing in the healthcare industry is the creation of prototypes or cells for immediate clinical use. However, their use has enormous potential in Indian healthcare and research. Both current and potential applications of 3D printing in medicine fall into several broad categories. This chapter provides an overview of 3D printing with a wide range of growth potential and brings together researchers from the engineering and healthcare fields.

Keywords: 3D printing, healthcare, 3D-printing revolution engineering, additive manufacturing, healthcare industry

1.1 Introduction

In healthcare, 3D printing has yielded several advancements that, while remarkable now, might seem boring in a few years when even more spectacular breakthroughs are made. Titanium cranial implants have been 3D-printed at Walter Reed Army Medical Center [1], and a woman's jaw was replaced with a 3D-printed prosthesis there as well [1]. In 2013, surgeons used an implant fabricated by the 3D printing company Oxford Performance Materials to replace 75% of a man's skull [2]. After discovering a rare kind of cancer in a man's pelvis, surgeons in the United Kingdom had to replace half of his pelvis [3]. Replacement hip cups have been made and put into tens of thousands of patients [4]. Other pharmacological treatments of 3D printing include the fabrication of bionic ears [5], attractive ears [6], and prosthetic ears. Almost all hearing aid housings are now 3D-printed [7]. In the United States alone, over 17 million

Rishabha Malviya and Rishav Sharma. 3D Printing in Healthcare: Novel Applications, (1–18)

teeth aligner molds are 3D-produced annually [8]. Newborns with life-threatening respiratory issues are being saved nearly routinely by tracheas and tracheal splints created using 3D printing technology [9]. It is not usually high-end, pricey 3D printers that are employed for these kinds of jobs. Surgical tracheal implants have been made using 3D printers and materials available to the general public. Custom scaffolding for a tracheal implant wa being 3D-printed by doctors at the Feinstein Institute for Medical Research using a Maker-Bot machine (about US$2,000) and PLA filament [10]. Using MakerBot machines, biodegradable medical implants made for each patient have been 3D-printed to treat bone infections and cancers [11]. There have been significant 3D printing initiatives focused on the human heart. Sabanci University in Turkey has 3D-printed aortic cells [12]. By 2023 [13], researchers at the University of Louisville hope to have successfully 3D-printed a human heart. Advanced Solutions, located out of Kentucky, plans to employ its bio assembly-Bot printer to pull it off [14]. In 2013, a high school student in California used a 3D printer to create a functional prototype of a patient-specific artificial heart [15]. Washington University in St. Louis is working on a 3D-printed membrane that can be stretched to fit over a patient's current heart like a glove to keep it beating. Built-in sensors identify approaching issues, and electrodes shock out potentially fatal arrhythmias [16]. San Diego, California-based company Organovo is 3D-printing drug-testing tissue and is developing a 3D-printed human liver, both of which have the potential to eliminate the need for the current standard of care and the use of animals to ensure a drug's safety and efficacy before it hits the market [17]. Some scientists are trying to develop drugs that can be printed out in 3D and used locally or at home [18]. Due to the high number of amputees in war-torn countries, such as the Sudan (where there are 50,000) and Uganda, low-cost 3D printers are being employed to create prostheses for these individuals [19]. The United States Army is also interested in applying 3D-printing technology to mitigate some of the negative effects of combat. The army and the University of Nevada are working together on a project to 3D-scan soldiers from head to toe and save the information in case a soldier loses an arm or a leg in a battle. The lightweight, inexpensive 3D-printed hand developed at Oak Ridge National Laboratory has potential applications in robotics, prosthetics, surgery, and the handling of hazardous chemicals [20]. To produce a gripping action, the finger joints receive pressurized fluid from a hydraulic pump driven by an electric motor that is housed in the palm. The fingers open and shut because of a cam driven by an electric motor, which is coupled to two master pistons through five slave pistons. The fingers' hydraulic coupling means they will easily shape themselves to anything they grab. Facial reconstructive surgery has also benefited greatly from the use of 3D printers, including a full-face replacement performed in Belgium [21]. Reconstructing injured nerve tissue with graphene and 3D-printed scaffolds is the focus of research at Michigan Technological University [22]. Surgical guides and models are excellent examples of medical use for 3D printing. Surgeons are now 3D-printing models of a patient's organs to study in advance of the operation. Instead of operating on a live patient, it is preferable to study models to spot anatomical irregularities and plan a course of action [23]. Doctors at Miami Children's Hospital 3D-printed an identical copy of a 4-year-old girl's heart so that they could practice for such a tough operation on the organ. Before functioning on an actual teen's brain, doctors at Boston Children's Hospital practiced on a 3D-printed variant of one. The organs of conjoined twins were successfully 3D-printed and used by surgeons at Texas Children's Hospital to plan and rehearse the separation of the babies [24]. Chinese scientists have used a 3D-printed replica of a human body to practice separating conjoined twins sharing a digestive track. Surgeons used the model to practice cutting through bone joints and skin connections to identify the most effective method for separating newborns. Moreover, 3D-printed models are being employed to train the next generation of neurosurgeons. For medical techniques, such as knee replacement, 3D-printed surgical guidance is invaluable [25]. Software that can transform 2D x-rays into 3D models can be employed to print such instructions. Surgical guidelines and models are increasingly being printed by certain hospitals using 3D printers—for instance, Materialise, a Belgian 3D-printing startup, has set up shop in Fuwai Hospital, China's largest cardiovascular institution. For medical uses, 3D printing appears to be a technology that evolves in waves. Researchers quickly saw the potential for CAD/CAM in the medical area, not long after its initial use in fields like mechanical engineering and design. The first patient-specific implants, such as those used to repair holes in the skull, became accessible just a few short years later. Compositional methods, such as CNC milling, were still in use at the outset, but as time went on, new additive manufacturing (AM) possibilities became popular. Selective laser sintering (SLS) and three-dimensional powder printing (also known as "additive manufacturing") were the most common laser-based techniques utilized for biomedical applications, although they were initially restricted to metals and ceramics, respectively [26]. The emergence of fused-deposition modeling (FDM) as the first advanced manufacturing methodology based on extrusion and using polymeric materials was a crucial first step. FDM of poly(lactic acid) or polycaprolactone has been studied a lot as a way to make porous 3D scaffolds with a certain shape on the outside and inside for use in biological applications like tissue engineering. These polymers were also the earliest examples of AM using biodegradable ingredients [27]. It was possibly due to the inadequate materials that could be utilized (the majority of the initial AM machines could only perform with a minimal number of different materials) and the high expense of the machines. However, things have changed radically since a wide range of inexpensive 3D printers became accessible. Many of these printers can print in several materials, providing the versatility needed for innovations [28]. The ability to directly manufacture artificial tissues was made possible by the development of ink-jet and extrusion-based technologies that allow for the incorporation of living cells in the printing process ("bioprinting"). As a result, the last few years have witnessed a surge in the number of papers on the issue of 3D printing in medicine from academics all over the world as well as the launch of several conferences dedicated specifically to the subject.

These are the current trends that investigators see as having the most momentum:

- New biomaterials that can be used with various AM techniques are being developed.
- Increased cell integration for therapeutically relevant cell-laden structures.
- Production of highly regulated spatial patterns for the assembly of more complex structures, including those made of several materials and/or distinct types of cells.

The private sector has already supplied us with advanced AM machines, many of which are adaptable to a wide range of biomaterials and working circumstances. Most modern extrusion-based devices have various dosing systems, allowing for the application of several materials inside a single scaffold. Combining materials from various classes, such as ceramics and polymers, can provide interesting new features in a structure or be utilized to create a structure that is a good match for a defect at an anatomical interface (where two or more types of tissue meet) [29]. In the past 20 years, the multidisciplinary field of 3D printing in medicine and surgery has grown steadily and quickly, providing a step toward an emerging revolution in precision medicine that is now simpler to realize and put into practice. Three-dimensional printing bridges traditional medical specializations to facilitate individualized care. Recent years have seen a rise in studies aimed at adapting 3D-printing technology for use in medicine. The application of cutting-edge technology like 3D printing has made it possible to provide patients with individualized treatment.

The hopes of doctors, the hypotheses of creative scientists, and the skill of avant-garde doctors all played a part. Researchers should think about using innovative approaches that will aid many patients today and in the future. Conventional preoperative and interoperative models have given way to the 3D printing of personalized implants and regenerative tissue systems. Researchers begin with patient-centered models and utilize them to construct intricate geometries that reflect the form and function of the human body. Researchers from many different scientific and medical fields as well as engineers and physicists work together to further 3D printing's applications in medicine and surgery [30]. When put together, it provides a quick way to profit from the growth of 3D printing beyond the realm of traditional engineering. In a fascinating twist, 3D printing has the potential to be more than a quick fix in the medical field. Creativity, originality, and a willingness to take risks are needed to create a paradigm shift in healthcare delivery. Experts in the field of 3D printing are constantly refining their techniques, and readers will go through them. In addition to cutting-edge, cutting-edge materials are employed as printed substrates. Developing the tools to make science fiction a reality is essential to bringing about a long-term change in the healthcare industry [31]—a time when medical care is tailored to each individual rather than being generic and applied to everyone. There are substantial benefits to be gained in terms of delivering long-term treatment. To become a reality, researchers need to develop 3D-printable applications that make use of high-performance materials. The most promising technique for improving and prolonging human life is 3D bioprinting. Even though the technology is just getting started, its potential is quite promising. Even though 3D printing as a whole is classified as an additive process, as it develops complex things and geometries layer by layer, it is not an additive process in and of itself. The most promising future lies in entrusting the idea to bold and innovative thinkers who will take it to new heights. The addition of increasingly complicated materials to 3D printing yields fascinating and adaptable results, even if polymers remain the primary material [32]. With 3D printing, it is possible to readily personalize medical components without breaking the bank. In a short amount of time, custom-made implants and parts may be produced. Modern polymers allow for the production of lighter and more robust parts. In addition, 3D-printed components with embedded mechanisms may be produced locally. The recent years have seen a paradigm shift toward the creation of individualized medication delivery methods due to additive manufacturing [33] and other technological advancements in the field of dosage form design for improved therapeutic efficacy. When compared to traditional drug delivery methods, the capacity to create individualized medication products with extensive control over the quantity, shape, and size of the dosage form to suit individual patients is a major benefit. Furthermore, manufacturing does not require any such adjustment of the formula or number of parts in advance, whereas traditional manufacturing sometimes necessitates such optimization for batch manufacture. When compared to additive manufacturing, conventional production takes more time, requires more resources, and costs more money. On top of that, instead of using a population-centric strategy, the quick design and development of individualized medication therapy for specific patients are now possible with the use of additive manufacturing technology [34]. In the 1980s, the aerospace, automotive, electronics, and medical device sectors were the first to use additive manufacturing. The pharmaceutical and healthcare sectors, for example, have shown increased interest in the science of additive manufacturing over the past few decades for the creation of a wide range of medicinal items and medical equipment [35]. Nearly three decades ago, in [36], 3D printing was invented as a means of producing complex medical devices and drug delivery systems by the deposition, binding, or polymerization of materials in consecutive layers. Infinite possibilities exist for creating medicine delivery systems tailored to each patient. Medication formulation design may be directly translated from the drug dose provided to a patient based on their age, gender, weight, body surface area, and other physiological characteristics [37]. The versatility of 3D printing allows for the creation of objects of a wide range of geometric shapes and sizes, and the technology also has the added advantages of low manufacturing costs and almost nonexistent variation from one unit to the next. Therefore, 3D printing is helpful in the production of artificial tissues and organs for biomedical purposes as well as the design and manufacture of different drug delivery systems for therapeutic uses. Because of its many uses, 3D printing is increasingly being considered for use in mass production, and there has been an uptick in efforts to develop more adaptable and reliable approaches to printing using the technology [38]. The first 3D-printed medicine, Spritam® (levetiracetam), was granted FDA approval on August 3, 2015 to treat provisional, myoclonic, or generalizable tonic–clonic seizures. The dosage form was an orodispersible tablet, created and patented by Aprecia Pharmaceuticals of the United States and distributed under the ZipDose® technology platform. 3D printing makes it possible to make a highly flexible composition with a drug loading capacity of up to 1,000 mg per dose, with the option of personalized distribution based on the patient's requirement and at a significantly reduced cost compared to traditional production methods [39]. Figure 1.1 summarizes a schematic depiction of the aforementioned standard 3D-printing procedure.

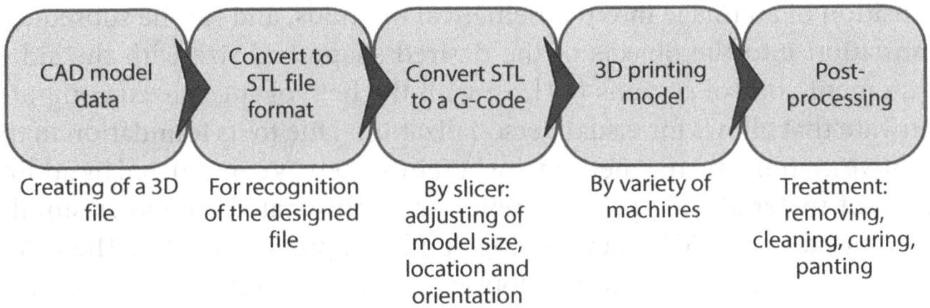

Figure 1.1 Common stages in 3D-printed format.

1.2 The Revolutionary Rise of 3D Printing Technology

In the 1980s, a group of scientists at the Massachusetts Institute of Technology in Boston, United States, led by Emanuel Sachs, developed the first functional 3D printer. 3D printing has followed the guidelines of binder jet technology [40], which entails first depositing a layer of powder and then spraying the solidified areas with a liquid binder. Several adjustments to the underlying science of 3D printing were later made to facilitate the creation of items with great process efficiency for a wide range of uses. Additional developments were made to enhance the effective use of materials, allowing for more adaptability and precision in the creation of items. In 1986, computer-aided drawing techniques and programs were merged with the method of "3D printing," in which materials are stacked onto a substrate to produce an item with three dimensions. In an x–y plane, the technique is similar to that employed to adhere to printed material [41]. To print the complete item to the desired thickness, the printer must travel along with the z-axis. By carefully adjusting the nozzle geometry and motion, an approach may be used to print objects of varied sizes and shapes. Additive manufacturing relies heavily on 3D printing, rapid prototyping, and scaling up applications [42].

1.3 3D Printing Revolution Engineering

Although printers first started making flat items in the 1970s and 1980s, they used simple processes including casting, molding, shaping, joining, and processing [43]. Researchers have developed a wide variety of novel ways to process 3D printing. Many different methods have been developed for the layout and customization options of 3D geometries, for the transition of an image into mathematical methods, and for the subsequent translation into the objects of the desired shape and size with the aid of equipment control systems [44], all with the help of specialized computer software that allows for visual personalization. Due to its foundation in the additive manufacturing method—wherein an item is constructed by adding layers of material—3D printing relies on sophisticated computer simulations based on the 3D's methodology outlined previously [45]. The three-pronged strategy of design, development, and distribution is important to the practice of effective tailored medicine therapy. Computer-simulated or CAD-designed models of the objects of interest are used to prepare the artwork in the preceding three stages of production. The printer examines the file the program generates, deciphers the command, and constructs the 3D-printed item or therapeutic items, which are then sent directly to the client or patients. There are several kinds of 3D printing used in fields like drug distribution and biomedicine. Some of the most well-known techniques are stereolithography (SLA), selective laser sintering (SLS), semi-solid extrusion (SSE), and binder jet printing (BJP) [46]. Emanuel Sachs is credited with developing the BJP method, which has been characterized as the "first generation" of 3D printing. This technique requires first laying down a powder layer but instead dumping the adhesive on top of it to harden it into the desired form. The printer creates items by depositing material layer by layer, just like in traditional inkjet printing (IJP). S. Scott Crump invented SEM as a second-generation 3D-printing method in 1989 (patent 5121329 was granted in 1992). Extrusion is the technique through which a substance is produced. The materials for 3D printing are typically melted or mixed into a slurry before being extruded through a nozzle to form the desired 3D shapes. Molding items from liquid plastic or metal by forcing them through a nozzle is another possible use of the method. Aside from the additive manufacturing process, FDM is another common method of 3D printing. The term "fused filament manufacturing" describes another name for this process. The thermoplastic filament is heated and passed between rollers to create the 3D objects, which are then extruded through a nozzle. The objects' three-dimensional geometry is modeled in CAD software before being printed in a filament, one layer at a time. Michael Feygin invented sheet lamination (SLM), commonly known as laminated item production (patent 4752352 submitted in 1987, granted in 1988). This process utilizes a high-powered laser beam to vaporize many layers of material before revealing the desired three-dimensional form, making it possible to fabricate objects from a variety of materials. Direct energy deposition (DED) and powder bed fusion (PBF) are the final two techniques for creating three-dimensional structures, and they are identical in that they both utilize a high energy flow on a powder bed of building material to create the required items. There are several different 3D-printing techniques now in use, each with its own set of pros and cons. Strong mechanical durability, biocompatibility, and human safety are necessities in the pharmaceutical industry. Furthermore, the additive manufacturing building materials employed are crucial to a successful printing process [47].

1.4 3D Printer Types for Additive Manufacturing

To create an item with the specified geometrical and functional properties, 3D printers are utilized to supply external energy in the form of casting, thermal ablation, or laser energy. The techniques of additive manufacturing, which will be discussed further on, serve as the basis for the creation of commercially available printers. As stated in [19, 20], speed, efficiency, and cost-effectiveness in printing are the most important factors to consider when choosing a 3D printer for routine use and commercial usage. As an additional need, the commercial manufacturing of printed products needs access to scaled models of 3D printers. Only FDM, SLA, SLS, and PBD-based 3D printers are now commercially accessible for use in the pharmaceutical industry, and these printers come in a range of maximum capacity configurations.

1.5 3D Printing in the Healthcare Industry

Since 3D printing eliminates the need for human intervention, it can boost production efficiency while decreasing the cost and number of flaws in manufactured goods [17]. 3D printing shifted not only the focus of industrial automation but also the nature of industrial production due to its versatility and ability to change and manufacture a wide range of geometries. Rapid advances in 3D-printing technology are reshaping the pharmaceutical industry by allowing manufacturers to produce more consistent medicinal items of higher quality [7, 11]. This is especially true in biopharmaceutical product development, which relies on creating pharmaceuticals using traditional manufacturing procedures. The field of biomedical engineering, which focuses on the development of surgical and diagnostic medical tools, has also profited from 3D printing. This chapter is an updated version of earlier reviews [21] on the use of 3D printing in the development of pharmaceutical products and other biological applications.

1.6 Early-Phase Drug Development

It is important to create a workable formulation of the active component in the first stages of drug development so that clinical safety and effectiveness studies may be conducted. To formulate a dosage form for assessing the therapeutic effects of the new medicine, one must first conduct a comprehensive examination of the physiochemical characteristics of the active ingredient. Early in the medication development process, 3D printing may be employed to construct dosage forms with less overhead [12, 22]. However, it enables the fast printing of pharmaceutical formulations with high dose flexibility and bioavailability characteristics, which have been necessary for formulations designed for various patient groups in various geographic regions and for achieving the different requirements of clinical sites to expedite the progression of clinical studies within constrained time frames. Traditional manufacturing methods do not offer these advantages since they require more time and money to complete extensive preformulation studies to improve and scale up the process before making the dosage forms [13, 14].

1.7 Customized Drugs

Although 3D printing can create unique medications for specific patient populations, it allows for more individualized and effective treatment plans. As a result, 3D printing has great potential as a therapeutic solution for the treatment of complicated disorders, including epilepsy, Alzheimer's disease, and cancer, in both young and old patients [48]. The goal of customized treatment is to optimize pharmacokinetic and pharmacodynamic responses by administering the optimal dose at the optimal time for each patient. In addition to a patient's genetic composition, gender, age, and weight are taken into account during dose titration and formulation of the dosage forms in this type of therapy. In contrast, the bulk of the patient population can only be served by conventional dose forms since they are based only on set strengths. Also, 3D printing allows for on-site fabrication, whereas traditional treatment typically requires setting up a whole manufacturing set-up with high-end machinery. Therefore, 3D printing has the potential to shift therapy away from a population-based focus and toward a more individualized one [49].

1.8 Advanced Pharmacological Treatments

Advanced dosage forms including numerous doses of narrow therapeutic index medications to assist long-acting pharmacological therapy may benefit from 3D printing. Patients using standard dose forms typically need to take numerous tablets for one illness indication to keep the medication levels in the blood for longer periods for the intended therapeutic activity [50]. Reduced patient compliance, missed doses leading to blood level changes, and high expenditures are only some of the disadvantages of this method. 3D printing instead allows for the creation of polypills that can contain several dosages of a medicine or other substances [51]. Therefore, the 3D-printing method of medicine distribution is highly advantageous for various conditions where polypills are indicated for patients, including asthma, cancer, cardiovascular disorders, tuberculosis, and epilepsy.

1.9 Community Medicine

Community medicine or the cultivation of self-reliant medicinal practices within a community is gaining traction. It would be especially helpful in places where there is a shortage of medical personnel. The 3D-printing method can help establish important milestones in the development of community healthcare delivery. Patients can tailor their dose needs to meet their illness requirements [52] rather than depending solely on the advice of healthcare providers. Drugs can be printed using personal 3D-printing equipment at the community pharmacy level or even at home with the help of specialized software that generates the data given by the patient. This method might be used in regions in need, such as outlying communities, military bases, and locations dealing with natural disasters. A few of the benefits of this strategy include less need for doctors and nurses, less medication waste, and simpler medication availability.

1.10 Clinical Pharmacy Practice

The 3D-printing method has applications in clinical pharmacy practice, just like it does in community medicine. Patients often visit a dispenser (chemist or pharmacist) with prescriptions given by their doctor to receive the final dosage forms [26]. Using the doctor's instructions and 3D-printing technology, a contemporary pharmacist might have the drug ready in an individual dose within minutes. Medication scarcity might be avoided, and individualized pharmacological therapy could be implemented more easily into standard clinical practice [16, 27].

1.11 3D Printing Process and Product Variable Optimization

There are still certain obstacles to overcome in 3D printing despite the many advancements and automation that have been made in the field. Due to the large array of printers based on various printing processes, it is crucial to have a comprehensive awareness of the factors that need altering for optimal 3D printing to manufacture high-quality dosage forms with adequate durability, safety, and effectiveness [28]. As an added note, the ability to create and maintain 3D printers is crucial for the creation of tailored pharmaceuticals [53, 54]. Producing 3D-printed items also requires a solid grounding in polymer chemistry and excipient characterization.

1.12 Recent Trends in 3D Printing Regulation

In 2015, the Food and Drug Administration (FDA) authorized the first 3D-printing product, providing a major boost to the industry and encouraging biopharmaceutical manufacturers to utilize 3D printing as a cutting-edge technique in the creation of new pharmaceuticals and biomedical equipment [30–35]. The FDA published Technological Considerations for Additive Manufacturing of Medical Devices in December 2017 in answer to the need to "provide significant policy insights, the operating mindset of the agency, as well as key chemistry, manufacturing, and control necessities for the approval of 3D-printed drug products and medicines" [36]. In contrast, there are still a lot of unknowns when it comes to printer specs and formulation quality control requirements for dosage form development. There is a wide variety of printers available today, each with its own set of technological criteria (OS compatibility, hardware specifications, print speed, and print quality), manufacturer's ethos, and price point. As a result, there is a wide range in the quality of dosage forms made with these machines. As a result, designers employ a QbD methodology to guarantee that the final product is consistently of high quality. Critical material attributes (CMAs), critical process parameters (CPPs), or diagnostic parameters utilized throughout the manufacturing process and in the inspection of the final product are all given special attention in this approach to quality control. In addition, it is suggested to look into the connections between the shapes of 3D-printed devices and the *in vitro–in vivo* product performance of characteristics like drug release and PK drug absorption. More than a hundred different biomedical devices are already available, all made possible by 3D printing. In a recent statement, the United States Food and Drug Administration's Center for Drug Evaluation and Research (CDERUSFDA) addressed several concerns regarding the use of 3D printing in the pharmaceutical and medical industries. The Food and Drug Administration's Centers for Evaluation and Research, Center for Biologics Evaluation and Research, and Center for Devices and Radiological Health are cooperating to create a strategy for bringing about this paradigm shift in medicine as a result of the promise that 3D printing holds for a new era of highly individualized healthcare. Health Canada has assessed that the printed materials are sophisticated enough to warrant review under the Innovative Pharmaceutical Products Pathway [55]. The pathway is designed for assessing products that integrate biologics and medical device components into a single manufacturing process to create individualized therapeutic solutions. In a similar vein, the European Medicines Agency (EMA) has taken moves toward authorizing newly manufactured medicinal goods made by utilizing 3D-printing techniques, which make use of software programming and electrical hardware equipment. As part of its role, the government agency also required comprehensive CE marking certification of electronic components. To ensure effective oversight, the MHRA has also agreed to draft such comprehensive guidelines that suppliers must adhere to while developing an electronic master file for submission to regulators. For regulatory purposes in Japan, new goods developed by the 3D-printing method have been labeled regenerative medicines by the PMDA. HSA's regulations on the use of 3D-printed medications and medical equipment are quite similar to those established by PMDS in that they treat such items as novel products that must be produced per cGMP guidelines [56].

1.13 Conclusion

The use of 3D printing in the medical industry holds a great deal of potential, particularly due to the technology's capacity to generate highly individualized products at the point of treatment. Having said that, this scenario also poses difficulties in terms of exercising sufficient monitoring. As the use of 3D printing becomes more widespread, regulatory monitoring will need to evolve to keep up with the technology and guarantee that the advantages of using this technology outweigh any potential drawbacks.

References

1. Hornick, J., 3D printing in healthcare. *J. 3D Print. Med.*, 1, 1, 13–7, Jan. 2017. https://www.engineering.com/story/chinese-dr-creates-3d-printed-skull-implant (accessed on January 2023).
2. Maxey, K., Chinese Dr. creates 3D printed skull implant, 2013. engineering.com.
3. Bhargav, A., Regulatory framework in 3D printing. *J. 3D Print. Med.*, 1, 4, 213–4, Oct. 2017.
4. Kianian, B., *Wohlers Report 2017: 3d Printing And Additive Manufacturing State Of The Industry, Annual Worldwide Progress Report: Chapters Titles: The Middle East, And Other Countries*. https://portal.research.lu.se/en/publications/wohlers-report-2017-3d-printing-and-additive-manufacturing-state- (accessed on January 2023).
5. Kuneinen, E., *Medical Application: 3D Printing A New Nose*, 3D Printing Industry.
6. Dankar, I., Haddarah, A., Omar, F.E., Sepulcre, F., Pujolà, M., 3D printing technology: The new era for food customization and elaboration. *Trends Food Sci. Ttechnol.*, 75, 231–42, May 1, 2018.
7. Heater, B., Cornell scientists 3D print ears with help from rat tails and cow ears. https://www.engadget.com/2013-02-22-3d-printed-ear.html. (accessed on February 2023)
8. Hornick, J.F., 3D printing and the future (or demise) of intellectual property. *3D Print. Addit. Manuf.*, 1, 1, 34–43, Mar. 1, 2014.
9. Paxton, N.C., *Designing Patient-Specific Melt-Electrospun Scaffolds For Bone Regeneration*, Doctoral Dissertation, Queensland University of Technology, 2017.
10. Hornick, J., 3D printing in healthcare. *J. 3D Print. Med.*, 1, 1, 13–17, 2017.
11. Hornick, J.F., 3D printing and the future (or demise) of intellectual property. *3D Print. Addit. Manuf.*, 1, 1, 34–43, 2014.
12. Bechtold, S., *3D Printing And The Intellectual Property System (Vol. 28)*, WIPO, Geneva, Switzerland, 2015.
13. Michigan, U.O., Baby's life saved with groundbreaking 3D printed device from University of Michigan that restored his breathing. https://www.prnewswire.com/news-releases/babys-life-saved-with-groundbreaking-3d-printed-device-from-u-m-that-restored-his-breathing-208656041.html (accessed on January 2023)
14. Stein, R., Doctors use 3-D printing to help a baby breathe. *Natl. Public Radio, Shots: Health News From NPR*, 4, 2013. available at (Mar. 17, 2014). https://www.npr.org/sections/health-shots/2014/03/17/289042381/doctors-use-3-d-printing-to-help-a-baby-breathe#:~:text=Race-,Doctors%20Use%203%2DD%20Printing%20To%20Help%20A%20Baby%20Breathe,Garrett%20should%20soon%20breathe%20normally. (accessed on January 2023)
15. Kolitsky, M.A., Reshaping teaching and learning with 3D printing technologies. *e-mentor*, 56, 4, 84–94, 2014.

16. Molitch-Hou, M., *Trachea 3D Printed With Ordinary Makerbotpla*, 3D Printing Industry, 2015.
17. Bechthold, L., Fischer, V., Hainzlmaier, A., Hugenroth, D., Ivanova, L., Kroth, K., Römer, B., Sikorska, E., Sitzmann, V., 3D printing: A qualitative assessment of applications, recent trends and the technology's future potential, in: *Studien zum deutschen Innovations System*, 2015.
18. Molitch-Hou, M., *Anatomically Accurate Aorta Cells 3D Printed at Sabancı University in Turkey*, 3D Printing Industry, 2014.
19. Edelson, R.D., The 3D blueprint file dilemma: The inherent dangers of digital creative expression and a techno-logical approach to regulation. *Intellect. Prop. Technol. Law J.*, 24, 153, 2019.
20. Clark, L., Bioengineer: The heart is one of the easiest organs to bioprint, we'll do it in a decade. *Wired*, Nov. 21, 2013. https://www.wired.co.uk/article/3d-printed-whole-heart (accessed on January 2023)
21. Barroso, W.F., *Proposta de Viabilidade Técnica-Econômica Para Bioimpressão 3D Auxiliada por Manipulador Robótico.* https://www.oasisbr.ibict.br/vufind/Record/BRCRIS_94de33b21d7d75159f96c766468e5195 (accessed on February 2023)
22. Jewell, C., 3-D printing and the future of stuff. *WIPO Mag.*, 1, 2, 2–6, Apr. 2013.
23. Bhargav, A., Regulatory framework in 3D printing. *J. 3D Print. Med.*, 1, 4, 213–4, Oct. 2017.
24. Clark, L., Bioengineers 3D print tiny functioning human liver. *Wired UK*, April 2013. https://www.wired.co.uk/article/3d-printed-liver (accessed on January 2023)
25. Knowlton, S., Yenilmez, B., Tasoglu, S., Towards single-step biofabrication of organs on a chip via 3D printing. *Trends Biotechnol.*, 34, 9, 685–8, Sep. 1, 2016.
26. Kuneinen, E., *3D Printing a Vaccine?*, 3D Printing Industry.
27. Bhasin, V. and Bodla, M.R., *Impact of 3D Printing on Global Supply Chains By 2020*, Doctoral Dissertation, Massachusetts Institute of Technology, 2020.
28. Gelinsky, M., Current research directions in 3D printing in medicine. *J. 3D Print. Med.*, 1, 1, 5–7, Jan 2017.
29. LaFrance, A., To help solve challenging cardiac problems, doctors at Children's Press 'print'. *Washington Post*, 2013. https://www.washingtonpost.com/national/health-science/to-help-solve-challenging-cardiac-problems-doctors-at-childrens-press-print/2013/05/13/b2eee214-8d9b-11e2-9838-d62f083ba93f_story.html (accessed on January 2023).
30. Nikitakos, N., Dagkinis, I., Papachristos, D., Georgantis, G., Kostidi, E., Economics in 3D printing, in: *3D Printing: Applications in Medicine and Surgery*, pp. 85–95, Elsevier, Amsterdam, Netherlands, Jan. 1, 2020.
31. Morris, H. and Murray, R., *Medical Textiles*, CRC Press, Dec. 21, 2021.
32. Molitch-Hou, M., *Complex Separation of Conjoined Twins Successfully Planned with 3D Printing*, 3D Printing Industry.

33. Eshkalak, S.K., Ghomi, E.R., Dai, Y., Choudhury, D., Ramakrishna, S., The role of three-dimensional printing in healthcare and medicine. *Mater. Des.*, 194, 108940, Sep. 1, 2020.
34. Gelinsky, M., Current research directions in 3D printing in medicine. *J. 3D Print. Med.*, 1, 1, 5–7, Jan. 2017.
35. Coelho, A.I., *A 3D Computer Assisted Orthopedic Surgery Planning Approach Based on Planar Radiography*, Doctoral Dissertation, Austria.
36. Chua, C.K. and Leong, K.F., *3D Printing and Additive Manufacturing: Principles and Applications (With Companion Media Pack)-of Rapid Prototyping*, World Scientific Publishing Company, Aug. 6, 2014.
37. Kumar, L.J., Pandey, P.M., Wimpenny, D.I. (Eds.), *3D Printing and Additive Manufacturing Technologies*, Springer, Singapore, 2019.
38. Van Hede, D., Liang, B., Anania, S., Barzegari, M., Verlee, B., Nolens, G., Pirson, J., Geris, L., Lambert, F., 3D-printed synthetic hydroxyapatite scaffold with in silico optimized macrostructure enhances bone formation in vivo. *Adv. Funct. Mater.*, 32, 6, 2105002, Feb. 2022.
39. Luo, Y., Lode, A., Sonntag, F., Nies, B., Gelinsky, M., Well-ordered biphasic calcium phosphate–alginate scaffolds fabricated by multi-channel 3D plotting under mild conditions. *J. Mater. Chem. B*, 1, 33, 4088–98, 2013.
40. Dadhich, P., Das, B., Pal, P., Srivas, P.K., Dutta, J., Ray, S., Dhara, S., A simple approach for an eggshell-based 3D-printed osteoinductive multiphasic calcium phosphate scaffold. *ACS Appl. Mater. Interfaces*, 8, 19, 11910–24, May 18, 2016.
41. Luo, Y., Wu, C., Lode, A., Gelinsky, M., Hierarchical mesoporous bioactive glass/alginate composite scaffolds fabricated by three-dimensional plotting for bone tissue engineering. *Biofabrication*, 5, 1, 015005, Dec. 11, 2012.
42. Agarwal, T., Kabiraj, P., Narayana, G.H., Kulanthaivel, S., Kasiviswanathan, U., Pal, K., Giri, S., Maiti, T.K., Banerjee, I., Alginate bead based hexagonal close packed 3D implant for bone tissue engineering. *ACS Appl. Mater. Interfaces*, 8, 47, 32132–45, Nov. 30, 2016.
43. Pérez-Sanpablo, A.I., Romero-Ávila, E., González-Mendoza, A., Three-dimensional printing in healthcare. *Rev. Mex. Ing. Bioméd.*, 42, 2, 32–48, Aug. 2021.
44. Costello, J.P., Olivieri, L.J., Su, L., Krieger, A., Alfares, F., Thabit, O., Marshall, M.B., Yoo, S.J., Kim, P.C., Jonas, R.A., Nath, D.S., Incorporating three-dimensional printing into a simulation-based congenital heart disease and critical care training curriculum for resident physicians. *Congenit. Heart Dis.*, 10, 2, 185–90, Mar. 2015.
45. Singh, S., Prakash, C., Ramakrishna, S., Three-dimensional printing in the fight against novel virus COVID-19: Technology helping society during an infectious disease pandemic. *Technol. Soc., Aug. 1*, 62, 101305, 2020.
46. Cui, M., Pan, H., Su, Y., Fang, D., Qiao, S., Ding, P., Pan, W., Opportunities and challenges of three-dimensional printing technology in pharmaceutical

formulation development. *Acta Pharm. Sin. B*, 11, 8, 2488–504, Aug. 1, 2021.

47. Salazar-Gamarra, R., Contreras-Pulache, H., Cruz-Gonzales, G., Binasco, S., Cruz-Gonzales, W., Moya-Salazar, J., Three-dimensional printing and digital flow in human medicine: A review and state-of-the-art. *Appl. Syst. Innov.*, 5, 6, 126, Dec. 15, 2022.
48. Roopavath, U.K. and Kalaskar, D.M., Introduction to three-dimensional printing in medicine, in: *3D Printing in Medicine*, pp. 1–27, Woodhead Publishing, United Kingdom, Jan. 1, 2023.
49. Javaid, M., Haleem, A., Singh, R.P., Suman, R., 3D printing applications for healthcare research and development. *GHJ*, 6, 217–226, Nov. 3, 2022.
50. Eshkalak, S.K., Ghomi, E.R., Dai, Y., Choudhury, D., Ramakrishna, S., The role of three-dimensional printing in healthcare and medicine. *Mater. Des.*, 194, 108940, Sep. 1, 2020.
51. Sharma, S. and Goel, S.A., 3D printing and its future in medical world. *JMRI*, 3, 1, e000141, 2019.
52. Mammadov, E., Three-dimensional printing in medicine: Current status and future perspectives. *Cyprus J. Med. Sci.*, 3, 3, 186–8, Dec. 1, 2018.
53. Mardis, N.J., Emerging technology and applications of 3D printing in the medical field. *Mo. Med.*, 115, 4, 368, Jul. 2018.
54. Rath, S.N. and Sankar, S., 3D printers for surgical practice, in: *3D Printing in Medicine*, pp. 127–147, Woodhead Publishing, United Kingdom, Jan. 1, 2023.
55. Bhat, S., 3D printing equipment in medicine, in: *3D Printing in Medicine and Surgery: Applications in Healthcare*, vol. 14, p. 223, Aug. 2020.
56. Eshkalak, S.K., Ghomi, E.R., Dai, Y., Choudhury, D., Ramakrishna, S., The role of three-dimensional printing in healthcare and medicine. *Mater. Des.*, 194, 108940, Sep. 1, 2020.

2

3D Printing in Medical Science

Abstract

Customizable, biocompatible, and sterile components are in high demand in the healthcare industry. When it comes to healthcare, 3D printing is a game-changer that opens up vast new possibilities for study and innovation. A straightforward 3D printing service provides patients with inexpensive, customized prostheses, implants, and devices; aids surgeons in performing more precise procedures with individualized tools and models; and helps medical device makers create cutting-edge, time-saving products. The use of 3D-printed tissue components has the potential to simplify drug development and help overcome several obstacles. Possible future benefits include making drugs more affordable for all people and expanding their availability. The literature on the benefits of using 3D-printed anatomic models in education and training is expanding rapidly. This chapter, however, focuses on recent advances in medical science using 3D printing.

Keywords: 3D printing, 3D-printed models, cardiovascular disease models, 3D-printed kidney models, pre-surgical programming, CT scans

2.1 Introduction

In recent years, noninvasive imaging techniques including computed tomography (CT), magnetic resonance imaging (MRI), nuclear medicine, and ultrasound have shown great diagnostic promise. These imaging modalities may be quantitatively analyzed for the identification and diagnosis of a wide range of disorders [1–10]. Traditional 2D and 3D projection approaches, currently restricted to a 2D screen, prevent the accurate portrayal of morphological traits and disorders of 3D information, despite encouraging results presented in the literature. The complexity of illnesses makes the point abundantly clear. Because of this, 3D printing is now a method that might be used in the field of medicine. The medical uses of 3D printing have grown rapidly over the past several decades, with numerous studies reporting success in fields as diverse

Rishabha Malviya and Rishav Sharma. 3D Printing in Healthcare: Novel Applications, (19–36)

as orthopedics, cardiology, and even tumor imaging [11–15]. In 2016, the Radiological Society of North America created a 3D Printing SIG to improve patient care through additive manufacturing [16, 17]. SIG guidelines, ideas, and training sessions enable safe and successful medical 3D printing. It is becoming increasingly clear that 3D-printed models help doctors better manage their patients, leading to better clinical outcomes. The fast growth of 3D printing's medical applications is the major topic of the editorial. Particular attention is paid to its potential in the treatment of CHD, vascular illness, and malignancies. Future research prospects are also emphasized, including the new field of employing 3D-printed models to build effective CT scanning techniques. The concept of "3D printing" is commonly used to refer to the process of creating an object layer by layer, but other terms have evolved, such as "rapid prototyping," "solid free-form fabrication," and "additive manufacturing," which are all equivalent. To convey the unique nature of 3D product creation, manufacturers have coined these words. Figure 2.1 depicts the 3D printing process.

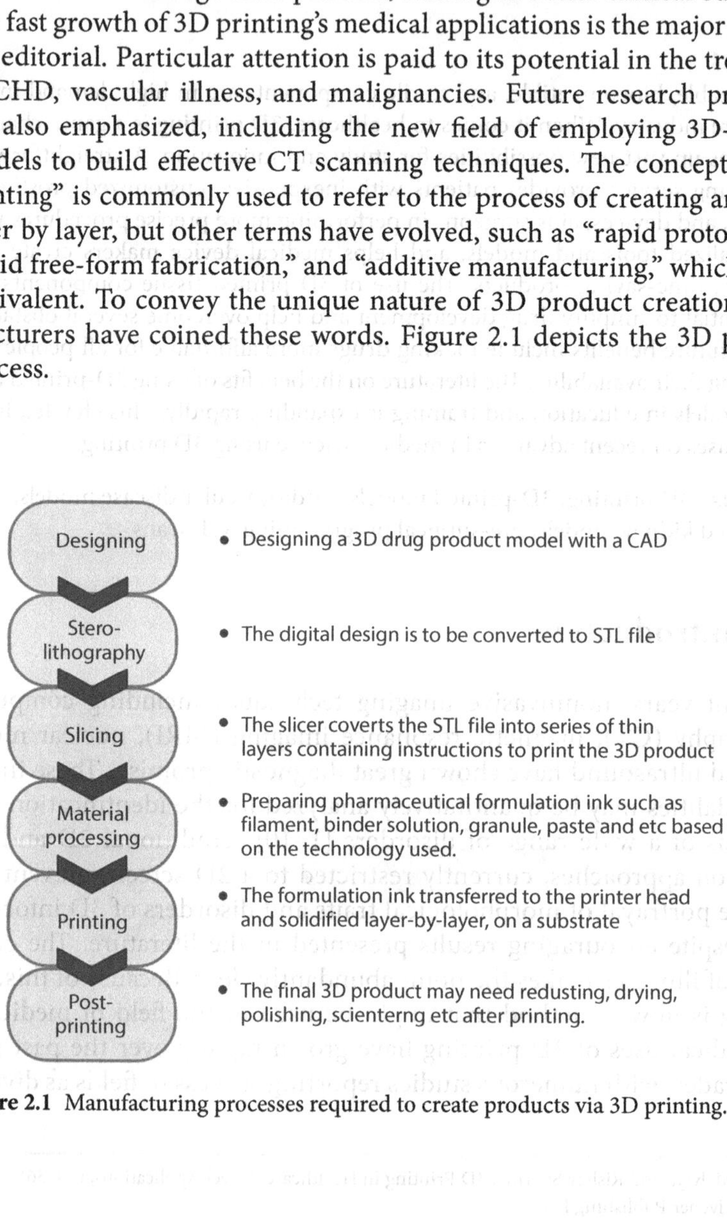

Figure 2.1 Manufacturing processes required to create products via 3D printing.

2.2 Present Clinical Applications

A patient-specific 3D-printed model is generated by running CT or MRI scan data through various image post-processing and segmented algorithms to isolate the regions of interest (specific anatomical structures and disorders). Normal and pathological anatomical structures and disorders are both accurately represented in 3D printed models [18–20]. Three-dimensional printed models of the craniomaxillofacial region have been shown to have therapeutic value since the late 1980s [21, 22]. The SIG has confirmed that patients with difficult cranium, facial, and mandible fractures, as well as those suffering from temporomandibular joint disorders, benign, and malignant tumors, can benefit greatly from the use of 3D-printed models [16]. There are already enough studies in the literature to prove this, so the investigator would not be discussing it further here. Since the most promising new uses are in the fields of cardiovascular illness, tumor imaging, and optimizing CT scanning techniques, those topics will be discussed in detail below.

2.3 3D-Printed Models in CHD

Although CHD is connected to a complex heart design, 3D printing offers a promising method for investigating the disease [9, 18]. The ability of 3D-printed models to help in pre-surgical assessment and simulation of difficult circumstances suggests that they may have therapeutic utility in CHD [23–25]. Although randomized controlled trials and multicenter studies are just beginning to establish their added benefit above standard visualization methodologies [26–31], case reports and case series make up the bulk of the present research on 3D printing in CHD. Loke *et al.* [28] investigated the utilization of 3D-printed cardiac models to study complicated CHDs such as the tetralogy of Fallot (ToF). Thirty-five second-year pediatric residents were split into two groups: 17 utilized the more typical 2D method of demonstrating ToF, while the remaining 18 used a 3D-printed replica of the heart defect. Pre- and post-session questionnaires were given to both sets of participants to gauge their levels of background knowledge, happiness with the learning process, and confidence in their ability to address cardiac abnormalities in patients. The use of 3D-printed models during training sessions improved the residents' learning and satisfaction compared to 2D photos and also boosted their self-assurance in caring for patients with ToF. White *et al.* [29] report similar results after randomly assigning 30 pediatric residents to the intervention group and the remaining to the control group. The identical 20-min lecture was presented to both groups, complete with 2D photos of VSDs and ToFs; however, 3D-printed replicas of normal and CHD hearts were given to the intervention group. 3D-printed models increased the participants' confidence and skill in treating severe CHD such as ToF, whereas they had minimal value when treating less complex CHD such as VSD. It provides more evidence that 3D-printed physical models are preferable to standard image representations when it comes to explaining complicated heart lesions. Valverde *et al.* [30] recently conducted a large-scale study demonstrating that 3D-printed models of CHD have aided in both treatment planning and surgical therapy. Forty patients with complex CHD from 10 hospitals throughout the world were included. 3D-printable models were made using CT and MRI images, and they were exceptionally realistic depictions of the basic anatomical characteristics (mean bias: 0.27–0.73 mm). Due to the relative simplicity of the CHD cases, the 3D-printed models did not influence the surgical choice in 52.5% of the instances. However, the therapeutic usefulness of 3D-printed models cannot be overstated since they were responsible for redefining the surgical strategy in nearly half of the instances (48%). Ryan *et al.* [31] just completed research detailing their localized practice with 3D-printed models for CHD. There were 928 cardiothoracic operations conducted at their pediatric hospital during 3 years, and 164 anatomical models were created for various objectives, including teaching, patient–doctor interaction, pre-surgical therapy, and preparation. In 79 cases with congenital heart disease, 3D models were created specifically to help in the preoperative planning of surgery. The historical analysis shows how 3D printing has been incorporated into clinical practice and how it has impacted patient care, namely, through shortening the recovery times and operating times with the use of 3D-printed models. Re-admission and mortality rates were lower after 30 days when 3D-printed models were used instead of the standard of care. These results need to be confirmed by prospective multicenter studies; however, it has already been proven that 3D-printed models are helpful in surgical planning for patients with complex CHD.

2.4 Cardiovascular Disease Models in 3D Printing

Case reports and short case series [23, 32–36] can provide most of the evidence for the efficacy of 3D printing in the management of cardiovascular and cerebrovascular disease [23]. Recent systematic assessments of CHD studies suggested that between 42% and 61% of studies incorporated case studies using 3D-printed heart or vascular models [32–34]. Stent graft insertion, assessing coronary lumen constriction owing to calcified plaques, simulating vascular diseases like aortic/cerebral aneurysms, and planning and simulating surgery are all possible with the use of 3D-printed models [35–38]. Patient-specific CT imaging data was used to determine very well how 3D-printed replicas of aortic aneurysms and aortic dissections mimicked the real thing [33, 34], but there were some discrepancies between the predicted sites and the actual lumen in terms of the measurements taken (more than 1.0 mm). Even though the intimal flap's microscopic nature makes it challenging to replicate it on 3D printing models. Hossein *et al.* [35] succeeded in doing so. Models of three individuals with type A acute aortic dissection were 3D-printed by the authors. In these patients, the aortic tear started in the ascending aorta and extended into the aortic branches.

2.5 Tumor in 3D-Printed Models

The diagnostic evaluation of tumors in terms of their size, location, and extent, which is crucial for surgical planning and the selection of tumor removal, is greatly aided by imaging technologies. A 3D printing technology may be of significant aid in enabling pre-surgical design and simulation for a range of tumor types, including those that affect the brain, liver, kidneys, and heart [39–45] due to the intricacy of linkages between tumors and surrounding systems—for example, 3D printing is getting prominence for modeling hepatic and renal malignant tumors before surgery. Nineteen studies on the pharmacological usage of 3D-printed liver models were reviewed in a comprehensive study [39]. Although the bulk of the papers used in the study were case reports, both quantitative and qualitative data proved the efficacy of three-dimensional models for pre-surgical and simulation of surgical procedures of liver lesions as well as in medical education and training. A new report analyzing 15 individual 3D models to CT scans shows that the 3D-printed models accurately represent hepatic structures and tumors [20]. Quantitative results were reported in over half of the investigations, with topics including the effectiveness of 3D-printed models in illustrating renal structures and renal tumors and the efficiency with which preoperative examinations could be completed. The additional empirical research only provided qualitative data, such as the therapeutic use of 3D-printed kidney models in pre-surgical programming or re-operation simulation. Despite these promising results, more large-scale clinical investigations involving several sites are needed.

2.6 3D-Printed Models in the Development of CT Scanning Procedures

The development of appropriate scanning techniques with minimal radiation dosage and acceptable picture quality [46] is an emerging research topic in the use of 3D-printed models. The standard method of optimizing imaging methods involves using anthropomorphic phantoms, which can only be used to simulate adults or children. Patient-specific CT scan reliability may be enhanced with the use of 3D-printed models that accurately depict patient anatomy and disease. Numerous strategies for decreasing radiation exposure during CT scans were evaluated using 3D-printed models of the cardiac and pulmonary veins [47, 48]. Comparable to the unique approach of using a 3D-printed cardiac insert phantom to maximize cardiac CT protocols [48], the strategy employed by Aldosari *et al.*, who simulated main and peripheral pulmonary embolism using a 3D-printed pulmonary artery model to maximize CT pulmonary angiography protocols, is also novel [49]. Diagnostic scans for pulmonary embolism tracking at the primary and peripheral pulmonary arteries could be generated utilizing a 3D-printed lung model with a significant reduction in dose of up to 80%, proving the viability of the technique [48].

2.7 Pharmaceutical 3D-Printing Technologies

Several examples of 3D-printed healthcare products are available today [50]. Such examples include ibuprofen hydrogels and various drug delivery systems for progesterone and pseudoephedrine, guaifenesin polypills, and the multi-active combinations of nifedipine, captopril, and glipizide. There are now five primary methods used for making such products: extrusion molding printing (EMP), drop-on powder printing, selective laser sintering (SLS), stereolithography, and electrohydrodynamic 3D printing [6]. In consideration of the most frequently widely used techniques, EMP includes both fused deposition model and semisolid extrusion modeling (SSE). The FDM process entails bringing drug-loaded polymers to a semi-liquid condition, extruding them via a printing nozzle, and then letting them cool and crystallize on a printing substrate. There is a risk of API thermal degradation during heating, which is worsened by low drug loading, limiting the process's cost-effectiveness and ease of operation [51]. When using SSE, however, the material is deposited on the printing platform by applying pressure to an extruding paste inside a syringe-shaped print head.

One example is guaifenesin, a bilayered polypill with a controlled release mechanism that is manufactured using this technique. DOP printing, also known as binder jetting, includes depositing powder in layers onto a build platform and then bonding the powders together using drops of a binding agent expelled from the print head. It is cheap, simple to scale up, and yields very porous tablets, but it has drawbacks in terms of resolution, durability, and fragility [51]. Selective laser sintering (SLS) is a kind of powder bed fusion that employs a CO_2 laser to selectively sinter (heat to make solid material) chosen regions of layered powders, making the powders solid in those places. Although SLS is slow and can potentially harm medical products because of the heat generated by the laser, its precision allows manufacturers to exert significant control over the microstructures of the medicines that they develop [51]. New high-density (EHD) techniques use computer-guided material deposition to mold fibrous materials into finished pharmaceuticals. It paves the way for nanoscale fiber engineering, which, in turn, makes it possible to create complex structures with bespoke geometries and a high degree of order. Scientists think that it has the potential to pave the way for individualized medication production, where each patient's specific demands are met, whether in terms of dose form specifications or active pharmaceutical ingredient release. EHD is a one-step technique that can be applied with many different substances, but it comes with a variety of limitations, particularly low efficiency, the presence of the solvent system in the pharmaceutical formulations, and stringent criteria for solution properties [51]. Organ models are physical models that duplicate the anatomy of a patient to aid in clinical treatment or teaching; they are distinct from tissue models and implants in that they are not biologically active and are not placed into human bodies (Figure 2.2).

2.8 Challenges Facing Printed Pharmaceuticals

Although 3D printing could drastically alter pharmaceutical companies, its general acceptance has been slowed by four factors: necessity excipients, advancements in printing technology, enhancements to mechanical characteristics, and regulatory framework. When compared to more conventional production methods, especially those involving heat or highly specific dose forms, the availability of excipients for use in pharmaceutical 3D printing is still somewhat low. More research on safe, biodegradable, biocompatible, and stable excipients is needed to increase their use in the pharmaceutical industry [51]. Modeling and slicing technology, which is

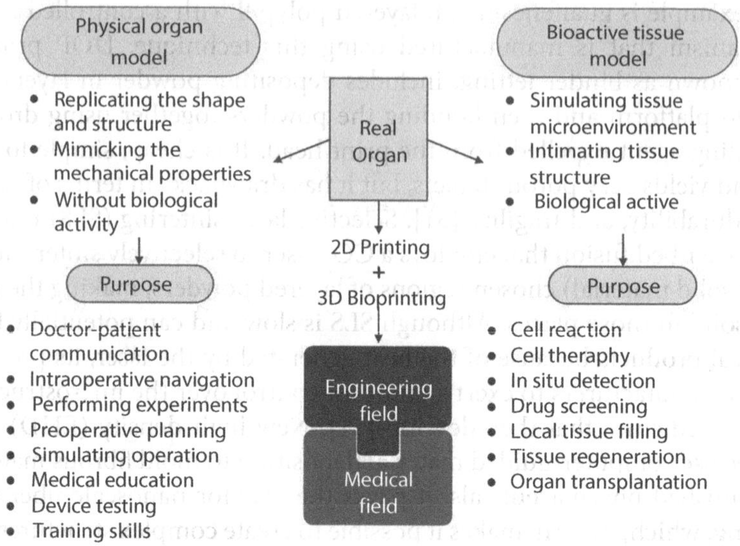

Figure 2.2 Dissimilarities between organ models and tissue models (such as tissue/organ combinations).

utilized to design and direct the manufacture of dosage forms, requires frequent updates as their complexity grows. To meet the needs of the different activities, it is also required to update and optimize the mechanical equipment, operating methods, and control system. The important safety criteria of 3D printing employed in the development of pharmaceutical formulations need to be examined since they do not currently satisfy good manufacturing practice (GMP) standards. Dosage form reproducibility and processing viability depend on the mechanical qualities that are measured as part of quality control. In 3D manufacturing, several variables, such as nozzle fineness, adhesive viscosity, drying techniques, and temperature, can affect the final product's characteristics. Equipment and control programs need to be improved, adhesive nozzles need to be modified, and printing process parameters need to be optimized to guarantee the desired mechanical qualities [51]. There are numerous unanswered problems about how the quality of 3D-printed drugs should be regulated. The Food and Drug Administration (FDA) presented its final assessment of technical factors for the clearance of 3D-printed medical devices in 2017 [52]. A further examination of safety and efficacy may be necessary, especially for unique goods; hence, these criteria might not apply to all 3D-printed medical equipment. Whether or not 3D printing is considered manufacturing or compounding will also affect the regulatory advice for goods that are tailored to individual patients. Although the FDA has granted its stamp of acceptance to 3D-printed medications, no regulations or guidelines have yet been established for the emerging industry. The FDA's Office of Research and Testing is currently investigating potential answers to several regulatory problems, such as how to assess the effectiveness and guarantee the quality of 3D-printed drugs [53].

2.8.1 A Developing Sector

Powder jetting, material extrusion, and SLS are just a few of the 3D printing technologies being tested at Merck's Innovation Center, making the company one of the leaders in the pharmaceutical 3D printing space. Dr. Christoph Huels, Merck's pioneer of additive tablet production, told the investigator at PHARMAP 2021 that perhaps the company is focused on SLS because it produces tablets with homogenous API content and comparable dissolving [54]. Oral solid dosage forms made using SLS have the right density, toughness, roughness, and shape that the manufacturer needs. According to Huels, Merck's present objective is to establish 3D printing as a reliable source of supplies for clinical trials. Within the next year, the company intends to make the technology available to clients for exploratory research before introducing a GMP solution to the market in the following 2 to 3 years. Experts say that scaling up from the hundreds of pills needed for clinical trials to the commercial level should be easy, but he anticipates it to take 10–15 years until additive manufacturing is mature enough for drug production [54, 55]. In a recent interview, Huels told the 3D Printing Industry [56] that "blockbuster drugs" and "billions of pills each year for international supply" are necessities for commercial manufacture. Unfortunately, the present throughput of 3D printing technology is insufficient to guarantee a steady supply. That can only be accomplished with substantial future enhancements. However, the present production is already sufficient to meet the need for orphan or mild cancer indications, where almost millions of tablets are needed annually. The investigators added that lesser indications are where 3D printing will likely have the most economical viability, at least in the short run [57, 58]. The M3DIMAKER, which FabRx claims to be the first GMP-ready 3D printer for medicines, will be released for research use in 2020. Co-founder and Director Alvaro Goyanes said: "Researchers are in discussion with the MHRA to facilitate regulatory development for the cutting-edge technology." The M3DIMAKER is now involved in national and international partnerships that will entail future clinical studies. It incorporates many different types of 3D printing onto a single machine, expanding the range of applications and customizability [59]. In general, 3D printing might dramatically alter the pharmaceutical industry by facilitating the distributed and individualized creation of medicines. However, the technology's full therapeutic promise remains unrealized until the obstacles plaguing the industry are resolved [60].

2.9 Opportunities and Limitations of Using 3D Printing in Healthcare

Due to their focus on mass manufacturing, pharmaceutical companies were unable to respond to requests for a shift toward individualized treatment and thus fell behind the consistently accelerating speed of development in this area. Recent advancements in 3D printing mean that it may soon be possible to fill the void in personalized medicine by producing medications in small quantities with individualized dosing and release profiles. Since the FDA greenlit 3D-printed Spritam by Aprecia in 2015, there has been a rapid uptick in its use for dispensing pharmaceuticals. Triastek, a company, has obtained approval from the FDA for the production of a dosage form that is created using 3D printing technology and contains the medicine T19 for the treatment of rheumatoid arthritis. For customized medication, the product is made to contain a wide variety of infills, each of which may produce a unique dosage and release profile. It is possible that 3D printing might be used in the early stages of the pharmaceutical sector because of the drug's flexibility and adaptability in production to suit that stage. Producing the medicine in tiny amounts, dosages, and different additives to alter the right dosage is necessary for the early stage of drug research [61]. In the preclinical stage of drug development, the method has been tested by several studies—for instance, rats have been given FDM-produced warfarin sodium to examine the effectiveness of prescribed dosages of the drug as an anticoagulant and to determine whether or not it could replace the practice of splitting commercially available tablets [62]. For the treatment of maple syrup urine illness, a rare metabolic ailment, FabRx has completed the first clinical research evaluating the efficacy of the 3D-printed medication isoleucine (MSUD). The medication requires a precise dosage based on the patient's age, weight, and blood profile. Blood levels of isoleucine were found to be comparable between the study group and those who received hospital-formulated preparations with means closer to the planned dosage and less variability [63]. The pharmaceutical industry is not interested in developing orphan medications because of the low demand and the high cost of setting up dedicated production lines. When compared to traditional industrial procedures, 3D printing's ability to produce in tiny numbers makes it an attractive option for ensuring a steady supply of much-needed orphan pharmaceuticals. Aprecia, the maker of Spritam, has established a partnership with Cambridge, Massachusetts's Cycle Team, a business that specializes in orphan medications. The two companies will work together to develop orphan medications based on the ZipdoseTM technology developed by Aprecia [64]. Pharmacists have shown a strong desire to use the technology as a means of medication distribution due to their conviction in the efficacy and safety of customized medicines [65], despite their fears that doing so will need a shift in their usual workflow in clinical practice. Although there is a lot of enthusiasm for the technology and its bright theoretical potential, it still has a long way to go before it can be implemented in the healthcare system. The shortage of specified regulatory guidelines is a major obstacle to the broad use of 3D printing in the pharmaceutical sector. Due to their emphasis on the creation of medical devices and implants, the Food and Drug Administration's rules for 3D printing in medicine do not permit the production of drugs [66]. The personalized medication made on demand cannot be governed by the same rules that govern mass-produced drugs since 3D-printing drugs is not considered a manufacturing process. FDA's Emerging Technology Team (EET) has begun working on the front. The primary goal of EET is to stimulate the development of cutting-edge manufacturing and design technologies, such as the use of 3D printing in the field of pharmaceutical research [67]. The MHRA plans to build a manufacturing master file to more precisely supervise production for regulatory compliance at the point of care. The idea proposes that a single, fully licensed hub may more easily ensure that its affiliates meet all applicable rules and regulations by acting as a guarantor for their credentials. Personalized therapy strategies may be developed through the combination of biologics and medical device components and production processes, which is why Health Canada considers printed goods to be complex products requiring consideration through the Advanced Therapeutic Products Pathway [68]. Layers are stacked using elements including heat, solvents, and light to create the 3D form in 3D printing. Because of these variables, the quality and stability of the printed medicine may be compromised. As a result, it is important to maintain high standards of quality and develop methods for assessing the finished product after printing, especially if the medicine is made in hospitals and pharmacies rather than in factories. The traditional pharmaceutical manufacturing and business processes typically perform harmful, labor-intensive, and costly quality checks of pharmaceutical items, which is inconsistent with the notion of on-demand development of individualized treatment. Non-invasive infrared (NIR) spectroscopy and reliable Raman spectroscopy have already been proposed for use in determining drug concentration in printed dosage forms, enabling real-time monitoring of pharmaceutical product quality in environments like clinics and hospital pharmacists [69]. Some 3D printers, such as the powder bed fusion (FDM) and powder bed additive manufacturing (PAM), are preferred over others for making pharmaceutical dosage forms due to their versatility, user-friendly features, and potential to use the excipients that meet the criteria for generally regarded as safe (GRAS) safety. While there are a variety of printers in the market, none of them is GMP-compliant because they were not created with the pharmaceutical industry in mind. Since the technology is envisioned as being used for medication dispensing in the healthcare system rather than factories, small, user-friendly printers that can reliably and securely generate drugs must be produced. Several enterprising businesses saw an opportunity in the gap in the market and have since built 3D printers that are both GMP-compliant and capable of generating high-quality pharmaceuticals. Companies like Vitae [70] and Triastek, as well as FabRx [70], which created the M3DIMakerTM printer for usage in hospitals and medical centers, are two such examples. Merck's recent partnership with AMCM (Additive Manufacturing Customized Machines) is aimed at bringing GMP-conforming industrial 3D printing to the drug development process. Novel medication delivery methods are another promising area for 3D printing's expanding range of applications—nanosuspension, multilayer drug delivery systems, microcapsules made from synthetic extracellular matrix based on hyaluronan, micropatterns printed with antibiotics, bioactive glass scaffolds with mesopores, and so on. Mucoadhesive films and similar multilayer structures have been proposed by various studies, and the technology appears to be a promising way for their development [71]. Thus, the quick prototyping tool is presenting the possibility of constructing infinite dose forms, which will gradually push the production of therapeutic administration systems to a whole new level, notwithstanding certain limits. When the technology is mature and the materials are plentiful, however, 3D printing will become a commonplace production method. The promise of 3D technology rests on the accessibility of 3D printing methods that can provide on-demand customized dosages in real-time at dispersed places. Traditional pharmaceutical manufacturing is predicted to be retooled for more adaptable 3D-printed items and a plethora of new formulas shortly. The last requirement for 3D printing to achieve commercial success will be the accuracy with which individual dose geometries are translated to meet patient needs while staying under budget [72].

2.10 Conclusion and Future Direction

A wide variety of medical applications have been found for 3D-printed models, including but not limited to pre-operative planning and simulation of complex surgical or interventional procedures, medical student and patient education, and doctor–patient communication. In addition, 3D-printed models customized for each patient can be used as a practical and economical resource for creating superior CT scanning protocols. Studies evaluating the effects of 3D printing on clinical decision-making and patient outcomes should receive more attention than those examining the accuracy of the models themselves in the current research landscape. To confirm these results, prospective studies with a larger sample size at multiple sites would be ideal. With the continued development of 3D printing technology, as well as decreases in printing cost and picture post-processing time, 3D printing will soon become a standard part of clinical diagnostics.

References

1. Loughborough, W.W., Yeong, M., Hamilton, M., Manghat, N., Computed tomography in congenital heart disease: How generic principles can be applied to create bespoke protocols in the Fontan circuit. *Quant. Imaging Med. Surg.*, 7, 1, 79, Feb. 2017.
2. Liu, D., Fan, Z., Li, Y., Zhang, N., Sun, Z., An, J., Stalder, A.F., Greiser, A., Liu, J., Quantitative study of abdominal blood flow patterns in patients with aortic dissection by 4-dimensional flow MRI. *Sci. Rep.*, 8, 1, 9111, Jun. 14, 2018.
3. Wang, R., Liu, X., Schoepf, U.J., van Assen, M., Alimohamed, I., Griffith, L.P., Luo, T., Sun, Z., Fan, Z., Xu, L., Extracellular volume quantitation using dual-energy CT in patients with heart failure: Comparison with 3T cardiac MR. *Int. J. Cardiol.*, 268, 236–40, Oct. 1, 2018.
4. Sun, Z., 3D printing in medicine: Current applications and future directions. *Quant. Imaging Med. Surg.*, 8, 11, 1069, Dec. 2018.
5. D'Errico, L., Salituri, F., Ciardetti, M., Favilla, R., Mazzarisi, A., Coppini, G., Bartolozzi, C., Marraccini, P., Quantitative analysis of epicardial fat volume: effects of scanning protocol and reproducibility of measurements in non-contrast cardiac CT vs. coronary CT angiography. *Quant. Imaging Med. Surg.*, 7, 3, 326, Jun. 2017.
6. Almutairi, A., Al Safran, Z., AlZaabi, S.A., Sun, Z., Dual energy CT angiography in peripheral arterial stents: Optimal scanning protocols with regard to image quality and radiation dose. *Quant. Imaging Med. Surg.*, 7, 5, 520, Oct. 2017.

7. Sun, Z. and Chaichana, T., An investigation of correlation between left coronary bifurcation angle and hemodynamic changes in coronary stenosis by coronary computed tomography angiography-derived computational fluid dynamics. *Quant. Imaging Med. Surg.*, 7, 5, 537, Oct. 2017.
8. Hidrovo, I., Dey, J., Chesal, M.E., Shumilov, D., Bhusal, N., Mathis, J.M., Experimental method and statistical analysis to fit tumor growth model using SPECT/CT imaging: A preclinical study. *Quant. Imaging Med. Surg.*, 7, 3, 299, Jun. 2017.
9. Mustapha, F.A., Bashah, F.A., Yassin, I.M., Fikri, A.S., Nordin, A.J., Razak, H.R., Estimation of kidneys and urinary bladder doses based on the region of interest in 18fluorine-fluorodeoxyglucose positron emission tomography/computed tomography examination: A preliminary study. *Quant. Imaging Med. Surg.*, 7, 3, 310, Jun. 2017.
10. Esposito, F., Mamone, R., Di Serafino, M., Mercogliano, C., Vitale, V., Vallone, G., Oresta, P., Diagnostic imaging features of necrotizing enterocolitis: A narrative review. *Quant. Imaging Med. Surg.*, 7, 3, 336, Jun. 2017.
11. Zanetti, E.M., Aldieri, A., Terzini, M., Calì, M., Franceschini, G., Bignardi, C., Additively manufactured custom load-bearing implantable devices: Grounds for caution. *Australas. Med. J.*, 10, 8, 694–700, Aug. 1, 2017.
12. Giannopoulos, A.A., Steigner, M.L., George, E., Barile, M., Hunsaker, A.R., Rybicki, F.J., Mitsouras, D., Cardiothoracic applications of 3D printing. *J. Thorac. Imaging*, 31, 5, 253, Sep. 2016.
13. Zanetti, E.M. and Bignardi, C., Mock-up in hip arthroplasty pre-operative planning. *Acta Bioeng. Biomech.*, 15, 3, 123–128, 2013.
14. Speranza, D., Citro, D., Padula, F., Motyl, B., Marcolin, F., Calì, M., Martorelli, M., Additive manufacturing techniques for the reconstruction of 3D fetal faces. *Appl. Bionics Biomech.*, 2017, 1–10, Dec. 19, 2017.
15. Sun, Z. and Liu, D., A systematic review of clinical value of three-dimensional printing in renal disease. *Quant. Imaging Med. Surg.*, 8, 3, 311, Apr. 2018.
16. Chepelev, L., Wake, N., Ryan, J., Althobaity, W., Gupta, A., Arribas, E., Santiago, L., Ballard, D.H., Wang, K.C., Weadock, W., Ionita, C.N., Radiological society of North America (RSNA) 3D printing Special Interest Group (SIG): Guidelines for medical 3D printing and appropriateness for clinical scenarios. *3D Print. Med.*, 4, 1, 1–38, Dec. 2018.
17. Chepelev, L., Souza, C., Althobaity, W., Miguel, O., Krishna, S., Akyuz, E., Hodgdon, T., Torres, C., Wake, N., Alexander, A., George, E., Preoperative planning and tracheal stent design in thoracic surgery: A primer for the 2017 Radiological Society of North America (RSNA) hands-on course in 3D printing. *3D Print. Med.*, 3, 1–26, Mar. 2017.
18. Lau, I.W., Liu, D., Xu, L., Fan, Z., Sun, Z., Clinical value of patient-specific three-dimensional printing of congenital heart disease: Quantitative and qualitative assessments. *PloS One*, 13, 3, e0194333, Mar. 21, 2018.
19. Aldosari, S., Jansen, S., Sun, Z., Patient-specific 3D printed pulmonary artery model with simulation of peripheral pulmonary embolism for developing

optimal computed tomography pulmonary angiography protocols. *Quant. Imaging Med. Surg.*, 9, 1, 75, Jan. 2019.

20. Witowski, J., Wake, N., Grochowska, A., Sun, Z., Budzyński, A., Major, P., Popiela, T.J., Pędziwiatr, M., Investigating accuracy of 3D printed liver models with computed tomography. *Quant. Imaging Med. Surg.*, 9, 1, 43, Jan. 2019.
21. Mankovich, N.J., Cheeseman, A.M., Stoker, N.G., The display of three-dimensional anatomy with stereolithographic models. *J. Digit. Imaging*, 3, 200–3, Aug. 1990.
22. Winder, J., Cooke, R.S., Gray, J., Fannin, T., Fegan, T., Medical rapid prototyping and 3D CT in the manufacture of custom made cranial titanium plates. *J. Med. Eng. Technol.*, 23, 1, 26–8, Jan. 1, 1999.
23. Lau, I. and Sun, Z., Three-dimensional printing in congenital heart disease: A systematic review. *J. Med. Radiat. Sci.*, 65, 3, 226–36, Sep. 2018.
24. Costello, J.P., Olivieri, L.J., Krieger, A., Thabit, O., Marshall, M.B., Yoo, S.J., Kim, P.C., Jonas, R.A., Nath, D.S., Utilizing three-dimensional printing technology to assess the feasibility of high-fidelity synthetic ventricular septal defect models for simulation in medical education. *World J. Pediatr. Congenit. Heart Surg.*, 5, 3, 421–6, Jul. 2014.
25. Costello, J.P., Olivieri, L.J., Su, L., Krieger, A., Alfares, F., Thabit, O., Marshall, M.B., Yoo, S.J., Kim, P.C., Jonas, R.A., Nath, D.S., Incorporating three-dimensional printing into a simulation-based congenital heart disease and critical care training curriculum for resident physicians. *Congenit. Heart Dis.*, 10, 2, 185–90, Mar. 2015.
26. Jones, T.W. and Seckeler, M.D., Use of 3D models of vascular rings and slings to improve resident education. *Congenit. Heart Dis.*, 12, 5, 578–82, Sep. 2017.
27. Lim, K.H., Loo, Z.Y., Goldie, S.J., Adams, J.W., McMenamin, P.G., Use of 3D printed models in medical education: A randomized control trial comparing 3D prints versus cadaveric materials for learning external cardiac anatomy. *Anat. Sci. Educ.*, 9, 3, 213–21, May 6, 2016.
28. Loke, Y.H., Harahsheh, A.S., Krieger, A., Olivieri, L.J., Usage of 3D models of tetralogy of Fallot for medical education: Impact on learning congenital heart disease. *BMC Med. Educ.*, 17, 1, 1–8, Dec. 2017.
29. White, S.C., Sedler, J., Jones, T.W., Seckeler, M., Utility of three-dimensional models in resident education on simple and complex intracardiac congenital heart defects. *Congenit. Heart Dis.*, 13, 6, 1045–9, Nov. 2018.
30. Valverde, I., Gomez-Ciriza, G., Hussain, T., Suarez-Mejias, C., Velasco-Forte, M.N., Byrne, N., Ordoñez, A., Gonzalez-Calle, A., Anderson, D., Hazekamp, M.G., Roest, A.A., Three-dimensional printed models for surgical planning of complex congenital heart defects: An international multicentre study. *Eur. J. Cardiothorac. Surg.*, 52, 6, 1139–48, Dec. 1, 2017.
31. Ryan, J., Plasencia, J., Richardson, R., Velez, D., Nigro, J.J., Pophal, S., Frakes, D., 3D printing for congenital heart disease: A single site's initial three-year-experience. *3D Print. Med.*, 4, 1, 1–9, Dec. 2018.

32. Sun, Z. and Shen-Yuan, L., A systematic review of 3-D printing in cardiovascular and cerebrovascular diseases. *Anatol. J. Cardiol.*, 17, 6, 423–35, 2017.
33. Ho, D., Squelch, A., Sun, Z., Modelling of aortic aneurysm and aortic dissection through 3D printing. *J. Med. Radiat. Sci.*, 64, 1, 10–7, Mar. 2017.
34. Sun, Z. and Squelch, A., Patient-specific 3D printed models of aortic aneurysm and aortic dissection. *J. Med. Imaging Health Inform.*, 7, 4, 886–9, Aug. 1, 2017.
35. Hossien, A., Gelsomino, S., Maessen, J., Autschbach, R., The interactive use of multi-dimensional modeling and 3D printing in preplanning of type A aortic dissection. *J. Card. Surg.*, 31, 7, 441–5, Jul. 2016.
36. Wang, H., Liu, J., Zheng, X., Rong, X., Zheng, X., Peng, H., Silber-Li, Z., Li, M., Liu, L., Three-dimensional virtual surgery models for percutaneous coronary intervention (PCI) optimization strategies. *Sci. Rep.*, 5, 1, 10945, Jun. 4, 2015.
37. Huang, J., Li, G., Wang, W., Wu, K., Le, T., 3D printing guiding stent graft fenestration: A novel technique for fenestration in endovascular aneurysm repair. *Vascular*, 25, 4, 442–6, Aug. 2017.
38. Ganau, M., Syrmos, N., Martin, A.R., Jiang, F., Fehlings, M.G., Intraoperative ultrasound in spine surgery: history, current applications, future developments. *Quant. Imaging Med. Surg.*, 8, 3, 261, Apr. 2018.
39. Perica, E.R. and Sun, Z., A systematic review of three-dimensional printing in liver disease. *J. Digit. Imaging*, 31, 692–701, Oct. 2018.
40. Javan, R. and Zeman, M.N., A prototype educational model for hepatobiliary interventions: Unveiling the role of graphic designers in medical 3D printing. *J. Digit. Imaging*, 31, 133–43, Feb. 2018.
41. Javan, R., Herrin, D., Tangestanipoor, A., Understanding spatially complex segmental and branch anatomy using 3D printing: Liver, lung, prostate, coronary arteries, and circle of Willis. *Acad. Radiol.*, 23, 9, 1183–9, Sep. 1, 2016.
42. Perica, E. and Sun, Z., Patient-specific three-dimensional printing for presurgical planning in hepatocellular carcinoma treatment. *Quant. Imaging Med. Surg.*, 7, 6, 668, Dec. 2017.
43. Lau, I., Squelch, A., Wan, Y.L., Wong, A.M., Ducke, W., Sun., Z., Patient-specific 3D printed model in delineating brain glioma and surrounding structures in a pediatric patient. *Digit. Med.*, 3, 2, 86, Apr. 1, 2017.
44. Al Jabbari, O., Abu Saleh, W.K., Patel, A.P., Igo, S.R., Reardon, M.J., Use of three-dimensional models to assist in the resection of malignant cardiac tumors. *J. Card. Surg.*, 31, 9, 581–3, Sep. 2016.
45. Thawani, J.P., Singh, N., Pisapia, J.M., Abdullah, K.G., Parker, D., Pukenas, B.A., Zager, E.L., Verma, R., Brem, S., Three-dimensional printed modeling of diffuse low-grade gliomas and associated white matter tract anatomy. *Neurosurgery*, 80, 4, 635–45, Apr. 1, 2017.
46. Sun, Z. and Aldosari, S., Three-dimensional printing in medicine: Opportunities for development of optimal CT scanning protocols. *Australas. Med. J. (Online)*, 11, 11, 529–32, 2018.
47. Abdullah, K.A., McEntee, M.F., Reed, W., Kench, P.L., Development of an organ-specific insert phantom generated using a 3D printer for investigations

of cardiac computed tomography protocols. *J. Med. Radiat. Sci.*, 65, 3, 175–83, Sep. 2018.
48. Aldosari, S., Jansen, S., Sun, Z., Optimization of computed tomography pulmonary angiography protocols using 3D printed model with simulation of pulmonary embolism. *Quant. Imaging Med. Surg.*, 9, 1, 53, Jan. 2019.
49. Aldosari, S., Jansen, S., Sun, Z., Patient-specific 3D printed pulmonary artery model with simulation of peripheral pulmonary embolism for developing optimal computed tomography pulmonary angiography protocols. *Quant. Imaging Med. Surg.*, 9, 1, 75, Jan. 2019.
50. Seoane-Viaño, I., Trenfield, S.J., Basit, A.W., Goyanes, A., Translating 3D printed pharmaceuticals: From hype to real-world clinical applications. *Adv. Drug Deliv. Rev.*, 174, 553–75, Jul. 1, 2021.
51. Dharmamoorthy, G., Sabareesh, M., Balaji, A., Reddy, Y.K., Monika, B., Hema, A.N., Reddy, P.S., Kartheek, U., A overview on 3d printing–current pharmaceutical applications and future directions. *YMER*, 21, 11, 749–765, 2022.
52. Gioumouxouzis, C.I., Karavasili, C., Fatouros, D.G., Recent advances in pharmaceutical dosage forms and devices using additive manufacturing technologies. *Drug Discov. Today*, 24, 2, 636–43, Feb. 1, 2019.
53. Market, A.C., *Global Forecast to 2021*, Maharashtra, India, 2019, URL: https://www.meticulousresearch.com/product/healthcare-analytics-market/ (accessed 15.05. 2021).
54. Dharmamoorthy, G., Sabareesh, M., Balaji, A., Reddy, Y.K., Monika, B., Hema, A.N., Reddy, P.S., Kartheek, U., A overview on 3D printing – current pharmaceutical applications and future directions. https://www.european-pharmaceuticalreview.com/article/162544/3d-printing-current-pharmaceutical-applications-and-future-directions/ (accessed on Jan 2023).
55. Cui, M., Pan, H., Su, Y., Fang, D., Qiao, S., Ding, P., Pan, W., Opportunities and challenges of three-dimensional printing technology in pharmaceutical formulation development. *Acta Pharm. Sin. B*, 11, 8, 2488–504, Aug. 1, 2021.
56. Beitler, B.G., Abraham, P.F., Glennon, A.R., Tommasini, S.M., Lattanza, L.L., Morris, J.M., Wiznia, D.H., Interpretation of regulatory factors for 3D printing at hospitals and medical centers, or at the point of care. *3D Print. Med.*, 8, 1, 7, Feb. 1, 2022.
57. Zidan, A., *CDER Researchers Explore The Promise And Potential Of 3D Printed Pharmaceuticals*, Spotlight on CDER Science, US Food & Drug Administration, Maryland, USA, 2017.
58. Dhyani, A., Singh, N., Kumar, V., Dhyani, A., Applications of 3 dimensional (3D) printing in biomedical field. *Int. J. Curr. Res. Rev.*, 12, 71–5, Oct. 2020.
59. Desai, H., Shah, N., Saiyad, M., Dwivedi, A., Joshipura, M., Polymers for 3D printing in biomedical engineering applications. *J. Pharm. Negat. Results*, 12, 1870–80, Oct. 2022.

60. Mohammed, A.A., Algahtani, M.S., Ahmad, M.Z., Ahmad, J., Kotta, S., 3D printing in medicine: Technology overview and drug delivery applications. *Ann. 3D Print. Med.*, 4, 100037, Dec. 1, 2021.
61. Seoane-Viaño, I., Trenfield, S.J., Basit, A.W., Goyanes, A., Translating 3D printed pharmaceuticals: From hype to real-world clinical applications. *Adv. Drug Deliv. Rev.*, 174, 553–75, Jul. 1, 2021.
62. Arafat, B., Qinna, N., Cieszynska, M., Forbes, R.T., Alhnan, M.A., Tailored on demand anti-coagulant dosing: An in vitro and in vivo evaluation of 3D printed purpose-designed oral dosage forms. *Eur. J. Pharm. Biopharm.*, 128, 282–9, Jul. 1, 2018.
63. Goyanes, A., Madla, C.M., Umerji, A., Piñeiro, G.D., Montero, J.M., Diaz, M.J., Barcia, M.G., Taherali, F., Sánchez-Pintos, P., Couce, M.L., Gaisford, S., Automated therapy preparation of isoleucine formulations using 3D printing for the treatment of MSUD: First single-centre, prospective, crossover study in patients. *Int. J. Pharm.*, 567, 118497, Aug. 15, 2019.
64. Global, B., Aprecia pharmaceuticals and cycle pharmaceuticals partner to develop 3D-printed orphan drugs. https://www.cambridgeindependent.co.uk/business/cycle-pharmaceuticals-to-use-3d-printing-to-develop-orphan-drugs-9053341/ (accessed on January 2023).
65. Algahtani, M.S., Assessment of pharmacist's knowledge and perception toward 3D printing technology as a dispensing method for personalized medicine and the readiness for implementation. *Pharmacy*, 9, 1, 68, Mar. 23, 2021.
66. Christensen, A. and Wake, N., Regulatory perspectives for 3D printing in hospitals, in: *3D Printing for the Radiologist*, vol. 1, pp. 109–16, Jan. 2022.
67. Madla, C.M., Trenfield, S.J., Goyanes, A., Gaisford, S., Basit, A.W., 3D printing technologies, implementation and regulation: An overview, in: *3D Printing of Pharmaceuticals*, pp. 21–40, 2018.
68. Markarian, J., FDA and the emerging technology of 3D printing. *Pharm. Technol.*, 40, 8, 1–36, 2016.
69. Beg, S., Almalki, W.H., Malik, A., Farhan, M., Aatif, M., Rahman, Z., Alruwaili, N.K., Alrobaian, M., Tarique, M., Rahman, M., 3D printing for drug delivery and biomedical applications. *Drug Discov. Today*, 25, 9, 1668–81, Sep. 1, 2020.
70. Sekar, M.P., Budharaju, H., Zennifer, A., Sethuraman, S., Vermeulen, N., Sundaramurthi, D., Kalaskar, D.M., Current standards and ethical landscape of engineered tissues—3D bioprinting perspective. *J. Tissue Eng.*, 12, 1–33, 20417314211027677, Jul. 2021.
71. Trenfield, S.J., Goyanes, A., Telford, R., Wilsdon, D., Rowland, M., Gaisford, S., Basit, A.W., 3D printed drug products: Non-destructive dose verification using a rapid point-and-shoot approach. *Int. J. Pharm.*, 549, 1-2, 283–92, Oct. 5, 2018.
72. Trenfield, S.J., Tan, H.X., Goyanes, A., Wilsdon, D., Rowland, M., Gaisford, S., Basit, A.W., Non-destructive dose verification of two drugs within 3D printed polyprintlets. *Int. J. Pharm.*, 577, 119066, Mar. 15, 2020.

3

3D Printing in Fabrication of Dosage Form

Abstract

Complicated biological structures, such as tissues and organs, may be printed out of digital designs using the additive manufacturing process of 3D printing. As a result of the success of Spritam®, the first 3D medicinal product approved by the FDA, a large number of researchers have been interested in the topic, and work is currently underway to produce a wide range of individualized dose forms. The aim of this overview is to familiarize readers with 3D printing, its background, advantages, and obstacles, and the numerous manufacturing techniques utilized to create pharmaceutical goods. The benefits and relevance of 3D-printed, patient-specific dose forms are evaluated as well. The necessity of tailored dosing and the utilization of anatomical models, tissue and organ fabrication, and other 3D printing applications in the treatment of diseases like cancer, diabetes, cardiovascular problems, and neurodegenerative disorders are highlighted. There is a wide range of discussions regarding the potential disruptions in healthcare and manufacturing that 3D printing may cause as well as the regulatory issues that may arise as a result. This analysis of 3D printing technology has discussed its current and future manufacturing and medicinal applications, both of which hold great promise for improving the quality of life for humans.

Keywords: 3D printing, CAD model, stereolithography, fused deposition melting, bio-inks, customized dosage forms, binder deposition, material jetting

3.1 Introduction

A 3D printer model [1] is an example of a type of manufacturing known as additive manufacturing. The method involves gradually adding new layers of material to build the final product. The United States Government Accountability Office (GAO) claims that the additive manufacturing technique made possible by 3D printing allows for the creation of 3D structures from digital models [2]. The medical, automotive, aerospace, culinary, chemical, and toy industries are just a few of the many that might benefit from its use. Medicine, prostheses, medical gadgets, and even synthetic

Rishabha Malviya and Rishav Sharma. 3D Printing in Healthcare: Novel Applications, (37–58)

tissues and organs have all been created via 3D printing in the healthcare sector. In addition, conventional pharmaceutical 2D printing entails printing hundreds of thousands of dots made from pharmaceutical ink onto a flat surface or substrate. Optimization parameters are scalable to 3D printing and can be screened with a 2D printing method [3–6], which can be used to evaluate a variety of medications, drug loadings, and release qualities in a variety of dosage forms. 4D printing is a subset of 3D printing in which the fourth dimension refers to the object's ability to adjust its shape after manufacturing, as demonstrated by tethered microgrippers that react to pressure, temperature, light, water, wind, and enzymes [7, 8]. By adding cells, biomaterials, and bio-inks like endotoxin-free low-acyl gellan gum [9], for example, to a 3D printer's build plate layer by layer, a Regenova [7] can create a viable artificial tissue or organ. Additive manufacturing (also referred to as "layer manufacturing" or "solid free-form fabrication") is a type of rapid prototyping that may be used to create complex structures from a wide range of materials [10]. Making a CAD model that represents the geometry and size of the eventual thing is a standard first step in fast prototyping and fabrication of solid objects [11]. Optimal medication absorption and distribution, as well as safety and efficacy, can be guaranteed with a more compliant patient population by using a dosage form with a predetermined release profile [12]. The first FDA-approved 3D printed drug, Spritam® (levetiracetam, an antiepileptic drug), has sparked a surge of interest in the investigation of 3D printing technology's potential for application in the production of other medications. Several factors must be considered in light of the invention to mitigate the potential for disruption. It is expected that 3D printing will cause several changes in industries including medicine and industry. More than 20 years have passed since 3D printing was used for anything beyond the prototype stage. Some examples of 3D-printed products in the healthcare and manufacturing sectors include prostheses, dental crowns and bridges, artificial kidneys and hearts for scientific study, and implants. Pete Basiliere, a member of the Gartner Blog Network, has established the following strategic planning assumptions based on current research. More than 10% of the industrialized world's population will be using 3D-printed things in their everyday lives by 2019. Over 35% of surgeries that include prostheses, implants, or artificial organs will use 3D printing in some capacity. Thanks to developments in technology and innovation, counterfeit medications, which account for 10% of the market, will increasingly be produced using 3D printers [13]. Ten percent of producers of discrete goods will utilize 3D printers to create diverse elements of their goods, and 10% of consumers will 3D-print components for goods such as automobiles, trucks, military equipment, and drones that are no longer manufactured [14].

3.2 History

Although the idea of 3D printing was developed quite some time ago, it is only recently that technology has gained widespread attention and been used in several practical contexts. Dr. Kodama's early work in rapid prototyping, beginning in 1980, is widely regarded as a watershed moment in the field. He was an innovator in the field of additive manufacturing, having developed the process of stereolithography, which involves the use of photosensitive resin polymerized by UV radiation. Unfortunately, a patent application for the invention was never submitted to him [15, 16]. When a group of French engineers tried stereolithography in 1984, they quickly gave up because they saw no future for it [15]. Charles Hull began working on stereolithography in 1983 when he patented the technique and produced the first SLA-I machine. [17]. Selective laser sintering (SLS) technology, a type of 3D printing in which a laser is used to fuse the powder material, was patented in 1988 by Charles Deckard [15]. Stratasys's creator, in 1989, came up with the revolutionary fused deposition melting (FDM) technique, which was patented in 1992 [18]. In the years between 1993 and 1999, several companies were developing innovative approaches to 3D printing, including ZCorp binder jetting at MIT, Arcam MCP technology, and selective laser melting. In 1999, advances in medicine were made possible by laboratory-created organs. Despite advances in 3D printing, transplantation research is still in its infancy. The first functional 3D-printed kidney was made in 2000. The advent of 3D printing technology has allowed for several developments to occur since [15].

3.3 Advantages

The dosage form's administration of the API can be tailored to the drug's intended release profile. The effectiveness of dosage forms can be increased by designing them with complex yet realizable geometries [18]. The versatility and complexity of release patterns in formulations are facilitated by 3D printing [19]. Novel drug delivery systems, such as the polypill and fixed dose combination (FDC), are encouraged, in which the release properties of each drug are predetermined. As a result, researchers may go on with creating better and more innovative ways to administer medications [20]. A 3D-printed levofloxacin implant, for example, enables the combined pulsatile and steady-state release of pharmaceuticals via predefined microstructures [21], paving the way for the production of medication on demand and in individualized dosages. Savings in time and money,

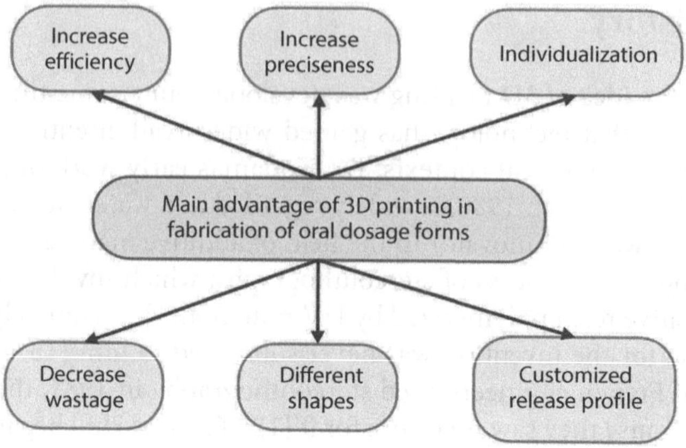

Figure 3.1 Main advantages of 3D printing technology in the fabrication of oral dosage forms.

increased output, creative leeway throughout production, and broader partnerships are all additional benefits [22]. The benefits of 3D printing for pharmaceutical manufacturing are shown in Figure 3.1.

3.4 Limitations and Challenges

Since 1993, researchers have been meticulously evaluating the procedure by discussing its shortcomings. Patient approval was shown to be worse when large, irregular forms were used for oral administration, as opposed to smaller, smoother ones. It was the case because the larger, irregular shapes were harder to swallow. Some production methods, such as ink-jet-based printing, subject the dosage form to heat for an extended duration, which increases the time required to produce the product [23]. It can cause crucial parameters, including residual solvents, to rise over acceptable levels. FDM is a solvent-free alternative to conventional modeling; however, it has a very poor drug loading capacity and still requires a drying phase. FDM is a thermal procedure that melts all main pharmaceuticals, excipients, and carriers, restricting its application to just a small number of suitable excipients and preventing the integration of thermolabile medications [24]. The use of ultraviolet light (UV) to cure the polymerization step that sets the final drug formulation in stereolithography poses a risk of drug degradation. Research has been ongoing to find solutions to these problems and expand the capabilities of 3D printing so that it can be used safely and effectively.

3.5 Personalized Dosage Form

The term "personalized medicine" [25] describes the practice of tailoring medical care to each patient's unique set of circumstances. The idea originated long ago when doctors saw a pattern of shared symptoms across diseases with varying origins and treatments. Because of the ease and accuracy with which modern diagnostic tools could determine the root of the problem, the industry prospered [26]. 3D printing's contribution to the medical and medical device industries has been in the creation of individualized dosages, dosage forms, implants, and other goods to increase the patients' likelihood of taking their medication as prescribed [20].

3.6 Bio-Inks

To facilitate the bio-printing of biological products, bio-inks are biomaterial formulations that mimic ink. Bio-inks are often cell suspensions, decellularized extra-cellular matrix-based solutions, or hydrogels (such as chitosan, gelatin, or poloxamer) loaded with cells for bio-printing [27]. These bio-inks provide an environment similar to that seen in a living cell, which permits typical cell functions including migration, proliferation, and division [28]. Bio-inks should be biocompatible, non-immunogenic, mechanically stable, and have a low modulus of elasticity [29]. The essential characteristics of an effective scaffold for engineering an artificial organ include the ability to transport nutrients, the presence of blood vessel integration for systemic circulation, mechanical strength, and cell type compatibility. Traditional fabrication techniques [30] include seeding cells onto a scaffold and molding bio-ink-based cells in a 3D bio-printer. Because of this, bio-inks are crucial to the success of 3D bio-printers in producing a wide range of biological products (tissues and organs).

3.7 Applications in Healthcare

Customized dosage forms, drug manufacture, and distribution, prostheses, medical gadgets and models, tissue and organ fabrication, and specialist surgical equipment all fall under the category [30]. By using 3D printing reaction ware, Lee Cronin's team was able to successfully print the medicine ibuprofen. Aprecia Pharmaceuticals' Spritam® (levetiracetam) is a good example of the production of high-dose tablets that dissolve and disintegrate rapidly due to their porous structure. According to Phil Reeves' 2013 research on 3D printing, over 10 million 3D-printed hearing aids have already been distributed. Dental equipment producers include Stratasys [31], Envisiontec [32], Zenith, etc [5]. It includes crowns, bridges, plaster/stone models, and a plethora of orthodontic instruments. Fully personalized, lightweight, and cheap 3D prostheses are all the rage compared to conventional prosthetics [5]. Helpful applications of 3D-printed anatomical models include the verification and validation of algorithms, the verification and education of students, and the design of virtual surgeries [33]. Small amounts of 3D bio-printed tissue culture for drug, glucose, bile acid, and lipid metabolism have been produced by the scaffold-free 3D bioprinter Regenova to aid in the discovery of novel drugs [34]. It is also being attempted to develop a fully functional artificial liver for transplant [35].

3.8 3D Printing Techniques

Solid dosage forms are traditionally difficult to formulate using traditional methods due to the extensive processing stages involved, including milling, mixing, granulating, etc. There may be an increased risk of batch failure or inadequate quality if more steps are required for preparation. Since there are fewer moving parts, there are fewer regulatory and quality control issues to worry about when using 3D printing [36]. The manufacturing strategies that make use of 3D printers are discussed below.

3.8.1 Binder Deposition

For the most part, this method is what is employed when 3D printing medicines. The method involves spraying a powder bed with tiny droplets of binder ink, like polyvinyl alcohol or maltodextrin, at a controlled and predetermined speed, movement, and size. A simple drug product formulation could involve using an ink composed entirely of a binder solution and a powder bed composed of an API and excipients. Binders in solution or nanoparticle suspension are alternatives to the API [20]. In the Biopharmaceutical Classification System, this method is used mostly for medications in classes II and IV due to their low solubility (BCS). Pardeike *et al.* [37] designed a nanosuspension of folic acid (a BCS class IV medicine) and other excipients, printed it on a substrate (edible paper), and then coiled it up and inserted it within a capsule to match individual dose needs. In many ways, the process of wet granulation can be compared to the solidification of the medicinal product. The approach has a similar evaluation scope due to the similarity in methodologies, and it can be quickly approved by regulators.

3.8.2 Material Jetting

Using a powder bed for printing with an inkjet printer is optional. By ejecting the material drop by drop, which hardens all at once like stalagmites, the printer can create free-form structures. Many different substances, including waxes, molten polymers, various resins, suspensions, solutions, and multi-component fluids, can be used as jet materials. Since jetting is integral to the formulation, the final shape is determined by the droplet's trajectory during ejection, the force of impact, and the moisture content of the surface [20]. Buanz *et al.* [38] used thermal inkjet printing to deposit single and multiple layers of salbutamol sulfate on a potato starch film, achieving an accuracy of within 5% of the predicted dose. Inkjet printing was used to deposit a nanosuspension of ciprofloxacin (a drug in the BCS class IV) and dextran sulfate onto a cellulose substrate. The formulation of microparticles is facilitated by the thinner layer thickness, which is an advantage over binder deposition [20].

3.8.3 Extrusion

The pharmaceutical industry has taken a keen interest in 3D printing, specifically the extrusion technique that is most widely utilized. Melt is extruded using mechanical nozzles to accomplish the desired effect [39]. Instead of requiring a powder bed, it is capable of printing on a wide variety of media. Extruded materials like Eudragit E and tribasic calcium phosphate [40] need scaffolds for support when printing drugs with the method. Tablets containing captopril, theophylline, and prednisolone with immediate release were created by Sadia *et al.* using a hot-melt extrusion technique [40]. A wide variety of materials, from molten formulations to semisolids and pastes to colloidal suspensions and silicones, can all be extruded using this technology. Medicines that break down at high temperatures, like bovine serum albumin [41], adalimumab, and abatacept [42], may not be suited for this method [20].

3.8.4 Powder Bed Fusion

Using a laser as a source of heat, this approach can be used to either sinter high-melting-point compounds or bind them with a low-melting-point binder [43]. Tayel *et al.* [44] created a sublingual tablet form of the anti-asthma medication ketotifen fumarate by combining polyethylene glycols

400 and 600 with a starch/mannitol mixture for fast dissolution. As an alternative to extrusion, quick and sophisticated technology can be used [20].

3.8.5 Photopolymerization (Stereolithography)

Polymerization of liquid resins like polylactic acid (PLA) and polyvinyl alcohol (PVA) [32] can occur when these substances are subjected to a high-energy light source like UV radiation. Wang *et al.* [45] used polyethylene glycol diacrylate as the monomer and diphenyl (2,4,6-trimethyl benzoyl) phosphine oxide as the photo-initiator in the development of modified-release tablets containing paracetamol and 4-amino salicylic acid. The lack of readily available photopolymerizable materials is a major limitation of the approach. The polymerization process leaves behind residual resins that are distinct from the finished product and may have their own set of toxicity problems, including genotoxicity. The only benefits are a high print resolution and fast printing speed [20].

3.8.6 Pen-Based 3D Printing

It is modernized handheld extrusion equipment for preparing insufficient but desired structures. Researchers are also thinking about how useful it could be for depositing materials for 3D constructions during surgery.

3.9 Comparison to the Conventional Manufacturing Technique

The introduction of 3D printing in the pharmaceutical business has led to an increase in the complexity of dosage forms created on a layer-by-layer basis. Since it is digitally planned and on-demand generated using automated and low-cost operational methods, it paves the way for customization in the medical sphere [20].

3.10 Comparisons between Various 3D Printing Techniques

3.10.1 Basic 3D Printing Procedure

Many 3D printing methods that are introduced are based on diverse concepts and can employ a wide variety of raw materials (such as thermoplastics, wax, metal, etc.) [46], but the majority of them share the procedure detailed below.

3.10.1.1 Designing

Using 3D photos of specimens and computer-aided design (CAD) tools like Optistruct by Altair or Millipede by Grasshopper [47], the necessary dosage form is designed digitally.

3.10.1.2 Creating a Machine-Readable Format

As a result of conversion to a more practical format (STL), the 3D model takes on its final form. Models are produced by digitally slicing them into many layers, which are then sent to a printer such as a MakerBot Replicator 2 or a Regenova [7] to be added together.

3.10.1.3 Raw Material Processing

APIs such as salbutamol sulfate [38], captopril, etc., and additives such as Eudragit E [40], PLA and PVA, etc. [32], can be processed into granules, hot-melt, filaments, and binder ink.

3.10.1.4 Actual Printing

Tablets, capsules, implants, and other finished goods can be made by the procedure by adding raw ingredients in the required shape and then automatically solidifying these layers [48, 49].

3.10.2 Various Dosage Forms

Many studies have been conducted toward the creation of various dosage formulations, and many more are in the works. The numerous 3D-printed dosage forms for medicines are described below.

3.10.3 Immediate-Release Tablet

The term "immediate-release tablet" refers to a specific type of tablet that dissolves or breaks apart rapidly to release its contents rapidly [50]. A paracetamol immediate-release medication formulation was manufactured using the selective laser sintering method of 3D printing, as was the case in one of the many studies on immediate-release tablets conducted by Goyanes *et al.* [51]. Paracetamol formulations with drug loadings of 5%, 20%, and 35% were made, and none of the finished products showed any signs of deterioration. Drug content-dependent release at a pH-independent rate was observed [51]. Theophylline immediate-release tablets in the shape of caplets were 3D-printed by Okwuosa *et al.* [52] using hot-melt extrusion, followed by fused deposition melting and a polyvinylpyrrolidone polymer excipient.

3.11 Bilayer Tablets

The term "bilayer tablet" refers to a type of biphasic delivery mechanism that is intended to simultaneously release two medicines at two distinct rates. One drug can have two different release patterns printed on different layers, increasing treatment efficacy through a synergistic effect while reducing the number of units required for treatment, lowering costs, and simplifying manufacture [53]. Khaled *et al.* [36] attempted to replicate the commonly produced bilayer tablet of guaifenesin (600 mg dose used for the diagnosis of respiratory tract infections) and were successful. Their tablet has an immediate release layer to relieve symptoms speedily and a sustained release layer to maintain therapeutic concentrations for an extended period.

3.11.1 Capsule

There are two types of capsules, those that dissolve slowly and those that dissolve quickly [54]. Size variations in capsules make it possible to pack various amounts of powder, granules, solution, emulsion, or other pharmacological preparations into a single pill. The application of fused deposition modeling led to the development of hydroxypropyl cellulose (HPC) erodible capsules (ChronoCap®) that can pulsatile release a wide range of pharmaceutical formulations, notwithstanding their size and thickness (using MakerBot Replicator 2). A wide range of powders, pellets, solutions, dispersions, and other materials can be stored in it [55, 56].

3.11.2 Polypill

The term "polypill" refers to a specific type of medication delivery system that combines many pharmaceuticals into one pill, known as FDC [57]. Using the 3D printing process, it can be produced in either mass quantities to meet the demands of a big population or in a uniquely crafted shape to meet the needs of an individual. A successful room-temperature 3D-printed tablet (polypill) comprising captopril, nifedipine, and glipizide (with a specific controlled release profile) has been produced for the treatment of diabetic hypertension using means of extrusion [58]. Another five-in-one polypill for the treatment of cardiovascular disorders was developed by Khaled *et al.* [59]. It contains the immediate-release medications aspirin and hydrochlorothiazide as well as the slow-release medications pravastatin, atenolol, and ramipril.

3.11.3 SEDDS

Self-emulsifying drug delivery systems (SEDDS) are amorphous combinations of oil, surfactant, cosolvents, and drugs. By enhancing the solubility of the medicine and the permeability of the membrane, SEDDS are used to improve the drug's bioavailability [60]. 3D printing was used to create a SEDDS formulation by coating an inert tablet with a self-emulsifying mixture of celecoxib and glacier 44/14 (10:90 w/w) heated to 70 °C [61].

3.11.4 Implants

Implants are devices that are placed inside or on the body to release medication gradually and safely. Nonbiodegradable polymers include polyurethane, silicone rubber, and ethylene vinyl acetate [62–64]. Biodegradable polymers, such as polylactide (PLA) and polyglycolic acid (PGA), can be used to construct implants with the desired features of medication release and safety for the body. Using a polylactic acid polymer, Water *et al.* [65] designed an implant of nitrofurantoin for controlled release over 45 days. Multilayer medicine implants containing isoniazid and rifampicin were created by Wu *et al.* [66] for the treatment of tuberculosis of the bone. Gbureck *et al.* [67] developed a method to create antibiotic sustained-release implants by adsorbing antibiotic solutions such as vancomycin, ofloxacin, and tetracycline onto substrates such as hydroxyapatite, brushite, etc.

3.12 Benefits of Various Disorders

3.12.1 Cancer

The National Cancer Institute defines cancer as "a disease characterized by abnormal and unregulated cell division that can infiltrate surrounding tissues and may or may not spread to other sections of the body via systemic circulation and the lymphatic system" [68]. Although the disease's mechanism and etiology have been better understood since its discovery, there are still challenges to its treatment [69]. The creation of a personalized replica model to practice and preplan surgery on the cancer patient posed a significant challenge [70]. *In vitro* models of tumor growth and metastasis can now be created with the use of 3D printing advancements [71]. It is especially helpful in cell microenvironment engineering because it permits fine-grained spatial control over cell structure and biomolecule insertion [72]. To simulate specific organs or tissues, additional components, such as cells, polymers, vasculature, and microchannels, can be added to the basic framework [73]. The ability to forecast the pattern of tumor cell proliferation and precisely detect the malignancy using a clinical platform improves the accuracy of treatment techniques and opens up new avenues for research into the causes of and potential cures for cancer [74].

3.12.2 Diabetes

Hyperglycemia is a hallmark of diabetes, which is a metabolic condition characterized by elevated blood glucose levels (typical pre-prandial: 72–108 mg/dl and post-prandial, i.e., 2 h after eating: 140 mg/dl) [75]. The treatment methods for diabetes have benefited greatly from the application of 3D printing technology. With the use of 3D printing, scientists have been able to overcome significant obstacles in the manufacturing of insulin-producing islet cells [76] and in the creation of individualized drug dosages. Scientists from Boston University have created a synthetic pancreas that can secrete insulin by using stem cells and other associated proteins [77]. Islet cells have been transported via an extrahepatic pathway, improving their viability and usefulness, according to the work of Marchioli *et al.*, who used a 3D alginate-based porous scaffold [78]. Nano-glands were produced by Sabek *et al.* by utilizing a 3D printer to encapsulate islet-like insulin-generating aggregates to produce stable amounts of insulin for at least 4 weeks [79]. Because people with diabetes have widely varying rates of insulin production and insulin responsiveness, personalized approaches and personalized medicine are becoming important for maximizing treatment efficacy while minimizing adverse effects [80].

3.13 Cardiovascular Diseases

Despite their prevalence, heart and vascular diseases are largely preventable [81], they are often debilitating [82], and no solution has yet been found. The diagnostic and treatment processes commonly utilize a variety of modalities for 2D imaging, such as magnetic resonance imaging (MRI), computerized tomography (CT), angiography (angioscopy), and echocardiography. The problem with these methods is that they cannot faithfully portray the true size structure in three dimensions [83]. To create a duplicate of the heart's architecture, a 3D printer uses a large amount of data collected via imaging techniques [84]. Having a 3D duplicate model of the heart's structure and pathophysiology allows for highly precise therapy planning [85]. To determine the optimal placement, size, and length of a stent, Valverde *et al.* [86] used MRI data to 3D-print a duplicate of a hypoplastic aortic arch. Human cells and other substances could be 3D-printed into a heart for transplantation [87] by utilizing 3D printing technology.

3.14 Neurodegenerative Diseases

Neurodegenerative diseases, which include Alzheimer's, Parkinson's, and dementia, are a group of conditions affecting the CNS and PNS and are defined by the gradual deterioration of the structure and function of the nervous system [88]. Three imaging and *in vitro* modeling have their advantages, but they have significant limitations when it comes to studying the brain and other sections and planning the treatment of various neurological diseases. By using peptide-modified gellan gum as bio-ink and neural cells enclosed in hydrogels, Lozano *et al.* [89] developed a method for 3D bio-printing brain-like structures. It permits the precise modeling of microstructures for enhanced surgical preparation and the development of more effective treatment strategies. Ploch *et al.* [90] suggested making an anatomically and physiologically accurate 3D model of the brain out of soft gelatin, which would be both inexpensive and individualized. Ormabera *et al.* [91] used CT scan data and a 3D printed model of the skull made of acrylonitrile butadiene styrene plastic to plan a skull resection. Owens *et al.* [92] used a rat model for sciatic nerve injury to bio-print a multi-layer nerve graft by deposition of cellular cylinders of mouse bone marrow stem cells and Schwann cells onto a support framework. To treat a debilitating neurological disorder, Hsieh *et al.* [93] used 3D bio-printing to encase neural stem cells in a thermo-responsive biodegradable polyurethane dispersion, which they then injected into a zebrafish embryo brain injury model.

3.15 Other Diseases

Ackland *et al.* [94] utilized a SIEMENS® CT scan to construct a 3D-printed musculoskeletal model for the production of a custom prosthetic joint replacement for the temporomandibular joint. Using a desktop 3D printer (Makerbot Replicator 2X), Cevenini *et al.* [95] developed a smartphone-based bioanalytical application that relied on bioluminescent sentinel cells enclosed in a 3D printer cartridge and smartphone adaptor. Researchers are developing 3D hepatic cultures of liver fibrosis to aid in the development of *in vitro* models for the identification of potent antifibrotic medications [96]. To deal with C2-level Ewing's sarcoma, a titanium C2-level vertebral body made by utilizing 3D printing technology was created and implanted [97].

3.16 Regulatory Issues

Tablets, capsules, implants, and other dose forms, as well as medical equipment like prosthetics and anatomical models, could all benefit from the usage of 3D printing in the pharmaceutical industry [98]. The FDA has already given its stamp of approval to several 3D-printed products, including a medicine product [53] and numerous pieces of medical equipment [5, 31], including orthodontic implants, prostheses, anatomical models, and reaction-wares. According to Recommendations Agenda [99], the FDA could have compiled recommendations tailored to 3D printing in Guideline Agenda 2015 but instead chose to forego the opportunity. The Food and Drug Administration (FDA) has approved certain 3D-printed products via emergency procedures, while it has also followed its long-standing protocols for drugs and medical devices of moderate risk. In the conventional model, a new medicine receives NDA approval only after it is safe and effective when used by the label's instructions. Aprecia Pharmaceuticals Co.'s Spritam® (levetiracetam, an antiepileptic drug) [5], Oxford Performance Materials Inc.'s OsteoFab® (patient-specific facial device, an orthodontic implant) [100], Zimmer Biomet Holdings' Unite3DTM Bridge Fixation System [100], and 85 other products approved via 510(k) pathways [101, 102] are just some of the 3D printed drugs and devices that have been approved by the FDA [102].

3.17 Conclusions

The remarkable variety of medical uses for 3D printing has attracted the attention of numerous researchers and sparked new developments in the field. With the ability to print out customized solutions, 3D printing can improve the standard of care provided in the medical field. Drugs of varying shapes, sizes, dosages, and dosage forms can be printed with a wide range of customizability, down to the drug release profile and FDC. Drug toxicity and other unwanted consequences induced by an overdose can be minimized or eliminated with personalized formulations. Also, 3D printers' ability to produce medicine at the point of care expands the therapeutic alternatives available to medical professionals and makes it easier for them to select the most appropriate treatment. In addition, it can produce a wide range of medical equipment and implants as well as anatomical models and artificial organs, among other things, which might greatly advance healthcare and healthcare education. In August 2015, the first FDA-approved medicine product confirmed the commercial viability of 3D-printed items, and since then, many medical devices have been made using this technology. Thus, it appears that the ever-increasing sophistication of 3D printing technology and its uses will significantly alter medical practice and raise the standards of living.

References

1. Prasad, L.K. and Smyth, H., 3D printing technologies for drug delivery: A review. *Drug Dev. Ind. Pharm.*, 42, 7, 1019–31, Jul. 2, 2016.
2. Pravin, S. and Sudhir, A., Integration of 3D printing with dosage forms: A new perspective for modern healthcare. *Biomed. Pharmacother.*, 107, 146–54, Nov. 1, 2018.
3. Sandler, N., Määttänen, A., Ihalainen, P., Kronberg, L., Meierjohann, A., Viitala, T., Peltonen, J., Inkjet printing of drug substances and use of porous substrates-towards individualized dosing. *J. Pharm. Sci.*, 100, 8, 3386–95, Aug. 1, 2011.
4. Leong, T.G., Randall, C.L., Benson, B.R., Bassik, N., Stern, G.M., Gracias, D.H., Tetherless thermochemically actuated microgrippers. *Proc. Natl. Acad. Sci.*, 106, 3, 703–8, Jan. 20, 2009.
5. Dodziuk, H., Applications of 3D printing in healthcare. *Kardiochir. Torakochirurgia Pol.*, 13, 3, 283–93, Sep. 30, 2016.
6. Choi, J., Kwon, O.C., Jo, W., Lee, H.J., Moon, M.W., 4D printing technology: A review. *3D Print. Addit. Manuf.*, 2, 4, 159–67, Dec. 1, 2015.
7. Kizawa, H., Nagao, E., Shimamura, M., Zhang, G., Torii, H., Scaffold-free 3D bio-printed human liver tissue stably maintains metabolic functions useful for drug discovery. *Biochem. Biophys. Rep.*, 10, 186–91, Jul. 1, 2017.
8. Munoz-Abraham, A.S., Rodriguez-Davalos, M.I., Bertacco, A., Wengerter, B., Geibel, J.P., Mulligan, D.C., 3D printing of organs for transplantation: where are we and where are we heading? *Curr. Transplant. Rep.*, 3, 93–9, Mar. 2016.
9. Ferris, C.J., Gilmore, K.J., Beirne, S., McCallum, D., Wallace, G.G., Bio-ink for on-demand printing of living cells. *Biomater. Sci.*, 1, 2, 224–30, 2013.

10. Guo, N. and Leu, M.C., Additive manufacturing: Technology, applications and research needs. *Front. Mech. Eng.*, 8, 215–43, Sep. 2013.
11. Goyanes, A., Wang, J., Buanz, A., Martínez-Pacheco, R., Telford, R., Gaisford, S., Basit, A.W., 3D printing of medicines: Engineering novel oral devices with unique design and drug release characteristics. *Mol. Pharm.*, 12, 11, 4077–84, Nov. 2, 2015.
12. Moulton, S.E. and Wallace, G.G., 3-dimensional (3D) fabricated polymer based drug delivery systems. *J. Control. Release*, 193, 27–34, Nov. 10, 2014.
13. Pravin, S. and Sudhir, A., Integration of 3D printing with dosage forms: A new perspective for modern healthcare. *Biomed. Pharmacother.*, 107, 146–54, 2018.
14. Basiliere, P., Predicts 2016: 3D printing disrupts healthcare and manufacturing. *Gartner*. https://www.gartner.com/en/documents/3171223 (accessed on February 2023).
15. Bell, D., Fallat, J., Sterley, G., Alsuhibani, E., *The Future of Additive Manufacturing in the US Military*, Air Command and Staff College, Air University Maxwell AFB United States, Mar. 17, 2017.
16. Prince, J.D., 3D printing: An industrial revolution. *J. Electron. Resour. Med. Libr.*, 11, 1, 39–45, Jan 1, 2014.
17. Papaioannou, T.G., Manolesou, D., Dimakakos, E., Tsoucalas, G., Vavuranakis, M., Tousoulis, D., 3D bioprinting methods and techniques: applications on artificial blood vessel fabrication. *Acta Cardiol. Sin.*, 35, 3, 284, May 2019.
18. Reis Silva, M., Pereira, A.M., Alves, N., Mateus, G., Mateus, A., Malça, C., Development of an additive manufacturing system for the deposition of thermoplastics impregnated with carbon fibers. *J. Manuf. Mater. Process.*, 3, 2, 35, Apr. 27, 2019.
19. Katstra, W.E., Palazzolo, R.D., Rowe, C.W., Giritlioglu, B., Teung, P., Cima, M.J., Oral dosage forms fabricated by three dimensional printing™. *J. Control. Release*, 66, 1, 1–9, May 3, 2000.
20. Norman, J., Madurawe, R.D., Moore, C.M., Khan, M.A., Khairuzzaman, A., A new chapter in pharmaceutical manufacturing: 3D-printed drug products. *Adv. Drug Deliv. Rev.*, 108, 39–50, Jan. 1, 2017.
21. Huang, W., Zheng, Q., Sun, W., Xu, H., Yang, X., Levofloxacin implants with predefined microstructure fabricated by three-dimensional printing technique. *Int. J. Pharm.*, 339, 1-2, 33–8, Jul. 18, 2007.
22. Sadia, M., Arafat, B., Ahmed, W., Forbes, R.T., Alhnan, M.A., Channelled tablets: An innovative approach to accelerating drug release from 3D printed tablets. *J. Control. Release*, 269, 355–63, Jan. 10, 2018.
23. Goole, J. and Amighi, K., 3D printing in pharmaceutics: A new tool for designing customized drug delivery systems. *Int. J. Pharm.*, 499, 1-2, 376–94, Feb. 29, 2016.
24. Alhnan, M.A., Okwuosa, T.C., Sadia, M., Wan, K.W., Ahmed, W., Arafat, B., Emergence of 3D printed dosage forms: Opportunities and challenges. *Pharm. Res.*, 33, 1817–32, Aug 2016.

25. Redekop, W.K. and Mladsi, D., The faces of personalized medicine: A framework for understanding its meaning and scope. *Value Health*, 16, 6, S4–9, Sep. 1, 2013.
26. Kichko, K., Marschall, P., Flessa, S., Personalized medicine in the US and Germany: Awareness, acceptance, use and preconditions for the wide implementation into the medical standard. *J. Pers. Med.*, 6, 2, 15, May 2, 2016.
27. Ji, S. and Guvendiren, M., Recent advances in bioink design for 3D bioprinting of tissues and organs. *Front. Bioeng. Biotechnol.*, 5, 23, Apr. 5, 2017.
28. Fisher, O.Z., Khademhosseini, A., Langer, R., Peppas, N.A., Bioinspired materials for controlling stem cell fate. *Acc. Chem. Res.*, 43, 3, 419–28, Mar. 16, 2010.
29. Chimene, D., Lennox, K.K., Kaunas, R.R., Gaharwar, A.K., Advanced bioinks for 3D printing: A materials science perspective. *Ann. Biomed. Eng.*, 44, 2090–102, Jun. 2016.
30. Fedorovich, N.E., Alblas, J., de Wijn, J.R., Hennink, W.E., Verbout, A.J., Dhert, W.J., Hydrogels as extracellular matrices for skeletal tissue engineering: State-of-the-art and novel application in organ printing. *Tissue Eng.*, 13, 8, 1905–25, Aug. 1, 2007.
31. Ali, A., Ahmad, U., Akhtar, J., 3D printing in pharmaceutical sector: An overview, in: *Pharmaceutical Formulation Design-Recent Practices*, Jan. 3, 2020.
32. Camardella, L.T., de Vasconcellos Vilella, O., Breuning, H., Accuracy of printed dental models made with 2 prototype technologies and different designs of model bases. *Am. J. Orthod. Dentofac. Orthop.*, 151, 6, 1178–87, Jun. 1, 2017.
33. Wang, K., Ho, C.C., Zhang, C., Wang, B., A review on the 3D printing of functional structures for medical phantoms and regenerated tissue and organ applications. *Engineering*, 3, 5, 653–62, Oct. 1, 2017.
34. Kizawa, H., Nagao, E., Shimamura, M., Zhang, G., Torii, H., Scaffold-free 3D bio-printed human liver tissue stably maintains metabolic functions useful for drug discovery. *Biochem. Biophys. Rep.*, 10, 186–91, Jul. 1, 2017.
35. Zhong, C., Xie, H.Y., Zhou, L., Xu, X., Zheng, S.S., Human hepatocytes loaded in 3D bioprinting generate mini-liver. *HBPD Int.*, 15, 5, 512–8, Oct. 15, 2016.
36. Khaled, S.A., Burley, J.C., Alexander, M.R., Roberts, C.J., Desktop 3D printing of controlled release pharmaceutical bilayer tablets. *Int. J. Pharm.*, 461, 1-2, 105–11, Jan. 30, 2014.
37. Pardeike, J., Strohmeier, D.M., Schrödl, N., Voura, C., Gruber, M., Khinast, J.G., Zimmer, A., Nanosuspensions as advanced printing ink for accurate dosing of poorly soluble drugs in personalized medicines. *Int. J. Pharm.*, 420, 1, 93–100, Nov. 25, 2011.
38. Buanz, A.B., Saunders, M.H., Basit, A.W., Gaisford, S., Preparation of personalized-dose salbutamol sulphate oral films with thermal ink-jet printing. *Pharm. Res.*, 28, 2386–92, Oct. 2011.

39. Cheow, W.S., Kiew, T.Y., Hadinoto, K., Combining inkjet printing and amorphous nanonization to prepare personalized dosage forms of poorly-soluble drugs. *Eur. J. Pharm. Biopharm.*, 96, 314–21, Oct. 1, 2015.
40. Sadia, M., Sośnicka, A., Arafat, B., Isreb, A., Ahmed, W., Kelarakis, A., Alhnan, M.A., Adaptation of pharmaceutical excipients to FDM 3D printing for the fabrication of patient-tailored immediate release tablets. *Int. J. Pharm.*, 513, 1-2, 659–68, Nov. 20, 2016.
41. Adami, R., Liparoti, S., Reverchon, E., A new supercritical assisted atomization configuration, for the micronization of thermolabile compounds. *Chem. Eng. J.*, 173, 1, 55–61, Sep. 1, 2011.
42. Ferreira, C.N., Squiassi, H.B., Santana, C.F., Cost of wastage in logistic management: thermolabile drugs in the treatment of rheumatoid arthritis in Brazil. *Value Health*, 19, 3, A240, May 1, 2016.
43. Kruth, J.P., Mercelis, P., Van Vaerenbergh, J., Froyen, L., Rombouts, M., Binding mechanisms in selective laser sintering and selective laser melting. *Rapid Prototyp. J.*, 11, 26–36, Feb. 1, 2005.
44. Tayel, S.A., Soliman, I.I., Louis, D., Formulation of ketotifen fumarate fast-melt granulation sublingual tablet. *AAPS PharmSciTech*, 11, 679–85, Jun. 2010.
45. Wang, J., Goyanes, A., Gaisford, S., Basit, A.W., Stereolithographic (SLA) 3D printing of oral modified-release dosage forms. *Int. J. Pharm.*, 503, 1-2, 207–12, Apr. 30, 2016.
46. Gu, Q., Hao, J., Lu, Y., Wang, L., Wallace, G.G., Zhou, Q., Three-dimensional bio-printing. *Sci. China Life Sci.*, 58, 411–9, May 2015.
47. García-Domínguez, A., Claver, J., Sebastián, M.A., Study for the selection of design software for 3D printing topological optimization. *Proc. Manuf.*, 13, 903–9, Jan. 1, 2017.
48. Edgar, J. and Tint, S., Additive manufacturing technologies: 3D printing, rapid prototyping, and direct digital manufacturing. *Johnson Matthey Technol. Rev.*, 59, 3, 193–8, Jul. 1, 2015.
49. Palo, M., Holländer, J., Suominen, J., Yliruusi, J., Sandler, N., 3D printed drug delivery devices: Perspectives and technical challenges. *Expert Rev. Med. Devices*, 14, 9, 685–96, Sep. 2, 2017.
50. Nyol, S. and Gupta, M.M., Immediate drug release dosage form: A review. *J. Drug Deliv. Ther.*, 3, 2, 155–161, Mar. 15, 2013.
51. Goyanes, A., Hatton, G.B., Merchant, H.A., Basit, A.W., Gastrointestinal release behaviour of modified-release drug products: Dynamic dissolution testing of mesalazine formulations. *Int. J. Pharm.*, 484, 1-2, 103–8, Apr. 30, 2015.
52. Okwuosa, T.C., Stefaniak, D., Arafat, B., Isreb, A., Wan, K.W., Alhnan, M.A., A lower temperature FDM 3D printing for the manufacture of patient-specific immediate release tablets. *Pharm. Res.*, 33, 2704–12, Nov. 2016.
53. He, W., Huang, S., Zhou, C., Cao, L., Yao, J., Zhou, J., Wang, G., Yin, L., Bilayer matrix tablets for prolonged actions of metformin hydrochloride and repaglinide. *AAPS PharmSciTech*, 16, 344–53, Apr. 2015.

54. Varghese, R., Sood, P., Salvi, S., Karsiya, J., Kumar, D., 3D printing in the pharmaceutical sector: Advances and evidences. *Sens. Int.*, 25, 100177, Apr. 2022.
55. Maroni, A., Zema, L., Del Curto, M.D., Loreti, G., Gazzaniga, A., Oral pulsatile delivery: Rationale and chronopharmaceutical formulations. *Int. J. Pharm.*, 398, 1-2, 1–8, Oct. 15, 2010.
56. Maroni, A., Melocchi, A., Parietti, F., Foppoli, A., Zema, L., Gazzaniga, A., 3D printed multi-compartment capsular devices for two-pulse oral drug delivery. *J. Control. Release*, 268, 10–8, Dec. 28, 2017.
57. Parhi, R. and Jena, G.K., An updated review on application of 3D printing in fabricating pharmaceutical dosage forms. *Drug Deliv. Transl. Res.*, 12, 1–35, Oct. 6, 2021.
58. Khaled, S.A., Burley, J.C., Alexander, M.R., Yang, J., Roberts, C.J., 3D printing of tablets containing multiple drugs with defined release profiles. *Int. J. Pharm.*, 494, 2, 643–50, Oct. 30, 2015.
59. Khaled, S.A., Burley, J.C., Alexander, M.R., Yang, J., Roberts, C.J., 3D printing of five-in-one dose combination polypill with defined immediate and sustained release profiles. *J. Control. Release*, 217, 308–14, Nov. 10, 2015.
60. Khaled, S.A., Burley, J.C., Alexander, M.R., Yang, J., Roberts, C.J., 3D printing of five-in-one dose combination polypill with defined immediate and sustained release profiles. *J. Control. Release*, 217, 308–14, Nov. 10, 2015.
61. Içten, E., Purohit, H.S., Wallace, C., Giridhar, A., Taylor, L.S., Nagy, Z.K., Reklaitis, G.V., Dropwise additive manufacturing of pharmaceutical products for amorphous and self emulsifying drug delivery systems. *Int. J. Pharm.*, 524, 1-2, 424–32, May 30, 2017.
62. Wu, P. and Grainger, D.W., Drug/device combinations for local drug therapies and infection prophylaxis. *Biomaterials*, 27, 11, 2450–67, Apr. 1, 2006.
63. Fu, Y. and Kao, W.J., Drug release kinetics and transport mechanisms of non-degradable and degradable polymeric delivery systems. *Expert Opin. Drug Deliv.*, 7, 4, 429–44, Apr. 1, 2010.
64. Genina, N., Holländer, J., Jukarainen, H., Mäkilä, E., Salonen, J., Sandler, N., Ethylene vinyl acetate (EVA) as a new drug carrier for 3D printed medical drug delivery devices. *Eur. J. Pharm. Sci.*, 90, 53–63, Jul. 30, 2016.
65. Water, J.J., Bohr, A., Boetker, J., Aho, J., Sandler, N., Nielsen, H.M., Rantanen, J., Three-dimensional printing of drug-eluting implants: Preparation of an antimicrobial polylactide feedstock material. *J. Pharm. Sci.*, 104, 3, 1099–107, Mar. 1, 2015.
66. Wu, W., Zheng, Q., Guo, X., Sun, J., Liu, Y., A programmed release multi-drug implant fabricated by three-dimensional printing technology for bone tuberculosis therapy. *Biomed. Mater.*, 4, 6, 065005, Nov. 9, 2009.
67. Gbureck, U., Vorndran, E., Müller, F.A., Barralet, J.E., Low temperature direct 3D printed bioceramics and biocomposites as drug release matrices. *J. Control. Release*, 122, 2, 173–80, Sep. 26, 2007.

68. Stal, M., *Differences in Fatigue, Depression, and Hemoglobin as a Function of MPN Diagnosis Types (Polycythemia Vera, Essential Thrombocythemia, and Myelofibrosis)*, Doctoral Dissertation, Northcentral University, 2018.
69. Ventola, C.L., Cancer immunotherapy, part 3: challenges and future trends. *PT*, 42, 8, 514, Aug. 2017.
70. Ginsburg, G.S. and Phillips, K.A., Precision medicine: From science to value. *Health Aff.*, 37, 5, 694–701, May 1, 2018.
71. Ceylan, S. and Bolgen, N., A review on three dimensional scaffolds for tumor engineering. *Biomater. Biomech. Bioeng.*, 3, 3, 141–55, Sep. 1, 2016.
72. Wüst, S., Müller, R., Hofmann, S., Controlled positioning of cells in biomaterials—approaches towards 3D tissue printing. *J. Funct. Biomater.*, 2, 3, 119–54, Aug. 4, 2011.
73. Kang, H.W., Lee, S.J., Ko, I.K., Kengla, C., Yoo, J.J., Atala, A., A 3D bioprinting system to produce human-scale tissue constructs with structural integrity. *Nat. Biotechnol.*, 34, 3, 312–9, Mar. 2016.
74. Samavedi, S. and Joy, N., 3D printing for the development of in vitro cancer models. *Curr. Opin. Biomed. Eng.*, 2, 35–42, Jun. 1, 2017.
75. Lamichhane, S., Bashyal, S., Keum, T., Noh, G., Seo, J.E., Bastola, R., Choi, J., Sohn, D.H., Lee, S., Complex formulations, simple techniques: Can 3D printing technology be the Midas touch in pharmaceutical industry? *Asian J. Pharm. Sci.*, 14, 5, 465–79, Sep. 1, 2019.
76. Andreadis, I.I., Gioumouxouzis, C.I., Eleftheriadis, G.K., Fatouros, D.G., The advent of a new era in digital healthcare: A role for 3d printing technologies in drug manufacturing? *Pharmaceutics*, 14, 3, 609, Mar. 10, 2022.
77. Chandekar, A., Mishra, D.K., Sharma, S., Saraogi, G.K., Gupta, U., Gupta, G., 3D printing technology: A new milestone in the development of pharmaceuticals. *Curr. Pharm. Des.*, 25, 9, 937–45, Mar. 1, 2019.
78. Marchioli, G., van Gurp, L., Van Krieken, P.P., Stamatialis, D., Engelse, M., Van Blitterswijk, C.A., Karperien, M.B., de Koning, E., Alblas, J., Moroni, L., van Apeldoorn, A.A., Fabrication of three-dimensional bioplotted hydrogel scaffolds for islets of Langerhans transplantation. *Biofabrication*, 7, 2, 025009, May 28, 2015.
79. Sabek, O.M., Farina, M., Fraga, D.W., Afshar, S., Ballerini, A., Filgueira, C.S., Thekkedath, U.R., Grattoni, A., Gaber, A.O., Three-dimensional printed polymeric system to encapsulate human mesenchymal stem cells differentiated into islet-like insulin-producing aggregates for diabetes treatment. *J. Tissue Eng.*, 7, 2041731416638198, Apr. 21, 2016.
80. Scheen, A.J., Precision medicine: The future in diabetes care? *Diabetes Res. Clin. Pract.*, 117, 12–21, Jul. 1, 2016.
81. Monib, U. and Riaz, M.A., Risk factors associated to cardiovascular diseases in Kyrgyzstan. *J. Asian Med. Stud. Assoc.*, 7, 2, 42–9, Jun. 1, 2019.
82. Franco, M., Cooper, R.S., Bilal, U., Fuster, V., Challenges and opportunities for cardiovascular disease prevention. *Am. J. Med.*, 124, 2, 95–102, Feb. 1, 2011.

83. Valverde, I., Three-dimensional printed cardiac models: applications in the field of medical education, cardiovascular surgery, and structural heart interventions. *Rev. Esp. Cardiol. (English Edition)*, 70, 4, 282–91, Apr. 1, 2017.
84. Vukicevic, M., Mosadegh, B., Min, J.K., Little, S.H., Cardiac 3D printing and its future directions. *JACC: Cardiovasc. Imaging*, 10, 2, 171–84, Feb. 2017.
85. Giannopoulos, A.A., Mitsouras, D., Yoo, S.J., Liu, P.P., Chatzizisis, Y.S., Rybicki, F.J., Applications of 3D printing in cardiovascular diseases. *Nat. Rev. Cardiol.*, 13, 12, 701–18, Dec. 2016.
86. Valverde, I., Gomez, G., Coserria, J.F., Suarez-Mejias, C., Uribe, S., Sotelo, J., Velasco, M.N., Santos De Soto, J., Hosseinpour, A.R., Gomez-Cia, T., 3D printed models for planning endovascular stenting in transverse aortic arch hypoplasia. *Catheter. Cardiovasc. Interv.*, 85, 6, 1006–12, May 2015.
87. Wang, J.Z., Li, Z.Y., Zhang, J.P., Guo, X.H., Could personalized bio-3D printing rescue the cardiovascular system? *Int. J. Cardiol.*, 223, 561–3, Nov. 15, 2016.
88. Malhotra, R.K., Neurodegenerative disorders and sleep. *Sleep Med. Clin.*, 13, 1, 63–70, Mar. 1, 2018.
89. Lozano, R., Stevens, L., Thompson, B.C., Gilmore, K.J., Gorkin III, R., Stewart, E.M., in het Panhuis, M., Romero-Ortega, M., Wallace, G.G., 3D printing of layered brain-like structures using peptide modified gellan gum substrates. *Biomaterials*, 67, 264–73, Oct. 1, 2015.
90. Ploch, C.C., Mansi, C.S., Jayamohan, J., Kuhl, E., Using 3D printing to create personalized brain models for neurosurgical training and preoperative planning. *World Neurosurg.*, 90, 668–74, Jun. 1, 2016.
91. Ormabera, B.J., Valle, R.D., Fernández, J.Z., Ortega, M.L., Inurritegui, X.U., Solís, S.T., Impresión 3D en neurocirugía: Modelo específico para pacientes con craneosinostosis. *Neurocirugia*, 28, 6, 260–5, Nov. 1, 2017.
92. Owens, C.M., Marga, F., Forgacs, G., Heesch, C.M., Biofabrication and testing of a fully cellular nerve graft. *Biofabrication*, 5, 4, 045007, Nov. 6, 2013.
93. Hsieh, F.Y., Lin, H.H., Hsu, S.H., 3D bioprinting of neural stem cell-laden thermoresponsive biodegradable polyurethane hydrogel and potential in central nervous system repair. *Biomaterials*, 71, 48–57, Dec. 1, 2015.
94. Ackland, D.C., Robinson, D., Redhead, M., Lee, P.V., Moskaljuk, A., Dimitroulis, G., A personalized 3D-printed prosthetic joint replacement for the human temporomandibular joint: From implant design to implantation. *J. Mech. Behav. Biomed. Mater.*, 69, 404–11, May 1, 2017.
95. Cevenini, L., Calabretta, M.M., Tarantino, G., Michelini, E., Roda, A., Smartphone-interfaced 3D printed toxicity biosensor integrating bioluminescent "sentinel cells". *Sens. Actuators B Chem.*, 225, 249–57, Mar. 31, 2016.
96. van Grunsven, L.A., 3D in vitro models of liver fibrosis. *Adv. Drug Deliv. Rev.*, 121, 133–46, Nov. 1, 2017.
97. Xu, N., Wei, F., Liu, X., Jiang, L., Cai, H., Li, Z., Yu, M., Wu, F., Liu, Z., Reconstruction of the upper cervical spine using a personalized 3D-printed

vertebral body in an adolescent with Ewing sarcoma. *Spine*, 41, 1, E50–4, Jan. 1, 2016.

98. Pravin, S. and Sudhir, A., Integration of 3D printing with dosage forms: A new perspective for modern healthcare. *Biomed. Pharmacother.*, 107, 146–54, Nov. 1, 2018.
99. Saleem, N., Ismail, M.K., Tombazzi, C.R., Soin, S., Dhruva, S.S., Endoscopic transmission of carbapenem-resistant Enterobacteriaceae: Implications for US Food and Drug Administration approval and postmarket surveillance of endoscopic devices. *Gastrointest. Endosc.*, 93, 1, 231–8, Jan. 1, 2021.
100. Durfee, W.K. and Iaizzo, P.A., Medical applications of 3D printing, in: *Engineering in Medicine*, pp. 527–543, Academic Press, USA, Jan 1, 2019.
101. Andreadis, I.I., Gioumouxouzis, C.I., Eleftheriadis, G.K., Fatouros, D.G., The advent of a new era in digital healthcare: A role for 3D printing technologies in drug manufacturing? *Pharmaceutics*, 14, 3, 609, Mar. 10, 2022.
102. Fda.gov, [online] Available at: Recently-Approved Devices (2017) (Accessed 2 February 2022).

4
The Potential of 3D-Printed Anatomical Model for Surgical Planning

Abstract
The possible surgical applications of 3D printing for anatomical simulations are discussed in this chapter. Since its introduction, 3D printing has revolutionized several industries and fields. Orthopedic, neurological, heart valve, and cancerous tissue surgeries are all listed as potential applications for 3D-printed models. Congenital anomaly surgical planning has also been considered. The use of 3D-printed models to teach surgical anatomy has been outlined. The notion of bone grinding has highlighted the central importance of 3D-printed models during the treatment of benign and malignant malignancies. Finally, several potential problems and benefits of using 3D-printed models in surgery, as well as certain ethical considerations, are discussed.

Keywords: 3D-printed, anatomical model, surgical planning, virtual models, orthopedic tissue, heart valve, neurosurgery, additive manufacturing techniques

4.1 Introduction

The indeterminate nature of surgical operations presents difficulties for inexperienced surgeons in terms of both unexpected outcomes and timely decisions. However, the issue of representing three-dimensional anatomical structures on a two-dimensional screen contributes to the complexity of congenital defects [1]. Anatomical models generated on a 3D printer could be used to fight it. Thus, it is possible to create personalized models for each patient, low-cost anatomical models, and surgical guidance templates [2]. It is also essential to use 3D models for precise preoperative planning during the surgical process. Using 3D-printed models, surgeons could see how their operations fared on both soft and hard tissues. A 3D-printed anatomical head model is useful for researching neurosurgical procedures such as facial nerve injury, brain bleeding, and dissection of delicate neural tissues. The prosthesis was created by

Rishabha Malviya and Rishav Sharma. 3D Printing in Healthcare: Novel Applications, (59–84)

Zhang *et al.* [3] using osseous morphonology. Complete joint prostheses made to order from the design have already been produced. Significant improvements in patients' healing times have been seen. With complete support for patients in their teens, Galasso *et al.* [4] create a distal prosthesis. Understanding the entire intricate anatomical structure is much easier with the background information, which, in turn, decreases surgical complications and saves time during the procedure. The study provides a thorough overview of the many 3D-printed models used in various anatomical procedures, including those involving orthopedic tissues, neurosurgery, malignant tissues, and heart valve surgery. The next parts also talk about the positives, negatives, and ethical issues surrounding the topic. Successful surgeries often involve careful preoperative planning, which can lessen the need for emergency measures and shorten the total operating time [5]. Traditional preoperative planning relies heavily on prior expertise and medical imaging; however, these methods may not provide surgeons with the necessary hands-on practice and visualization. Commonly performed planning techniques such as magnetic resonance imaging (MRI) and computed tomography (CT) cannot properly display the diversity of anatomical characteristics, forcing clinicians to extrapolate from 2D pictures. Even though surgical planning is greatly aided by 3D virtual models, but still it does not always provide a precise depiction of the patient's anatomy [6]. In addition, their transient nature complicates surgical modeling, especially for more involved procedures [7]. Preoperative planning can be improved with the help of 3D printing, which provides a new perspective and helps to circumvent some of the shortcomings of more conventional approaches. Advanced 3D-printing technology now permits the painstaking construction of multilayered replicas of human anatomy [8]. It has many uses in the medical field, including patient-specific model building for surgical procedure planning. The majority of research (82%) reported that using 3D-printed models instead of traditional preoperative planning improved the surgical results, and more than half of the studies showed a reduction in operation duration [7]. Three-dimensional printing or additive manufacturing (AM) is a manufacturing technique that has gained traction in the corporate environment due to its distinctive advantages in the digital fabrication process. AM has been making inroads into the medical field for some time now by developing novel solutions to everyday problems. The most common approaches to dealing with the problem comprise the use of AM either (1) before surgery, (2) during surgery, or (3) as a potential replacement or implant [8, 9]. Doctors and engineers have encountered challenges in each of these domains, and as a result, newly built solutions have already been established and integrated into the healthcare profession to be used in items like the construction and design of surgical robotic devices as well as anatomical training modeling procedures [10–17]. Medical practitioners and surgeons now have a simple yet effective tool to utilize in preparation for surgery with the introduction of AM: tangible 3D-printed models [18]. Virtual models with high levels of realism can be developed by reverse-engineering the methods used to collect 3D medical data [10]. These models will be used by surgeons for preoperative planning, giving them a realistic representation of the anatomy they would see during operations [19]. Using 3D-printed anatomical models has many advantages, including increased precision and accuracy during surgery, reduced expenses, and a faster recovery time [20]. Since the emergence of 3D printing in the 1990s to educate both patients and doctors, the surgical industry has grown at an accelerating pace. As of late, it has also been used in the development of artificial organs. Therefore, researchers from all surgical subfields decided to look into the current status and future potential of 3D printing in pre-operative, during, and post-operative surgical conditions. The primary objective of the study was to increase knowledge of the emerging subject so that a team of surgeons and engineers could create innovative 3D technologies and advocate for their usage in conjunction with high-resolution scans like MRI, CT, and US to improve patient health [21].

4.2 3D-Printed Approaches: Anatomical Simulations

4.2.1 Orthopedic Tissue

3D-printed models have been utilized in orthopedic treatments, including aesthetic surgery including the repair of facial characteristics. On the operating table, doctors can check for and treat any issues that have not been anticipated [22]. Bone drilling is a common procedure in orthopedic surgery when a hole is drilled into the bone to facilitate repair. When bone and drill bit come into proximity to one another, abrasion can occur. Thus, it produces a rise in body temperature, which, in turn, can lead to thermal necrosis and the destruction of bone tissue. The patient is harmed by the bone's irreparable deterioration. Bone drilling procedures can be adjusted with foresight into the effects and repercussions of drill bit geometry. In this case, 3D-printed bone can be used for *in-vitro* testing before undergoing clinical procedures on living patients. Orthopedic simulation with the 3D-printed bone facilitates *in-vivo* surgical operation planning.

4.2.2 Heart Valve

One of the most difficult operations is replacing a patient's heart valve. It is not clear yet what the best graft is or what surgical approach is best. Using echocardiographic pictures, 3D-printed models might be fabricated [23]. A more positive outcome from surgery is possible by using incisions to indicate the actual spatial gap. In the case of angiosarcoma, knowing the tumor's exact position might reduce the likelihood of infection and shorten the length of surgery. Heart valve surgery, whether for replacement or repair, can be better planned with the help of 3D-printed models in such circumstances.

4.2.3 Neurosurgery

The elimination of a flap of bone through bone grinding is a standard procedure in neurosurgical procedures; however, it has been associated with heat necrosis and bone death. Additional concerns include color-blindness, disruption to the optic nerve, and facial nerve injury [24]. A 3D-printed model can be used for the procedure, allowing researchers to monitor and regulate the temperature as it rises during the bone grinding process. Even inexperienced surgeons can improve patient outcomes and speed up rehabilitation by practicing on 3D-printed replicas of complex neurological procedures. Neurosurgical temperature monitoring can be performed using either thermocouples or thermography. Drilling holes into the workpiece and inserting thermocouples at a predetermined distance from the cutting zone constitutes the thermocouple technique. However, in the thermography method, the temperature is measured by keeping an infrared red camera at a fixed distance from the machining zone.

4.2.4 Malignant Tissues

Due to the proximity of healthy, critical tissues to the cancerous ones, treating cancer might be difficult. The dissection of these tissues requires extreme caution to protect adjacent nerves and other structures. Despite preoperative risk assessments, additional challenges may emerge that the operating team must address. The use of prefabricated 3D-printed models could be quite useful. For the surgical planning of tumor dissection, the malignant lesion has been demonstrated.

4.3 Congenital Anomalies: Surgical Planning

Blood vessels in the vicinity of diseased regions are often unpredictable in people with congenital abnormalities. More accurate prenatal diagnoses are possible with the use of 3D-printed models that are size- and shape-precise replicas of the patient. It is possible to construct precise 3D models using high-resolution CT scans and MRI scans (MRI). By employing 3D-printed models, surgeons may plan out their whole procedure in meticulous detail. Cardiac MRI scans are used to produce a 3D model of the heart, which is then the lumen segmented, the blood volume reconstructed, the heart sectioned, and finally, the heart 3D-printed. If the assessment is neglected, nerves may be damaged during surgery. Here, 3D-printed models help surgeons arrange the entire procedure more precisely [25].

4.4 Anatomical Training With 3D-Printed Models

3D-printed models have the potential for application in anatomy education. In today's medical schools, human cadaver bone is used for teaching and learning purposes. In some nations, however, there are moral constraints that prevent the use of human cadavers. Plastic replicas have too many flaws to be trusted. On the flip side, 3D-printed models have benefits including speedy mass production, portability (can print a model anywhere with a 3D printer), lack of ethical considerations, and few health and safety risks. As a result of practicing anatomical models, surgeons can improve their techniques for *in-vivo* procedures. The implementation of a three-dimensional printer enables the creation of a unique model for each patient. When making an implant, a 3D scanner is used to capture the complete skull area so that an STL file can be transmitted to the printer. The 3D-printed component can then be implanted at the injury site. A variety of materials and methods [26, 27] are used in the production of training surgical instruments.

4.5 Advantages, Challenges, and Ethical Concerns

The ability to adapt a model to the needs of a single patient is a major benefit of 3D printing. Quick recovery, decreased trauma and surgical time, and a lower chance of infection are further benefits. 3D printing allows for the rapid production of components of virtually any shape and size. The whole procedure can be repeated with good results and at a low expense. In the following three contexts [28], 3D printing plays a significant role:

- The degree of difficulty and individualization is dependent on the patient's circumstances.
- Fewer requirements of products.
- Urgent design adjustments are required in response to user input.

3D-printed models also have their own set of difficulties, such as variable skin elasticity and stiff, fragile tissue. Putting together several components also takes a long time and often results in inconsistent results. The 3D-manufactured dura mater lacks crucial blood arteries for neurosurgery procedures. However, they can be printed individually and then diffused to create a more lifelike imitation. Because of the serious consequences that can result from incorrect customization, the relevant legal challenges must be resolved to advance the use of 3D printing in surgical procedures.

4.6 Fundamentals of 3D Printing

Doctors must understand the technologies, materials, and processes of 3D printing to better integrate the method into therapeutic settings. 3D-printing techniques vary according to the final product, and some are more suitable than others for replicating specific anatomical structures. If a researcher wants to make a model that can be used in the clinic, there is a need to make sure that he/she employs the right methods and materials. Consequently, doctors need to acquire a comprehensive knowledge of 3D printing's technological features. 3D printing, also known as additive manufacturing or rapid prototyping, was first developed in the 1980s for usage in business and engineering [29]. 3D printing is finding more and more uses in the medical field as technology improves. Two-dimensional medical images can be transformed into a three-dimensional printable model. 3D printers interpret digital models as "pieces" limited by surfaces and volume throughout the printing process. Therefore, it is necessary to transform medical photos into stereolithography (STL) files or any appropriate 3D file format. All surfaces in STL files are represented by a triangular "facets" structure. The exhibited anatomies need to be accurately segmented by tissue and pathology before medical imaging data like CT scans and MRIs may be converted to STL format. A 3D model cannot be made or printed until it is done. As a result, there are three distinct phases involved in making 3D-printed medical models:

- The process of obtaining the diagnostic images of a patient is called "image acquisition."
- Post-processing and image segmentation, when a 2D image is turned into a 3D format.
- Three-dimensional printing is when a physical object is created from a digital model [5, 29].

4.7 Additive Manufacturing Techniques

The development of CT and MRI has allowed doctors to see precise geometries inside patients' bodies without resorting to invasive procedures [30, 31]. Healthcare providers could model the topography of the human body, from the heart's vascular system to the skeleton, using CAD software [32, 33]. It is possible to diagnose medical conditions and create models in engineering by identifying the area of interest (ROI) [34] using the 16-bit maps that can be generated from CT and MRI scans, each of which has around 65,536 shades of gray. Standard triangle language (STL) [34, 35] is used to get a quantity representation of the ROI, which is then used to generate a physical model through AMT. Techniques of additive manufacturing technology that are currently in wide usage include fused deposition modeling, stereolithography, selective laser sintering, selective laser melting, electron beam melting, and direct energy deposition. Fused deposition modeling (FDM) is the most widely spread additive manufacturing technique. The technology utilizes a heated nozzle to melt engineered thermoplastics like lactic polyacid (PLA) and acrylonitrile butadiene styrene. To construct 3D objects layer by layer, an extrusion nozzle is mounted on a robot platform with X, Y, and Z axes [31]. The process of FDM requires no particular ventilation; however, it might be negatively impacted by excessive temperature fluctuations in the environment [36, 37]. Patient-specific implants of varied densities were successfully made using FDM for cranial deformities and femur portions [33], as were biocompatible nanocomposites for tissue engineering purposes [38]. Stereolithography (also termed photo-solidification or resin printing) is a method for creating three-dimensional objects by layering a photo-polymerization process. In SLA, a pool of light-curable resin is scanned with an optical light source to cause localized molecular linking and solidification of the resin's surface. Among the types of cavities that SLA may successfully print are sinuses and neurovascular channels [36, 37]. The SLA model's construction has several drawbacks, including weak mechanical strength and a lengthy production time [38, 39]. The process of selective laser sintering begins with the fusion of powder (SLS). Powder materials (often nylon, polyamide, or metal) are fused in consecutive layers using a strong laser as a heat source [40]. To improve the model's mechanical qualities and topological surface, try switching out the granular material with a powder material with a diameter in the order of 50 m. Each layer is deposited over the previous one in the method, making it self-supporting in contrast to SLA. Oral, maxillofacial, neurological, and orthopedic surgeries are only a few of the areas where SLS could be useful [41]. Selective laser melting (SLM), a variant of SLS, is used to melt the powder material and bind them in layers, as opposed to simply fusing the metal powder to link certain locations. In electron beam melting (EBM), an electron beam is used to melt metal powder in a high-temperature, high-vacuum environment to create metal parts in a layer-by-layer process [42–44]. Surgery is a significant field for EBM's use, and it frequently involves commercial pure titanium (CP-Ti), titanium alloys, stainless steel, magnesium alloys, and nickel alloys [42–44]. To create three-dimensional things, scientists have developed a technique called directed energy deposition (DED), which uses a laser or electron beam to melt powder delivered onsite. DED is not limited to just fabricating 3D objects one layer at a time; it can also repair broken components, augment preexisting structures, and modify surfaces [45]. The cooling impact and refabricating capabilities of DED procedures are enhanced [46]. When compared to EBM and SLM, DED's inferior fabrication efficiency is a major drawback. Finally, patient-specific surgical implants are necessary because they facilitate bone in-growth and decrease the elastic modulus disparity between bone and metal, leading to greater long-term stability. Selective laser sintering, selective laser melting, electron beam melting, and direct electron deposition are all viable options for producing these implants. Interlayer de-bonding or cracking could occur if the stress is not released. To do it, CP-Ti and titanium alloys are typically employed [43, 47].

4.8 Surgical Applications

4.8.1 Craniofacial and Nervous Systems

4.8.1.1 Head and Neck

During craniofacial and head and neck surgery, 3D printing provides the opportunity to learn about intricate anatomy, fractures, and anomalies. In addition, when combined with virtual preoperative planning, the technology can have a profound effect. Thus, patient-specific implants (PSI) and CAD/computer-aided manufacturing (CAM) guidance for surgery can be developed to increase the accuracy and decrease the amount of time spent in surgery despite the growing complexity of reconstructions [48, 49]. Since the area serves a significant cosmetic purpose and has a complex anatomy, 3DP is making a significant impact there. According to a 2019 study published by Pettersson *et al.* [50], the Craniomaxillofacial Surgery Department in Finland is responsible for the design of 73.5 annual 3D-printed implant usage there. In craniomaxillofacial trauma, the method is most often used to repair the orbital floor following a fracture. The objectives of the procedure are to avoid further damage to the orbit, restore its function, improve its appearance, and cure any aesthetic impairment. As part of the process, either a premade mesh or a PSI will be placed. The most frequent forms of PSI are those that are physically pre-bent in a 3D model tailored to the individual patient and those that are built to the exact specifications of the patient. According to traditionally prepared ones, PSI was observed to restore orbital volume more accurately in the ORBITA III randomized multi-centric clinical trial [51]. The orbital volume difference between the PSI groups was $p = 0.029$ [52], suggesting that patient-specific manufactured implants may be advantageous for orbital reconstruction. Thus, it appears that the degree to which an implant is individualized is connected to its success. 3D printing has also demonstrated its efficacy in congenital surgery. Monobloc craniofacial advancement and Le Fort osteotomies are effective operations that benefit from virtual planning and surgical assistance. Computer-assisted surgery has been successful in treating severe cranial deformities such as plagiocephaly, oxycephaly, hypertelorism, Crouzon disease, and Treacher–Collins syndrome [53, 54]. Additionally, orthognathic surgery and temporomandibular joint reconstruction can be performed simultaneously with these sorts of procedures. Given that orthognathic surgery pioneered the use of computer simulations in surgical planning and that TMJ reconstruction surgery was an early adopter of 3D-printed prostheses, it is not surprising that 3D printing is having such a profound effect on these operations today [55, 56]. Accelerated AM is also useful in head and neck surgery [53]. Bone resection and repair in oncological surgery is the most common use. Virtual planning of fibular flaps and the subsequent printing of guides have been shown to improve surgical accuracy and decrease procedure time in such circumstances [57, 58]. Additionally, dental implants allow for simultaneous dental rehabilitation [58]. In addition, 3D printing can have a unique effect in the classroom. Despite its inexperience, there have been numerous potential initiatives for imparting head and neck anatomy at the graduate and undergraduate levels [59, 60], which should increase students' anatomical understanding and reduce their dependency on cadaveric workshops. The benefits of 3DP in terms of cost-effectiveness have not yet been determined in many medical fields. Although multiple clinical trials have proven the efficacy of the technology, maxillofacial surgery has been at the forefront of advancement. As an example, a 2014 clinical trial conducted by Ayoub *et al.* revealed that CAD surgery drastically reduced the time needed for transplant ischemia and defect reconstruction [61]. According to Dumas *et al.* [62], the total cost of producing a 3D-printed model of a human skull is $200 (labor cost included). These articles argue that 3D printing can be done affordably [63]. Tissue engineering and bioprinting are being discussed in the context of potential future applications in head and neck reconstructive surgery. Recent research has demonstrated that microtia, alveolar cleft, and other congenital diseases, as well as acquired tissue abnormalities, may benefit from the use of new biomaterials and polymeric 3DP [64, 65]. In conclusion, fast AM is revolutionizing head and neck surgery for the better. For illnesses that need precise 3D conformation, the economical method enhances surgical outcomes while cutting down on surgical time.

4.8.1.2 Brain and Spinal Cord

Neurosurgery is an example of a very demanding, precise, and sophisticated profession that stands to benefit greatly from the rapid development of 3DP. There is no longer a need to practice on a live patient, thanks to 3D printing and other similar technologies. 3DP is used in neurosurgery in three main ways: (a) patient-specific anatomical and pathological models created on a 3D printer, (b) 3D-printed neurosurgical equipment, gadgets, and implants, and (c) bio-printed scaffolding for tissue engineering and research. The most crucial application of 3D printing is the creation of patient-specific models for use in pre-operative planning, surgical simulation by recreating scenarios and complications (such as intraoperative dural sinus injury), surgical training, patient education, and interdisciplinary communication [66–71].

4.9 Cardiovascular System

4.9.1 Cardiothoracic

Congenital heart defects (CHD) can cause a wide range of unusual and complex structures. Conventional imaging modalities such as CT, ultrasound, and MRI are not very helpful for analyzing the unique and typically complicated spatial connections associated with CHD [72–74] due to their two-dimensional projection, which substantially deviates from the reality of the operating room. Thus, 3D-printed models offer substantial benefits for pre-surgical planning and simulation of cardiac operations [75]. These models exhibit the intricate anatomical anomalies of patients with CHD with great accuracy and permit a thorough study of the one-of-a-kind spatial linkages that cannot be obtained by other approaches [76]. Several investigations [73, 75, 77] highlight the usefulness of 3D-printed models for a variety of purposes, including but not limited to enhancing medical and surgical education, enhancing communication between doctors and patients, and aiding clinical decision-making. The most recent systematic reviews examined the present applications and accuracy of 3DP for CHD [78], and they found that patient-specific 3D models which replicate complex cardiac anatomies with high accuracy indicate a significant value in preoperative planning, surgical simulation, decision-making, and intraoperative orientation. The anatomical complexity of the mitral valve stems from its posterior placement and the delicate relationship it has with the ventricle, the sub-valvular apparatus, and the left ventricular outflow tract (LVOT). Patients with severe mitral valve regurgitation are forced to undergo potentially life-threatening surgery to have the valve repaired or replaced because no viable medical therapy exists [79]. The success of the treatment depends on the surgeon's competence, and it is difficult to determine the anatomy of the valve from 2D or 3D echocardiographic projections, which complicates pre-intervention planning [80]. Several publications have made use of 3DP to replicate various mitral valve pathological processes using stiff plastic and silicon cast based on 3D transoesophageal echocardiography. These models give doctors a way to practice minimally invasive valve surgery on simulated patients [81] by allowing them to plan and try out new tools. Transcatheter mitral valve replacement is an alternate treatment for severe symptomatic mitral valve disease in circumstances where surgery is not an option owing to higher intraoperative risk, and 3DP preoperative planning is helpful for the procedure [82]. LVOT blockage is a common complication of TMVR, occurring between 8.2% and 11.2% of the time. To prevent an obstruction following neo-LVOT deployment, the surgeon can utilize a 3D anatomical model to replicate the neo-LVOT and place a transcatheter valve within the model [83]. When dealing with serious lung conditions, 3DP is indispensable. Especially for stent implantation, standardizing interventional treatments is difficult due to the tracheobronchial tree's significant anatomical diversity [84].

4.9.2 Vascular

Since the initial utilization of 3D printing in vascular surgery, which involved creating a duplicate of an aneurysm before endovascular therapy for surgical planning [85], several studies have been undertaken on the topic. The majority of the existing literature on 3D prototyping for vascular surgery is descriptive or case series, and there is yet no known randomized controlled trial. Cardiovascular surgeons frequently use 3D printing for (a) infrarenal and juxtarenal approaches to abdominal aortic aneurysms, (b) thoracic aortic aneurysms, and (c) additional approaches to big arteries such as the celiac trunk and splenic artery, carotid artery, subclavian artery, femoral artery, and portal vein. The preoperative planning process for vascular surgery often involves CT scans, MRI scans, and Doppler ultrasound for good measure [86]. FDM is a widely used and inexpensive printing method [87]. Vascular and endovascular surgery is benefiting from the development of 3D printing, which provides images of vessels of various sizes and enables precise surgical planning. In difficult cases of thoracoabdominal aortic aneurysm, 3DP can be used to work aortic fenestrations, shortening the length of surgery and improving the accuracy of measurements. It is made possible by combining the knowledge and insight gained from both the actual surgery and the planning process.

4.10 Clinical Applications in Preoperative Planning

New advancements have allowed 3D printing to be widely used in surgical planning. Based on a thorough literature review, preoperative planning using 3D models was mentioned in about 40% of articles about medical 3D printing. Studies in cardiothoracic, neurothoracic, craniomaxillofacial, orthopedic, and interventional radiology indicated that 3D models correlated with patient-specific anatomical features, shortened procedures, lowered ionizing radiation exposure, and improved patient outcomes [88].

4.11 Cardiovascular Surgery

The most common types of cardiac imaging are MRI, CT, and echocardiography. These imaging techniques, despite their great resolution, have limitations when dealing with a wide variety of heart disease shapes. Since routine imaging often fails to detect preexisting conditions in patients with a history of cardiac surgery, these patients are at an increased risk for unforeseen surgical outcomes. As a result, a doctor's pre-op preparation can benefit substantially by having access to patient-specific models. The use of 3D models has been shown to be useful in a variety of conditions, including surgical planning for patients with congenital cardiac anomalies such as atrium and ventricle septal defects [88–93]. Transcatheter closure of diseases like muscular ventricular septal defects is planned using 3D-printed models based on CT angiography, allowing doctors to properly predict the catheter size before the procedure [94]. Using CT images and a 3D-printed model, researchers Ryan *et al.* successfully managed an intervention in a newborn demonstrating tetralogy of Fallot (TOF) with pulmonary valve atresia and several aortopulmonary collateral arteries. Due to the severe nature of TOF, a full invasive assessment of patient morphology is generally required before surgery [95]. Nevertheless, 3D printing has proven to be a feasible alternative to traditional TOF diagnostic approaches [95]. Increased adoption of 3D cardiac models has led to the development of cutting-edge enhancements to 3D printing processes. Improved 3D echocardiography has allowed for more detailed models to be created, which may now be used to illustrate subtle heart defects such as valve leakage. 3D-printed mitral valves were developed in research [96] using a variety of elastomeric materials, which allowed them to closely mimic the physical properties of a natural valve. One potential benefit of 3D printing with several materials is the potential for more accurate surgical simulation.

4.12 Neurosurgery

In neurosurgery, 3D printing is used to plan successful surgeries. In-depth familiarity with the nearby anatomical structures is required for success in the endeavor. Brain and spinal cord MRIs provide a wealth of information because of their high contrast and spatial resolution. Improvements in 3D imaging techniques in conjunction with virtual reality simulations have further aided preoperative preparation [97]. It is because 2D displays of such representations do not adequately replicate 3D dimensions and lack haptic feedback, which would later benefit a physician in the operating room. Multicolored models made with 3D printing processes like binder jetting [5] can shed light on minute anatomical components that may not be easily discernible with medical imaging. Preoperative planning for neurovascular therapies has been shown to benefit from the use of patient-specific vascular models in several studies [98–101]. Intracranial aneurysms present a unique challenge for neurosurgeons, who must resort to microsurgical clipping to obstruct blood flow when embolization is not an option. CT angiography was used to create 3D-printed models, and their viability as surgical rehearsal aids was evaluated retrospectively. The models helped successfully replicate patient morphology and showed the correct sizing of aneurysm clips compared to those utilized in surgery [102]. Also, 3D-printed vascular networks have made possible the modeling of cerebrovascular intervention for both educational and clinical objectives. It has been shown by Mashiko *et al.* [103] that such networks may effectively replicate aneurysm clipping, allowing students to get valuable hands-on experience. Functional neurological procedures, such as subdural electrode implantation for epilepsy patients, are typically planned without considering the optimal placement of the patient for evaluation. With the advent of high-precision 3D-printed models of patients' brains, however, doctors now can tailor electrode arrays to each patient's unique gyral and sulcal characteristics. In addition, Morris and coworkers were able to adjust the number of electrodes in each array, which allowed them to concentrate electrodes on certain anatomical regions—for instance, each array had a higher density of electrodes surrounding the motor bank of a patient's central sulcus [104] to zero in on the physiology of the motor cortex.

4.13 Craniomaxillofacial Surgery

Similar to its use in neurosurgery, preoperative surgical simulation is routinely employed in craniomaxillofacial surgery to plan the most appropriate intervention. Unfortunately, there are several caveats associated with virtual simulations that may lead to incorrect evaluations of bone deformations, growth, and location. Inaccurate anatomical data is especially problematic in the preoperative planning of osteotomies, where it is essential. The use of 3D-printed models has allowed surgeons to practice osteotomies and mold titanium implants, which are otherwise impossible to modify during surgery [105]. Preoperative planning for otologic therapies like tympanoplasty can be difficult because of the ear's complex shape. Multiple studies [106–110] document the development of 3D-printed models to simulate ear deformation for use in surgical simulation and training. 3D-printed models of temporal bones were found to be more successful than virtual models for surgical simulation by Hochman *et al.* [107], who employed 3D-printing to create the models.

4.14 Orthopedic Surgery

Orthopedic surgeons now routinely use 3D-printed implants and other surgical tools. Research shows that orthopedic operations account for more than a quarter of all studies exploring the advantages of 3D printing in surgery. An area of particular interest is the surgical treatment of fractures, with models suggesting improvements in the time of the procedure and minimal blood loss [111–113]. The study showed that 3D-printed models helped surgeons better plan how to repair fractures at the end of the tibia. Whenever presented with a 3D-printed model of the patient's anatomy, less experienced surgeons were more likely to modify their plate selection for distal tibial fractures surgery (74% vs. 9%, respectively) [114]. To help in the removal of tumors, orthopedists have begun using 3D-printed oncologic models. These models are perfect replicas of the lesion of interest and its surrounding anatomy. 3D-printed models may also be used to create allografts, which are utilized to replace cancerous tissue.

4.15 Interventional Radiology

Interventional radiology relies heavily on the use of precise models to direct medical practitioners (IR). Three-dimensional images cannot provide the spatial resolution required to perform embolization and other IR operations that benefit from a thorough familiarity with the patient's anatomy for optimal results [115]. In addition, Giannopoulos *et al.* [116] 3D-printed a patient's ascending aorta and aortic arch to mimic an endovascular repair, expanding the range of applications of IR in cardiovascular surgery. Splenic artery aneurysms were modeled using 3D printing, and different catheterized techniques were used. By figuring out the optimal course of action ahead of time, doctors cut down on the amount of time spent operating and the amount of radiation their patients were subjected to. Furthermore, several attempted techniques may have resulted in vascular harm if evaluated in the operating room [117], such as coil embolization.

4.16 Other Interventions

Anatomical compatibility between the recipient and donor is crucial for a successful surgical outcome in whole organ transplantation; thus, it is important to gain that information before the procedure begins. Before performing a liver transplant, researchers Zein *et al.* looked at the potential of 3D-printed livers for preoperative planning. These models were accurate representations of the biliary and vascular systems of specific patients [118]. Three patients with stage 5 chronic renal insufficiency had 3D-printed kidneys evaluated for transplant viability by Chandak *et al.* [119]. These printed models were able to assess a patient's kidney transplant eligibility where conventional imaging had failed. Renal tumors were removed by Silberstein *et al.* using 3D printing. Preoperative surgical planning was aided by 3D models of kidneys and malignancies [120]. By offering a visual aid, these models improved patient education throughout the intervention process [119]. Similarly, 3D models could speed up cath lab planning before stenting pulmonary branches or the aortic arch and pinpointing aortopulmonary collateral arteries to be embolized (Figure 4.1). Optimizing percutaneous procedures necessitates the development of a combination of 3D models and fusion imaging in the cath lab. Despite that, it appears that the actual utility of these 3D models is limited when used to guide treatments on extracardiac structures. MRI and CT, which provide 3D visualization of the vasculature and clearly illustrate the interactions with nearby thoracic structures, are typically used to provide an unambiguous demonstration of the anatomy. In pulmonary atresia with ventricular septal defect, the geolocalization of the main aortopulmonary

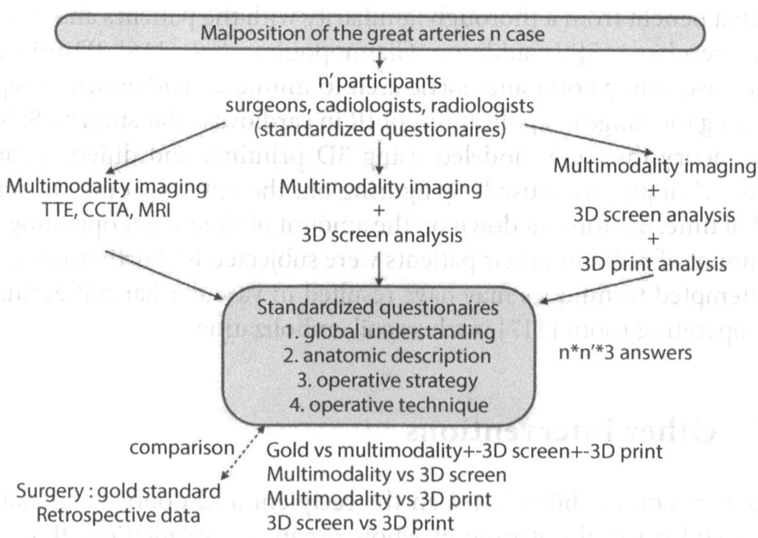

Figure 4.1 Design proposal for a retrospective study.

collateral arteries (MAPCAs) could be a breakthrough application of 3D models. Although conventional imaging techniques can characterize the genesis and propagation of the MAPCAs, they may prove difficult to monitor, suggesting that the required cross-clamping duration in the defect may be overly long.

4.17 Conclusion

The 3D-printed replicas can be used for practice and planning before the actual surgery. Inexperienced doctors may have to deal with unexpected complications that arise during surgical procedures. There is still a lot of room for research into 3D printing with several layers and materials. With 3D-printed models, which are exact replicas of the actual surgical situations, the actual surgery can be organized realistically. Many models have made substantial advancements in the quality of surgical planning. Results that are consistent with the correct interpretation and those with similar mechanical properties of the tissues are promising. The surgeons' self-assurance will be bolstered through simulation training before the actual surgery. The application of 3D-printing technology to surgical simulation and planning, however, requires the establishment of appropriate criteria.

References

1. Johnson, B.N., Lancaster, K.Z., Zhen, G., He, J., Gupta, M.K., Kong, Y.L., Engel, E.A., Krick, K.D., Ju, A., Meng, F., Enquist, L.W., 3D printed anatomical nerve regeneration pathways. *Adv. Funct. Mater.*, 25, 39, 6205–17, Oct. 2015.
2. Liaw, C.Y. and Guvendiren, M., Current and emerging applications of 3D printing in medicine. *Biofabrication*, 9, 2, 024102, Jun. 7, 2017.
3. Zhang, Y., Yang, Z., Li, X., Chen, Y., Zhang, S., Du, M., Li, J., Custom prosthetic reconstruction for proximal tibial osteosarcoma with proximal tibiofibular joint involved. *Surg. Oncol.*, 17, 2, 87–95, Aug. 1, 2008.
4. Galasso, O., Mariconda, M., Brando, A., Iannò, B., Disassembly of a distal femur modular prosthesis after tumor resection. *J. Arthroplasty*, 25, 2, 334–e5, Feb. 1, 2010.
5. Tejo-Otero, A., Buj-Corral, I., Fenollosa-Artés, F., 3D printing in medicine for preoperative surgical planning: A review. *Ann. Biomed. Eng.*, 48, 2, 536–55, Feb. 2020.

6. Segaran, N., Saini, G., Mayer, J.L., Naidu, S., Patel, I., Alzubaidi, S., Oklu, R., Application of 3D printing in preoperative planning. *J. Clin. Med.*, 10, 5, 917, Feb. 26, 2021.
7. Tack, P., Victor, J., Gemmel, P., Annemans, L., 3D-printing techniques in a medical setting: A systematic literature review. *Biomed. Eng. Online*, 15, 1–21, Dec. 2016.
8. Martelli, N., Serrano, C., van den Brink, H., Pineau, J., Prognon, P., Borget, I., El Batti, S., Advantages and disadvantages of 3-dimensional printing in surgery: A systematic review. *Surgery*, 159, 6, 1485–500, Jun. 1, 2016.
9. I. Gibson, *Additive Manufacturing Technologies 3D Printing, Rapid Prototyping, and Direct Digital Manufacturing*, Springer, New York, 2016.
10. Nasab, M.H. (Ed.), *Handbook of Robotic and Image-Guided Surgery*, Elsevier, USA, Sep. 25, 2019.
11. Cornejo, J., Cornejo-Aguilar, J.A., Perales-Villarroel, J.P., Innovaciones internacionales en robótica médica para mejorar el manejo del paciente en Perú. *Rev. Fac. Med. Hum.*, 19, 4, 105–13, Oct. 2019.
12. Desai, J.P., *The Encyclopedia Of Medical Robotics, (In 4 Volumes)*, World Scientific, Singapore, Aug. 28, 2018.
13. Cornejo, J., Cornejo-Aguilar, J.A., Palomares, R., Biomedik surgeon: Surgical robotic system for training and simulation by medical students in Peru, in: *2019 International Conference on Control of Dynamical and Aerospace Systems (XPOTRON)*, IEEE, pp. 1–4, Apr. 23, 2019.
14. Cornejo, J., Cornejo-Aguilar, J.A., Sebastian, R., Perales, P., Gonzalez, C., Vargas, M., Elli, E.F., Mechanical design of a novel surgical laparoscopic simulator for telemedicine assistance and physician training during aerospace applications, in: *2021 IEEE 3rd Eurasia Conference on Biomedical Engineering, Healthcare and Sustainability (ECBIOS)*, IEEE, pp. 53–56, May 28, 2021.
15. Cornejo, J., Perales-Villarroel, J.P., Sebastian, R., Cornejo-Aguilar, J.A., Conceptual design of space biosurgeon for robotic surgery and aerospace medicine, in: *2020 IEEE ANDESCON*, IEEE, pp. 1–6, Oct. 13, 2020.
16. Cornejo, J., Cornejo-Aguilar, J.A., Gonzalez, C., Sebastian, R., Mechanical and kinematic design of surgical mini robotic manipulator used into SP-LAP multi-DOF platform for training and simulation, in: *2021 IEEE XXVIII International Conference on Electronics, Electrical Engineering and Computing (INTERCON)*, IEEE, pp. 1–4, Aug. 5, 2021.
17. Mitsouras, D., Liacouras, P.C., Wake, N., Rybicki, F.J., RadioGraphics update: Medical 3D printing for the radiologist. *Radiographics*, 40, 4, E21–3, Jul. 2020.
18. Bücking, T.M., Hill, E.R., Robertson, J.L., Maneas, E., Plumb, A.A., Nikitichev, D.I., From medical imaging data to 3D printed anatomical models. *PloS One*, 12, 5, e0178540, May 31, 2017.
19. Liaw, C.Y. and Guvendiren, M., Current and emerging applications of 3D printing in medicine. *Biofabrication*, 9, 2, 024102, Jun. 7, 2017.

20. Christensen, A. and Rybicki, F.J., Maintaining safety and efficacy for 3D printing in medicine. *3D Print. Med.*, 3, 1, 1–0, Mar. 2017.
21. Gibson, I. and Srinath, A., Simplifying medical additive manufacturing: Making the surgeon the designer. *Proc. Technol.*, 20, 237–42, Jan. 1, 2015.
22. Bücking, T.M., Hill, E.R., Robertson, J.L., Maneas, E., Plumb, A.A., Nikitichev, D.I., From medical imaging data to 3D printed anatomical models. *PloS One*, 12, 5, e0178540, May 31, 2017.
23. Giannopoulos, A.A., Mitsouras, D., Yoo, S.J., Liu, P.P., Chatzizisis, Y.S., Rybicki, F.J., Applications of 3D printing in cardiovascular diseases. *Nat. Rev. Cardiol.*, 13, 12, 701–18, Dec. 2016.
24. Babbar, A., Jain, V., Gupta, D., Thermogenesis mitigation using ultrasonic actuation during bone grinding: A hybrid approach using CEM43 C and Arrhenius model. *J. Braz. Soc. Mech. Sci. Eng.*, 41, 1–4, Oct. 2019.
25. Jacobs, S., Grunert, R., Mohr, F.W., Falk, V., 3D-Imaging of cardiac structures using 3D heart models for planning in heart surgery: A preliminary study. *Interact. Cardiovasc. Thorac. Surg.*, 7, 1, 6–9, Feb. 1, 2008.
26. Kumar, M., Babbar, A., Sharma, A., Shahi, A.S., Effect of post weld thermal aging (PWTA) sensitization on micro-hardness and corrosion behavior of AISI 304 weld joints. *J. Phys. Conf. Ser. IOP Publishing*, 1240, 1, 012078, Jul. 1, 2019.
27. Babbar, A., Singh, P.A., Farwaha, H.S., Parametric study of magnetic abrasive finishing of UNS C26000 flat brass plate. *Int. J. Adv. Mechatron. Robot.*, 9, 83–9, 2017.
28. Kang, H.W., Lee, S.J., Ko, I.K., Kengla, C., Yoo, J.J., Atala, A., A 3D bioprinting system to produce human-scale tissue constructs with structural integrity. *Nat. Biotechnol.*, 34, 3, 312–9, Mar. 2016.
29. Mitsouras, D., Liacouras, P., Imanzadeh, A., Giannopoulos, A.A., Cai, T., Kumamaru, K.K., George, E., Wake, N., Caterson, E.J., Pomahac, B., Ho, V.B., Medical 3D printing for the radiologist. *Radiographics*, 35, 7, 1965–88, Nov. 2015.
30. Edelman, R.R., The history of MR imaging as seen through the pages of radiology. *Radiology*, 273, 2S, S181–200, Nov. 2014.
31. Thomas, A.M. and Banerjee, A.K., *The History of Radiology*, OUP, Oxford, May 9, 2013.
32. Tahmaseb, A., Wu, V., Wismeijer, D., Coucke, W., Evans, C., The accuracy of static computer-aided implant surgery: A systematic review and meta-analysis. *Clin. Oral. Implants Res.*, 29, 416–35, Oct. 2018.
33. Gao, C., Wang, C., Jin, H., Wang, Z., Li, Z., Shi, C., Leng, Y., Yang, F., Liu, H., Wang, J., Additive manufacturing technique-designed metallic porous implants for clinical application in orthopedics. *RSC Adv.*, 8, 44, 25210–27, 2018.
34. Kimpe, T. and Tuytschaever, T., Increasing the number of gray shades in medical display systems—how much is enough? *J. Digit. Imaging*, 20, 4, 422–32, Dec. 2007.

35. Pieper, S., Halle, M., Kikinis, R., 3D Slicer, in: *2004 2nd IEEE International Symposium on Biomedical Imaging: Nano To Macro (IEEE Cat No. 04EX821)*, pp. 632–635, Apr. 18, 2004IEEE.
36. Esses, S.J., Berman, P., Bloom, A.I., Sosna, J., Clinical applications of physical 3D models derived from MDCT data and created by rapid prototyping. *Am. J. Roentgenol.*, 196, 6, W683–8, Jun. 2011.
37. Mohan, N., Senthil, P., Vinodh, S., Jayanth, N., A review on composite materials and process parameters optimisation for the fused deposition modelling process. *Virtual Phys. Prototyp.*, 12, 1, 47–59, Jan. 2, 2017.
38. Jin, Y.A., Li, H., He, Y., Fu, J.Z., Quantitative analysis of surface profile in fused deposition modelling. *Addit. Manuf.*, 8, 142–8, Oct. 1, 2015.
39. Espalin, D., Arcaute, K., Rodriguez, D., Medina, F., Posner, M., Wicker, R., Fused deposition modeling of patient-specific polymethylmethacrylate implants. *Rapid Prototyp. J.*, 16, 3, 164–73, Apr. 27, 2010.
40. Mazzoli, A., Selective laser sintering in biomedical engineering. *Med. Biol. Eng. Comput.*, 51, 245–56, Mar. 2013.
41. Choi, J.W. and Kim, N., Clinical application of three-dimensional printing technology in craniofacial plastic surgery. *Arch. Plast. Surg.*, 42, 03, 267–77, May 2015.
42. Murr, L.E., Esquivel, E.V., Quinones, S.A., Gaytan, S.M., Lopez, M.I., Martinez, E.Y., Medina, F., Hernandez, D.H., Martinez, E., Martinez, J.L., Stafford, S.W., Microstructures and mechanical properties of electron beam-rapid manufactured Ti–6Al–4V biomedical prototypes compared to wrought Ti–6Al–4V. *Mater. Charact.*, 60, 2, 96–105, Feb. 1, 2009.
43. Grover, T., Pandey, A., Kumari, S.T., Awasthi, A., Singh, B., Dixit, P., Singhal, P., Saxena, K.K., Role of titanium in bio implants and additive manufacturing: An overview. *Mater. Today Proc.*, 26, 3071–80, Jan. 1, 2020.
44. Zhao, X., Li, S., Zhang, M., Liu, Y., Sercombe, T.B., Wang, S., Hao, Y., Yang, R., Murr, L.E., Comparison of the microstructures and mechanical properties of Ti–6Al–4V fabricated by selective laser melting and electron beam melting. *Mater. Des.*, 95, 21–31, Apr. 5, 2016.
45. Nematollahi, M., Baghbaderani, K.S., Amerinatanzi, A., Zamanian, H., Elahinia, M., Application of NiTi in assistive and rehabilitation devices: A review. *Bioengineering*, 6, 2, 37, Apr. 29, 2019.
46. Li, Y., Hu, Y., Cong, W., Zhi, L., Guo, Z., Additive manufacturing of alumina using laser engineered net shaping: Effects of deposition variables. *Ceram. Int.*, 43, 10, 7768–75, Jul. 1, 2017.
47. Zhang, L.C., Klemm, D., Eckert, J., Hao, Y.L., Sercombe, T.B., Manufacture by selective laser melting and mechanical behavior of a biomedical Ti–24Nb–4Zr–8Sn alloy. *Scr. Mater.*, 65, 1, 21–4, Jun. 1, 2011.
48. Ghai, S., Sharma, Y., Jain, N., Satpathy, M., Pillai, A.K., Use of 3-D printing technologies in craniomaxillofacial surgery: A review. *Oral. Maxillofac. Surg.*, 22, 249–59, Sep. 2018.

49. Crafts, T.D., Ellsperman, S.E., Wannemuehler, T.J., Bellicchi, T.D., Shipchandler, T.Z., Mantravadi, A.V., Three-dimensional printing and its applications in otorhinolaryngology–head and neck surgery. *Otolaryngol. Head Neck Surg.*, 156, 6, 999–1010, Jun. 2017.
50. Pettersson, A.B., Salmi, M., Vallittu, P., Serlo, W., Tuomi, J., Mäkitie, A.A., Main clinical use of additive manufacturing (three-dimensional printing) in Finland restricted to the head and neck area in 2016–2017. *Scand. J. Surg.*, 109, 2, 166–73, Jun. 2020.
51. Zimmerer, R.M., Ellis III, E., Aniceto, G.S., Schramm, A., Wagner, M.E., Grant, M.P., Cornelius, C.P., Strong, E.B., Rana, M., Chye, L.T., Calle, A.R., A prospective multicenter study to compare the precision of posttraumatic internal orbital reconstruction with standard preformed and individualized orbital implants. *J. Craniomaxillofac. Surg.*, 44, 9, 1485–97, Sep. 1, 2016.
52. Rana, M., Chui, C.H., Wagner, M., Zimmerer, R., Rana, M., Gellrich, N.C., Increasing the accuracy of orbital reconstruction with selective laser-melted patient-specific implants combined with intraoperative navigation. *J. Oral. Maxillofac. Surg.*, 73, 6, 1113–8, Jun. 1, 2015.
53. Mazzoni, S., Bianchi, A., Schiariti, G., Badiali, G., Marchetti, C., Computer-aided design and computer-aided manufacturing cutting guides and customized titanium plates are useful in upper maxilla waferless repositioning. *J. Oral. Maxillofac. Surg.*, 73, 4, 701–7, Apr. 1, 2015.
54. Laure, B., Louisy, A., Joly, A., Travers, N., Listrat, A., Pare, A., Virtual 3D planning of osteotomies for craniosynostoses and complex craniofacial malformations. *Neurochirurgie*, 65, 5, 269–78, Nov. 1, 2019.
55. Lin, H.H., Lonic, D., Lo, L.J., 3D printing in orthognathic surgery–a literature review. *J. Formos. Med. Assoc.*, 117, 7, 547–58, Jul. 1, 2018.
56. Mercuri, L.G., The role of custom-made prosthesis for temporomandibular joint replacement. *Rev. Esp. Cir. Oral. Maxilofac.*, 35, 1, 1–10, Jan. 1, 2013.
57. Avraham, T., Franco, P., Brecht, L.E., Ceradini, D.J., Saadeh, P.B., Hirsch, D.L., Levine, J.P., Functional outcomes of virtually planned free fibula flap reconstruction of the mandible. *Plast. Reconstr. Surg.*, 134, 4, 628e–34e, Oct. 1, 2014.
58. Shenaq, D.S. and Matros, E., Virtual planning and navigational technology in reconstructive surgery. *J. Surg. Oncol.*, 118, 5, 845–52, Oct. 2018.
59. Nicot, R., Druelle, C., Schlund, M., Roland-Billecart, T., Gwénaël, R., Ferri, J., Gosset, D., Use of 3D printed models in student education of craniofacial traumas. *Dent. Traumatol.*, 35, 4–5, 296–9, Oct. 2019.
60. Low, C.M., Morris, J.M., Matsumoto, J.S., Stokken, J.K., O'Brien, E.K., Choby, G., Use of 3D-printed and 2D-illustrated international frontal sinus anatomy classification anatomic models for resident education. *Otolaryngol. Head Neck Surg.*, 161, 4, 705–13, Oct. 2019.
61. Ayoub, N., Ghassemi, A., Rana, M., Gerressen, M., Riediger, D., Hölzle, F., Modabber, A., Evaluation of computer-assisted mandibular reconstruction

with vascularized iliac crest bone graft compared to conventional surgery: A randomized prospective clinical trial. *Trials*, 15, 1, 1–4, Dec. 2014.
62. Dumas, B.M., Nava, A., Law, H.Z., Smartt, J., Derderian, C., Seaward, J.R., Kane, A.A., Hallac, R.R., Three-dimensional printing for craniofacial surgery: A single institution's 5-year experience. *Cleft Palate Craniofac. J.*, 56, 6, 729–34, Jul. 2019.
63. Berner, A., Woodruff, M.A., Lam, C.X., Arafat, M.T., Saifzadeh, S., Steck, R., Ren, J., Nerlich, M., Ekaputra, A.K., Gibson, I., Hutmacher, D.W., Effects of scaffold architecture on cranial bone healing. *Int. J. Oral. Maxillofac. Surg.*, 43, 4, 506–13, Apr. 1, 2014.
64. Tao, O., Kort-Mascort, J., Lin, Y., Pham, H.M., Charbonneau, A.M., ElKashty, O.A., Kinsella, J.M., Tran, S.D., The applications of 3D printing for craniofacial tissue engineering. *Micromachines*, 10, 7, 480, Jul. 17, 2019.
65. Nyberg, E.L., Farris, A.L., Hung, B.P., Dias, M., Garcia, J.R., Dorafshar, A.H., Grayson, W.L., 3D-printing technologies for craniofacial rehabilitation, reconstruction, and regeneration. *Ann. Biomed. Eng.*, 45, 45–57, Jan. 2017.
66. Clifton, W., Damon, A., Valero-Moreno, F., Nottmeier, E., Pichelmann, M., The SpineBox: A freely available, open-access, 3D-printed simulator design for lumbar pedicle screw placement. *Cureus*, 12, 4, 1–9, Apr. 20, 2020.
67. Damon, A., Clifton, W., Valero-Moreno, F., Quinones-Hinojosa, A., Cost-effective method for 3-dimensional printing dynamic multiobject and patient-specific brain tumor models. *World Neurosurg.*, 140, 173–9, Aug. 1, 2020.
68. Panesar, S.S., Magnetta, M., Mukherjee, D., Abhinav, K., Branstetter, B.F., Gardner, P.A., Iv, M., Fernandez-Miranda, J.C., Patient-specific 3-dimensionally printed models for neurosurgical planning and education. *Neurosurg. Focus*, 47, 6, E12, Dec. 1, 2019.
69. Mashiko, T., Otani, K., Kawano, R., Konno, T., Kaneko, N., Ito, Y., Watanabe, E., Development of three-dimensional hollow elastic model for cerebral aneurysm clipping simulation enabling rapid and low cost prototyping. *World Neurosurg.*, 83, 3, 351-61, Mar. 1, 2015.
70. Colaguori, F., Marin-Mera, M., McDonnell, M., Martínez, J., Valero-Moreno, F., Damon, A., Domingo, R.A., Clifton, W., Fox, W.C., Chaichana, K., Middlebrooks, E.H., Three-dimensionally printed surgical simulation tool for brain mapping training and preoperative planning. *Oper. Neurosurg.*, 21, 6, 523-32, Nov. 15, 2021.
71. Martinez, J.L., Damon, A., Domingo, R.A., Valero-Moreno, F., Quiñones-Hinojosa, A., Retrosigmoid craniectomy and suprameatal drilling—3-dimensionally printed microneurosurgical simulation: 2-dimensional operative video. *Oper. Neurosurg.*, 21, E355–E356, Sep. 15, 2021.
72. Vukicevic, M., Mosadegh, B., Min, J.K., Little, S.H., Cardiac 3D printing and its future directions. *JACC: Cardiovasc. Imaging*, 10, 2, 171–84, Feb. 2017.

73. Ryan, J., Plasencia, J., Richardson, R., Velez, D., Nigro, J.J., Pophal, S., Frakes, D., 3D printing for congenital heart disease: A single site's initial three-year-experience. *3D Print. Med.*, 4, 1, 1–9, Dec, 2018.
74. Hermsen, J.L., Roldan-Alzate, A., Anagnostopoulos, P.V., Three-dimensional printing in congenital heart disease. *J. Thorac. Dis.*, 12, 3, 1194, Mar. 2020.
75. Biglino, G., Koniordou, D., Gasparini, M., Capelli, C., Leaver, L.K., Khambadkone, S., Schievano, S., Taylor, A.M., Wray, J., Piloting the use of patient-specific cardiac models as a novel tool to facilitate communication during cinical consultations. *Pediatr. Cardiol.*, 38, 813–8, Apr. 2017.
76. Valverde, I., Three-dimensional printed cardiac models: Applications in the field of medical education, cardiovascular surgery, and structural heart interventions. *Rev. Esp. Cardiol. (English Edition)*, 70, 4, 282–91, Apr. 1, 2017.
77. Costello, J.P., Olivieri, L.J., Su, L., Krieger, A., Alfares, F., Thabit, O., Marshall, M.B., Yoo, S.J., Kim, P.C., Jonas, R.A., Nath, D.S., Incorporating three-dimensional printing into a simulation-based congenital heart disease and critical care training curriculum for resident physicians. *Congenit. Heart Dis.*, 10, 2, 185–90, Mar. 2015.
78. Lau, I., Sun, Z., Three-dimensional printing in congenital heart disease: A systematic review. *J. Med. Radiat. Sci.*, 65, 3, 226–36, Sep. 2018.
79. Nishimura, R.A., Vahanian, A., Eleid, M.F., Mack, M.J., Mitral valve disease—current management and future challenges. *Lancet*, 387, 10025, 1324–34, Mar. 26, 2016.
80. Daemen, J.H., Heuts, S., Olsthoorn, J.R., Maessen, J.G., SardariNia, P., Mitral valve modelling and three-dimensional printing for planning and simulation of mitral valve repair. *Eur. J. Cardiothorac. Surg.*, 55, 3, 543–51, Mar. 1, 2019.
81. Tuncay, V., van Ooijen, P., 3D printing for heart valve disease: A systematic review. *Eur. Radiol. Exp.*, 3, 1, 1-0, Dec. 2019.
82. Yoon, S.H., Bleiziffer, S., Latib, A., Eschenbach, L., Ancona, M., Vincent, F., Kim, W.K., Unbehaum, A., Asami, M., Dhoble, A., Silaschi, M., Predictors of left ventricular outflow tract obstruction after transcatheter mitral valve replacement. *JACC Cardiovasc. Interv.*, 12, 2, 182–93, Jan. 28, 2019.
83. Kohli, K., Wei, Z.A., Yoganathan, A.P., Oshinski, J.N., Leipsic, J., Blanke, P., Transcatheter mitral valve planning and the neo-LVOT: utilization of virtual simulation models and 3D printing. *Curr. Treat. Options Cardiovasc. Med.*, 20, 1–4, Dec. 2018.
84. Christou, S., Chatziathanasiou, T., Angeli, S., Koullapis, P., Stylianou, F., Sznitman, J., Guo, H.H., Kassinos, S.C., Anatomical variability in the upper tracheobronchial tree: Sex-based differences and implications for personalized inhalation therapies. *J. Appl. Physiol.*, 130, 3, 678–707, Mar. 1, 2021.
85. Lermusiaux, P., Leroux, C., Tasse, J.C., Castellani, L., Martinez, R., Aortic aneurysm: Construction of a life-size model by rapid prototyping. *Ann. Vasc. Surg.*, 15, 2, 131–5, Mar. 1, 2001.
86. Marti, P., Lampus, F., Benevento, D., Setacci, C., Trends in use of 3D printing in vascular surgery: A survey. *Int. Angiol.*, 38, 5, 418–24, Sep. 20, 2019.

87. Sheth, R., Balesh, E.R., Zhang, Y.S., Hirsch, J.A., Khademhosseini, A., Oklu, R., Three-dimensional printing: An enabling technology for IR. *J. Vasc. Interv. Radiol.*, 27, 6, 859–65, Jun. 1, 2016.
88. He, L., Cheng, G.S., Du, Y.J., Zhang, Y.S., Feasibility of device closure for multiple atrial septal defects with an inferior sinus venosus defect: Procedural planning using three-dimensional printed models. *Heart Lung Circ.*, 29, 6, 914–20, Jun. 1, 2020.
89. Thakkar, A.N., Chinnadurai, P., Breinholt, J.P., Lin, C.H., Transcatheter closure of a sinus venosus atrial septal defect using 3D printing and image fusion guidance. *Catheter. Cardiovasc. Interv.*, 92, 2, 353–7, Aug. 1, 2018.
90. Forte, M.N.V., Byrne, N., Valverde, I., Gomez Ciriza, G., Hermuzi, A., Prachasilchai, P., Mainzer, G., Pushparajah, K., Henningsson, M., Hussain, T., Qureshi, S., Interventional correction of sinus venosus atrial septal defect and partial anomalous pulmonary venous drainage: Procedural planning using 3D printed models. *JACC Cardiovasc. Imaging*, 11, 2 Part 1, 275–8, Feb. 2018.
91. Bhatla P, Mosca RS, Tretter JT. Altering management decisions with gained anatomical insight from a 3D printed model of a complex ventricular septal defect. *Cardiol. Young*, 27, 2, 377–80, Mar. 2017.
92. Costello JP, Olivieri LJ, Krieger A, Thabit O, Marshall MB, Yoo SJ, Kim PC, Jonas RA, Nath DS. Utilizing three-dimensional printing technology to assess the feasibility of high-fidelity synthetic ventricular septal defect models for simulation in medical education. *World J. Pediatr. Congenit. Heart Surg.*, 5, 3, 421–6, Jul. 2014.
93. Garekar, S., Bharati, A., Chokhandre, M., Mali, S., Trivedi, B., Changela, V.P., Solanki, N., Gaikwad, S., Agarwal, V., Clinical application and multidisciplinary assessment of three dimensional printing in double outlet right ventricle with remote ventricular septal defect. *World J. Pediatr. Congenit. Heart Surg.*, 7, 3, 344–50, May 2016.
94. Kim, M.S., Hansgen, A.R., Wink, O., Quaife, R.A., Carroll, J.D., Rapid prototyping: A new tool in understanding and treating structural heart disease. *Circulation*, 117, 18, 2388–94, May 6, 2008.
95. Ryan, J.R., Moe, T.G., Richardson, R., Frakes, D.H., Nigro, J.J., Pophal, S., A novel approach to neonatal management of tetralogy of Fallot, with pulmonary atresia, and multiple aortopulmonary collaterals. *JACC Cardiovasc. Imaging*, 8, 1, 103–4, Jan. 2015.
96. Vukicevic, M., Puperi, D.S., Jane Grande-Allen, K., Little, S.H., 3D printed modeling of the mitral valve for catheter-based structural interventions. *Ann. Biomed. Eng.*, 45, 508–19, Feb. 2017.
97. Randazzo, M., Pisapia, J.M., Singh, N., Thawani, J.P., 3D printing in neurosurgery: A systematic review. *Surg. Neurol. Int.*, 7, Suppl 33, S801, 2016.
98. Nagesh, S.S., Hinaman, J., Sommer, K., Xiong, Z., Ionita, C.N., Bednarek, D.R., Rudin, S., A simulation platform using 3D printed neurovascular phantoms for clinical utility evaluation of new imaging technologies, in:

Medical Imaging 2018: Biomedical Applications in Molecular, Structural, and Functional Imaging, vol. 10578, SPIE, pp. 157–165, Mar. 12, 2018.

99. Nagesh, S.S., Russ, M., Ionita, C.N., Bednarek, D., Rudin, S., Use of patient specific 3D printed neurovascular phantoms to evaluate the clinical utility of a high resolution x-ray imager, in: *Medical Imaging 2017: Biomedical Applications in Molecular, Structural, and Functional Imaging*, vol. 10137, SPIE, pp. 114–122, Mar. 13, 2017.
100. Potjewyd, G., Moxon, S., Wang, T., Domingos, M., Hooper, N.M., Tissue engineering 3D neurovascular units: A biomaterials and bioprinting perspective. *Trends Biotechnol.*, 36, 4, 457–72, Apr. 1, 2018.
101. Nawka MT, Spallek J, Kuhl J, Krause D, Buhk JH, Fiehler J, Frölich A. Evaluation of a modular in vitro neurovascular procedure simulation for intracranial aneurysm embolization. *J. Neurointerv. Surg.*, 12, 2, 214–9, Feb. 1, 2020.
102. Leal, A., Souza, M., Nohama, P., Additive manufacturing of 3D biomodels as adjuvant in intracranial aneurysm clipping. *Artif. Organs*, 43, 1, E9–15, Jan. 2019.
103. Mashiko, T., Otani, K., Kawano, R., Konno, T., Kaneko, N., Ito, Y., Watanabe, E., Development of three-dimensional hollow elastic model for cerebral aneurysm clipping simulation enabling rapid and low cost prototyping. *World Neurosurg.*, 83, 3, 351–61, Mar. 1, 2015.
104. Morris, S., Hirata, M., Sugata, H., Goto, T., Matsushita, K., Yanagisawa, T., Saitoh, Y., Kishima, H., Yoshimine, T., Patient-specific cortical electrodes for sulcal and gyral implantation. *IEEE Trans. Biomed. Eng.*, 62, 4, 1034–41, Jul. 11, 2014.
105. Kozakiewicz, M., Elgalal, M., Loba, P., Komuński, P., Arkuszewski, P., Broniarczyk-Loba, A., Stefańczyk, L., Clinical application of 3D pre-bent titanium implants for orbital floor fractures. *J. Craniomaxillofac. Surg.*, 37, 4, 229–34, Jun. 1, 2009.
106. Da Cruz, M.J., Francis, H.W., Face and content validation of a novel three-dimensional printed temporal bone for surgical skills development. *J. Laryngol. Otol.*, 129, S3, S23–9, Jul. 2015.
107. Hochman, J.B., Rhodes, C., Kraut, J., Pisa, J., Unger, B., End user comparison of anatomically matched 3-dimensional printed and virtual haptic temporal bone simulation: A pilot study. *Otolaryngol. Head Neck Surg.*, 153, 2, 263–8, Aug. 2015.
108. Hochman, J.B., Rhodes, C., Wong, D., Kraut, J., Pisa, J., Unger, B., Comparison of cadaveric and isomorphic three-dimensional printed models in temporal bone education. *Laryngoscope*, 125, 10, 2353–7, Oct. 2015.
109. Longfield, E.A., Brickman, T.M., Jeyakumar, A., 3D printed pediatric temporal bone: A novel training model. *Otol. Neurotol.*, 36, 5, 793-5, Jun. 1, 2015.
110. Rose, A.S., Kimbell, J.S., Webster, C.E., Harrysson, O.L., Formeister, E.J., Buchman, C.A., Multi-material 3D models for temporal bone surgical simulation. *Ann. Otol. Rhinol. Laryngol.*, 124, 7, 528–36, Jul. 2015.

111. Xiong, L., Li, X., Li, H., Chen, Z., Xiao, T., The efficacy of 3D printing-assisted surgery for traumatic fracture: A meta-analysis. *Postgrad. Med. J.*, 95, 1126, 414-9, Aug. 1, 2019.
112. Yang, L., Shang, X.W., Fan, J.N., He, Z.X., Wang, J.J., Liu, M., Zhuang, Y., Ye, C., Application of 3D printing in the surgical planning of trimalleolar fracture and doctor-patient communication. *BioMed Res. Int.*, 2016, 1–5, Oct. 2016.
113. Hung, C.C., Li, Y.T., Chou, Y.C., Chen, J.E., Wu, C.C., Shen, H.C., Yeh, T.T., Conventional plate fixation method versus pre-operative virtual simulation and three-dimensional printing-assisted contoured plate fixation method in the treatment of anterior pelvic ring fracture. *Int. Orthop.*, 43, 425–31, Feb. 14, 2019.
114. Kang, H.J., Kim, B.S., Kim, S.M., Kim, Y.M., Kim, H.N., Park, J.Y., Cho, J.H., Choi, Y., Can preoperative 3D printing change surgeon's operative plan for distal tibia fracture?. *BioMed Res. Int.*, 2019, 1–7, Feb. 11, 2019.
115. Sheth, R., Balesh, E.R., Zhang, Y.S., Hirsch, J.A., Khademhosseini, A., Oklu, R., Three-dimensional printing: An enabling technology for IR. *J. Vasc. Interv. Radiol.*, 27, 6, 859–65, Jun. 1, 2016.
116. Giannopoulos, A.A., Steigner, M.L., George, E., Barile, M., Hunsaker, A.R., Rybicki, F.J., Mitsouras, D., Cardiothoracic applications of 3D printing. *J. Thorac. Imaging*, 31, 5, 253, Sep. 2016.
117. Itagaki, M.W., Using 3D printed models for planning and guidance during endovascular intervention: A technical advance. *Diagn. Interv. Radiol.*, 21, 4, 338, Jul. 2015.
118. Zein, N.N., Hanouneh, I.A., Bishop, P.D., Samaan, M., Eghtesad, B., Quintini, C., Miller, C., Yerian, L., Klatte, R., Three-dimensional print of a liver for preoperative planning in living donor liver transplantation. *Liver Transplant.*, 19, 12, 1304–10, Dec. 2013.
119. Chandak, P., Byrne, N., Coleman, A., Karunanithy, N., Carmichael, J., Marks, S.D., Stojanovic, J., Kessaris, N., Mamode, N., Patient-specific 3D printing: A novel technique for complex pediatric renal transplantation. *Ann. Surg.*, 269, 2, e18–23, Feb. 1, 2019.
120. Silberstein, J.L., Maddox, M.M., Dorsey, P., Feibus, A., Thomas, R., Lee, B.R., Physical models of renal malignancies using standard cross-sectional imaging and 3-dimensional printers: A pilot study. *Urology*, 84, 2, 268–73, Aug. 1, 2014.

5

Customized Implants and Prosthetics with 3D Printing

Abstract

Due to a lack of effective tools, doctors must frequently rely on intuition, experience, and imaging studies to design surgical procedures. Clinicians need to learn about 3D printing and its applications as the technology becomes more commonplace in healthcare settings. Here, researchers go over the basics of 3D printing and its workflow. In this chapter, the investigator takes a look at the benefits and drawbacks of using 3D printing for preoperative planning as well as for creating customized implants and prosthetics.

Keyword: 3D printing, customized implants, prosthesis design, image acquisition, CT scan, digital imaging, fused deposition modeling

5.1 Introduction

Many different reconstruction techniques have been used for limb salvage over the past few decades [1]. These techniques include autografts, allografts, and specialized or modular prostheses. There are benefits and drawbacks to each option. Due to its strong osteoconductive and osteoinductive qualities, autograft has an exceptional capacity for wound healing. Unfortunately, supply is low, and invasive collection is necessary [2]. Allografts provide both immediate structural support and a place for muscles and ligaments to join again. Possible disease transfer and sluggish absorption into the host bone are two disadvantages [3]. Also, autografts and allografts must be carefully carved to precisely match the flaws. It takes a lot of time and effort to do the task. While prostheses can give immediate support and allow for a speedy recovery to weight bearing, they are also prone to problems such as aseptic loosening, infection, and periprosthetic fracture [4]. Analysis of the advantages and disadvantages of each possible rebuild is necessary in order to decide the best course of action. The use of 3D printing in medicine is fast growing and has the

Rishabha Malviya and Rishav Sharma. 3D Printing in Healthcare: Novel Applications, (85–100)

potential to completely alter the medical industry [5]. Tissue and organ fabrication; construction of bespoke prosthetics, implants, and anatomical models; pharmaceutical research regarding drug dosage forms, distribution, and discovery—these are only some of the many potentials and existing medical applications of 3D printing [6]. There are several potential advantages to using 3D printing in the medical field, including the ability to tailor treatments to an individual's needs, lower costs, boost efficiency, broaden participation in the creative process, and improve teamwork [7]. Notwithstanding recent exciting medical discoveries involving 3D printing, it is important to note that considerable scientific and regulatory difficulties remain and that the most transformational applications for the technology will require time to evolve [8–10]. Because the first prosthesis will be constructed specifically for the patient, treatment time may be extended. Modular prostheses have become increasingly popular in limb-salvage operations in recent years due to their low cost and high availability. After receiving modular hemipelvis prostheses, patients in trials [5, 6] had an MSTS 93 score of 57.2%–62% on average. Patients with tailored prostheses had similar functional scores (ranging from 50% to 59.4%) [7, 8]. The means Toronto Extremity Salvage (TES) score for proximal femoral reconstruction was 61 points out of 100 (90.7% survival rate) [9]. However, bespoke prostheses had a higher rate of long-term success: 77% at 10 years and 57% at 20 years [10]. It means that patients with extremity and pelvic sarcomas can benefit from adaptable reconstructions and functionalities provided by modular prostheses. However, a modular prosthesis that might replace the clavicle, the shoulder blade, and the pelvis is not currently in the market. Although many methods have been explored, the best repair following the removal of these bones remains unknown. An ideal biological rebuilding would involve a large-scale bone graft (allograft or recycled autograft). Nonetheless, there are still separate issues to worry about [11, 12], such as bone resorption, fracture, infection, and immunological rejection. Another promising method of regaining lost function after surgery is prosthetics [13, 14]. The primary issue with the method, besides the need for complex surgical techniques, is the scarcity of appropriate prostheses. Modern prostheses are made by milling down a solid block of titanium and then treating the surface and geometry in various ways to boost stability and osteointegration. There is currently no single-step method for creating an implant with a fully regulated geometry and surface morphology using any of the usual methods. The term "rapid prototyping" (RP) refers to a technique that uses data from a digital model to create a physical replica of the model. Stereolithography (SLA), selective laser sintering (SLS), fused deposition modeling (FDM), laminated object manufacturing (LOM), inkjet printing, and electron beam melting (EBM) are all typical RP processes. EBM, which is essentially a form of 3D printing, is becoming increasingly popular. Metallic components with intricate geometries and pore networks can be fabricated using the method [15]. The clavicle, scapula, and ilium are all aberrant bones with unusual measurements. As a result, designing a unique prosthesis and having it manufactured quickly may be a workable option. Complete osteointegration of EBM-made Ti–6Al–4V (TAV) alloy scaffolds was shown in an animal investigation after only 60 days [16]. For zygomatic–orbital deformities, EBM-made TAV implants were used in patients undergoing maxillofacial reconstruction. Digital planning processes, quick prototyping, and titanium implants have all been shown to be successful in clinical trials [17]. However, until recently, there have been relatively few studies examining the use of 3D-printed TAV prostheses in limb salvage procedures. Likewise, details regarding the prosthesis' longevity, functionality, and potential issues are scarce [18, 19]. The designer used medical image data to create a three-dimensional computer model from which researchers fashioned titanium prosthetics in the study. After the tumor was removed, an osseous defect was left; therefore, a prosthesis was made from EBM and implanted to fill it. The purpose of this chapter was twofold: (i) to detail the process involved in the procedure and (ii) to display the outcomes of patients who had received prostheses after their first implantation. Additive manufacturing involves building up an object by laying down successive layers of raw materials in the correct pattern. Several distinct fabrication technologies comprise additive manufacturing, sometimes referred to as "3D printing." Extrusion printing, material sintering, material binding, and object lamination are the four main types of additive manufacturing based on the 3D-printing process used. More than three decades have passed with 3D-printing technology already in use in the automotive and aerospace industries. Before, the only medical use of 3D printing was to make models of the human body that were used to teach and learn about medicine. Since the discovery of new biodegradable materials, the use of 3D printing in the healthcare and pharmaceutical industries has gone through the roof. Additive manufacturing is a rapidly growing field with numerous potential medical uses today [20]. Bioprinting tissues and living scaffolds for regenerative medicine, as well as personalizing implants and prosthetics and creating patient-specific biomedical models and surgical aids, has fundamentally changed the healthcare system [21]. Figure 5.1 presents several distinct categories of customized implants.

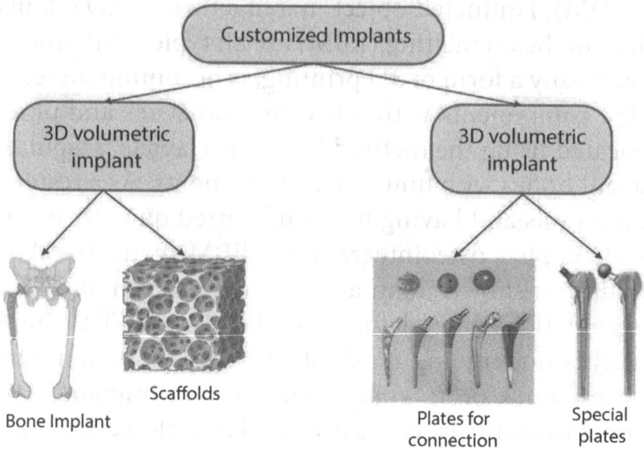

Figure 5.1 Different types of customized implants.

5.2 Image Acquisition and Prosthesis Design

All patients started with a CT scan (Mutislice 64, GE Healthcare, USA). Digital Imaging and Communication in Medicine (DICOM) files were created from a soft tissue standard filter (a 512 × 512-pixel matrix) to capture magnified slices of 0.625 mm in thickness. Specifically, mimics were used for the picture segmentation procedure (Leuven, Belgium). The bone was separated from the surrounding tissue and structures, including the muscle, fat, skin, and even the metal table of the CT scanner. DICOM image pixel data was pseudo-colored, and segmented images were then used to rebuild the 3D model. Bone structures were often completely or partially obliterated by tumor invasion, leaving the 3D models seemingly unfinished. They could not use it to create prosthetics. Here, a three-dimensional mirror model was developed using photographs of the opposite anatomical region to aid in prosthesis development. The tumor was virtually removed, and the prosthesis was virtually placed at the simulated defect site. The authors were able to experiment with several prosthetic designs, thanks to the rotatable 3D model. Titanium has a low modulus (110 GPa) compared to other metals like stainless steel (190 GPa) and cobalt-chrome (230 GPa). The modulus is still significantly higher, being six times that of cortical bone (7–30 GPa). A phenomenon similar to stress protection is produced by an asymmetry in Young's modulus [18]. The titanium prosthesis design was modified to include a porous component to lower the modulus and to address the issue. After determining the optimal surgical approach and exposure, a 3D model was created, and the safe margin, cutting plane, implant position, and screw sites were designated before surgery.

5.3 Manufacturing the TAV Prosthesis

With EBM, the following steps were taken to make the porous TAV prosthetic. After the prosthesis was finished being designed, the information was sent to a template library and then put into the EBM S12 system (Arcam AB, Sweden). The EBM equipment was then used to melt the TAV alloy powder in layers. The prosthesis' framework was modified following the CAD model. After that, acid treatment and ultrasonic cleaning were used to get rid of any lingering particles in the prosthesis. The prosthesis was then packaged after it had been sterilized.

5.4 Patient Information

Surgical procedures were performed on three female patients with malignant tumors in a clinic between November 2018 and June 2019. All patients underwent imaging tests such as X-rays, CT scans, MRIs, and SPECT/CT scans to identify the tumor's edge, its stage, and the optimal cutting plane. Before surgery, needle biopsies were performed on all patients to confirm a pathological diagnosis. Preoperative diagnoses included Ewing's sarcoma (ES) of the clavicle in one patient, ES of the scapula in another, and CS of the pelvis in the third. The patients diagnosed with ES received adjuvant chemotherapy. The ethics committee of Xi-Jing Hospital, Fourth Military Medical University, gave its stamp of approval to the study (FMMU). The Xi-Jing Hospital Ethics Committee has a copy of all of the patients' written informed permission forms [18].

5.5 Commonly Used 3D Printing Technologies in the Medical Field

The most popular additive manufacturing techniques utilized in medicine are FDM, extrusion-based bioprinting, inkjet, and polyjet.

5.5.1 Fused Deposition Modeling or Free Form Fabrication

FDM is the most widely used and cost-effective additive manufacturing technique. The thermoplastic filament is fed through a heated print head and deposited layer by layer onto a build platform until the desired object is created. Some examples of low-cost desktop 3D printers available in the market are the MakerBot, Ultimaker, Flashforge, and Prusa. Print quality with these printers is lower because of the wide range of materials available. Expensive FDM printers, such as Stratasys 3D printers, are also available, and they have the added benefit of being able to print with a wider range of materials and at a greater resolution. Due to the FDM printer's ability to house many print heads, it can print from a wide variety of materials simultaneously. One print head on these multi-head printers often holds a supporting filament that can be withdrawn and dissolved in water [21]. The FDM procedure is typically employed using ABS, the most popular thermoplastic material. In addition to polylactic acid (PLA), nylon, polycarbonate (PC), and polyvinyl alcohol (PVA) are frequently used as printing filaments. PLA and polylactic co-polymer (PCL) are two of the most popular biocompatible polymers utilized in the medical and pharmaceutical industries. Because of their low melting points (175°C and 65°C, respectively), PLA and PCL are ideal for drug loading because they prevent medicines from being deactivated by heat. These polymers are broken down by hydrolysis *in vivo* and flushed out by the kidneys and intestines, respectively [22, 23]. PCL is employed for non-load-bearing applications due to its lesser mechanical strength compared to PLA.

5.5.2 Extrusion-Based Bioprinting

Pneumatic or mechanical pressure is used to extrude the material through a print head. In a manner analogous to FDM, materials are constantly placed in layers until the desired shape is created. The method is preferred for the production of cell- and growth hormone-laden tissue engineering structures because it does not require any heating operations. To print cells and other biological materials in three dimensions, scientists have developed bio-inks. These 3D-printed structures may deposit single cells or small groups of cells with high precision and minimum process-induced cell harm. The advantages of the method in the fabrication of live scaffolds are numerous and include more accurate cell deposition, more manageable cell distribution, and a faster process. The technique of 3D printing allows for the printing of a wide variety of materials, including those with a wide range of viscosities and high cell-density aggregates. Nowadays, scientists are investigating a wide range of polymers for potential application in bioprinting. Bio-inks for 3D printing often consist of natural polymers including collagen [24], gelatin [25], alginate [26], and hyaluronic acid (HA) [27] as well as synthetic polymers like PVA [28] and polyethylene glycol (PEG). To improve the mechanical properties of the build, these bio-inks are often subjected to further processing, most frequently chemical or UV crosslinking. Bio-inks can be made from a wide variety of polymers, allowing for the fabrication of biological tissues and scaffolds with varying degrees of complexity. The method allows for the use of several print heads, each of which can transport a distinct cell line, allowing for the printing of complicated multicellular constructs. To create a functional human ear, Lee *et al.* [29] used a six-extrusion-headed 3D printer with six distinct bio-inks, one of which (PEG) served as a sacrificial ink. Using extrusion bioprinting, mice that had been surgically sterilized were able to reproduce after receiving these implants [29]. Scaffolds for the repair of many tissues, including bone [30], cartilage [26], aortic valve [31], skeletal muscle [32], and neural [33], have been fabricated via extrusion bioprinting. Nonetheless, bioprinting still faces significant challenges in areas like material choice and mechanical strength. There is still the challenge of how to fabricate vascularization within a complicated tissue using the technology. Scientists have been working on a solution to the problem by using sacrificial materials, which are added to the construct during 3D printing and then removed afterward, leaving blank spaces to serve as vascularization channels [34].

5.6 Material Sintering

Sintering is a type of 3D printing in which physical (ultraviolet/laser/electron beam) or chemical (binding liquid) sources fuse powdered printing material in a reservoir into a solid product. When it comes to metal sintering 3D printers, the SLA variety is the most established and used technology. In contrast to extrusion-based printers, the print head does not physically touch the object being printed. The method allows for highly precise and detailed 3D printing of the products. The main problem with the technology is that there are not many photocurable polymer resins out there. The majority of commercially available SLA resins are derived from epoxy or low-molecular-weight polyacrylate resins. Calcium phosphate salts derived from hydroxyapatite are the main component of the polymer ceramic composite resins utilized in biomedical applications.

5.7 Process Chain for Customized Prosthetics and Implants

5.7.1 Product Requirements

The primary objective of the personalized prosthetics and implants process chain is to meet the needs of the consumers, i.e., the patients (Figure 5.2). Such necessities are limited by the specifics of each patient's clinical scenario. Throughout product creation, numerous choices must be taken about—factors like the product's purpose, shape, composition, and user interface.

5.7.2 Design Process

Prosthetics and implants used in series are typically designed using a CAD method. The typical human body is used as a starting point for designing products that fulfill specific needs and are then further segmented into various sizes to accommodate a wide range of consumers. Nonetheless, a reverse engineering approach forms the backbone of the medical device design process for individualized products [35]. The process begins with recording and then transferring the individual patient's clinical situation into a digital model. Using the one-of-a-kind set of information, a customized solution

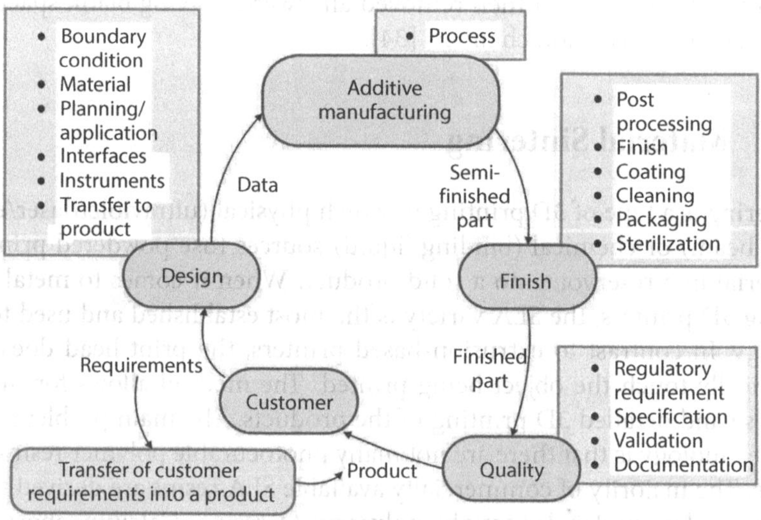

Figure 5.2 Additive manufacturing for medical applications and the difficulties of customization.

is developed for the individual patient. Recent developments in imaging technology have made such implementations possible [36]. Today, imaging modalities like computed tomography (CT) and magnetic resonance imaging (MRI) are used for either 3D surface scanning or volume scanning (MRI). Prosthetics and orthodontics often only require a 3D surface scan of the affected area. It is possible to perform the scan either directly on the patient or indirectly by using an impression. CT and MRI are examples of volume scanning techniques that record a series of cross-sectional images of the patient's body. Several sets of imaging data are collected and fed into a software algorithm for analysis. It enables the reconstruction of a 3D virtual model that faithfully represents the patient's condition. Segmentation creates a paradigm in which CT and MRI images can be interpreted in terms of tissue type. The design procedure that follows is very interdisciplinary when creating a bespoke endoprosthesis. With the help of the generated model and the underlying clinical scenario, clinicians and design engineers work together to plan the implant and decide on its characteristics, such as the implant's kind, placement, bone resection lines, and form of fixation. A design is then derived from the data and refined and improved upon as needed. Processing the virtual model presents a significant challenge for design engineers due to the complex anatomic structure it represents with free-form surfaces [37]. The usage of traditional CAD programs to arrive at a solution is extremely limited. Complex surface modeling and the creation of osseointegration cell structures require a suite of software tools that have not yet been acquired. More than just the implant itself, operation planning, including resection lines, individual instrumentation, and screw placement, is a part of the design process for bespoke endoprostheses. During the design phase, it is necessary to account for the design space and medical boundary conditions as well as the AM process and any following finishing procedures. Training designers in AM and developing a constant process of information transfer between the design and production teams produce the best results. Customized implants can be created accurately from the start, without the need for prototypes or testing, when manufacturing knowledge is incorporated into the design phase [38].

5.8 Applications

5.8.1 Endoprostheses

Endoprostheses are implants that are designed to act inside the body to repair damaged bones or joints. Because they must bear weight, artificial bones and joints have stringent limitations. These days, titanium alloy Ti–6Al–4V is the most commonly used material for making cement-free metallic LAM implants. Here, polymethylmethacrylate is not used to create the implant fixture (so-called bone cement). Instead, osseointegration is aided by a porous structure at the bone–implant interface, and secondary stability is achieved after the loss of primary stability due to press-fit insertion. Only the largest or most complicated abnormalities, however, can be addressed effectively with off-the-shelf implants [38]. Trauma, revision of implants, and malignancies are all examples of extreme conditions. Custom endoprostheses account for a tiny fraction of the market compared to mass-produced series implants. In today's world, LAM technology is utilized to produce a wide range of products, including one-offs and mass-produced items, for use in the operating room. The sections that follow introduce several noteworthy implementations.

5.8.2 Patient-Specific Surgical Guides

Custom instruments can help when implanting a series of implants or a single implant. Patient-specific implants (PSIs) are used to objectively define anatomic landmarks for surgical guidance. PSIs are tailored to a specific position based on preoperative patient imaging data (CT and MRI), orienting a drilling or cutting guide in the direction of travel. Although it is a contentious topic among surgeons, the proponents argue that it improves implant alignment, cuts down on tissue loss, requires fewer instruments, and cuts down on operating time [39]. Selective laser sintering allows the use of a biocompatible polymeric material like PA because of the low mechanical stress experienced by PSIs during application. PSIs may have a metallic cover at the contact with the drilling or sawing guide to prevent plastic particles from flying off during use.

5.8.3 Knee Implants

Primary knee endoprostheses can now be tailored on a mass scale before implantation. Reportedly, an indirect manufacturing process is used rather than LAM [40]. After an additively made wax design is created for the personalized knee implant, investment casting can begin. The clinical evidence for individualized partial knee replacements is promising [41]. It has not yet been stated to the public what steps would be taken to create a bespoke knee replacement using LAM as a direct manufacturing method. LAM's future as a viable production technology is bright because of the intricate geometry of the knee's articulating surface. With a significant bone and joint deformity, a preliminary trial demonstrated the efficacy of a partial knee arthroplasty [42].

5.8.4 Spinal Implants

During spinal arthrodesis, surgeons employ fusion cages to fuse vertebrae. Because of its compact size, intricate shape, and surface modification requirements for osseointegration, LAM has emerged as a practical approach for mass manufacture. The results from an analysis of the structural and mechanical qualities of LAM's spinal implant [43] were favorable. The introduction of a porous structure to lower the particular Young's modulus permits reduced stress shielding and promises a better therapeutic outcome. It was proposed [44] that a process chain may be used to manufacture intervertebral disc implants that are tailored to each patient's anatomy. By analyzing imaging data, researchers were able to locate important landmarks in the patient's skeleton and use those points as inspiration for the disc's shape. Biomechanical data of the patient was used to guide the development and placement of an artificial ball-and-socket joint.

5.9 3D Printing Technology for a Customized Implant and Prosthesis Production

Additive manufacturing, which encompasses 3D printing, is a layered production method in which a physical model is generated by overlapping successive layers of material [45]. Among these substances are metals, ceramics, polymers, liquids, powders, and even live cells [46]. While the procedure relies significantly on computer technology to create the physical model from digital information, it is an essential part of the process. The 3D-printing industry has grown quickly in recent years due to falling production costs and increased productivity of printers [45]. The technology is still in its infancy, but it has shown great promise in the medical field. The bioprinting of skin and organs, as well as the fabrication of individualized implants and prostheses, is just an example of the many ways in which 3D printing is being put to use in the medical field today [47]. Many 3D-printing techniques exist, each with its own set of pros and cons. They are printed using a wide range of substrates and methods. 3D-printing methods like SLS and FDM are frequently utilized for making one-of-a-kind prosthetics and implants [46]. Powdered metal, ceramic, and plastic can be utilized in an SLS printer to make finely detailed, three-dimensional items. Piece by piece, the powder is fused in the form of an object using a laser [46]. The print head of a FDM printer, analogous to an inkjet printer's nozzle, releases heated plastic beads. The object is constructed from many successive thin layers, which solidify and join together as the plastic cools. FDM printers are more widespread and cheaper than SLS printers and can print with a wider range of polymers [46].

5.10 Benefits of 3D-Printing-Customized Implants and Prostheses

The fabrication of dental implants and individualized prostheses was one of the earliest uses of 3D printing in the medical field, dating back to the early 2000s [46, 47]. As compared to other uses of the technology, such as bioprinting, it can be said that this one is fairly well developed. With the use of 3D printing technology, a wide range of unique implants and prosthetics are now possible. Bone implants to replace ribs, jaws, spines, and skulls; knee and hip replacement implants; and prosthetic limbs to replace hands and feet are only a few examples [48]. They can be made from metals, polymers, ceramics, or even a hybrid of those materials [45]. When compared to more conventional procedures, 3D printing offers several advantages when it comes to making individualized implants and prostheses. The ability to make goods that are tailored to the patient in terms of anatomy and pathology is one of the most crucial [49]—for instance, prosthetic limbs can be adjusted for a more precise fit, enhancing both comfort and performance. Accurately fabricating complex structures is another perk. It has ramifications for orthopedic implants when fitting required surgical modification of the implant or the surrounding bone. It shortens the length of the procedure and reduces the amount of damage done to the body during the process. One of the greatest advantages of 3D printing is the reduced expense of mass production. One-of-a-kind custom prostheses and implants can be manufactured with substantially lower setup costs than with conventional manufacturing. Small-batch and low-volume production benefits from this as well, lowering the overall costs [46]. Machining has long been the standard method for creating prosthetics and implants. It is possible that casting flaws and machining the finished product for a better fit will be necessary steps in the manufacturing process. There is a significant amount of time required for all of these steps. Since 3D printing can be done in real time, production times can be shortened [45].

5.11 Limitations and Future Directions

As it has been previously mentioned, 3D printing is already at a point where it is widely used to create personalized implants and prostheses. However, as is the case with any technological advancement, future enhancements are always possible. The current constraints in implant and prosthetic design are mostly attributable to the materials that can be used to construct them. Many of the metals utilized, for instance, have a high elastic modulus, making them exceptionally resistant to elastic deformation. The implant and the grafted bone may not have the same elastic properties, which might lead to stress issues in the bone. The future of 3D printing in the field depends on the discovery and development of new materials.

5.12 Conclusion

While 3D printing is still a young manufacturing technique, its popularity has grown dramatically in recent years, and the trend is only expected to continue as new technologies become available. Throughout the entire procedure, digital information is used to inform the physical model's development. One of the first medical applications of 3D printing was the production of individual implants and prostheses. It still has many uses, such as the capacity to mass-produce complex and precise things that can be adapted to each customer's preferences. Moreover, production costs are kept to a minimum, and turnaround times are shortened. Existing restrictions may be the result of material incompatibilities between 3D-printed things and the human tissue they are attached to. To address these concerns and maximize the cost savings, improved quality, and time-saving efficiencies that 3D printing of personalized implants and prostheses offers, researchers must create novel materials and printing processes.

References

1. Lietman, S.A. and Joyce, M.J., Bone sarcomas: Overview of management, with a focus on surgical treatment considerations. *Clev. Clin. J. Med.*, 77, S8–12, Mar. 1, 2010.
2. Schuh, R., Panotopoulos, J., Puchner, S.E., Willegger, M., Hobusch, G.M., Windhager, R., Funovics, P.T., Vascularised or non-vascularised autologous fibular grafting for the reconstruction of a diaphyseal bone defect after resection of a musculoskeletal tumor. *Bone Joint J.*, 96, 9, 1258–63, Sep. 1, 2014.

3. Fan, H., Guo, Z., Wang, Z., Li, J., Li, X., Surgical technique: Unicondylarosteoallograft prosthesis composite in tumor limb salvage surgery. *Clin. Orthop. Relat. Res.*, 470, 3577–86, Dec. 2012.
4. Pala, E., Henderson, E.R., Calabrò, T., Angelini, A., Abati, C.N., Trovarelli, G., Ruggieri, P., Survival of current production tumor endoprostheses: Complications, functional results, and comparative statistical analysis. *J. Surg. Oncol.*, 108, 6, 403–8, Nov. 2013.
5. Schubert, C., Van Langeveld, M.C., Donoso, L.A., Innovations in 3D printing: A 3D overview from optics to organs. *Br. J. Ophthalmol.*, 98, 2, 159–61, Feb. 1, 2014.
6. Klein, G.T., Lu, Y., Wang, M.Y., 3D printing and neurosurgery–ready for prime time? *World Neurosurg.*, 80, 3-4, 233–5, Jul. 16, 2013.
7. Banks, J., Adding value in additive manufacturing: Researchers in the United Kingdom and Europe look to 3D printing for customization. *IEEE Pulse*, 4, 6, 22–6, Nov. 6, 2013.
8. Mertz, L., Dream it, design it, print it in 3-D: What can 3-D printing do for you? *IEEE Pulse*, 4, 6, 15–21, 2013.
9. Ursan, I.D., Chiu, L., Pierce, A., Three-dimensional drug printing: A structured review. *J. Am. Pharm. Assoc.*, 53, 2, 136–44, Mar. 1, 2013.
10. Gross, B.C., Erkal, J.L., Lockwood, S.Y., Chen, C., Spence, D.M., Evaluation of 3D printing and its potential impact on biotechnology and the chemical sciences. *Anal. Chem.*, 86, 3240–3253, 2014.
11. Bartlett, S., Printing organs on demand. *Lancet Respir. Med.*, 1, 9, 684, Nov. 1, 2013.
12. Desarda, R.V., The Third Dimension: 3D Printing in Medical Science. *Int. J. Comput. Biol. Bioinf.*, 6, 1, 12–5, Sep. 18, 2020.
13. Lipson, H. and Kurman, M., *Fabricated: The New World of 3D Printing*, John Wiley & Sons, New Jersey, U.S.A., Jan. 22, 2013.
14. Cui, X., Boland, T., DD'Lima, D., Lotz, M.K., Thermal inkjet printing in tissue engineering and regenerative medicine. *Recent Pat. Drug Deliv. Formul.*, 6, 2, 149–55, Aug. 1, 2012.
15. Hoy, M.B., 3D printing: Making things at the library. *Med. Ref. Serv. Q.*, 32, 1, 93–9, Jan. 1, 2013.
16. Coakley, M. and Hurt, D.E., 3D printing in the laboratory: Maximize time and funds with customized and open-source labware. *SLAS Technol.*, 21, 4, 489–95, Aug. 1, 2016.
17. Ozbolat, I.T. and Yu, Y., Bioprinting toward organ fabrication: Challenges and future trends. *IEEE Trans. Biomed. Eng.*, 60, 3, 691–9, Jan. 30, 2013.
18. Bertassoni, L.E., Cecconi, M., Manoharan, V., Nikkhah, M., Hjortnaes, J., Cristino, A.L., Barabaschi, G., Demarchi, D., Dokmeci, M.R., Yang, Y., Khademhosseini, A., Hydrogel bioprintedmicrochannel networks for vascularization of tissue engineering constructs. *Lab. Chip*, 14, 13, 2202–11, 2014.
19. Yaldo, A., Seal, B.S., Lage, M.J., The cost of absenteeism and short-term disability associated with colorectal cancer. *J. Occup. Environ. Med.*, 56, 8, 848–51, Aug. 1, 2014.

20. Khaled, S.A., Burley, J.C., Alexander, M.R., Roberts, C.J., Desktop 3D printing of controlled release pharmaceutical bilayer tablets. *Int. J. Pharm.*, 461, 1-2, 105–11, Jan. 30, 2014.
21. Sparrow, N., FDA tackles opportunities, challenges of 3D-printed medical devices. *Plastics today: Med.*, 2014. https://www.plasticstoday.com/fda-tackles-opportunities-challenges-3d-printed-medical-devices (accessed on February 2023).
22. Rezwan, K., Chen, Q.Z., Blaker, J.J., Boccaccini, A.R., Biodegradable and bioactive porous polymer/inorganic composite scaffolds for bone tissue engineering. *Biomaterials*, 27, 18, 3413–31, Jun. 1, 2006.
23. Godbey, W.T. and Atala, A., In vitro systems for tissue engineering. *Ann. N. Y. Acad. Sci.*, 961, 1, 10–26, Jun. 2002.
24. Rhee, S., Puetzer, J.L., Mason, B.N., Reinhart-King, C.A., Bonassar, L.J., 3D bioprinting of spatially heterogeneous collagen constructs for cartilage tissue engineering. *ACS Biomater. Sci. Eng.*, 2, 10, 1800–5, Oct. 10, 2016.
25. Laronda, M.M., Rutz, A.L., Xiao, S., Whelan, K.A., Duncan, F.E., Roth, E.W., Woodruff, T.K., Shah, R.N., A bioprosthetic ovary created using 3D printed microporous scaffolds restores ovarian function in sterilized mice. *Nat. Commun.*, 8, 1, 15261, May 16, 2017.
26. Markstedt, K., Mantas, A., Tournier, I., Martínez Ávila, H., Hagg, D., Gatenholm, P., 3D bioprinting human chondrocytes with nanocellulose–alginate bioink for cartilage tissue engineering applications. *Biomacromolecules*, 16, 5, 1489–96, May 11, 2015.
27. Nguyen, D., Hägg, D.A., Forsman, A., Ekholm, J., Nimkingratana, P., Brantsing, C., Kalogeropoulos, T., Zaunz, S., Concaro, S., Brittberg, M., Lindahl, A., Cartilage tissue engineering by the 3D bioprinting of iPS cells in a nanocellulose/alginate bioink. *Sci. Rep.*, 7, 1, 1–10, Apr. 6, 2017.
28. Tan, Z., Parisi, C., Di Silvio, L., Dini, D., Forte, A.E., Cryogenic 3D printing of super soft hydrogels. *Sci. Rep.*, 7, 1, 16293, Nov. 24, 2017.
29. Lee, J.S., Hong, J.M., Jung, J.W., Shim, J.H., Oh, J.H., Cho, D.W., 3D printing of composite tissue with complex shape applied to ear regeneration. *Biofabrication*, 6, 2, 024103, Jan. 24, 2014.
30. Phillippi, J.A., Miller, E., Weiss, L., Huard, J., Waggoner, A., Campbell, P., Microenvironments engineered by inkjet bioprinting spatially direct adult stem cells toward muscle-and bone-like subpopulations. *Stem Cells*, 26, 1, 127–34, Jan. 2008.
31. Duan, B., Hockaday, L.A., Kang, K.H., Butcher, J.T., 3D bioprinting of heterogeneous aortic valve conduits with alginate/gelatin hydrogels. *J. Biomed. Mater. Res. A*, 101, 5, 1255–64, May 2013.
32. Fedorovich, N.E., Alblas, J., de Wijn, J.R., Hennink, W.E., Verbout, A.J., Dhert, W.J., Hydrogels as extracellular matrices for skeletal tissue engineering: State-of-the-art and novel application in organ printing. *Tissue Eng.*, 13, 8, 1905–25, Aug. 1, 2007.

33. Hsieh, F.Y., Lin, H.H., Hsu, S.H., 3D bioprinting of neural stem cell-laden thermoresponsive biodegradable polyurethane hydrogel and potential in central nervous system repair. *Biomaterials*, 71, 48–57, Dec. 1, 2015.
34. Suntornnond, R., An, J., Chua, C.K., Roles of support materials in 3D bio-printing-present and future. *Int. J. Bioprint.*, 3, 1, 83–86, 2017.
35. Ntintakis, I., Stavroulakis, G.E., Plakia, N., Topology optimization by the use of 3D printing technology in the product design process. *HighTech Innov. J.*, 1, 4, 161–71, Dec. 1, 2020.
36. Kim, S., Shin, Y., Park, J., Lee, S.W., An, K., Exploring the potential of 3D printing technology in landscape design process. *Land*, 10, 3, 259, Mar. 4, 2021.
37. Berman, B., 3-D printing: The new industrial revolution. *Bus. Horiz.*, 55, 2, 155–62, Mar. 1, 2012.
38. Tawk, C. and Alici, G., Finite element modeling in the design process of 3D printed pneumatic soft actuators and sensors. *Robotics*, 9, 3, 52, Jul. 7, 2020.
39. Renson, L., Poilvache, P., Van den Wyngaert, H., Improved alignment and operating room efficiency with patient-specific instrumentation for TKA. *Knee*, 21, 6, 1216–20, Dec. 1, 2014.
40. Gregg, A., Perfect knee implants, courtesy of a 3D printer. *Washington Post*, 2015. http://www.washingtonpost.com/business/capitalbusiness/surgeons-turn-to-printed-implants/2014/12/23/0d5c353e-8486-11e4-9534-f79a23c40e6c_story. html (accessed on February 2023).
41. Demange, M.K., Von Keudell, A., Probst, C., Yoshioka, H., Gomoll, A.H., Patient-specific implants for lateral unicompartmental knee arthroplasty. *Int. Orthop.*, 39, 1519–26, Aug. 2015.
42. Stuyts, B., Peersman, G., Thienpont, E., Van den Eeden, E., Van der Bracht, H., Custom-made lateral femoral hemiarthroplasty for traumatic bone loss: A case report. *Knee*, 22, 5, 435–9, Oct. 1, 2015.
43. Lin, C.Y., Wirtz, T., LaMarca, F., Hollister, S.J., Structural and mechanical evaluations of a topology optimized titanium interbody fusion cage fabricated by selective laser melting process. *J. Biomed. Mater. Res. A*, 83, 2, 272–79, 2007.
44. de Beer, N. and van der Merwe, A., Patient-specific intervertebral disc implants using rapid manufacturing technology. *Rapid Prototyp. J.*, 19, 2, 126–39, Mar. 1, 2013.
45. Yan, Q., Dong, H., Su, J., Han, J., Song, B., Wei, Q., Shi, Y., A review of 3D printing technology for medical applications. *Engineering*, 4, 5, 729–42, Oct. 1, 2018.
46. Ventola, C.L., Medical applications for 3D printing: Current and projected uses. *PT*, 39, 10, 704, Oct. 2014.
47. Nadagouda, M.N., Rastogi, V., Ginn, M., A review on 3D printing techniques for medical applications. *Curr. Opin. Chem. Eng.*, 28, 152–7, Jun. 1, 2020.
48. Yan, Q., Dong, H., Su, J., Han, J., Song, B., Wei, Q., Shi, Y. A review of 3D printing technology for medical applications, *Engineering*, 4, 5, 729–42, 2018.
49. Schubert, C., Van Langeveld, M.C., Donoso, L.A., Innovations in 3D printing: A 3D overview from optics to organs. *Br. J. Ophthalmol.*, 98, 2, 159–61, Feb. 1, 2014.

6

Advanced Drug Delivery Systems with 3D Printing

Abstract

Using computer-aided design (CAD) and a variety of processes and materials, 3D printing (3DP) allows for the creation of novel geometries with promising potential in fields like pharmaceutical drug delivery treatment. With the Food and Drug Administration's (FDA) blessing (2015), printed medicine presents a once-in-a-generation chance to advance the pharmaceutical business through the discovery of novel substances and technology. The benefits, restrictions, problems, and prospects of 3DP of pharmaceutical-grade formulations and polymers used in drug delivery systems are discussed in this chapter.

Keywords: 3D printing, drug delivery systems, vat photopolymerization, stereolithography, DLP-printed drug delivery devices

6.1 Introduction

New drug delivery systems are urgently needing attention to improve therapeutic effects despite the rapid progress in a wide variety of APIs, particularly for big macromolecules (such as peptides and proteins) with limited bioavailability and hydrophobic medicinal substances with a restricted therapeutic window. Conventional drug delivery systems used a "one size fits all" approach, making them unable to account for variations in pharmacokinetic features across patients [1, 2]. In addition, underdose or overdose, two common problems with conventional medication delivery methods [3], can lead to undesirable side effects. Patient compliance may suffer in the case of geriatric and pediatric therapy when using conventional drug delivery systems because of inaccuracies in the dosing schedule caused by individual variances in the patients being treated [4, 5]. Concerns about the safety of implanted medication delivery devices include the possibility of adverse events such as foreign body responses [6]. The amount and kind of medicine (liquid vs. powder) present in the medical device are also crucial design

Rishabha Malviya and Rishav Sharma. 3D Printing in Healthcare: Novel Applications, (101–120)

factors. A drug's efficacy *in vivo* can be affected by how it is formulated [7]. Traditional drug delivery devices are limited in terms of both their size and the maximum dose that can be contained within them, both of which affect the devices' long-term viability and effectiveness. As a result, throughout the years, there has been a growing need for standardized systems of metered medication administration all across the world. The potential of additive manufacturing (AM) to tackle problems with conventional drug delivery technologies has made it the most attractive solution in the pharmaceutical sector for customizable treatment. The term "3D printing" refers to the technique of creating three-dimensional things from computer-aided design (CAD) models by layering components in successive layers on a created platform [8]. The initial applications of 3D printing, which developed from stereolithography in the late 1980s [9], were in industrial prototyping and process improvement. With the emergence of AM methods, 3D printing has been the focus of investigation in many different academic disciplines, such as bioengineering and pharmaceuticals [10–13]. Spritam, the first medication manufactured using 3D printing technology, was authorized by the Food and Drug Administration (FDA) in 2015 [14]. Research proved the viability of employing the technique to produce customized, complicated dose forms. Additionally, 3D printing technology is a preferable replacement for conventional fabrication methods since it facilitates the efficient and cost-effective realization of complex and adaptable structures. In addition, the AM-manufactured polypills comprise diverse drug and excipient compositions and display distinct drug release kinetics, initiating a revolution in the pharmaceutical sector [15–18]. As an added benefit, 3D-printed drug delivery devices allow for the gradual and precise release of various chemical components with specialized therapeutic effects. Even with all the progress that has been made, most 3D-printing methods still only produce structures using a single material through a standalone AM process. Emerging AM techniques, which include multi-material printing and 4D printing, have been motivated by the introduction of printable materials with unique physicochemical, mechanical, and biological characteristics. With multi-material printing, designers may print functional pieces from a wide range of materials all at once, opening up new possibilities for intricate and subtle 3D models [19]. In contrast, the AM method used in 4D printing is combined with stimuli-responsive materials to create 3D objects whose shapes may be altered in a predetermined manner in response to an applied stimulus [20]. Because of these characteristics, smart implants may be developed with tunable shapes to improve tissue adhesion [21]. The development of 3D-printed medication delivery systems is aided in special ways by these two types of AM processes. 3D printing has improved the design and production of drug delivery medical devices, which has paved the way for individualized treatment. Acne treatment patches containing salicylic acid have been 3D printed after being scanned in 3D [22]. These customized medication delivery patches, which might dramatically increase patient compliance compared to standard drug-loaded patches, permitted customization to the nasal architecture of individual patients. Moreover, each patch's medication dosage might be modified to account for variations in the patient's illness condition, reducing the likelihood of unwanted consequences caused by under- or overdosing. High biocompatibility, biosafety, and minimal cytotoxicity are important considerations for 3D printing in biomedical applications. Hydrogel is an excellent substance for use as biological 3D-printing ink because of its biocompatibility. Hydrogels that meet the criteria for biosafety, low toxicity, and sustained or triggered local drug release make promising drug delivery carriers. When combined with 3D printing technology, it can help bring about the tailoring of individual pharmaceuticals. Hydrogels can be employed for cell encapsulation to realize cell delivery while preserving exceptional cell viability because of their hydrophilicity and high expansion rate. Researchers have recently been able to heal tissue and alter the local microenvironment by delivering stem cells or immune cells using 3D-printed hydrogels. The recent developments and uses of 3D-printed hydrogels in the area of medication and cell administration are mostly discussed here (Figure 6.1).

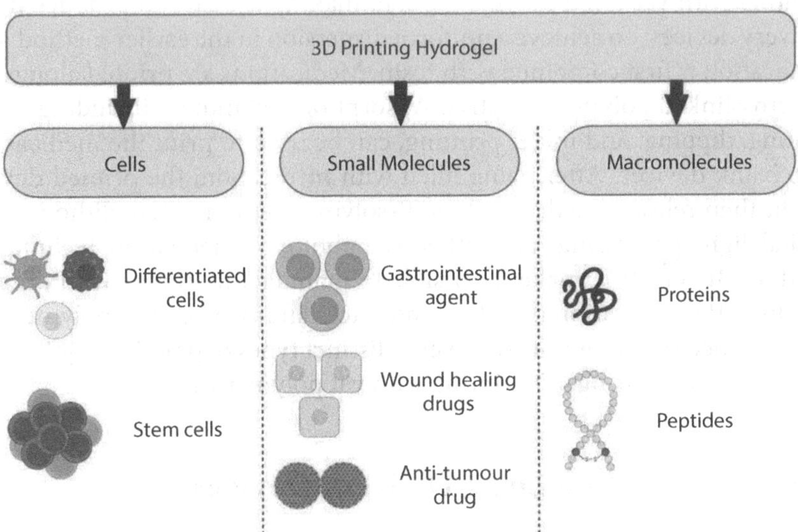

Figure 6.1 A 3D-printing system for hydrogel-based topical drug delivery. Administration of small molecules, macromolecules, and cells may all be printed in a polymeric hydrogel using 3D printing.

6.2 Modern 3D-Printing Technologies

6.2.1 Vat Photopolymerization-Based 3D Printing

To make three-dimensional solid things, high-energy light of a certain wavelength is shone over a vat of liquid photopolymer, a method known as vat photopolymerization-based 3D printing. The generation of reactive species under light irradiation is what drives the polymer chain development, and photoinitiators are utilized for its purpose. Several different types of photopolymers have been created and put to use in many different kinds of research. Photocurable compounds from methacrylate or acrylic ester monomers [23] are commonly employed in biomedical research. Thus, there has been a lot of work put into discovering and creating new photopolymers for usage in medical settings. There has been a surge in interest in studying shape-memory photopolymers recently. 3D structures that alter in response to water may be made by mixing hydrophobic materials like poly(ethylene glycol) diacrylate (PEGDA) with hydrophilic ones like poly(propylene glycol) methacrylate (PPGDA) [24]. Commercial applications for 3D printing using photopolymerization might arise in areas such as biomaterials, tissue engineering, and multifunction medication drug delivery system. Medications can be preloaded into a printed blank device or directly entrapped entering the polymeric network while printing with vat photopolymerization, making it easier to produce drug delivery devices. To achieve a uniform dispersion in the earlier method, the medication is first combined with resin. Medications are printed alongside the crosslinked polymeric matrix. Adsorption techniques, including spray coating, dipping, and inkjet printing, can be used to print the medication into blank devices. After being filled with medication, the printed device might then release the drug into a dissolving medium. Stereolithography, digital light processing, and other vat photopolymerization techniques used for 3D printing make it possible to manufacture things with unique features. The generation of optical interfaces and two-photon polymerization [25] occurs continuously. Several distinct types of practical equipment have been made using 3D printing with vat polymerization.

6.3 SLA-Printed Drug Delivery Devices

Popular stereolithography 3D printing was invented and registered by Chuck Hull in 1986. This method utilizes photopolymerization and can achieve a resolution as low as 10 mm [26]. To create 3D objects, SLA printers use UV laser beams controlled by computers to initiate the polymerization of photocurable resin at specific locations; the resulting solid layers are then piled one on top of the other. Post-curing is the process of washing and curing a structure that was printed using SLA to remove any residual resin and improve its mechanical characteristics [27]. Stereolithography is a common additive manufacturing technique used to make medical devices that distribute drugs (SLA). SLA printing has displayed a lot of promise in the development of personalized microneedles with improved medication delivery efficiency; therefore, many people are turning to it to get around the problems with traditional transdermal microneedles. Problems with bluntness, erratic medication delivery, and poor skin penetration are all examples. Using SLA printing, Uddin *et al.* [28] manufactured a microneedle array in the form of a cross.

6.4 DLP-Printed Drug Delivery Devices

Light-activated polymerization is used to selectively cure liquid photopolymers in the DLP printing system as well. DLP printing involves repeatedly dipping a construction platform into a resin bath to polymerize successive layers of resin, as seen in [29]. The printability and functionality of several additive compositions and printing parameters were analyzed and compared. PEGDA concentration, plasticizer addition, exposure time, and layer height were found to affect printability and mechanical strength. The optimum resin composition for exterior constructions was found to be 100% PEGDA, with the best layer thickness being 0.02 mm. For interior constructions, a 0.05-mm layer thickness was found to be ideal, with 25% PEGDA concentration and 0.25 mg/mL tartrazine addition yielding the best resin composition. The ideal sample had the highest levels of mechanical characteristics, the most favorable drug release profile, and the highest drug loading efficiency. These results show that DLP printing holds great promise as a tool for creating custom drug delivery implants and other forms of individualized healthcare [30].

6.5 CLIP-Printed Drug Delivery Devices

The inconsistency in the molecular structure that results from printing a single layer of a 3D object using SLA or DLP means that these objects are likely to have worse mechanical qualities. Nevertheless, CLIP employs a continuous manufacturing method rather than layer-by-layer manufacturing to create 3D objects with more consistent architecture and predictable mechanical properties. Joseph DeSimone *et al.* developed CLIP in 2014, and Carbon 3D has now brought it to market [31]. Using an oxygen-permeable window, the CLIP technology produces a dead zone [32] at the interface between the liquid resin and the printed pieces. The dead zone eliminates the need to recoat the resin between layers in DLP printing and inhibits interface photopolymerization, allowing the resin to flow freely under the surface of the window [33]. The protein cargo was deposited solely on the skin at the sites where the microneedles had been implanted to a specially developed coating mask. Examples of model proteins include ovalbumin, BSA, and lysozyme. It was found that coated microneedles could rapidly eject model proteins in an aqueous solution and on pig skin. Immunotherapies might gain significantly from the microneedle patch's ability to deliver several proteins for use in the co-delivery of multiple antigens and/or adjuvants. The capacity to keep proteins stable during microneedle coating was further demonstrated by the fact that lysozyme activity was maintained throughout the coating process. In addition, the protein-coated microneedle demonstrated sustained release kinetics for 72 h in an *in-vivo* protein delivery study. The study backed up the claim that CLIP can be used to make high-tech transdermal medication delivery systems on demand.

6.6 TPP-Printed Drug Delivery Devices

An initial step in TPP microfabrication comprises irradiating a little amount of photosensitive resin with a near-infrared femtosecond laser beam. Micro/nano 3D structures with custom morphologies can be made via a non-linear optical technique in which photosensitive polymers absorb multiple photons concurrently. The spatial resolution of TPP is determined by a number of factors, among which the most significant are the laser power density, the exposure time, and the effectiveness of the photoinitiator [34]. TPP microfabrication's [34] ability to construct micro/nano-scale structures with high accuracy and precision makes it a potent technique for use in drug delivery applications. Poly-lactide (PLA)-based photocurable polymers, which are used to create medication-encapsulated particles, have also been shown to be amenable to TPP. Insulin-loaded particles were manufactured by Shavkuta *et al.* utilizing methacrylate-functionalized PLA, thermoplastic polypropylene (TPP), and a micro-molding process [35]. The combination of micromolding and thermoplastic polymerization (TPP) creates a highly adaptable system for making drug carriers of arbitrary size and shape with controlled chemical release. Microneedles were made in a straightforward and reproducible fashion by Cordeiro *et al.* [36], who used TPP 3D printing to create microneedle array templates of varied patterns. The drug release kinetics of the printed drug delivery device was adjustable by changing the printing conditions, and it showed desirable cytocompatibility with several cell lines. This chapter added to the existing body of evidence on TPP's utility in the development of sophisticated, modulatable drug delivery systems.

6.7 FDM for Advanced Drug Delivery Applications

Drug-eluting medical devices may be made in several different ways due to FDM 3D-printing technology. These include implants used to replace organs or tissues, devices used to intervene after surgery, and devices used to provide drugs locally.

6.8 Local Drug Delivery Devices

Currently, most treatment platforms employ a non-targeted oral route of administration, although the route is plagued by problems such as increased gastrointestinal (GI) adverse effects and substantial first-pass metabolism [37, 38]. Although there are alternatives to conventional drug administration, most of the related platforms do not provide precise therapeutic delivery [39]. Current research is focusing on 3D-printed local drug delivery devices, which show potential for a more accurate drug delivery system [40] because they could release a therapeutically active chemical in the local vicinity of the implant. An increase in pharmacological efficacy is often observed when drugs are administered locally or at the location of interest [41]. The local distribution of antibiotics to regions affected by osteomyelitis, for example [42], has been proposed as a potentially more effective alternative to the more conventional method of administering antibiotics systemically. Scaffolds based on polycaprolactone (PCL) that release the antibiotic rifampicin were successfully FDM 3D-printed, as shown by Lee *et al.* [43].

6.8.1 Implanted Medical Medication Delivery Systems (Long-Term Organ and Drug-Eluting Devices)

However, difficulties can arise when patients do not take their medication as prescribed or when there are changes in plasma levels as a result of daily dosing [44]. Long-term implanted drug delivery methods that distribute the medication gradually and have their pharmacological effects elsewhere may relieve these difficulties [45, 46]. Probuphine, a subcutaneous implant containing buprenorphine used to treat opioid addiction, is one such medical product [47]. Although buprenorphine is administered subcutaneously, it predominantly affects the m receptors in the brain. Hormone replacement therapy for menopause, hypogonadism, and birth control generally involve daily dosing with progesterone, a naturally occurring steroid hormone that can be administered orally or intravenously [48]. First-pass metabolism reduces the oral bioavailability of progesterone to less than 10%, while injectable progesterone sometimes produces exaggerated adverse effects such as severe local pains and bruises. Vaginal rings containing polyethylene glycol (PEG), polylactic acid (PLA), and polycaprolactone (PCL) were 3D-printed for sustained vaginal progesterone administration by Fu *et al.* (1.75 mm in diameter). Making vaginal rings to order also allows for greater flexibility in catering to women's varying preferences, lifestyles, and anatomical characteristics. Diffusion-controlled release behavior [48] was seen for progesterone released from vaginal rings over more than 7 days. The vaginal rings' ability to deliver a steady stream of progesterone makes them an intriguing potential treatment option for gynecological issues. Implants used in patients who have had organ or tissue removal are at risk for bacterial infections that can cause the creation of biofilms and, in turn, serious consequences [49, 50]. There is great promise for the use of implanted devices that release drugs to promote healing and prevent infection. Non-union fractures, also known as fractures that do not heal completely, are common in patients who have undergone bone resection or who have suffered severe injuries [51].

6.9 Surgical Intervention and Postoperative Implants

Some study results have shown that postoperative infections caused by bacteria like *Staphylococcus aureus* [52] can worsen anywhere from 8% to 11% of cranial procedures, 1.1% to 1.5% of spinal procedures, and 5.7% of mandible fracture repairs in children with acquired or congenital cardiac disease [53, 54]. Catheter-associated urinary tract infections are another example of the half-a-million healthcare-associated infections generated annually by indwelling medical devices [55, 56]. Infections encountered before, during, or after surgery, especially those spread by artificial organs or other prosthetics, are rising to prominence as a primary source of morbidity and mortality in the medical industry. In recent years, there has been a proliferation of research investigating the viability of 3D printing anti-microbial drug-eluting stents, catheters, surgical screws, pins, bone plates, and vaginal implants [57–59, 60–62]. Weisman *et al.* established a bioabsorbable catheter that can be produced using fused deposition modeling to administer the medicines gentamicin sulfate and methotrexate. The catheter is made from PLA, a thermoplastic polymeric carrier (FDM). These devices effectively inhibited *Escherichia coli* growth in liquid nutritive broth and on agar plates for up to 5 days [60], demonstrating a continuous release of the anti-microbial agent.

6.10 Challenges and Future Perspectives

Various drug-loaded medical devices may be manufactured via FDM printing; however, the method has several drawbacks, including poor resolution, absence of appropriate materials/polymers, and lengthy processing periods. The lack of features required for acceptable quality structures [63] is the primary technical hurdle to the expansion of FDM printing in the pharmaceutical business. Long exposure to the high temperatures required for the extrusion of filaments and the creation of 3D-printed things can also drastically damage drugs. Moreover, the process is made more difficult since a special technology is needed to produce filaments appropriate for use in the FDM printing of medical equipment [64]. Although the HME and FDM printing processes are currently separated, integrating them more smoothly will increase productivity and make the process continuous. Researchers and medical professionals should take advantage of 3D printing to treat ailments with personalized therapies, as opposed to traditional "one size fits all" approaches, as it permits the development of devices that are tailored to the requirements and prognosis of the person by simple manipulation of the formulation composition or the structure of the devices.

6.11 The Multi-Material Additive Manufacturing Technique

Multi-material AM is a state-of-the-art production process built on AM. MMAM is at the forefront of the utilization of several materials in the manufacturing of an item in a single process, resulting in products with more complicated geometries and additional functionality [65]. AM's have many advantages such as reduce production time, more design and material flexibility and less waste throughout during production process. Initially, a 3D component is developed in CAD software for MMAM. The MMAM 3D model differs from the first stage in that it focuses less on the overall structure and more on the design of the joints between several materials. Subsequently, the MMAM machine reads the 3D model's sliced format to generate the parts. The MMAM machine uses a layer-by-layer approach to manufacture the 3D components on flat substrates.

6.11.1 Microneedles

Over the past two decades, the multi-microneedle array machining (MMAM) technology has become the standard for making microneedles. As MMAM enables the design of microneedles with complex topologies and multifunctional performance, it stands above other microscale production processes. In a similar vein, microneedles are utilized in MMAM after being coated in new biomaterials and functional polymers with distinct physical, chemical, biological, and mechanical properties. Microneedles can be further categorized into FDM-printed microneedles, SLA-printed microneedles, DLP-printed microneedles, bio-printed microneedles, and hybrid-printed microneedles, depending on the 3D printing technique used for manufacturing devices. However, because of its analgesic effectiveness, cheap cost, relative safety, and minimal risk of adverse effects [66–68], transdermal drug delivery (TDD) commonly utilize microneedles, which are flexible medical devices.

6.11.2 Soft Robots

The medical and pharmaceutical fields can now benefit from the wider availability of soft robots credited to MMAM's ability to simplify their construction while simultaneously increasing their load capacity, functionality, and energy efficiency. The soft robot is technically a 4D-printed device due to its use of a shape memory polymer that permits structural changes over time.

6.11.3 Implants

Compared to traditional 3D-printed implants, those made with MMAM provide several benefits, including the ability to load them with a wide variety of drugs and other useful substances, superior mechanical properties, and intricate designs. MMAM, as previously indicated, not only permits a variety of valuable products but also integrates prefabricated components onto implants in a single step [19, 69]. To perform its functional functions, tissue engineering often requires a micro/nanostructure that is not present in biological tissue. Traditional 3D printing methods with a single material make it challenging to create an implant that looks and functions like natural tissue. Therefore, MMAM offers a strategy for continuously fabricating an artificial tissue implant with a predetermined internal design. The use of 3D-printed bone implants, for example, has been shown to stimulate bone repair in an equine injury model.

6.12 Regulatory Issues of Drug Delivery Medical Device

Aside from the difficulty in obtaining regulatory approval, the unique capabilities of 3D printing to create complex and multifunctional structures may limit their use in biomedicine. Before being introduced to the commercial market, drug delivery devices produced using AM techniques must meet the regulatory requirements of the FDA, yet there are significant issues that must be addressed, including the device's biocompatibility and biodegradability, drug degradation, and hazardous responses. Spritam, the first 3D-printed medication to receive FDA approval, marked a major advance for the emerging field [14]. In addition, the ZipDose technology is used, which allows for high-dose medication and helps patients with swallowing difficulties. The basic idea is that when 3D-printed tablets come into contact with fluids, the bindings between the individual layers are quickly broken, allowing the tablet to dissolve into its constituent parts very quickly [70]. Instruments, implants, and prosthetics are the three main types of 3D-printed medical devices now in the market. Several copies of a typical item can be manufactured from a single CAD file, but patient-specific medical devices can be tailored to each individual's unique anatomy using 3D printing. Medical devices made with AM are subject to the same FDA regulations as traditional medical devices. Devices designed for individual patients can be 3D-printed with a continuous size range defining minimum and maximum dimensions [71]. The Food and Drug Administration assigns different risk levels to different types of medical devices. Medical devices are divided into three classes, known as I, II, and III, depending on the degree to which they constitute a risk to patients and how closely they are monitored by authorities. There is a lack of agreement on how to categorize additively manufactured medical devices; nevertheless, the FDA is now examining applications for innovative 3D-printed

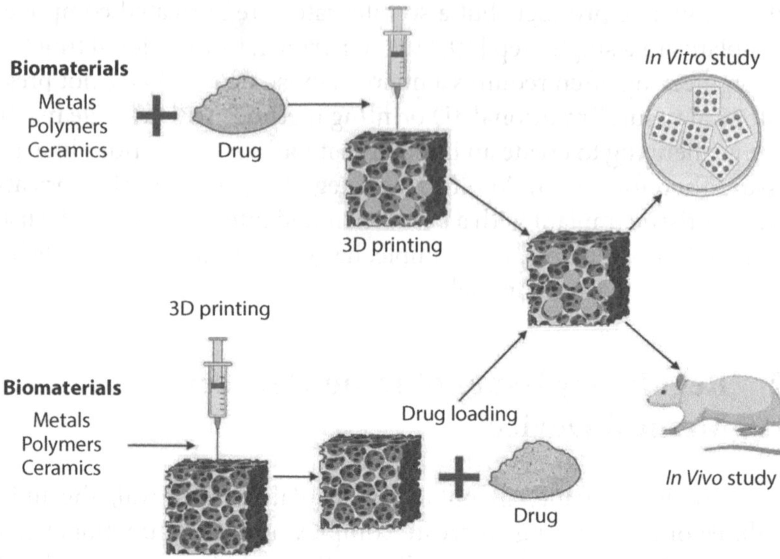

Figure 6.2 Three-dimensionally printed mesoporous scaffolds for drug delivery.

medical equipment to evaluate their safety and efficacy. The FDA released guidelines on the technical concerns for 3D-printed devices [72] in 2016. These recommendations included topics such as device design, materials management, manufacturing process, and testing challenges. There is an opportunity for public feedback on the proposed regulation, but it is not yet final. Until rules may be firmly established, several questions must be resolved: (1) Should they apply to the materials used, the printer itself, the production procedure, the finished goods, and any post-printing care, such as cleaning and sterilization? (2) Does a new regulatory road need to be taken if 3D-printed medical devices are used in conjunction with biological, cellular, or tissue-based products? (3) Should they be limited to use within the USA or not? Certainly, 3D-printed medical devices provide special difficulties in conforming to regulatory criteria related to manufacturing quality assurance due to their customizability and distinctive production procedures. As shown in Figure 6.2, 3DP mesoporous scaffolds can be printed in three dimensions and used for drug delivery.

6.13 Scalability and Cost Factors

For 3D printing to become widely used, AM processes must be upgraded to an industrial scale. The reliability of 3D-printed objects, including buildings and multipurpose tools like polypills, has improved significantly, but 3D printers still have a long way to go before they can compete with the scalability of traditional manufacturing methods [73, 74]. Powder compression, a standard method in tablet production, allows for fast turnaround times. Compared to existing 3D printers, the production efficiency of conventionally made tablets could reach up to 1.6 million per hour [75]. Here, numerous 3D printers must be used in tandem to meet the massive demand. Nevertheless, running a large number of 3D printers all at once requires a lot of power and results in a lot of carbon emissions, which is neither cheap nor good for the environment [76]. The vast amount of ink required for industrial production also makes it impractical to have on hand. Hence, significant energy consumption, chemical emission difficulties, and ink supply must be addressed if modern production is to compete with the high productivity of traditional manufacturing. The following are some potential answers: (1) tailoring large-scale 3D printers suitable for mass production and (2) reducing chemical emissions by printing more practical and eco-friendly materials. Furthermore, while the filaments travel through the heated printhead, some volatile organic compounds or particles may be emitted, which may be dangerous to the user's health [77], despite these attempts to expand the scalability of 3D printing. Additive manufacturing's primary value lies not in replacing or rendering obsolete conventional manufacturing methods but, rather, in the fabrication of individualized medicine with novel functionality. The use of AM in healthcare has been on the rise rapidly in recent years, yet 3D-printed goods are typically more expensive than their conventionally made counterparts. The majority of an AM project's budget will go into the machinery, tools, and supplies necessary to complete the job [78]. It was reported by Thomas and Gilbert that the price of AM gear fell by 51% between 2001 and 2010. Rapid technological advancements in 3D-printing systems are predicted to continue reducing the price of the necessary hardware. As hardware costs go down, more and more high-quality industrial AM systems that seamlessly combine hardware and software will become available. On the other hand, the material costs associated with the AM process might differ substantially depending on the printing method used. FDM filaments are less expensive than SLA resin and SLS powder [79, 80]. A kilogram of thermoplastic filaments is easier to create than 1 kg of UV-curable resin. The raw material cost has decreased because of technological advancements, but the expense of developing new, flexible materials for 4D printing and multi-material printing still accounts for a significant amount of the finished product's price tag. More research is required to develop more cost-effective strategies for generating multifunctional, 3D-printed medication delivery devices with cutting-edge designs. While deciding whether or not to upscale AM technology for industrial applications, it is important to weigh the high cost of the process against its scalability.

6.14 Conclusion

The rapid development of 3D printing technology and the abundance of printable materials have given rise to the exciting prospect of 3D-printed drug delivery systems with promising applications in pharmaceutical sciences and biomedicine. The advantages of multi-material printing and 3D printing over 3D-printed drug delivery devices, such as superior design and novel functionality, bode well for their usage in satisfying the growing need for personalized medicine. The limitations of AM-made medical devices are substantially alleviated, and their usefulness is broadened by their connectivity to other types of wearable technology, such as sensors. Despite significant progress, regulatory hurdles have limited the use of 3D-printed medication delivery devices in clinical settings. There is also a great deal of work that needs to be done to perfect the processes of mass production, quality assurance, and sterilization of 3D-printed medical equipment. Rapid advancements in printing technology and refined medical device legislation are necessary for 3D printing to be widely adopted in the drug delivery sector.

References

1. Elkomy, M.H., Changing the drug delivery system: Does it add to non-compliance ramifications control? A simulation study on the pharmacokinetics and pharmacodynamics of an atypical antipsychotic drug. *Pharmaceutics*, 12, 4, 297, Mar. 25, 2020.
2. Reddy, R.D. and Sharma, V., Additive manufacturing in drug delivery applications: A review. *Int. J. Pharm.*, 589, 119820, Nov. 15, 2020.
3. Shi, K., Aviles-Espinosa, R., Rendon-Morales, E., Woodbine, L., Maniruzzaman, M., Nokhodchi, A., Novel 3D printed device with integrated macroscale magnetic field triggerable anti-cancer drug delivery system. *Colloids Surf. B Biointerfaces*, 192, 111068, Aug. 1, 2020.
4. Menditto, E., Orlando, V., De Rosa, G., Minghetti, P., Musazzi, U.M., Cahir, C., Kurczewska-Michalak, M., Kardas, P., Costa, E., Sousa Lobo, J.M., Almeida, I.F., Patient centric pharmaceutical drug product design—The impact on medication adherence. *Pharmaceutics*, 12, 1, 44, 2020.

5. Stewart, S.A., Domínguez-Robles, J., McIlorum, V.J., Mancuso, E., Lamprou, D.A., Donnelly, R.F., Larrañeta, E., Development of a biodegradable subcutaneous implant for prolonged drug delivery using 3D printing. *Pharmaceutics*, 12, 2, 105, Jan. 28, 2020.
6. Lee, D., Park, K., Seo, J., Recent advances in anti-inflammatory strategies for implantable biosensors and medical implants. *BioChip J.*, 14, 48–62, Mar. 2020.
7. Lee, H.J., Choi, N., Yoon, E.S., Cho, I.J., MEMS devices for drug delivery. *Adv. Drug Deliv. Rev.*, 128, 132–47, Mar. 15, 2018.
8. Jacob, S., Nair, A.B., Shah, J., Emerging role of nanosuspensions in drug delivery systems. *Biomater. Res.*, 24, 1–6, Dec. 2020.
9. Singh, R., Gehlot, A., Akram, S.V., Gupta, L.R., Jena, M.K., Prakash, C., Singh, S., Kumar, R., Cloud manufacturing, internet of things-assisted manufacturing and 3D printing technology: Reliable tools for sustainable construction. *Sustainability*, 13, 13, 7327, Jun. 30, 2021.
10. Maniruzzaman, M., Pharmaceutical applications of hot-melt extrusion: Continuous manufacturing, twin-screw granulations, and 3D printing. *Pharmaceutics*, 11, 5, 218, May 7, 2019.
11. Maniruzzaman, M. (Ed.), *3D And 4D Printing In Biomedical Applications: Process Engineering And Additive Manufacturing*, John Wiley & Sons, Germany, ISBN: ISBN: 978-3-527-34443-7, Mar. 18, 2019.
12. Al-Dulimi, Z., Wallis, M., Tan, D.K., Maniruzzaman, M., Nokhodchi, A., 3D printing technology as innovative solutions for biomedical applications. *Drug Discovery Today*, 26, 2, 360–83, Nov. 16, 2020.
13. Vaut, L., Juszczyk, J.J., Kamguyan, K., Jensen, K.E., Tosello, G., Boisen, A., 3D printing of reservoir devices for oral drug delivery: From concept to functionality through design improvement for enhanced mucoadhesion. *ACS Biomater. Sci. Eng.*, 6, 4, 2478–86, Feb. 21, 2020.
14. Katstra, W.E., Palazzolo, R.D., Rowe, C.W., Giritlioglu, B., Teung, P., Cima, M.J., Oral dosage forms fabricated by Three Dimensional Printing™. *J. Control. Release*, 66, 1, 1–9, May 3, 2000.
15. Robles-Martinez, P., Xu, X., Trenfield, S.J., Awad, A., Goyanes, A., Telford, R., Basit, A.W., Gaisford, S., 3D printing of a multi-layered polypill containing six drugs using a novel stereolithographic method. *Pharmaceutics*, 11, 6, 274, Jun. 11, 2019.
16. Keikhosravi, N., Mirdamadian, S.Z., Varshosaz, J., Taheri, A., Preparation and characterization of polypills containing aspirin and simvastatin using 3D printing technology for the prevention of cardiovascular diseases. *Drug Dev. Ind. Pharm.*, 46, 10, 1665–75, Oct. 2, 2020.
17. Pereira, B.C., Isreb, A., Forbes, R.T., Dores, F., Habashy, R., Petit, J.B., Alhnan, M.A., Oga, E.F., 'Temporary Plasticiser': A novel solution to fabricate 3D printed patient-centred cardiovascular 'Polypill'architectures. *Eur. J. Pharm. Biopharm.*, 135, 94–103, Feb. 1, 2019.

18. Qi, S., Nasereddin, J., Alqahtani, F., Personalized polypills produced by fused deposition modeling 3d printing, in: *3D and 4D Printing in Biomedical Applications: Process Engineering and Additive Manufacturing*, pp. 273–95, Feb. 19, 2019.
19. Han, D. and Lee, H., Recent advances in multi-material additive manufacturing: methods and applications. *Curr. Opin. Chem. Eng.*, 28, 158–66, Jun. 1, 2020.
20. Joshi, S., Rawat, K., Karunakaran, C., Rajamohan, V., Mathew, A.T., Koziol, K., Thakur, V.K., Balan, A.S., 4D printing of materials for the future: Opportunities and challenges. *Appl. Mater. Today*, 18, 100490, Mar. 1, 2020.
21. Han, D., Morde, R.S., Mariani, S., La Mattina, A.A., Vignali, E., Yang, C., Barillaro, G., Lee, H., 4D printing of a bioinspired microneedle array with backward-facing barbs for enhanced tissue adhesion. *Adv. Funct. Mater.*, 30, 11, 1909197, Mar. 2020.
22. Goyanes, A., Det-Amornrat, U., Wang, J., Basit, A.W., Gaisford, S., 3D scanning and 3D printing as innovative technologies for fabricating personalized topical drug delivery systems. *J. Control. Release*, 234, 41–8, Jul. 28, 2016.
23. Xu, X., Awad, A., Robles-Martinez, P., Gaisford, S., Goyanes, A., Basit, A.W., Vat photopolymerization 3D printing for advanced drug delivery and medical device applications. *J. Control. Release*, 329, 743–57, Jan. 10, 2021.
24. Zhao, Z., Kuang, X., Yuan, C., Qi, H.J., Fang, D., Hydrophilic/hydrophobic composite shape-shifting structures. *ACS Appl. Mater. Interfaces*, 10, 23, 19932–9, May 8, 2018.
25. Bagheri, A. and Jin, J., Photopolymerization in 3D printing. *ACS Appl. Polym. Mater.*, 1, 4, 593–611, Feb. 20, 2019.
26. C.W. Hull, Apparatus for production of three-dimensional objects by stereolithography. United States Patent, Appl., No. 638905, Filed. 1984.
27. Davim, J.P. (Ed.), *Additive And Subtractive Manufacturing: Emergent Technologies*, Walter de Gruyter GmbH & Co KG, Berlin, Germany, ISBN: ISBN. 9783110548334, Jan. 20, 2020.
28. Uddin, M.J., Scoutaris, N., Economidou, S.N., Giraud, C., Chowdhry, B.Z., Donnelly, R.F., Douroumis, D., 3D printed microneedles for anticancer therapy of skin tumours. *Mater. Sci. Eng. C.*, 107, 110248, Feb. 1, 2020.
29. Yang, Y., Zhou, Y., Lin, X., Yang, Q., Yang, G., Printability of external and internal structures based on digital light processing 3D printing technique. *Pharmaceutics*, 12, 3, 207, Feb. 28, 2020.
30. Kadry, H., Wadnap, S., Xu, C., Ahsan, F., Digital light processing (DLP) 3D-printing technology and photoreactive polymers in fabrication of modified-release tablets. *Eur. J. Pharm. Sci.*, 135, 60–7, Jul. 1, 2019.
31. J.M. DeSimone, E.T. Samulski, J.P. Rolland, Inventors; Carbon Inc, assignee, Methods and apparatus for continuous liquid interface production with rotation. United States patent US 10,589,512, Mar. 17, 2020.

32. Taki, K., A simplified 2D numerical simulation of photopolymerization kinetics and oxygen diffusion–reaction for the continuous liquid interface production (CLIP) system. *Polymers*, 12, 4, 875, Apr. 10, 2020.
33. Janusziewicz, R., Tumbleston, J.R., Quintanilla, A.L., Mecham, S.J., DeSimone, J.M., Layerless fabrication with continuous liquid interface production. *Proc. Natl. Acad. Sci.*, 113, 42, 11703–8, Oct. 18, 2016.
34. Xing, J.F., Zheng, M.L., Duan, X.M., Two-photon polymerization microfabrication of hydrogels: an advanced 3D printing technology for tissue engineering and drug delivery. *Chem. Soc Rev.*, 44, 15, 5031–9, 2015.
35. Shavkuta, B., Bardakova, K., Khristidis, Y., Minaev, N.V., Frolova, A., Kotova, S., Aksenova, N., Heydari, Z., Semenova, E., Khlebnikova, T., Golubeva, E.N., Approach to tune drug release in particles fabricated from methacrylate functionalized polylactides. *Mol. Syst. Des. Eng.*, 6, 3, 202–13, 2021.
36. Cordeiro, A.S., Tekko, I.A., Jomaa, M.H., Vora, L., McAlister, E., Volpe-Zanutto, F., Nethery, M., Baine, P.T., Mitchell, N., McNeill, D.W., Donnelly, R.F., Two-photon polymerisation 3D printing of microneedle array templates with versatile designs: Application in the development of polymeric drug delivery systems. *Pharm. Res.*, 37, 1–5, Sep. 2020.
37. Homayun, B., Lin, X., Choi, H.J., Challenges and recent progress in oral drug delivery systems for biopharmaceuticals. *Pharmaceutics*, 11, 3, 129, Mar. 19, 2019.
38. Ensign, L.M., Cone, R., Hanes, J., Oral drug delivery with polymeric nanoparticles: the gastrointestinal mucus barriers. *Advanced Drug delivery Rev.*, 64, 6, 557–70, 2012.
39. Zunhammer, M., Ploner, M., Engelbrecht, C., Bock, J., Kessner, S.S., Bingel, U., The effects of treatment failure generalize across different routes of drug administration. *Sci. Transl. Med.*, 9, 393, eaal2999, Jun. 7, 2017.
40. Mondal, S. and Pal, U., 3D hydroxyapatite scaffold for bone regeneration and local drug delivery applications. *J. Drug Deliv. Sci. Technol.*, 53, 101131, Oct. 1, 2019.
41. Zhou, Y., Chen, X., Cao, J., Gao, H., Overcoming the biological barriers in the tumor microenvironment for improving drug delivery and efficacy. *J. Mater. Chem. B*, 8, 31, 6765–81, 2020.
42. Lee, J.H., Baik, J.M., Yu, Y.S., Kim, J.H., Ahn, C.B., Son, K.H., Kim, J.H., Choi, E.S., Lee, J.W., Development of a heat labile antibiotic eluting 3D printed scaffold for the treatment of osteomyelitis. *Sci. Rep.*, 10, 1, 7554, May 5, 2020.
43. Lee, J.W., Kang, K.S., Lee, S.H., Kim, J.Y., Lee, B.K., Cho, D.W., Bone regeneration using a microstereolithography-produced customized poly (propylene fumarate)/diethyl fumarate photopolymer 3D scaffold incorporating BMP-2 loaded PLGA microspheres. *Biomaterials*, 32, 3, 744–52, Jan. 1, 2011.
44. Timmer, C.J. and Mulders, T.M., Pharmacokinetics of etonogestrel and ethinylestradiol released from a combined contraceptive vaginal ring. *Clin. Pharmacokinetics*, 39, 233–42, Sep. 2000.

45. Wang, J., Zhang, Y., Aghda, N.H., Pillai, A.R., Thakkar, R., Nokhodchi, A., Maniruzzaman, M., Emerging 3D printing technologies for drug delivery devices: Current status and future perspective. *Adv. Drug Deliv. Rev.*, 174, 294–316, Jul. 1, 2021.
46. R.A. Patel, L.R. Bucalo, Inventors, Titan Pharmaceuticals Inc, assignee, Implantable polymeric device for sustained release of buprenorphine. United States patent US 7,736,665, Jun. 15, 2010.
47. Kleppner, S.R., Patel, R., Costantini, L.C., McDonough, J., In-vitro and in-vivo characterization of a buprenorphine delivery system. *J. Pharm. Pharmacol.*, 58, 3, 295–302, Mar, 2006.
48. Fu, J., Yu, X., Jin, Y., 3D printing of vaginal rings with personalized shapes for controlled release of progesterone. *Int. J. Pharm.*, 539, 1-2, 75–82, Mar. 25, 2018.
49. Pavithra, D. and Doble, M., Biofilm formation, bacterial adhesion and host response on polymeric implants—issues and prevention. *Biomed. Mater.*, 3, 3, 034003, Aug. 8, 2008.
50. Vivero-Lopez, M., Xu, X., Muras, A., Otero, A., Concheiro, A., Gaisford, S., Basit, A.W., Alvarez-Lorenzo, C., Goyanes, A., Anti-biofilm multi drug-loaded 3D printed hearing aids. *Mater. Sci. Eng. C.*, 119, 111606, Feb. 1, 2021.
51. Wu, Y., Woodbine, L., Carr, A.M., Pillai, A.R., Nokhodchi, A., Maniruzzaman, M., 3D printed calcium phosphate cement (CPC) scaffolds for anti-cancer drug delivery. *Pharmaceutics*, 12, 11, 1077, Nov. 11, 2020.
52. Deny, A., Loiez, C., Deken, V., Putman, S., Duhamel, A., Girard, J., Pasquier, G., Chantelot, C., Senneville, E., Migaud, H., Epidemiology of patients with MSSA versus MRSA infections of orthopedic implants: Retrospective study of 115 patients. *Orthop. Traumatol. Surg. Res.*, 102, 7, 919–23, Nov. 1, 2016.
53. Wang, J., Zhang, Y., Aghda, N.H., Pillai, A.R., Thakkar, R., Nokhodchi, A., Maniruzzaman, M., Emerging 3D printing technologies for drug delivery devices: Current status and future perspective. *Adv. Drug Deliv. Rev.*, 174, 294–316, Jul. 1, 2021.
54. Wang, J., Zhang, Y., Aghda, N.H., Pillai, A.R., Thakkar, R., Nokhodchi, A., Maniruzzaman, M., Emerging 3D printing technologies for drug delivery devices: Current status and future perspective. *Adv. Drug Deliv. Rev.*, 174, 294–316, Jul. 1, 2021.
55. Nanda, A. and Patra, D.P., Surgical complications in neurosurgery, in: *Complications in Neurosurgery*, pp. 17–22, Elsevier, Amsterdam, Netherlands, Jan. 1, 2018.
56. VanEpps, J.S. and Younger, J.G., Implantable device related infection. *Shock (Augusta, Ga.)*, 46, 6, 597, Dec. 2016.
57. Fouladian, P., Kohlhagen, J., Arafat, M., Afinjuomo, F., Workman, N., Abuhelwa, A.Y., Song, Y., Garg, S., Blencowe, A., Three-dimensional printed 5-fluorouracil eluting polyurethane stents for the treatment of oesophageal cancers. *Biomater. Sci.*, 8, 23, 6625–36, 2020.
58. Guerra, A.J., Cano, P., Rabionet, M., Puig, T., Ciurana, J., 3D-printed PCL/PLA composite stents: Towards a new solution to cardiovascular problems. *Materials*, 11, 9, 1679, Sep. 11, 2018.

59. Van Lith, R., Baker, E., Ware, H., Yang, J., Farsheed, A.C., Sun, C., Ameer, G., 3D-printing strong high-resolution antioxidant bioresorbable vascular stents. *Adv. Mater. Technol.*, 1, 9, 1600138, Dec. 2016.
60. Weisman, J.A., Ballard, D.H., Jammalamadaka, U., Tappa, K., Sumerel, J., D'Agostino, H.B., Mills, D.K., Woodard, P.K., 3D printed antibiotic and chemotherapeutic eluting catheters for potential use in interventional radiology: In vitro proof of concept study. *Acad. Radiol.*, 26, 2, 270–4, Feb. 1, 2019.
61. Tappa, K., Jammalamadaka, U., Weisman, J.A., Ballard, D.H., Wolford, D.D., Pascual-Garrido, C., Wolford, L.M., Woodard, P.K., Mills, D.K., 3D printing custom bioactive and absorbable surgical screws, pins, and bone plates for localized drug delivery. *J. Funct. Biomater.*, 10, 2, 17, Apr. 1, 2019.
62. Domínguez-Robles, J., Mancinelli, C., Mancuso, E., García-Romero, I., Gilmore, B.F., Casettari, L., Larrañeta, E., Lamprou, D.A., 3D printing of drug-loaded thermoplastic polyurethane meshes: A potential material for soft tissue reinforcement in vaginal surgery. *Pharmaceutics*, 12, 1, 63, Jan. 13, 2020.
63. Aduba Jr., D.C., Margaretta, E.D., Marnot, A.E., Heifferon, K.V., Surbey, W.R., Chartrain, N.A., Whittington, A.R., Long, T.E., Williams, C.B., Vat photopolymerization 3D printing of acid-cleavable PEG-methacrylate networks for biomaterial applications. *Mater. Today Commun.*, 19, 204–11, Jun. 1, 2019.
64. Ranganathan, S.I., Kohama, C., Mercurio, T., Salvatore, A., Benmassaoud, M.M., Kim, T.W., Effect of temperature and ultraviolet light on the bacterial kill effectiveness of antibiotic-infused 3D printed implants. *Biomed. Microdevices*, 22, 1–4, Sep. 2020.
65. Bandyopadhyay, A. and Heer, B., Additive manufacturing of multi-material structures. *Mater. Sci. Eng. R Rep.*, 129, 1–6, Jul. 1, 2018.
66. Chen, G., Xu, Y., Kwok, P.C., Kang, L., Pharmaceutical applications of 3D printing. *Addit. Manuf.*, 34, 101209, Aug. 1, 2020.
67. Yang, J., Liu, X., Fu, Y., Song, Y., Recent advances of microneedles for biomedical applications: drug delivery and beyond. *Acta Pharm. Sin. B*, 9, 3, 469–83, May 1, 2019.
68. Ma, G. and Wu, C., Microneedle, bio-microneedle and bio-inspired microneedle: A review. *J. Control. Release*, 251, 11–23, Apr. 10, 2017.
69. Joyee, E.B. and Pan, Y., Additive manufacturing of multi-material soft robot for on-demand drug delivery applications. *J. Manuf. Process.*, 56, 1178–84, Aug. 1, 2020.
70. West, T.G. and Bradbury, T.J., 3D printing: A case of zipdose® technology–world›s first 3d printing platform to obtain fda approval for a pharmaceutical product, in: *3D and 4D Printing in Biomedical Applications: Process Engineering and Additive Manufacturing*, pp. 53–79, Feb. 19, 2019.
71. Abdollahi, S., Boktor, J., Hibino, N., Bioprinting of freestanding vascular grafts and the regulatory considerations for additively manufactured vascular prostheses. *Transl. Res.*, 211, 123–38, Sep. 1, 2019.
72. Wang, J., Zhang, Y., Aghda, N.H., Pillai, A.R., Thakkar, R., Nokhodchi, A., Maniruzzaman, M., Emerging 3D printing technologies for drug delivery

devices: Current status and future perspective. *Adv. Drug Deliv. Rev.*, 174, 294–316, Jul. 1, 2021.

73. Shah, J., Snider, B., Clarke, T., Kozutsky, S., Lacki, M., Hosseini, A., Large-scale 3D printers for additive manufacturing: Design considerations and challenges. *Int. J. Adv. Manuf. Technol.*, 104, 9-12, 3679–93, Oct. 2019.
74. Shim, J.S., Kim, J.E., Jeong, S.H., Choi, Y.J., Ryu, J.J., Printing accuracy, mechanical properties, surface characteristics, and microbial adhesion of 3D-printed resins with various printing orientations. *J. Prosthet. Dent.*, 124, 4, 468–75, Oct. 1, 2020.
75. Kalyan, B.G.P. and Kumar, L., 3D printing: Applications in tissue engineering, medical devices, and drug delivery. *AAPS PharmSciTech*, 23, 4, 92, Mar. 17, 2022.
76. Zhu, J., Zhang, Q., Yang, T., Liu, Y., Liu, R., 3D printing of multi-scalable structures via high penetration near-infrared photopolymerization. *Nat. Commun.*, 11, 1, 3462, Jul. 10, 2020.
77. Gu, J., Wensing, M., Uhde, E., Salthammer, T., Characterization of particulate and gaseous pollutants emitted during operation of a desktop 3D printer. *Environ. Int.*, 123, 476–85, Feb. 1, 2019.
78. Lim, S.H., Kathuria, H., Tan, J.J., Kang, L., 3D printed drug delivery and testing systems—a passing fad or the future? *Adv. Drug Deliv. Rev.*, 132, 139–68, Jul. 1, 2018.
79. Thomas, D.S. and Gilbert, S.W., *Costs And Cost Effectiveness Of Additive Manufacturing*, vol. NIST Special Publication, National Institute of Standards and Technology, USA, 1176, p. 12, Dec. 4, 2014.
80. Danayat, S.S., *Investigating 3-D Printed Polymer Heat Exchanger*, Doctoral Dissertation, Arizona State University, 2019.

7

Exploring the Fabrication of 3D-Printed Scaffolds for Tissue Engineering

Abstract

The topic of tissue engineering is increasingly employing 3D-printing methods. The situation of 3D printing, as it pertains to tissue engineering, has been thoroughly examined in this study. Tissue engineering's end objective is functional tissue that can be used for things like drug testing and regenerative medicine. Recent studies into tissue formation have highlighted the potential of 3D printing's layer-by-layer method, which facilitates direction over structural components on scales ranging from the microscopic to the cosmic. 3D-printed scaffolds for tissue engineering provide a biomimetic structural environment that facilitates extracellular matrix incorporation and tissue synthesis, even when a scaffold is also used (e.g., cellular infiltration, vascularization, and active remodeling). The unique fabrication methods of tissue engineering structures are discussed, along with their impact on the development of 3D printing. It will also cover how 3D printing is being used to fabricate tissues from both synthetic and natural sources.

Keywords: 3D-printed, tissue engineering, scaffold library, scaffold architecture design, vascularization, three-dimensional scaffolds, selective laser sintering

7.1 Introduction

The term "tissue engineering" was formally established in a 1993 *Science* article by Langer and Vacanti, who described the properties and uses of biodegradable 3D scaffolds. Highly porous, linked pore networks and consistently sized pores are necessary for cell migration and infiltration into 3D scaffolds [1, 2]. Simple fabrication procedures, such as fiber binding, emulsification, solvent casting, particle leaching, membranes lamination, molding, and foaming, have additionally been utilized for creating porous 3D scaffolds since the research was first published a decade ago [3, 4]. The potential for 3D printing to offer a quick and robust method of assembling functional tissue *in vitro* is extremely exciting for the field of tissue

Rishabha Malviya and Rishav Sharma. 3D Printing in Healthcare: Novel Applications, (121–142)

engineering [4–8]. To function well as a macro-tissue, an implanted structure must first have the appropriate micro-architecture in place to supply it with the structural and mechanical support, nutrients, and cell types it needs [9–13]. The use of biomaterials, printing methods, and cell transport technologies is advocated by the field of 3D printing as an effective means of bringing these elements together. Scaffold-based designs or scaffold-less designs strive to eliminate stages and supply structure and cells concurrently as opposed to earlier efforts that involved printing complicated scaffolds followed by a cell seeding process [14–17]. The ideal 3D-printed construct for tissue engineering would be a structure that guides cell growth, allowing cells to migrate and multiply to build functional tissue. Even though genetics can regulate cell destiny, studying the phenomenon has been time-consuming and difficult [18, 19]. 3D printing's layer-by-layer technique has recently shown promising potential in tissue development since it provides structural control from micro- to macro-scale. 3D-printed structures for tissue engineering, whether they contain a scaffold or not, aim to do the same way: generate a biomimetic structural setting that promotes host tissue integration and tissue creation (e.g., cellular infiltration, vascularization, and active remodeling). It is clear from developmental biology that the microenvironment of a cell, without delving into the domain of genetics and epigenetics, is the natural ground for determining cell fate [20–22]. The cellular microenvironment's extracellular matrix (ECM) constitutes the substrate for mechanical and chemical stimulation generated *in vitro* through 3D printing [23, 24]. The engineered ecosystem is built from the bottom up, and the choice of materials (such as synthetic ECM) is vital to its success, but it is also a contested topic. In anticipation of their possible use in soft tissue engineering, a wide variety of chemically synthesized biodegradable materials [25, 26], natural polymers [27–32], and combinations thereof [33–35] have already been studied for their ability to be printable using layer-by-layer fused filament fabrication (SFF) techniques, such as 3D blotting. Powder-based 3D printing and other SFF technologies are extensively utilized to create ceramic materials like hydroxyapatite, which are regarded to be beneficial for bone ingrowth [35–38]. The possibility of utilizing these substances in hard tissue engineering has been investigated [39]. However, the biophysics of cellular self-assembly has led to the speculation that high cell concentration and cell spheroids (i.e., cellular aggregates) might serve as effective delivery vehicles for bio-ink, which might be employed in dispensing-based printers [16, 39]. In 1993, Langer and Vacanti established the foundation for the field of tissue engineering by publishing a seminal article in *Science* explaining the properties and uses of biodegradable 3D scaffolds. Three-dimensional scaffolds with large, consistently sized pores that facilitate cell migration and infiltration are recommended. Fiber bonding, solvent evaporation, solvent casting, particle leaching, membrane lamination, molding, and foaming are only some of the conventional manufacturing processes that have been employed to create porous 3D scaffolds in the decade after the announcement (1993–2002). Consistently inadequate 3D scaffolds are produced because of a lack of fine-grained control over the scaffold design, pore network, and pore size. Investigators have proposed the use of 3D-printing techniques (also known as rapid prototyping, solid free-form fabrication, or additive manufacturing) to create individualized scaffolds with tunable pore size and pore shape. Fused deposition modeling (FDM), stereolithography (SL), inkjet printing, selective laser sintering (SLS), and color jet printing represent a few of the more prominent polymer-processing 3D-printing methods [7, 8]. As a result, there was a huge uptick in the number of studies conducted on 3D printing as a tool for tissue engineering in the second decade of the discipline (2003–2012). These studies looked into a wide variety of topics, including novel scaffold materials for 3D printing, novel 3D-printing methods for scaffold fabrication, *in vitro* and *in vivo* applications of 3D-printed scaffolds as well as the emergence of an entirely new field, 3D bioprinting or organ printing. Although 3D-printed tissue engineering frameworks have been constructed based on the significant qualities of biodegradability, biocompatibility, and rapid prototyping [40, 41], further research is needed on tissue integration. The scaffold's biocompatibility and polymer–cell adhesion have indeed been adjusted to synchronize with biological maturation to ease remodeling and incorporation into the host tissue. [26, 37]. Figure 7.1 shows the production process for a 3D-printed scaffold: (a) CAD models of the scaffold, (b) processing of the precursors, and (c) 3D printing of the scaffold using an extrusion-based method. Investigators have begun printing networks of channels, which are subsequently implanted or printed with vascular cell types to address the vascularization difficulty. In this chapter, the authors explore the many 3D printing strategies, both scaffold-based and scaffold-free, which have been developed to tackle these major challenges to tissue engineering.

7.2 Scaffold Architecture Design

7.2.1 Scaffold Library

Scaffolds' mechanical characteristics and cell behaviors are very sensitive to scaffold architecture design [40, 41]. The bottom-up approach begins with

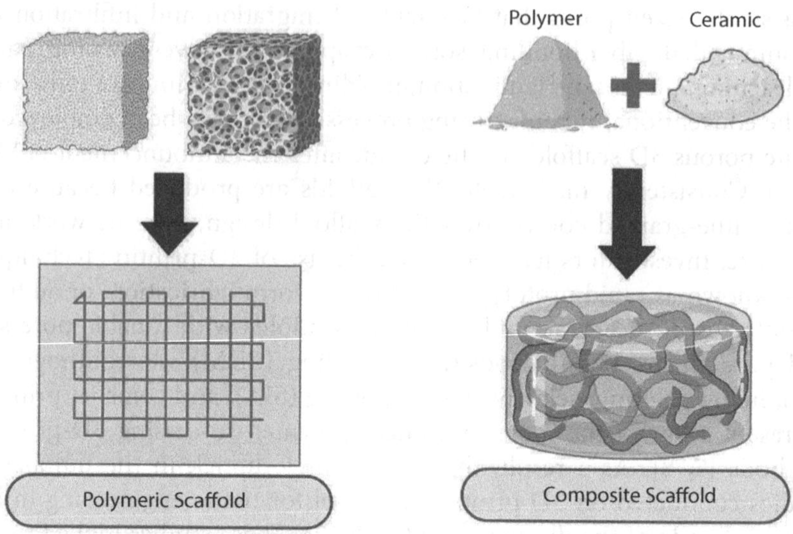

Figure 7.1 The process of making a 3D-printed scaffold. (a) Computer-aided design models of scaffolds, (b) processing of precursors, and (c) 3D printing of scaffolds using extrusion.

the fabrication of individual cells and continues with the assembly of the resulting 3D scaffold. By tailoring the mechanical property in this way, the designer can control the porous structure's overall design. The innovative computer-aided technique for tissue scaffolds (CASTS) allows us to design extremely porous 3D scaffold models with a controlled architecture and a surface profile that precisely matches a natural anatomic structure, such as bone [42, 43]. The unit cell's fundamental geometry is derived from a collection of around 20 polyhedral forms in the system. It is possible to consistently replicate each polyhedral unit in a given spatial configuration, scale it to form a block, and then modify the scaffold library and the properties from each unit cell, also including pore size and strut size, to suit the requirements of the intended scaffold application. It is possible to create a porous scaffold with the correct anatomical shape by performing a Boolean operation on the scaffold block and the actual surface model of the damaged tissue. An extensive set of mathematical formulas underpins the CASTS system [44] for designing and constructing tissue engineering scaffolds.

7.2.2 Functionally Graded Scaffold

The mechanical strength and stiffness of the porous scaffold design must be matched to the structure of the target tissue, which, in the case of bone and other natural tissues, generally has a porous structure with a gradient [45]. Stiffness rises radially in long bones but linearly in short, irregular bones. By stacking the cylinder unit cells in a concentric pattern, a radial gradient design is created, with porosity decreasing linearly from the core to the surface. By shifting the struts' diameter in the direction of the gradient, a linear gradient is produced. By manipulating the porosity–stiffness connection, the investigator can control the stiffness variation of CASTS scaffolds. Researchers successfully constructed a functional gradient bone scaffold for the human mandibular cancellous bone and a bone segment for the femur after adapting and upgrading the CASTS technology [46, 47]. The accuracy and reproducibility of the method are excellent. Gradient structures can also be designed using form functions and refined using an all-hexahedral mesh [48]. By using the technique, irregular hexahedral elements are used to represent a truncated bone, and these elements are further transformed into irregular pore elements using a shape function. The bone scaffold could be generated by first calculating the disparity of the contour model and the pore model and then adopting the union of the irregular pores to get the full pore model. The procedure allows the development of gradient bone scaffolds with a tunable pore size distribution. For 3D printing, these functionally graded structures can be created as STL files with the help of a new approach [49] that combines the sigmoid function and the Gaussian radial foundation function.

7.2.3 Design for Vascularization

Tissue engineers face challenges beyond just mechanical performance when trying to create thick or bulk tissues because of the difficulty of vascularizing them. Researchers have proposed several techniques to improve or speed up vascularization, many of which include modifications to the scaffold's architecture [50]. Pore sizes of 250 micrometer or more were found to promote blood vessel formation more than smaller pore sizes [51]. In addition, there is no guarantee that a higher porosity would result in more vascularization, as cell migration and vascularization may be stifled by a lack of interconnectivity between pores [52]. Some time ago, scientists created a set of tools for assessing 3D porous scaffolds [53]. The set of tools is predicated on a modular scaffold architecture that permits precise control over the scaffold's pore size and porosity to conduct a vascularization analysis [54]. The novel method comprises alternating layers of thin porous membranes and filament meshes to create a 3D scaffold.

7.3 Scaffold-Based Technique

7.3.1 Polymeric Scaffolds

Tissue-engineered scaffolds require a microenvironment that mimics the ECM's mechanical stability, but it is biodegradable to permit normal cellular ECM synthesis. Synthetic polymer scaffolds may be customized to print both soft and hard tissues, and their characteristics can be accurately tuned [55, 56]. They are also biodegradable and have well-defined nanoscale structures. Printing patterns were based on Griffith *et al.* [43] ceramic models, which used chloroform to combine a biodegradable polymer powder made of 25% poly-L-lactide (PLLA) and 75% polylactide-coglycolide (PLGA). The designers accounted for host implantation by making the intake and outflow resemble arteries and veins. Eventually, the "mini-liver" model's metabolism was enhanced [57, 58] immediately after the continual seeding of hepatocytes and some other types of liver cells *in vitro* underflow. Synthetic polymers, with their mechanical potential, have found uses in bone and cartilage tissue engineering. The characteristics of the final structure can be fine-tuned by adjusting the concentrations of polymers as well as other design variables in SFF (such as the concentration of pyrogens, the drying duration, and even the drying procedure). Sherwood *et al.* [23] used an SFF method to construct an osteochondral composite scaffold with a D,L-PLGA/L-PLA cartilage region and an L-PLGA/TCP composite bone section, with a material and porosity gradient between the two. The cartilage component of the novel design attracted chondrocytes more strongly, and the device's orthopedic mechanical qualities were at par with those of a conventional prosthesis. Macro-scale and micro-scale control are provided, just like in the industrial 3D production of inorganic materials, utilizing design resolution and porosity control. In addition, starch-based polymers permit prolonged breakdown and, thus, greater porosity with escalating cellular integration, making them well-suited for bone tissue creation [59]. Using a multilayered electrospun nanofiber mesh of polycaprolactone, Martins *et al.* [60] proved capable of demonstrating more command over the hierarchical structure by merging 3D predicted scaffolds of starch-polycaprolactone (SPCL) microfibers (PCL). Bone tissue engineering uses a nanofibrous mesh due to its starch-based polymer and nanoscale component. For polymer scaffold fabrication, both direct as well as indirect forms of 3D printing are already being studied. Sachlos and colleagues demonstrated that collagen and certain other natural polymers can sometimes be poured into a 3D-printed, ethanol-dissolvable mold with a defined internal shape [61]. Critical point drying replaced ethanol with liquid CO_2 after the construct was frozen during collagen dispersion casting. Freezing enables frost crystals to act as interstitial spacers, which, in turn, causes collagen to create a fibrillar network that promotes cell adhesion. Indirect 3D printing has the potential to increase printing resolution because organic solvents are not needed as a binder for polymer scaffold building. Molds were filled with sucrose particles (i.e., porogen), and the biodegradable polymer PLGA was poured on top to form the scaffolds. To improve tissue growth, a fibronectin solution was incubated with the scaffold after mold and porogen were washed away in water [53].

7.3.2 Hydrogel System

In a perfect scenario, a 3D-printed item would faithfully capture the intricacy of ECM in the wild. Despite the present lack of direction that investigators have over polymeric design, water-based hydrogel technology gives such a matrix framework for 3D tissue proliferation with comparable diffusion capacities for feeding and waste exchange [62]. They show great promise as a potential structural support material for cells and a delivery agent for cells. Gelatin, the major component of hydrolyzed collagen, has gained a lot of attention due to its capacity to keep cells in a gel at a relatively low temperature and its ECM origins. Despite the enhanced hydrogel structure, cell viability can be negatively impacted by the glutaraldehyde-crosslinker that has been widely utilized [63–65]. Yan and coworkers printed a liver tissue construct by mixing hepatocytes with gelatin and chitosan and then fixing the mixture in glutaraldehyde [66]. While using single cells or spheroids as a scaffold, longer glutaraldehyde crosslinking increased the hydrogel's endurance, and it also increased cell mortality near the hydrogel's perimeter. Skardal and coworkers [67] used gelatin, polyethylene glycol tetracrylates, and thiolated hyaluronic acid to create a synthetic ECM with adjustable modules that can be printed in the shape of a vessel using a microfilament stacking process [68]. At 4 weeks, cell viability and structure were still present, but no additional information on the development of vascular tissue was acquired. Regulated gelation using alginate has been employed in several printing methods to sidestep the indirect negative effects of hydrogel crosslinkers. Cell-adhesive ligands (including RGD peptides) have the capability of influencing cell motility and differentiation [69, 70] according to their adaptable physical and chemical properties [71, 72]. Photocrosslinking ligands, however, offer a different approach to gelation [73]. Calcium chloride ($CaCl_2$) solutions are frequently employed for alginate gelation after printing; these solutions are chelating agents and have shown excellent biocompatibility and processing qualities as cell delivery agents [74]. Using a 3D plotting device and high-viscosity alginate, Fedorovich and colleagues demonstrated the simultaneous delivery of scaffold and cells in a $CaCl_2$-containing petri dish. Cells were incorporated into the hydrogel fibers, and the location of the printed construct can be kept steady during the printing process by printing alginate-containing cells into a $CaCl_2$ solution with additional viscosity enhancers such as polyvinyl alcohol or hyaluronan [56]. Printing alginate mixtures onto a gelatin substrate doped with $CaCl_2$ to facilitate the timely upward migration of calcium ions to chelate is a technique developed by Pataky and colleagues to advance alginate inkjet technology [75]. Combining alginate, a fast-gelling hydrogel, with slower-gelling hydrogels having better cell-directing qualities, such as collagen, improves the material's lack of physiologically active features and allows for a broader range of physical applications in 3D printing [75]. Although alginate's non-adhesive characteristics can be conducive to host tissue integration, cell motility can be chemically altered by adding an RGD peptide. The ability of human cardiomyocyte progenitor cells placed in an unaltered alginate matrix to migrate and fully colonize a neighboring matrigel layer [76] is a stunning demonstration of the phenomenon. The composition of several polymers has been investigated as an alternative to using a single polymer in hydrogels to use the benefits of each. Xu *et al.* [77] proposed using a 3D-printed gelatin/alginate/fibrinogen matrix that is then seeded with adipose-derived stromal cells to examine the pathogenic pathways of the metabolic syndrome. Their approach integrated ECM analogs like gelatin and alginate with endogenous scaffold protein (protein) fibrinogen. The addition of $CaCl_2$ caused the alginate to crosslink, and the addition of thrombin caused the fibrinogen to polymerize, leading to gelation. Tissue engineers have an exciting new tool in their toolbox for creating channel networks as a result of the ability of cells seeded externally to differentiate into endothelial cells when cultivated with vascular endothelial growth factor (VEGF) [77]. The hydrogel system generates an aqueous ECM-like matrix for use in soft tissue engineering as a growth medium for cells and a delivery mechanism for drugs.

7.3.3 Inorganic Scaffolds

Although 3D printing was initially used for fabrication, its early applications in 3D bioprinting were in areas like orthopedic design and hard tissue engineering. Researchers in the field of orthopedic implants have turned to 3D printing techniques like powder-based selective laser sintering [58] and laser-engineered net shaping (LENS) [78] because they provide access to metal implant production processes that have a direct impact on mechanical qualities. Hard tissue scaffold designs often use the powder-based SFF process to print ceramic, resorbable materials (e.g., hydroxyapatite) with variable degrees of porosity to encourage cell infiltration and proliferation, in contrast to soft tissue engineering's use of synthetic, non-resorbable materials. Pores weaken a structure mechanically but allow for cellular incorporation and vascularization. While a biomolecular strategy is usually employed in tandem with the method, careful 3D design of porosity in exchange for mechanical strength can aid in vascularization and cellular integration [79]. Scaffolds that are regular and geometrically arranged have been demonstrated to induce organized bone growth [60], which necessitates the use of 3D printing techniques. Ceramic scaffolds frequently incorporate the inorganic component of bone, hydroxyapatite (HA), or a related compound, tricalcium phosphate (TCP) [80], due to their widespread use in orthopedic applications. Spraying a layer of powder with a specific binder, as instructed by a 2D layer breakdown of a 3D computer-aided design (CAD) file, is 3D printing. Toward the end of the operation, the density of the construct is increased through high heating (the process of sintering), which also improves the build's mechanical qualities [79]. Under both static and dynamic perfusion scenarios, Leukers *et al.* [81] fabricated a porous 3D scaffold made of HA linked with a soluble polymer and a polymer-based binder, which improved cell adhesion and proliferation. As the polymer is pyrolyzed during sintering, a microporous surface that facilitates bone incorporation is produced [82]. CAD models can only influence macropore size, but micropore size can be adjusted by changing the powder composition (the ratio of fine to coarse powder) and the sintering temperature [83]. Teixeira and colleagues achieved their goal of improving osteogenic differentiation and cellular integration of human sclerotic stem cells in HA porous scaffolds by inserting collagen [84]. It is still difficult to achieve a high level of resolution and organization in micropores, and the sintering process eventually limits the degree of control that can be exerted. Microwave sintering has recently been employed by Tarafder and others to increase heat homogeneity and save processing time as opposed to the surface heating of traditional sintering, which creates heat fluxes that are material dependent. It allows for tighter regulation of grain development and pore size, as well as greater densification, which, in turn, yields better mechanical qualities. The sintering procedure prevents cells or biomolecules from being incorporated into scaffolds until after they have been printed. Gbureck *et al.* [85] established a low-temperature method for synthesizing brushite (i.e., hydrated calcium phosphate) and HA scaffolds, which increases cellular and vascular responsiveness.

Researchers have found a revolutionary way to administer tiny quantities of inorganic copper, either alone or in combination with VEGF, that have shown potential vascular induction capabilities, using a mechanism similar to that of supplying vascular signals from within the scaffold. By 3D printing a calcium phosphate scaffold with a Y-shaped pore, Barralet and coworkers were able to inject VEGF and/or copper sulfate into the edge of the macropore [86]. Copper sulfate was implanted into a mouse model and afterward explanted after the mouse was sacrificed, revealing capillary development in the wound tissue. 3D printing of inorganic scaffolds has come a long way, with promising *in vitro* studies and early orthotopic applications [87–89]. However, significant problems persist in areas such as design resolution and vascular induction [86]. Three-dimensional printing of scaffold-based frameworks may prove beneficial in resolving some of the most irreconcilable issues associated with tissue formation and integration, as suggested by developments in printing technologies for scaffold designs; breakthroughs in materials science and characterization offer important implications for synthetic and natural biomaterials as well.

7.4 Scaffold-Free Approach

The scaffold-free approach aims to gain insight from the natural self-assembly process typical of embryonic biology, despite the reality that there has been a major accomplishment in the disciplines of scaffold-based tissue engineering designs. Cellular self-assembly has been the subject of extensive study and has been implemented in non-3D printing techniques like L'Heureux's cell-sheet approach to vessel building [90–93]. Studying the self-assembly properties of 100% cellular bio-ink for use in vessel construction, the lab of Gabor Forgac has found promising results. Utilizing agarose rods as a mold template, a layer-by-layer extrusion 3D printer dispenses the bio-ink as spheroids or cylindrical cellular rods [93]. At 2 to 4 days after printing, the bio-ink fused. The agar rods were then removed by hand, and the resulting vascular structures were placed in a perfusion bioreactor. To prove the method's viability for 3D-printing applications, the first step in the investigation involved using a desktop stereolithography setup to 3D-print scaffolds of several geometries: small hexagonal (SH), large hexagonal (LH), small square (SS), and large square (LS) (Figure 7.2).

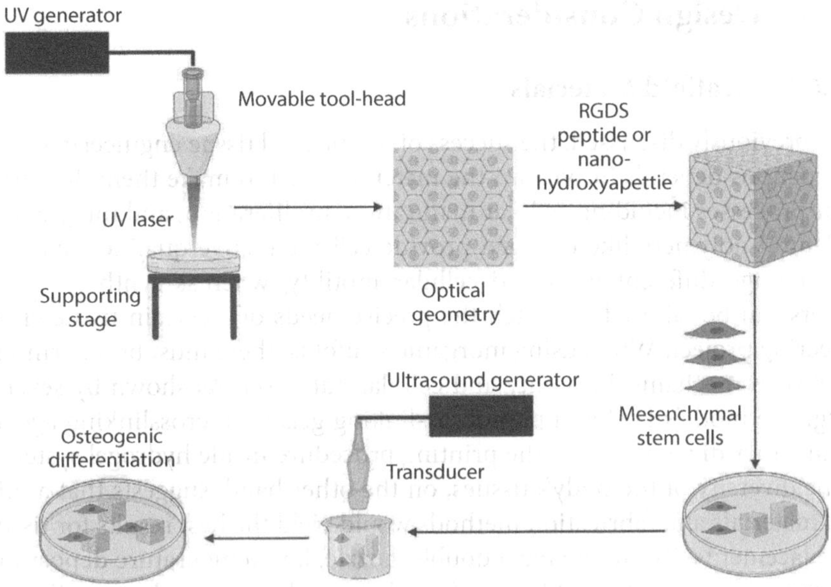

Figure 7.2 Schematic showing the construction of a 3D-printed scaffold and the excitation of MSCs using low-intensity pulsed ultrasound.

7.5 Bioreactor

Since the bioreactor offers a challenging environment for the cell-scaffold build, it serves a crucial role as a post-processing tool in tissue engineering, facilitating the maturation and complexation of the construct. Tissue engineering on a large scale yet requires the bioreactor as part of the automated line [94]. Further evidence to prove the use of a bioreactor comes from recent studies showing that the scaffold layout can influence cell differentiation in a bioreactor but not in static culture [95]. An intriguing new usage for a bioreactor is in the generation of induced pluripotent stem (iPS) cells for alveolar epithelium development [96]. It is accomplished by using the air–liquid contact typically present in a spinning bioreactor. Recent advances in bioreactor design [97] have seen the use of mechanical stimulation and a dual-flow arrangement. These cutting-edge bioreactors are perfect for generating gradients of nutrients and anabolic or catabolic chemicals, making them well-suited for use in the construction of interface tissues. Future bioreactors are expected to integrate several biological functions with credit to the use of various stimulation and non-invasive monitoring approaches.

7.6 Design Considerations

7.6.1 Scaffold Materials

As previously discussed, the success of 3D-printed tissue engineering constructions depends heavily on the materials used to make them. It is true for processes including cellular maturation, proliferation, and integration. Natural polymers like collagen provide cell-interactive qualities that can encourage differentiation and cellular motility, whereas synthetic polymers can be tailored to match the precise needs of a certain tissue engineering project. When using inorganic scaffolds, there must be a harmony between mechanical stability and cellular adhesion. As shown by several alginate models [11] and photocrosslinking gels [33], crosslinking agents can either dictate or limit the printing procedure inside hydrogel systems. The diversity of the body's tissues, on the other hand, suggests that a mix of materials and fabrication methods would yield the best results for tissue replacements. By employing a double-nozzle, low-temperature deposition technique [98] to deposit layers of synthetic and natural polymers, Xu was able to produce a mechanically stable structure with a larger matrix-like area for cell implantation and growth. Electrospun poly(caprolactone), collagen type I (PCL), and hydroxyapatite fiber meshes were used to create a bone substitute (hydroxyapatite). The study showed that several material properties, such as biodegradability, may be combined to enhance a biological interaction mold. By studying a wide range of biomaterials for 3D printing, unique ways can be developed to treat a wide range of tissues and disorders.

7.6.2 Bio-Ink

Scaffolds are used in tissue engineering to guide cell growth and give structural cues for tissue formation. Rather than relying on ECM-mimetic materials, scaffold-free methods advocate for cell aggregates to act as their delivery vehicle. The fusion and self-assembly of cellular aggregates (such as spheroids or cylinder rods) into architectural tissues have been proven by a range of investigators, including Norotte and Jakab [5, 6]. Monodispersed cells, on the other hand, have been proven to be just as efficient as spheroids at forming complicated forms [99]. In contrast, it has been established that the pre-culture period of spheroids, in which a shorter time contributes to a much more compact fusion, and varying combinations of mixed spheroids and cells may influence the tissues' structural characteristics and cellular sorting behavior [99]. Thus, identifying cells in bio-ink, either singly or as spheroids, alleviates the shortcomings of cell counting and provides a versatile criterion for cell distribution in heterotopic 3D tissues that require a scaffold or do not.

7.6.3 Bioprinters

The development of 3D printing technology has allowed scientists to create customized, patient-specific structures using CT scans, MRIs, and other medical imaging data as well as CAD models. Maintaining cytocompatibility while manipulating the architecture at the micro- and nano-scale is a significant difficulty in tissue engineering. Organic solvents used as crosslinkers in hydrogel systems might be hazardous to cells or add complexity to the construction process. While using UV crosslinking printers, it may cause genetic damage. Droplet dispersion governs the spatial control of volume-defined droplets used in dispensing and inkjet printing. Powder and a binder are used in the standard SFF way of building, and there have been major advancements in the area. Casting onto SFF-printed molds is an indirect printing technique that allows for scaffolds with a better resolution. Resolution constraints on constructions can be traced back to material features such as droplet dispersion and powder flowability. However, while the method could be useful in the lab, it is currently unsuitable for use in tissue genesis due to lengthy manufacturing times. High-density cells and self-assembling bio-ink were facilitated by scaffold-free cellular aggregate dispensing, although the resolution is still being enhanced [93]. It can save the time required for tissue synthesis and allow for more precise design micromanagement. Tissue construct maturation for orthotopic application can be achieved via post-printing management (i.e., dynamic bioreactors) in addition to the printing technique [100–103]. Tissue-specific bioprinter techniques will also benefit from future research into cellular positioning control [104–106]. Other fabrication techniques outside 3D printing may also hold promise—for example, Du and coworkers [82–84] have shown that cell-laden microgels with defined micro-architectures can self-assemble underneath controlled conditions. The DeSimone group has also created a method called PRINT (particles replicating in nonwetting templates) [107, 108] that shows promise for use in tissue engineering.

7.7 Conclusion

The goal of tissue engineering is to combine engineering with tissue genetics to produce functioning artificial tissue. Tissue engineering faces significant obstacles, but 3D printing offers hope for a solution because of its quick prototyping and inherent capacity for manufacturing on an industrial scale. Increased cellular integration, host integration, and vascularization can result from the preceding design considerations for 3D-printed tissue engineering constructs. More specifically, the size of implantable tissue constructs is constrained by the difficulty in vascularizing them. Many researchers have made important strides toward solving the problem, but more work is needed, as are improved *in vitro* and *in vivo* models. From a manufacturing point of view, good designs will have fewer components and processes in their ultimate assembly. Some of the above-mentioned techniques allow for the improved or simultaneous delivery of structure, cells, and biomolecules without the need for further purification stages and thus serve as a foundation for future studies aimed at further streamlining the process. Further investigation into 3D-printed tissues will not only help in the development of implantable tissue constructs but will also give cutting-edge medication delivery and diseased human models, hence decreasing the risk associated with moving from animal to human studies. It has been proven that 3D printing can be a potent tool for building functional tissue *in vitro*, speeding up the implementation of tissue engineering principles in regenerative medicine and drug testing.

References

1. Langer, R. and Vacanti, J.P., Tissue engineering. *Science*, 260, 5110, 920–6, 1993.
2. Loh, Q.L. and Choong, C., Three-dimensional scaffolds for tissue engineering applications: Role of porosity and pore size. *Tissue Eng. Part B Rev.*, 19, 6, 485–502, 2013. doi:10.1089/ten.TEB.2012.0437
3. Yang, S., Leong, K.F., Du, Z., Chua, C.K., The design of scaffolds for use in tissue engineering. Part I. Traditional factors. *Tissue Eng.*, 7, 6, 679–89, Dec. 1, 2001.
4. Elbert, D.L., Bottom-up tissue engineering. *Curr. Opin. Biotechnol.*, 22, 5, 674–80, Oct. 1, 2011.
5. Jakab, K., Norotte, C., Marga, F., Murphy, K., Vunjak-Novakovic, G., Forgacs, G., Tissue engineering by self-assembly and bio-printing of living cells. *Biofabrication*, 2, 2, 022001, Jun. 2, 2010.
6. Jakab, K., Norotte, C., Damon, B., Marga, F., Neagu, A., Besch-Williford, C.L., Kachurin, A., Church, K.H., Park, H., Mironov, V., Markwald, R., Tissue engineering by self-assembly of cells printed into topologically defined structures. *Tissue Eng. Part A*, 14, 3, 413–21, Mar. 1, 2008.

7. Wang, X., Yan, Y., Zhang, R., Rapid prototyping as a tool for manufacturing bioartificial livers. *Trends Biotechnol.*, 25, 11, 505–13, Nov. 1, 2007.
8. Guillotin, B. and Guillemot, F., Cell patterning technologies for organotypic tissue fabrication. *Trends Biotechnol.*, 29, 4, 183–90, Apr. 1, 2011.
9. Tsang, V.L. and Bhatia, S.N., Three-dimensional tissue fabrication. *Adv. Drug Deliv. Rev.*, 56, 11, 1635–47, Sep. 22, 2004.
10. Rivron, N.C., Rouwkema, J., Truckenmüller, R., Karperien, M., De Boer, J., Van Blitterswijk, C.A., Tissue assembly and organization: Developmental mechanisms in microfabricated tissues. *Biomaterials*, 30, 28, 4851–8, Oct. 1, 2009.
11. Perez-Castillejos, R., Replication of the 3D architecture of tissues. *Mater. Today*, 13, 1-2, 32–41, Jan. 1, 2010.
12. Langridge, B., Griffin, M., Butler, P.E., Regenerative medicine for skeletal muscle loss: A review of current tissue engineering approaches. *J. Mater. Sci. Mater. Med.*, 32, 1–6, Jan. 2021.
13. Lee, M., Wu, B.M., Dunn, J.C., Effect of scaffold architecture and pore size on smooth muscle cell growth. *J. Biomed. Mater. Res. A*, 87, 4, 1010–6, Dec. 15, 2008.
14. Kim, S.S., Utsunomiya, H., Koski, J.A., Wu, B.M., Cima, M.J., Sohn, J., Mukai, K., Griffith, L.G., Vacanti, J.P., Survival and function of hepatocytes on a novel three-dimensional synthetic biodegradable polymer scaffold with an intrinsic network of channels. *Ann. Surg.*, 228, 1, 8, Jul. 1998.
15. Griffith, L.G., Wu, B.E., Cima, M.J., Powers, M.J., Chaignaud, B.E., Vacanti, J.P., *In vitro* organogenesis of liver tissue. *Ann. N. Y. Acad. Sci.*, 831, 1, 382–97, Dec. 1997.
16. Miller, J.S., Stevens, K.R., Yang, M.T., Baker, B.M., Nguyen, D.H., Cohen, D.M., Toro, E., Chen, A.A., Galie, P.A., Yu, X., Chaturvedi, R., Rapid casting of patterned vascular networks for perfusable engineered three-dimensional tissues. *Nat. Mater.*, 11, 9, 768–74, Sep. 2012.
17. Norotte, C., Marga, F.S., Niklason, L.E., Forgacs, G., Scaffold-free vascular tissue engineering using bioprinting. *Biomaterials*, 30, 30, 5910–7, Oct. 1, 2009.
18. Porteus, M., Translating the lessons from gene therapy to the development of regenerative medicine. *Mol. Ther.*, 19, 3, 439–41, Mar. 1, 2011.
19. Barrett, A.J. and Melenhorst, J.J., Is human cell therapy research caught in a mousetrap? *Mol. Ther.*, 19, 2, 224–7, Feb. 1, 2011.
20. Goldberg, A.D., Allis, C.D., Bernstein, E., Epigenetics: A landscape takes shape. *Cell*, 128, 4, 635–8, Feb. 23, 2007.
21. Bernstein, B.E., Meissner, A., Lander, E.S., The mammalian epigenome. *Cell*, 128, 4, 669–81, Feb. 23, 2007.
22. Marga, F., Neagu, A., Kosztin, I., Forgacs, G., Developmental biology and tissue engineering. *Birth Defects Res. C Embryo Today Rev.*, 81, 4, 320–8, Dec. 2007.
23. Sherwood, J.K., Riley, S.L., Palazzolo, R., Brown, S.C., Monkhouse, D.C., Coates, M., Griffith, L.G., Landeen, L.K., Ratcliffe, A., A three-dimensional

osteochondral composite scaffold for articular cartilage repair. *Biomaterials*, 23, 24, 4739–51, Dec. 1, 2002.
24. Lee, M., Dunn, J.C., Wu, B.M., Scaffold fabrication by indirect three-dimensional printing. *Biomaterials*, 26, 20, 4281–9, Jul. 1, 2005.
25. Schumann, D., Ekaputra, A.K., Lam, C.X., Hutmacher, D.W., Biomaterials/Scaffolds, in: *Tissue Engineering*, pp. 101–24, 2007.
26. Sachlos, E., Reis, N., Ainsley, C., Derby, B., Czernuszka, J.T., Novel collagen scaffolds with predefined internal morphology made by solid freeform fabrication. *Biomaterials*, 24, 8, 1487–97, Apr. 1, 2003.
27. Gaetani, R., Doevendans, P.A., Metz, C.H., Alblas, J., Messina, E., Giacomello, A., Sluijter, J.P., Cardiac tissue engineering using tissue printing technology and human cardiac progenitor cells. *Biomaterials*, 33, 6, 1782–90, Feb. 1, 2012.
28. Kai, H., Wang, X., Madhukar, K.S., Qin, L., Yan, Y., Zhang, R., Wang, X., Fabrication of a two-level tumor bone repair biomaterial based on a rapid prototyping technique. *Biofabrication*, 1, 2, 025003, Jun. 10, 2009.
29. Wang, X., Yan, Y., Pan, Y., Xiong, Z., Liu, H., Cheng, J., Liu, F., Lin, F., Wu, R., Zhang, R., Lu, Q., Generation of three-dimensional hepatocyte/gelatin structures with rapid prototyping system. *Tissue Eng.*, 12, 1, 83–90, Jan. 1, 2006.
30. Nishiyama, Y., Nakamura, M., Henmi, C., *et al.*, Development of a three-dimensional bioprinter: Construction of cell supporting structures using hydrogel and state-of-the-art inkjet technology. *J. Biomech. Eng.*, 131, 3, 035001, 2009. doi:10.1115/1.3002759
31. De Colli, M., Massimi, M., Barbetta, A., Di Rosario, B.L., Nardecchia, S., Devirgiliis, L.C., Dentini, M., A biomimetic porous hydrogel of gelatin and glycosaminoglycans cross-linked with transglutaminase and its application in the culture of hepatocytes. *Biomed. Mater.*, 7, 5, 055005, Jul. 26, 2012.
32. Xu, M., Wang, X., Yan, Y., Yao, R., Ge, Y., An cell-assembly derived physiological 3D model of the metabolic syndrome, based on adipose-derived stromal cells and a gelatin/alginate/fibrinogen matrix. *Biomaterials*, 31, 14, 3868–77, May 1, 2010.
33. Skardal, A., Zhang, J., Prestwich, G.D., Bioprinting vessel-like constructs using hyaluronan hydrogels crosslinked with tetrahedral polyethylene glycol tetracrylates. *Biomaterials*, 31, 24, 6173–81, Aug. 1, 2010.
34. Martins, A., Chung, S., Pedro, A.J., Sousa, R.A., Marques, A.P., Reis, R.L., Neves, N.M., Hierarchical starch-based fibrous scaffold for bone tissue engineering applications. *J. Tissue Eng. Regen. Med.*, 3, 1, 37–42, Jan. 2009.
35. Xu, W., Wang, X., Yan., Y., Zhang, R., A polyurethane-gelatin hybrid construct for manufacturing implantable bioartificial livers. *J. Bioact. Compat. Polym.*, 23, 5, 409–22, Sep. 2008.
36. Seitz, H., Rieder, W., Irsen, S., Leukers, B., Tille, C., Three-dimensional printing of porous ceramic scaffolds for bone tissue engineering. *J. Biomed. Mater. Res. B*, 74, 2, 782–8, Aug. 2005.

37. Leukers, B., Gülkan, H., Irsen, S.H., Milz, S., Tille, C., Schieker, M., Seitz, H., Hydroxyapatite scaffolds for bone tissue engineering made by 3D printing. *J. Mater. Sci. Mater. Med.*, 16, 12, 1121–4, Dec. 2005.
38. Tarafder, S., Balla, V.K., Davies, N.M., Bandyopadhyay, A., Bose, S., Microwave-sintered 3D printed tricalcium phosphate scaffolds for bone tissue engineering. *J. Tissue Eng. Regen. Med.*, 7, 8, 631–41, Aug. 2013.
39. Butscher, A., Bohner, M., Hofmann, S., Gauckler, L., Müller, R., Structural and material approaches to bone tissue engineering in powder-based three-dimensional printing. *Actabiomaterialia*, 7, 3, 907–20, Mar. 1, 2011.
40. Neagu, A., Kosztin, I., Jakab, K., Barz, B., Neagu, M., Jamison, R., Forgacs, G., Computational modeling of tissue self-assembly. *Mod. Phys. Lett. B*, 20, 20, 1217–31, Aug. 30, 2006.
41. Hollister, S.J., Porous scaffold design for tissue engineering. *Nat. Mater.*, 4, 7, 518–24, Jul. 1, 2005.
42. Cheah, C.M., Chua, C.K., Leong, K.F., Chua, S.W., Development of a tissue engineering scaffold structure library for rapid prototyping. Part 1: investigation and classification. *Int. J. Adv. Manuf. Technol.*, 21, 291–301, Feb. 2003.
43. Griffith, L.G., Wu, B.E., Cima, M.J., Powers, M.J., Chaignaud, B.E., Vacanti, J.P., In vitro organogenesis of liver tissue. *Ann. N. Y. Acad. Sci.*, 831, 1, 382–97, Dec. 1997.
44. Naing, M.W., Chua, C.K., Leong, K.F., Wang, Y., Fabrication of customised scaffolds using computer-aided design and rapid prototyping techniques. *Rapid Prototyp. J.*, 11, 4, 249–59, Sep. 1, 2005.
45. Leong, K.F., Chua, S.C., Sudarmadji, N., Yeong, W.Y., Engineering functionally graded tissue engineering scaffolds. *J. Mech. Behav. Biomed. Mater.*, 1, 2, 140–52, Apr. 1, 2008.
46. Chua, C.K., Sudarmadji, N., Leong, K.F., Chou, S.M., Lim, S.C., Firdaus, W.M., Process flow for designing functionally graded tissue engineering scaffolds, in: *Innovative Developments in Design and Manufacturing*, pp. 63–68, CRC Press, Boca Raton, Florida, Sep. 22, 2009.
47. Chua, C.K., Leong, K.F., Sudarmadji, N., Liu, M.J., Chou, S.M., Selective laser sintering of functionally graded tissue scaffolds. *MRS Bull.*, 36, 12, 1006–14, Dec. 2011.
48. Cai, S., Xi, J., Chua, C.K., A novel bone scaffold design approach based on shape function and all-hexahedral mesh refinement, in: *Computer-Aided Tissue Engineering*, pp. 45–55, 2012.
49. Yang, N., Quan, Z., Zhang, D., Tian, Y., Multi-morphology transition hybridization CAD design of minimal surface porous structures for use in tissue engineering. *Comput.-Aided Des.*, 56, 11–21, Nov. 1, 2014.
50. Rouwkema, J., Rivron, N.C., van Blitterswijk, C.A., Vascularization in tissue engineering. *Trends Biotechnol.*, 26, 8, 434–41, Aug. 1, 2008.
51. Druecke, D., Langer, S., Lamme, E., Pieper, J., Ugarkovic, M., Steinau, H.U., Homann, H.H., Neovascularization of poly (ether ester) block-copolymer

scaffolds *in vivo*: Long-term investigations using intravital fluorescent microscopy. *J. Biomed. Mater. Res. A*, 68, 1, 10–8, Jan. 1, 2004.

52. Karageorgiou, V. and Kaplan, D., Porosity of 3D biomaterial scaffolds and osteogenesis. *Biomaterials*, 26, 27, 5474–91, Sep. 1, 2005.
53. Wang, M.O., Vorwald, C.E., Dreher, M.L., Mott, E.J., Cheng, M.H., Cinar, A., Mehdizadeh, H., Somo, S., Dean, D., Brey, E.M., Fisher, J.P., Evaluating 3D-Printed biomaterials as scaffolds for vascularized bone tissue engineering. *Adv. Mater.*, 27, 1, 138–44, Jan. 2015.
54. Suntornnond, R., An, J., Yeong, W., Chua, C., 3D hybrid membrane based structure: A novel approach for tissue engineering scaffold, in: *Tissue Engineering Part A*, vol. 20, pp. S66–S66, Mary Ann Liebert, INC, 140 Huguenot Street, 3rd Fl, New Rochelle, NY 10801 USA, Dec. 1, 2014.
55. Hutmacher, D.W., Schantz, T., Zein, I., Ng, K.W., Teoh, S.H., Tan, K.C., Mechanical properties and cell cultural response of polycaprolactone scaffolds designed and fabricated via fused deposition modeling. *J. Biomed. Mater. Res.*, 55, 2, 203–16, May 2001.
56. Leong, K.F., Chua, C.K., Gui, W.S., Building porous biopolymeric microstructures for controlled drug delivery devices using selective laser sintering. *Int. J. Adv. Manuf. Technol.*, 31, Dec. 15, 2006.
57. Kim, S.S., Utsunomiya, H., Koski, J.A., Wu, B.M., Cima, M.J., Sohn, J., Mukai, K., Griffith, L.G., Vacanti, J.P., Survival and function of hepatocytes on a novel three-dimensional synthetic biodegradable polymer scaffold with an intrinsic network of channels. *Ann. Surg.*, 228, 1, 8, Jul. 1998.
58. Chen, C.H., Shyu, V.B., Chen, J.P., Lee, M.Y., Selective laser sintered poly-ε-caprolactone scaffold hybridized with collagen hydrogel for cartilage tissue engineering. *Biofabrication*, 6, 1, 015004, Jan. 15, 2014.
59. Gomes, M.E., Azevedo, H.S., Moreira, A.R., Ellä, V., Kellomäki, M., Reis, R.L., Starch–poly (ε-caprolactone) and starch–poly (lactic acid) fibre-mesh scaffolds for bone tissue engineering applications: Structure, mechanical properties and degradation behaviour. *J. Tissue Eng. Regen. Med.*, 2, 5, 243–52, Jul. 2008.
60. Martin, I., Wendt, D., Heberer, M., The role of bioreactors in tissue engineering. *Trends Biotechnol.*, 22, 2, 80–6, Feb. 1, 2004.
61. Kinstlinger, I.S., Bastian, A., Paulsen, S.J., Hwang, D.H., Ta, A.H., Yalacki, D.R., Schmidt, T., Miller, J.S., Open-source selective laser sintering (OpenSLS) of nylon and biocompatible polycaprolactone. *PloS One*, 11, 2, e0147399, Feb. 3, 2016.
62. Modulevsky, D.J., Cuerrier, C.M., Pelling, A.E., Biocompatibility of subcutaneously implanted plant-derived cellulose biomaterials. *PloS One*, 11, 6, e0157894, Jun. 21, 2016.
63. Lewis, P.L. and Shah, R.N., 3D printing for liver tissue engineering: Current approaches and future challenges. *Curr. Transpl. Rep.*, 3, 100–8, Mar. 2016.
64. Wang, X., Yan, Y., Pan, Y., Xiong, Z., Liu, H., Cheng, J., Liu, F., Lin, F., Wu, R., Zhang, R., Lu, Q., Generation of three-dimensional hepatocyte/gelatin

structures with rapid prototyping system. *Tissue Eng.*, 12, 1, 83–90, Jan. 1, 2006.
65. Silva, T.H., Alves, A., Popa, E.G., Reys, L.L., Gomes, M.E., Sousa, R.A., Silva, S.S., Mano, J.F., Reis, R.L., Marine algae sulfated polysaccharides for tissue engineering and drug delivery approaches. *Biomatter*, 2, 4, 278–89, Oct. 1, 2012.
66. Yan, Y. Wang, X., Pan, Y., *et al.*, Fabrication of viable tissue-engineered constructs with 3D cell-assembly technique. *Biomaterials*, 26, 29, 5864–5871, 2005. doi:10.1016/j.biomaterials.2005.02.027.
67. Deegan, D.B., Zimmerman, C., Skardal, A., Atala, A., Shupe, T.D., Stiffness of hyaluronic acid gels containing liver extracellular matrix supports human hepatocyte function and alters cell morphology. *J. Mech. Behav. Biomed. Mater.*, 55, 87–103, Mar. 1, 2016.
68. Itoh, M., Nakayama, K., Noguchi, R., Kamohara, K., Furukawa, K., Uchihashi, K., Toda, S., Oyama, J.I., Node, K., Morita, S., Scaffold-free tubular tissues created by a bio-3D printer undergo remodeling and endothelialization when implanted in rat aortae. *PloS One*, 10, 9, e0136681, Sep. 1, 2015.
69. Poldervaart, M.T., Goversen, B., De Ruijter, M., Abbadessa, A., Melchels, F.P., Öner, F.C., Dhert, W.J., Vermonden, T., Alblas, J., 3D bioprinting of methacrylated hyaluronic acid (MeHA) hydrogel with intrinsic osteogenicity. *PloS One*, 12, 6, e0177628, Jun. 6, 2017.
70. Mousavi, S.J. and HamdyDoweidar, M., Role of mechanical cues in cell differentiation and proliferation: A 3D numerical model. *PloS One*, 10, 5, e0124529, May 1, 2015.
71. Augst, A.D., Kong, H.J. and Mooney, D.J., Alginate hydrogels as biomaterials. *Macromol. Biosci.*, 6, 623–33, 2006. https://doi.org/10.1002/mabi.200600069.
72. Claus, J., Brietzke, A., Lehnert, C., Oschatz, S., Grabow, N., Kragl, U., Swelling characteristics and biocompatibility of ionic liquid based hydrogels for biomedical applications. *PloS One*, 15, 4, e0231421, Apr. 20, 2020.
73. Rouillard, A.D., Berglund, C.M., Lee, J.Y., Polacheck, W.J., Tsui, Y., Bonassar, L.J., Kirby, B.J., Methods for photocrosslinking alginate hydrogel scaffolds with high cell viability. *Tissue Eng. Part C Methods*, 17, 2, 173–9, Feb. 1, 2011.
74. Nakamura, M., Nishiyama, Y., Henmi, C., Iwanaga, S., Nakagawa, H., Yamaguchi, K., Akita, K., Mochizuki, S., Takiura, K., Ink jet three-dimensional digital fabrication for biological tissue manufacturing: Analysis of alginate microgel beads produced by ink jet droplets for three dimensional tissue fabrication. *J. Imaging Sci. Technol.*, 52, 6, 060201, Nov. 1, 2008.
75. Pataky, K., Braschler, T., Negro, A., Renaud, P., Lutolf, M.P., Brugger, J., Microdrop printing of hydrogel bioinks into 3D tissue-like geometries. *Adv. Mater.*, 24, 3, 391–6, Jan. 17, 2012.
76. Gaetani, R., Doevendans, P.A., Metz, C.H., Alblas, J., Messina, E., Giacomello, A., Sluijter, J.P., Cardiac tissue engineering using tissue printing technology and human cardiac progenitor cells. *Biomaterials*, 33, 6, 1782–90, Feb. 1, 2012.

77. Xu, M., Wang, X., Yan, Y., Yao, R., Ge, Y., An cell-assembly derived physiological 3D model of the metabolic syndrome, based on adipose-derived stromal cells and a gelatin/alginate/fibrinogen matrix. *Biomaterials*, 31, 14, 3868–77, May 1, 2010.
78. Xue, W., Krishna, B.V., Bandyopadhyay, A., Bose, S., Processing and biocompatibility evaluation of laser processed porous titanium. *Actabiomaterialia*, 3, 6, 1007–18, Nov. 1, 2007.
79. Mengsteab, P.Y., Freeman, J., Barajaa, M.A., Nair, L.S., Laurencin, C.T., Ligament regenerative engineering: Braiding scalable and tunable bioengineered ligaments using a bench-top braiding machine. *Regen. Eng. Transl. Med.*, 7, 524–32, Dec. 2021.
80. Khan, Y., Yaszemski, M.J., Mikos, A.G., Laurencin, C.T., Tissue engineering of bone: Material and matrix considerations. *J. Bone Jt. Surg.*, 90, Supplement_1, 36–42, Feb. 1, 2008.
81. Leukers, B., Gülkan, H., Irsen, S.H., Milz, S., Tille, C., Schieker, M., Seitz, H., Hydroxyapatite scaffolds for bone tissue engineering made by 3D printing. *J. Mater. Sci. Mater. Med.*, 16, 12, 1121–4, 2005.
82. Du, Y., Lo, E., Vidula, M.K., Khabiry, M., Khademhosseini, A., Method of bottom-up directed assembly of cell-laden microgels. *Cell. Mol. Bioeng.*, 1, 157–62, Sep. 2008.
83. Du, Y., Ghodousi, M., Lo, E., Vidula, M.K., Emiroglu, O., Khademhosseini, A., Surface-directed assembly of cell-laden microgels. *Biotechnol. Bioeng.*, 105, 3, 655–62, Feb. 15, 2010.
84. Zamanian, B., Masaeli, M., Nichol, J.W., Khabiry, M., Hancock, M.J., Bae, H., Khademhosseini, A., Interface-directed self-assembly of cell-laden microgels. *Small*, 6, 8, 937–44, Apr. 23, 2010.
85. Gbureck, U., Hölzel, T., Doillon, C.J., Müller, F.A., Barralet, J.E., Direct printing of bioceramic implants with spatially localized angiogenic factors. *Adv. Mater.*, 19, 6, 795–800, Mar. 19, 2007.
86. Barralet, J., Gbureck, U., Habibovic, P., Vorndran, E., Gerard, C., Doillon, C.J., Angiogenesis in calcium phosphate scaffolds by inorganic copper ion release. *Tissue Eng. Part A*, 15, 7, 1601–9, Jul. 1, 2009.
87. Becker, S.T., Douglas, T., Acil, Y., Seitz, H., Sivananthan, S., Wiltfang, J., Warnke, P.H., Biocompatibility of individually designed scaffolds with human periosteum for use in tissue engineering. *J. Mater. Sci. Mater. Med.*, 21, 1255–62, Apr. 2010.
88. Guang-xi, Z.H., Shi-feng, L.I., Xin, Y.A., Ming-jun, S.H., Yao-jia, R.E., Research progress on preparation of biological implant materials by additive manufacturing. *Powder Metall. Technol.*, 37, 4, 312–8, Aug. 27, 2019.
89. Tamimi, F., Torres, J., Gbureck, U., Lopez-Cabarcos, E., Bassett, D.C., Alkhraisat, M.H., Barralet, J.E., Craniofacial vertical bone augmentation: a comparison between 3D printed monolithic monetite blocks and autologous onlay grafts in the rabbit. *Biomaterials*, 30, 31, 6318–26, 2009.

90. L'heureux, N., Pâquet, S., Labbé, R., Germain, L., Auger, F.A., A completely biological tissue-engineered human blood vessel. *FASEB J.*, 12, 1, 47–56, Jan. 1998.
91. L'Heureux, N., Dusserre, N., Konig, G., Victor, B., Keire, P., Wight, T.N., Chronos, N.A., Kyles, A.E., Gregory, C.R., Hoyt, G., Robbins, R.C., Human tissue-engineered blood vessels for adult arterial revascularization. *Nat. Med.*, 12, 3, 361–5, Mar. 1, 2006.
92. L'heureux, N., Dusserre, N., Marini, A., Garrido, S., De La Fuente, L., McAllister, T., Technology insight: The evolution of tissue-engineered vascular grafts—from research to clinical practice. *Nat. Clin. Pract. Cardiovasc. Med.*, 4, 7, 389–95, Jul. 2007.
93. Norotte, C., Marga, F.S., Niklason, L.E., Forgacs, G., Scaffold-free vascular tissue engineering using bioprinting. *Biomaterials*, 30, 30, 5910–7, Oct. 1, 2009.
94. Mironov, V., Kasyanov, V., Markwald, R.R., Organ printing: From bioprinter to organ biofabrication line. *Curr. Opin. Biotechnol.*, 22, 5, 667–73, Oct. 1, 2011.
95. Bartnikowski, M., Klein, T.J., Melchels, F.P., Woodruff, M.A., Effects of scaffold architecture on mechanical characteristics and osteoblast response to static and perfusion bioreactor cultures. *Biotechnol. Bioeng.*, 111, 7, 1440–51, Jul. 2014.
96. Ghaedi, M., Mendez, J.J., Bove, P.F., Sivarapatna, A., Raredon, M.S., Niklason, L.E., Alveolar epithelial differentiation of human induced pluripotent stem cells in a rotating bioreactor. *Biomaterials*, 35, 2, 699–710, Jan. 1, 2014.
97. Spitters, T.W., Leijten, J.C., Deus, F.D., Costa, I.B., van Apeldoorn, A.A., van Blitterswijk, C.A., Karperien, M., A dual flow bioreactor with controlled mechanical stimulation for cartilage tissue engineering. *Tissue Eng. Part C Methods*, 19, 10, 774–83, Oct. 1, 2013.
98. Xu, W., Wang, X., Yan, Y., Zhang, R., A polyurethane-gelatin hybrid construct for manufacturing implantable bioartificial livers. *J. Bioact. Compat. Polym.*, 23, 5, 409–22, Sep. 2008.
99. Kim, T.Y., Kofron, C.M., King, M.E., Markes, A.R., Okundaye, A.O., Qu, Z., Mende, U., Choi, B.R., Directed fusion of cardiac spheroids into larger heterocellularmicrotissues enables investigation of cardiac action potential propagation via cardiac fibroblasts. *PloS One*, 13, 5, e0196714, May 1, 2018.
100. Mayer, N., Lopa, S., Talò, G., Lovati, A.B., Pasdeloup, M., Riboldi, S.A., Moretti, M., Mallein-Gerin, F., Interstitial perfusion culture with specific soluble factors inhibits type I collagen production from human osteoarthritic chondrocytes in clinical-grade collagen sponges. *PloS One*, 11, 9, e0161479, Sep. 1, 2016.
101. Martin, I., Wendt, D., Heberer, M., The role of bioreactors in tissue engineering. *Trends Biotechnol.*, 22, 2, 80–6, Feb. 1, 2004.
102. Lu, J., Zhang, X., Li, J., Yu, L., Chen, E., Zhu, D., Zhang, Y., Li, L., A new fluidized bed bioreactor based on diversion-type microcapsule suspension for bioartificial liver systems. *PloS One*, 11, 2, e0147376, Feb. 3, 2016.

103. Rath, S., Salinas, M., Villegas, A.G., Ramaswamy, S., Differentiation and distribution of marrow stem cells in flex-flow environments demonstrate support of the valvular phenotype. *PloS One*, 10, 11, e0141802, Nov. 4, 2015.
104. Du, Y., Lo, E., Vidula, M.K., Khabiry, M., Khademhosseini, A., Method of bottom-up directed assembly of cell-laden microgels. *Cell. Mol. Bioeng.*, 1, 157–62, Sep. 2008.
105. Du, Y., Ghodousi, M., Lo, E., Vidula, M.K., Emiroglu, O., Khademhosseini, A., Surface-directed assembly of cell-laden microgels. *Biotechnol. Bioeng.*, 105, 3, 655–62, Feb. 15, 2010.
106. Zamanian, B., Masaeli, M., Nichol, J.W., Khabiry, M., Hancock, M.J., Bae, H., Khademhosseini, A., Interface-directed self-assembly of cell-laden microgels. *Small*, 6, 8, 937–44, Apr. 23, 2010.
107. Rolland, J.P., Maynor, B.W., Euliss, L.E., Exner, A.E., Denison, G.M., DeSimone, J.M., Direct fabrication and harvesting of monodisperse, shape-specific nanobiomaterials. *J. Am. Chem. Soc*, 127, 28, 10096–100, Jul. 20, 2005.
108. Sun, L., Su, T., Xu, J., Hao, D., Liao, W., Zhao, Y., Ren, W., Deng, C., Lü, H., Aerobic oxidative desulfurization coupling of Co polyanion catalysts and p-TsOH-based deep eutectic solvents through a biomimetic approach. *Green Chem.*, 21, 10, 2629–34, 2019.

8

Personalized Medicine with 3D Printing

Abstract
The purpose of personalized medicine is to treat each patient with medication that is specifically designed for them, taking into account their unique physiology, drug response, and genetic profile. Several new technologies, most notably 3D printing, are driving a change from mass-produced, "one-size-fits-all" medicine to individualized, patient-specific care. Using a variety of programs, 3D printing allows for the gradual construction of a three-dimensional item. The shape, release profile, and medication combination options for pharmaceutical dosage forms made using 3D printing are practically endless. Inkjet printing, binder jetting, fused filament fabrication, selective laser sintering, stereolithography, and pressure-assisted micro-syringe are a few of the 3D-printing technologies being studied for potential usage in the pharmaceutical industry. The technology may find future use in the medical field, namely, in the dispensing of prescription drugs on an individual basis. This chapter highlights the numerous 3D-printing methods, their uses in research for producing pharmaceutical items, and the benefits and drawbacks of each. Incorporating various medications into a single polypill also demonstrates its promise in individualized therapy. Insight into its care for different demographics is also presented. Its potential clinical application is also addressed. The many obstacles that stand in the way of the technology's application in customized medicine are also highlighted.

Keywords: 3D printing, personalized medicine, computer-aided design, transdermal patches, selective laser sintering, drug delivery systems

8.1 Introduction

The existing medical system is based on the "one size fits all" model, where the same medications are given to most patients at the same dosages and with the same regularity [1]. It became clear that the "one size fits all" approach did not work for all therapies. The same doses of the same active component given to different people have elicited a wide range of reactions. The response may be either excessively strong, leading to unwanted side

Rishabha Malviya and Rishav Sharma. 3D Printing in Healthcare: Novel Applications, (143–166)

effects (ADRs), or too weak, producing little or minimal pharmacological effects. Each of these scenarios has the potential to result in further patient problems [2]. Because of this, customized medicines are being developed, in which patients take pharmaceuticals that have been developed specifically for them or in which patients who share comparable genetic, physiological, or pathological characteristics take the same prescription [3]. Its mission is to provide the most appropriate medication to each patient at the most appropriate time for their condition, with the maxim "one size does not fit all" as its guiding principle [1]. In theory, personalized medicine should result in more targeted treatments. They have fewer adverse effects, greater effectiveness, higher patient compliance, and lower overall costs [4]. Three-dimensional printing, commonly known as additive manufacturing or 3D printing, is a process in which a solid form is built up from the bottom up in a series of successive layers. To use a computer-aided design (CAD) tool, information is sent to a 3D printer, which slices the digital model into 2D pieces, forms solid layers, and then manufactures the required objects [5]. It has found widespread use in fields as disparate as the car and aerospace industries and the medicinal and pharmaceutical fields. The building sector, the entertainment business, the fashion industry, the visual arts, and even the jewellery trade all make use of it. It has been used to make microneedles, transdermal patches, and micro-emulsifying drug delivery systems [6]. It has also been utilized in the fabrication of controlled-release tablets, polypills, oro-dispersible films, gastro-floating tablets as well as other drug delivery systems. A broad range of printing technologies is currently available [7], including inkjet printing, binder jet printers, fusion deposition, selective laser sintering, stereolithography, and pressure-assisted microsyringe printing. Several pharmaceutical items could benefit greatly from 3D printing, which has the potential to transform their creation, distribution, and use. Traditional manufacturing methods are often inexpensive, but when produced in big quantities, they can be labor-intensive and time-consuming. It is difficult to adjust dosages in traditional manufacturing techniques to meet individual patients' demands. Personalized medicine made possible by 3D printing has the potential to significantly improve patient outcomes by increasing drug adherence. It may be accomplished using clinical on-demand manufacturing [8] to provide the highest-quality medical treatment. Several studies have looked into the advantages of 3D printing for the distribution of medicines. While 3D printing has many potential applications in the pharmaceutical sector, few articles have been published about it. These applications range from their role in personalized treatment to their ability to serve a diverse spectrum of patients. Tumor heterogeneity is a significant challenge for cancer treatment, which is why personalized medicine is an ideal method for improving cancer care. By taking into account each individual's unique genetic makeup and way of life, personalized medicine develops treatments with fewer adverse effects and more effective drug delivery. Personalized medicine aspires to offer a comprehensive approach to healthcare, including diagnostics and therapy. The proven method of 3D printing, known for its precision, produces the personalization required in personalized medicine. Cancer drugs targeting breast, liver, thyroid, and kidney tumors have been successfully printed using a variety of 3D-printing methods. The field of cancer modeling, as well as research utilizing cancer models for treatment and diagnostics, has benefited greatly from the advent of 3D printing. Drug screening, metastasis, and prognosis studies all benefit from using 3D-printed tailored tumor models, including physical 3D models, printed models, and tumor-on-chip models. Cancer models benefit from the use of 3D printing, and the technology has also altered the way cancer is treated. Anticancer drugs can be delivered more effectively with the use of 3D-printed devices, implants, and dose forms designed specifically for each patient. The chapter discusses the current uses of 3D-printed personalized medication for different types of cancer and makes observations about potential future approaches, such as the use of 4D printing and the standardization of 3D-printed personalized medicine in healthcare. Figure 8.1 shows the potential benefits of 3D-printed personalized medicine in cancer diagnosis, prognosis, and treatment.

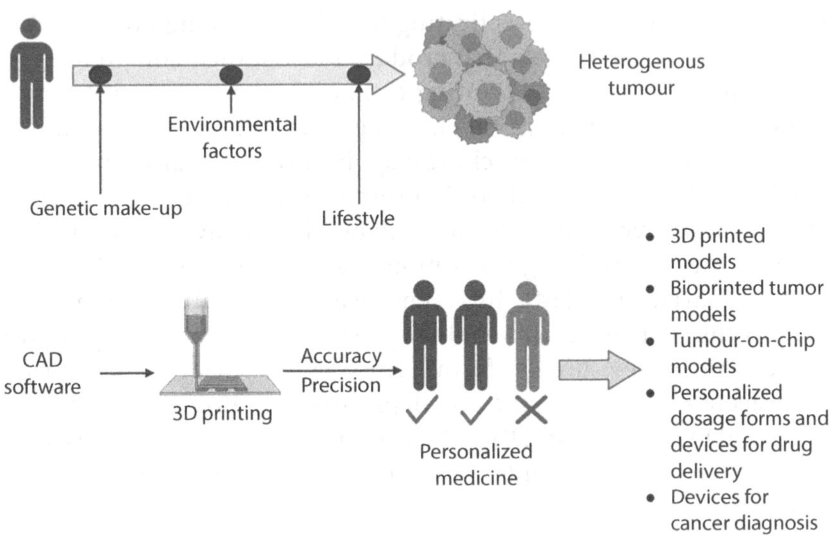

Figure 8.1 3D-printed personalized cancer medicine for better diagnosis, prognosis, and treatment.

8.2 History of 3D Printing

Patents covering various methods of computer-aided additive fabrication on a variety of platforms date back to the late 1970s, marking the beginning of 3D printing research [9]. Charles (Chuck) Hull is widely regarded as a pioneer in the field of 3D printing, and he is also credited with developing and patenting stereolithography (SLA) in the mid-1980s. Ultraviolet light polymerized resins were employed then to get the desired effect. The popularization of these SLA printers was accomplished by 3D Systems, a company that Hull helped start [10, 11]. Selective laser sintering is a method created in 1986 by a Texas University student named Carl Deckard. It uses a laser to fuse the powder. In 1989, Scott and Lisa Crump, the creators of Stratasys, acquired a patent for fused deposition modeling. With a nozzle, molten materials such as plastic or metal can be extruded. Emanuel Sachs and his colleagues at MIT modified an inkjet printer later that year (1989) to create "three-dimensional printing techniques" that used a binding solution injected over a powder bed. In the succeeding decades, the technique became known as binder jetting. To make 3D objects from digital models, Hans Langer focused on direct metal laser sintering in 1989 [10, 12]. There were several initiatives aimed at getting these low-cost, accessible printers into the hands of the people. With the assistance of many different collaborations, University of Bath researcher Andrew Bowyer was able to greatly expand his Replicating Rapid Prototyping project, which involves making 3D printers that produce most of their components [9]. Since its development, 3D-printing technology has been put to use in many different settings. Surgical planning and guiding, as well as implant manufacturing, were the first clinical applications in healthcare to make use of 3D printing. Also, there is promising potential for individualization in the development of implantable drug delivery systems [13]. Similarly, medical training institutions have incorporated 3D printing into their curriculum [14]. In recent years, 3D printing has made its way into the pharmaceutical industry, where it has been employed in the creation of new dosage forms. Aprecia Pharmaceuticals' Spritam (levetiracetam), a treatment for epilepsy that was manufactured in 3D, received FDA approval in 2015. As a result, its extremely porous structure, created using the binder jet printing technique, allows for quick oral dissolution [15].

8.3 Technologies for 3D Printing in Pharmaceutical Research and Development

8.3.1 The Inkjet Printing Process

Inkjet printing, in its broadest sense, applies to the use of pattern-generating machines to precisely control the placement of minute droplets of liquid on a surface. It is standard procedure in the pharmaceutical business to deposit the pharmaceutical and its excipients (often called "ink") as small drops on a suitable substrate, creating a multilayer structure. The two most prevalent kinds of inkjet printing are continuous inkjet printing (CIJ) and drop-on-demand (DoD) [16, 17].

8.3.2 Continuous Inkjet Printer

Continuous inkjet printers, as the name indicates, continually expel a spray of liquid droplets onto a substrate, even while printing is not taking place. Here, the nozzle is made to vibrate, generating a pressure wave that is introduced into the ink stream and causes the droplets of ink to split up into uniform sizes before being ejected. The method wastes ink since it constantly ejects droplets. High-speed, continuous droplet creation is one of the benefits of the printing process that helps prevent nozzle clogging. Low resolution and high upkeep costs are two major drawbacks [18].

8.3.3 Drop-on-Demand Inkjet Printer

Drops of liquid are released from the printhead and deposited onto a substrate in these printers based on a trigger signal, which is sent only when it is required to do so. While most inkjet printers have anywhere from 100 to 1,000 nozzles, others use single-nozzle printheads. Nevertheless, with a drop-on-demand inkjet printer, the kinetic energy of the drops comes from sources adjacent to each nozzle, within the printhead itself [19], whereas with a continuous inkjet printer the droplets are driven out of the nozzles by an external pressure source. The method can deposit precisely sized droplets and generate them with high precision. It also helps keep medication waste to a minimum. As a result, it has become the go-to method for printing [20, 21], even above continuous inkjet printing. Based on the printhead technology used, a drop-on-demand inkjet printer may be further broken down into two categories: thermal inkjet and piezoelectric [22].

8.3.4 Thermal Inkjet Printer

In thermal inkjet printer (TIJ), droplets are released from the nozzle as a result of heat energy. Resistors built into the printheads generate heat when an electric current is sent through them and into the fluid (ink). In the presence of heat, the volatile fluid bubbles up, expanding to push out a stream of fluid through the nozzle. The primary drawback to the approach is the need to heat the resistor to high temperatures (200–300°C), which could also cause the breakdown of thermo-labile active chemicals [18, 23].

8.3.5 Piezoelectric Inkjet Printer

Piezoelectric components or actuators, which change shape in response to an applied electric voltage, are crucial to the technology. Due to the pressure it generates, the fluid (ink) is expelled out to the nozzle. The fluid can be reintroduced into the nozzle and the system reactivated once the component has been restored to its original shape [23, 24]. The method's key benefits are that it may be carried out at room temperature using fluids that are less flammable and more biocompatible [23]. Miniature solenoid valves provide the basis of an intriguing printing method utilized in the pharmaceutical industry: "valve jet" or "electromagnetic" printing. Because of its durability and bigger orifice sizes, it would be more useful for printing coarser suspensions [25, 26] than a TIJ or piezoelectric inkjet printer (PIJ). For the rapid expulsion of droplets, scientists devised a glass inkjet tool. Being an inert material, the glass will not react with any of the substances found in pharmaceuticals, making it an ideal candidate for such uses [27]. Using UV photo-initiation with inkjet technology can advance the field. Inkjet printers have made extensive use of ultraviolet (UV) curing for the quick, on-demand hardening of various materials. The functional groups in the ink utilized here are designed to cross-link when exposed to light, and photo-initiators are typically utilized to speed up the procedure [28].

8.4 Medicinal Applications for Inkjet Printers

Orodispersible film (ODF) preparation is one area in which inkjet printing has proven very useful in the pharmaceutical business. The medication is printed on either a single sheet or a multilayer composition of the appropriate materials, and upon entering the mouth, the drug is rapidly released to form a solution or suspension in the saliva [29]. Thabet *et al.* employed

PIJ printing to add enalapril maleate to drug-free and hydrochlorothiazide-containing ODFs made from hydroxypropyl cellulose. Inks based on water or methanol were utilized for it. Fixed-dosage combinations of enalapril and hydrochlorothiazide might be made by adjusting the doses of the two drugs in enalapril on hydrochlorothiazide films [30]. Propranolol hydrochloride ODFs have been produced in water and glycerol using TIJ, and the results were subsequently evaluated on three different consumable substrates (rice paper, coated rice paper, and icing sheet). Saccharin was cast into the meal with only a casting knife to improve the flavor [31]. By making certain adjustments to a commercial TIJ printer, the researcher discussed an innovative method of administering two medications separately on ODFs. Ethanol, dimethyl sulfoxide (DMSO), and propylene glycol (PG) were all employed to prepare the ink formulations for printing T3 (liothyronine sodium) and T4 (levothyroxine sodium) [32, 33]. The substrates were made of hydroxypropyl methylcellulose. Moreover, TIJ was utilized in tandem with fused deposition modeling to create mucoadhesive buccal films (FDM). Here, HPMC films were created using the FDM technique, and ibuprofen ink was placed on them. PIJ was also used to generate an oromucosal dosage form [34] by printing lidocaine hydrochloride on an electrospun gelatin substrate with or without piroxicam. Thus, it has been shown that integrating two technologies into drug development is beneficial. When it comes to drug loading efficiency, most films employed for oral administration fall short. To get around the porous substrate, edible solid foam suitable for inkjet printing with more ink was produced [35]. The printing of biological drugs on a suitable substrate using an inkjet printer for buccal delivery has also been investigated [36, 37], in addition to the accumulation of tiny molecules. Inkjet printing technology is now used in transdermal delivery systems. Ink formulations of indomethacin in ethanol were loaded onto polythene films using the PIJ technique, resulting in films for transdermal distribution [38]. Microneedles used in transdermal distribution have also been coated via inkjet printing [39–41]. With the advancement of drop-on-demand technologies and dropwise additive manufacturing of pharmaceuticals (DAMPP), it has become feasible to mass-produce novel pharmaceutical formulations [20]. To increase drug solubility, researchers have created self-emulsifying drug delivery systems (SEDDS). The DAMPP method was utilized by Icten *et al.* [42] to develop a composition that includes a film of a self-emulsifying mixture, a tablet, and a film made from a polymer. Furthermore, inkjet with photoinitiation has been used to create tablets of carvedilol and ropinirole [28, 43]. Moreover, solvent inkjet printing was employed during the production of thiamine hydrochloride tablets [44]. Inkjet technology has also been used to generate formulations like drug-loaded mesoporous silica nanoparticles [45] and hydrogel microspheres for pulmonary delivery [46].

8.5 Binder Jet Printing

There is an inkjet printing technique called binder jet printing or the drop-on-powder method. Binder jet printers provide both thermal and piezoelectric printhead options. It is made up of a powder bed that is melted together layer by layer. The liquid binder (and/or medication) is squirted onto the bed of loose powder using a printer nozzle that is moved along the x–y axis. When the liquid drops land on the powder, they absorb moisture and cause the powder to solidify. The powder hardens in one of two ways: either the particles dissolve and re-crystallize or the binder bridges form. The powder supply platform travels upwards along the z-axis, while the manufacturing platform travels downwards. The powder is transferred from the bed to the surface of the bonded layer through a roller. Iteratively performing the process allows the 3D object to be built. Afterward, the item is extracted from the powder bed, and the surplus powder is swept away. To get rid of any trace of the volatile solvent, thermal sintering is commonly utilized. The binder jetting-based zip dosage technique was used in the creation of FDA-approved Spritam [15]. The TheriForm approach is a novel microfabrication method for synthesizing dosage forms by building them up in layers, utilizing a binder jetting [47] approach.

8.6 Medicinal Applications for Binder Jet Printing

Binder jetting has been studied extensively for its potential uses in tablet manufacturing. The characteristics of tablets produced using binder jetting are very sensitive to the excipients utilized and the concentrations at which they are employed. Research indicates that combining filling agents with high-water-solubility, moistening agents with a high water content and binders with high solution viscosity may increase the tablets' hardness, binding strength, and disintegration time [48]. Tablet friability was shown to be highly dependent on binder particle size in another investigation that revealed hydroxypropyl cellulose as a possible binder [49]. The binder linear and four-arm star polyvinyl pyrrolidone was the subject of another investigation. They determined that the proportion of polymer in the tablet's binder affected its compressive strength. The lower viscosity of four-arm star polymers compared to their linear counterparts allowed for their wettability at higher concentrations, resulting in more robust tablets. Additionally, at a concentration of 5% to 50%, acetaminophen in the tablets exhibited acceptable physical characteristics [50]. Tablets with active pharmaceutical ingredients (API) in a wide range of forms and significant characteristics have already been made using binder jetting. Tablets containing chlorpheniramine were manufactured utilizing ethanol and acetone-soluble Eudragit E-100 and Eudragit RLPO binder solutions. Each placebo tablet comprised eight layers, preceded by six of the active components, and then another six of the placebo [51]. Captopril dosage forms were developed in some other studies using the TheriForm technique [47]. Mannitol was employed as the main active ingredient, with maltitol, maltodextrin, and polyvinyl pyrrolidone added as powders. Furthermore, binder jetting has been used in the manufacturing of tablets containing pseudoephedrine [52], acetaminophen [53], 5-fluorouracil [54], or amitriptyline hydrochloride [55].

8.7 Fused Deposition Modeling

The most prevalent kind of 3D printing is fused deposition modeling (FDM), often recognized as fused filament fabrication. Polymeric filaments comprising thermoplastic pharmaceuticals are developed and then fed into a printer, in which they melt at a specified temperature and are extruded through a device. After the printhead has been moved around on a raster platform, the first layer of the object is unloaded from the extruder onto the printer platform. As the platform is lowered between each layer's deposition, the resulting structure becomes denser. As they cool, the filaments bond to the one below them. Each step is repeated until a finished 3D object is created. Most printers' printhead temperatures are adjustable, allowing for the use of a wide range of polymers and polymer blends [56]. Hot melt extrusion (HME) is commonly used to prepare the filaments for FDM, which incorporates the drug into the polymer along with several excipients. In the HME method, the mixture is melted using heat and pressure in a barrel-shaped extrusion system based on screws. The system is powered by an electric motor. As the mixture cools, it solidifies into the filament that will be used as the feedstock for FDM [56, 57]. Because of its low price, high-printing-precision-assured quality parameters, and incorporation of HME [58], FDM has found widespread application in the pharmaceutical industry. Since direct powder 3D printing (DPP) is a one-step FDM technique that eliminates the need for HME, investigations on it have been done. Furthermore, a powder blend was heated and printed to produce tablets with a honeycomb structure [59]. For this purpose, a stainless steel extrusion cartridge was filled with the powder.

8.8 Selective Laser Sintering

In selective laser sintering, a 3D solid is created by heating powder particles with a laser until they fuse. Selective laser sintering (SLS) systems typically consist of a spreading platform, powder bed, and laser system. Before using a roller blade to smooth down the surface, the spreading machine applies a homogeneous layer of powder throughout the deck. The characteristics of the final product dictate the predetermined scanning pattern for the two-dimensionally moving laser system. Fusion by melting is achieved by increasing the temperature of the material below its melting point and focusing the laser beam on the newly created surface by adjusting the height of the bed. Loose powder on the base helps sustain weight during the procedure. Every time a new layer of powder is deposited and fused, the bed is lowered by one layer's worth of height. The process is continued until the desired 3D-printed item is complete, at which point it is removed from the printer and allowed to cool before being collected from the loose powder by hand or with a sieve [60]. The approach is preferable since it just requires one simple step, the manufacturing time is shortened significantly, and no solvent is used. Because of the pinpoint accuracy of the laser, the resulting objects also have a great degree of detail [61].

8.9 Pressure-Assisted Micro-Syringe

Pressure-assisted micro-syringes operate by feeding a semi-solid material into a syringe-shaped head and, afterward, extruding the material in a continuous, layer-by-layer fashion to create a 3D-printed object. A piston mechanism, such as a mechanical one, a pneumatic one, or a solenoid one, can be used to effect the extrusion. A semi-solid mixture with print-friendly qualities is made by combining a polymer with a solvent and any other required excipients. Due to the use of solvents, drying time after printing is critical to prevent any shrinkage or distortion of the final product. A further risk is that the printed item will collapse if the deposited layer is not strong enough to support the weight of the subsequent layers. Lack of extreme heat is the method's key selling point [62].

8.10 The Possibility of 3D Printing in Individualized Medicine

The capacity to personalize dose forms for specific patients is one of the most exciting applications of 3D printing in the pharmaceutical industry. It can be achieved by tailoring the dosage forms' production, dosing, combination, and release patterns to the specific requirements of individual patients. The idea of using 3D printing to customize medicines provided by hospitals and community pharmacies is also highly cutting-edge. Although it has been shown that the technology can be used to create a variety of dose forms, the practical implementation of the technique requires adequate technological and legal backing. The technology undoubtedly paves the way for a future in which a patient's digital clinical data is delivered directly to a 3D printer, which then prints out a customized drug to fit the patient's specific therapeutic needs (Figure 8.2).

8.11 Dose Personalization

3D printing can help in achieving dosage flexibility based on individual patient demands. The therapeutic dose for children varies with their age and body weight; hence, the population is a prime candidate for dose variation. To provide the optimal dose for patients, 3D printers may be used to modify the aforementioned dosage forms. It is easily accomplished in ODF formulations by adjusting the volume of liquid API injected into the

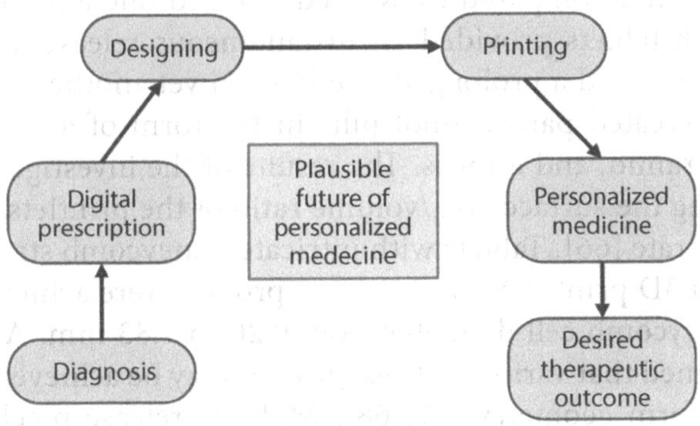

Figure 8.2 3D-printed medicine for individual patients.

film. Altering the size and form of ODFs is another way to tailor care for each patient [29]. Other dosage forms, such as pills or patches, also allow for the adjustment of dose strength to meet the individual requirements of patients. Pietrzak *et al.* [62] exploited FDM and HME to print theophylline tablets varied in strength from 60 to 300 mg by altering the print size. During the past few years, people have started breaking tablets in half by hand or using a splitter so they may adjust the dosage as needed. The numerous characterization criteria of the subdivided tablets do not always meet the pharmacopoeial requirements, proving the strategy to be useless. It was determined that the 3D-printed split tablets were more precise, secure, and adaptable than the traditional tablets [62]. Little tablets, sometimes known as "pellets" or "mini-prints," have been made using 3D printing technology, and they may be customized. They are also useful for combining two medications. Customization of the appropriate dosage may also be accomplished by the combination and encapsulation of mini-printlets [63].

8.12 Modifying Release Profiles

Dosage formulations with individualized release characteristics are now possible due to 3D printing. Changing the tablet's geometry and form is one method of achieving the goal. It was determined that lowering the tablet thickness or creating gaps in them boosted the drug release rates and that total release was attained at periods as low as 5 min [64]. It led to the development of immediate-release tablets of low-dosage medications. Several paracetamol tablet shapes, including ring and mesh, were created and compared by Khaled *et al.* to one another and solid tablets. Mesh tablets provided an instantaneous release, but ring and solid tablets showed a prolonged one [65]. In yet another investigation, researchers created paracetamol pills in the form of a cube, a disc, a sphere, a pyramid, and a torus. The results of the investigation showed that changing the surface area/volume ratio of the printlets affected the drug release rate [66]. Tablets with intricate honeycomb structures were printed on a 3D printer. Several release profiles were achieved by altering the honeycomb cell diameter from 0.20 to 1.83 mm. As a result, it was determined that various release profiles may be achieved by altering the dosage form geometry [67, 68]. Multiple-release mechanism tablets were also successfully manufactured. Several of these pills have two parts with different release mechanisms dependent on pH. It was possible to generate breakaway tablets that disintegrated into three pieces, each of which contained two drug subunits that eroded in 45 min in an environment resembling the GIT. Biphasic release pills with peaks at 1 and 8 h, known as enteric dual pulsatory tablets, were also produced. Moreover, dual pulsatory tablets were developed with two sections with contrasting pH-based solubility: one section eroded in the acid-dissolving stage within 30 min and the other section eroded in the higher pH stage at 5 h later [51].

8.13 Combination Tablets—Polypills

The idea of a "polypill" is one of 3D printing's most promising uses in the field of customized medicine. Specifically designed for someone taking many medications at once, a "polypill" combines multiple pills into one convenient pill. As a bonus, the dosage and timing of the medication delivery can be adjusted on an individual basis. The elderly population stands to gain the most from the idea since it has the potential to increase compliance and adherence to medicine while decreasing the total amount of tablets taken each day. Researchers Khaled *et al.* examined the effectiveness of 3D-printed polypills including three drugs as a possible treatment for diabetes with hypertension. Captopril serves as the osmotic compartment, while nifedipine and glipizide are included within the sustained-release portions of the tablet [69]. The same group of people also designed a five-part polypill that represents a cardiovascular treatment plan. Two of the chambers are designed for quick-release drugs like aspirin and hydrochlorothiazide, whereas the remaining three are dedicated to longer-acting drugs like pravastatin, atenolol, and ramipril [70]. Polypill capsules with variable release patterns for different medications were then developed using the 3D-printing technique. This was achieved with the help of FDM and hot-filling syringes. The research group developed multiple capsule skeletons, each with four compartments: one with a concentrical configuration, showing two external surface compartments for easy connection and two inner compartments for potential release, and another that had a parallel combination, designed to showcase non-dissolving compartment shells with special pass subways and decomposition rate-limiting pores, designed for use with the early and delayed release. Polyvinyl alcohol and polylactic acid are combined to create the capsule shell. By adjusting the layer thickness in the concentric arrangement and the diameter of the rate-limiting apertures in the parallel arrangement, researchers were able to create release profiles that met our specific objectives [71].

8.14 3D Printing for Everybody

8.14.1 Medical Pediatric Treatment

Children's varying preferences in dose, flavor, and appearance/scent make them the most finicky of customers. Although oral administration may first appear simpler, it may become rather complicated when dealing with youngsters. A young patient may be resistant to a certain dose form due to personal preferences in factors including appearance, flavor, and texture. Here's where 3D printing comes in, providing customized solutions [72]. One of the biggest challenges in treating kids is giving them the right dosages based on their weight, but 3D printing can help with that. ODF formulations, rapidly dissolving tablets, and mini-pills manufactured by 3D printing appear to be appropriate for administration, even though swallowing is a worry in younger children. Children, according to research focusing on their preferences for dose forms, showed a clear preference for mini-tablets of 4 mm in diameter [73]. Another study found that ODF formulations are preferable to unit dosage sachets of oral powder when treating children [74]. When children are given dose forms in the taste and color of their choosing, they are more likely to take their medication as prescribed. Chewable tablets of isoleucine were 3D-printed by Goyanes *et al.* in a trial for the treatment of maple syrup urine illness. They were able to print tablets in a variety of dosages to meet the needs of pediatric patients as well as tablets in flavors (lemon, coconut, banana, raspberry, etc.) and colors (yellow, black, light green, orange, etc.) to meet the preferences of those individuals [74]. Another research successfully created a variety of chewable chocolate-based dose forms [75, 76] that were safe for youngsters to use.

8.14.2 Tending to Geriatrics

As aging progresses, swallowing pills becomes more difficult for most elderly people, which might impact medication compliance [77]. Oro-dispersible film formulations and rapidly disintegrating tablets, both of which are possible to create with 3D printing, can overcome the problem. The problems associated with polypharmacy are exacerbated by the fact that the elderly population suffers from various diseases and requires several medications and extended therapy [77]. The problem of polypharmacy can be overcome with the help of polypills made to order using 3D-printing technology. Cognitive impairment (dementia) affects the ability of some of these patients to take their medicine as prescribed. 3D-printed dose forms which incorporate embossing patterns to signify administration time, administration date, and/or administration month are presently being considered as a potential solution to the problem [78].

8.15 3D Printing in a Clinical Setting

Research shows that people have no problems taking their medications in 3D-printed dose forms. The vast majority of people surveyed had a favorable impression of 3D-printed pharmaceuticals. The technology has the potential to play a significant role shortly in hospitals and hospital pharmacies to administer individualized medicinal items. It entails a thorough evaluation of each patient and the creation of custom dose forms [79]. A patient's medical condition is diagnosed and evaluated upon admission to the hospital in a hypothetical scenario. Age, weight, the existence of other diseases, previous treatments, and lifestyle choices will also be considered. Tests on bodily fluids would also factor in the hereditary factors. The information might be used to complete the person's profile with all relevant facts. The patient's unique treatment plan and medication would be determined by the information in the profile. Then, multiple databases and AI systems might be used to determine which dose forms were the most appropriate. The medication's dose form may then be manufactured with the use of a 3D printer already available at the hospital, thanks to the use of CAD software. The drug can be administered to the patient when it has undergone adequate quality assurance testing. After that, the patient was checked in again and the time asked for their opinion. All of it can go more quickly with the help of modern testing, data processing, and 3D-printing technologies, which might be useful in a clinical context.

8.15.1 Challenges

Although 3D printing offers many advantages in the pharmaceutical industry, it also has certain drawbacks. Significant issues exist in the fields of pharmacy technology, dosage form manufacture, patient safety, quality assurance, government regulation, and clinical pharmacy.

8.15.2 Technology

All the different kinds of 3D printers have their technological limitations, which have been discussed above. Systems based on nozzles run the risk of having their nozzles clog, while those reliant on heat or light might have their API degrade with time. The incompatibility between drugs and excipients is a significant difficulty that must be overcome. In addition, numerous production parameters must be optimized to solve structural and surface flaws in the final product.

8.15.3 Safety Aspects

The issue of safety also has to be resolved. When some materials are heated, extruded, or fused, they can release poisonous airborne debris that can irritate the lungs and skin. To lessen the potential for injury, standard operating procedures and other safety measures must be followed [80].

8.15.4 Clinical Pharmacy Practice

There are several obstacles to overcome when introducing 3D printing to hospitals. In the beginning, it may appear unrealistic because it calls for highly qualified technical operators to be present at the site to manage the technical components. Another difficulty is ensuring the quality of the printed dosage forms, which necessitates the development of processes that are both practical and non-destructive. To combat this, several process analytical technologies (PAT) have been implemented to keep tabs on the product's quality. Near-infrared spectroscopy and Raman confocal microscopy, two aspects of the PAT model, have been demonstrated to be highly reliable for tracking the concentration of drugs and distribution in tablets and oral films [81]. The expense of putting 3D printers in hospitals needs to be weighed as well, of course. To fulfill the needs of customized medicine in a clinical context, packaging and labeling regulations must also be considered [80]. The aforementioned drawbacks and benefits of each printing platform mean that it is impossible to say with certainty which printer would be most suited for use in a healthcare context. Hence, innovations in technology are needed to create "the perfect 3D printer" for clinical applications, one that is rapid, user-friendly, affordable, and has great resolution.

8.16 Regulatory Aspects

The lack of a regulatory framework is also a key roadblock to the widespread use of technology in the pharmaceutical industry. The FDA released regulations for the production of medical devices in 2017 [82] in the form of guidelines. Many 3D-printed medical equipment have been cleared for use by the Food and Drug Administration, but only one drug has been authorized for 3D printing so far. As of yet, no regulatory body has set standards for the production of 3D-printed dosage forms. Furthermore, it is unclear at the moment if regulatory approval will be provided only for the final version or for an entire set of requirements that would apply to all parts and stages of a manufacturer's development and production [80, 81]. To ensure patient safety and efficacy, the FDA would need significant clinical trials if a tablet included more than one medicine, as it would be deemed a new combination drug composition. Every organization which intends to use a 3D printer for the manufacture or distribution of pharmaceuticals should additionally have their facility certified as meeting the Good Manufacturing Practice (GMP) standards. To end, it is necessary to establish uniform regulations for the production and distribution of pharmaceuticals [82].

8.17 Conclusion

The pharmaceutical sector is going to benefit greatly from the recent explosion of 3D-printing technology, which might lead to a transition from mass production to on-demand individualized dose forms, ultimately providing patients with easy accessibility to safer and more effective medications. The healthcare system may hinge on its ability to revolutionize traditional pharmacy. The technique has applications outside the clinic since it may be used to create novel dosage forms with sophisticated geometric and pharmacokinetic properties. The Food and Drug Administration's green light for Spritam was a watershed moment for 3D printing, and the sector has seen a flood of promising studies in the years afterward. The pharmaceutical industry may benefit tremendously from the use of 3D printing because of the rapid manufacturing speed, low cost, and formulation flexibility it offers. Moreover, to develop a 3D printer appropriate to be utilized in a healthcare setting, it is necessary to assess the advantages and disadvantages of various platforms. Despite the benefits and considerable developments, the pharmaceutical sector has yet to fully adopt this technology. The many challenges, particularly those that have a technical, quality control, and regulatory character, are to blame. Also, appropriate regulatory criteria for the application of this technology in clinical settings must be developed. Once these issues are resolved, the pharmaceutical industry will have no choice but to fully adopt the technology. Once this is achieved, customized medicine, with the potential to completely transform the healthcare system, may be viewed as part of a bright, technological future.

References

1. Litman, T., Personalized medicine—Concepts, technologies, and applications in inflammatory skin diseases. *APMIS*, 127, 5, 386–424, 2019 May.
2. Žitnik, I.P., Černe, D., Mancini, I., Simi, L., Pazzagli, M., Di Resta, C., Podgornik, H., Lampret, B.R., Podkrajšek, K.T., Sipeky, C., Van Schaik, R., Personalized laboratory medicine: A patient-centered future approach. *Clin. Chem. Lab. Med. (CCLM)*, 56, 12, 1981–91, 2018 Dec 1.
3. Florence, A.T. and Siepmann, J., Dosage forms for personalized medicine: From the simple to the complex, in: *Modern Pharmaceutics*, vol. 2, pp. 511–530, CRC Press, Boca Raton, Florida, 2016 Apr 19.
4. Mathur, S. and Sutton, J., Personalized medicine could transform healthcare. *Biomed. Rep.*, 7, 1, 3–5, 2017 Jul 1.
5. Yao, R., Xu, G., Mao, S.S., Yang, H.Y., Sang, X.T., Sun, W., Mao, Y.L., Three-dimensional printing: Review of application in medicine and hepatic surgery. *Cancer Biol. Med.*, 13, 4, 443, 2016 Dec.
6. Robles Martinez, P., Pharmaceutical applications of stereolithography (SLA) 3D printing, Doctoral dissertation, UCL (University College London), London, 2019.
7. Pandey, M., Choudhury, H., Fern, J.L., Kee, A.T., Kou, J., Jing, J.L., Her, H.C., Yong, H.S., Ming, H.C., Bhattamisra, S.K., Gorain, B., 3D printing for oral drug delivery: A new tool to customize drug delivery. *Drug Deliv. Transl. Res.*, 10, 986–1001, 2020 Aug.
8. Trenfield, S.J., Awad, A., Goyanes, A., Gaisford, S., Basit, A.W., 3D printing pharmaceuticals: Drug development to frontline care. *Trends Pharmacol. Sci.*, 39, 5, 440–51, 2018 May 1.
9. Savini, A. and Savini, G.G., A short history of 3D printing, a technological revolution just started, in: *2015 ICOHTEC/IEEE International History of High-Technologies and Their Socio-Cultural Contexts Conference (HISTELCON)*, 2015 Aug 18, IEEE, pp. 1–8.
10. Min, J.K., Mosadegh, B., Dunham, S., Al'Aref, S.J. (Eds.), *3D Printing Applications in Cardiovascular Medicine*, Academic Press, London, United Kingdom, 2018 Jul 4.
11. Prasad, L.K. and Smyth, H., 3D Printing technologies for drug delivery: A review. *Drug Dev. Ind. Pharm.*, 42, 7, 1019–31, 2016 Jul 2.
12. Jiménez, M., Romero, L., Domínguez, I.A., Espinosa, M.D., Domínguez, M., Additive manufacturing technologies: An overview about 3D printing methods and future prospects. *Complexity*, 2019, 1–30, 2019 Feb 19.
13. Water, J.J., Bohr, A., Boetker, J., Aho, J., Sandler, N., Nielsen, H.M., Rantanen, J., Three-dimensional printing of drug-eluting implants: Preparation of an antimicrobial polylactide feedstock material. *J. Pharm. Sci.*, 104, 3, 1099–107, 2015 Mar 1.
14. Ballard, D.H., Trace, A.P., Ali, S., Hodgdon, T., Zygmont, M.E., DeBenedectis, C.M., Smith, S.E., Richardson, M.L., Patel, M.J., Decker, S.J., Lenchik, L.,

Clinical applications of 3D printing: Primer for radiologists. *Acad. Radiol.*, 25, 1, 52–65, 2018 Jan 1.
15. Trenfield, S.J., Madla, C.M., Basit, A.W., Gaisford, S., Binder jet printing in pharmaceutical manufacturing, in: *3D Printing of Pharmaceuticals*, pp. 41–54, 2018.
16. Goole, J. and Amighi, K., 3D printing in pharmaceutics: A new tool for designing customized drug delivery systems. *Int. J. Pharm.*, 499, 1-2, 376–94, 2016 Feb 29.
17. Kotta, S., Nair, A., Alsabeelah, N., 3D printing technology in drug delivery: Recent progress and application. *Curr. Pharm. Des.*, 24, 42, 5039–48, 2018 Nov 1.
18. AziziMachekposhti, S., Mohaved, S., Narayan, R.J., Inkjet dispensing technologies: Recent advances for novel drug discovery. *Expert Opin. Drug Discov.*, 14, 2, 101–13, 2019 Feb 1.
19. Daly, R., Harrington, T.S., Martin, G.D., Hutchings, I.M., Inkjet printing for pharmaceutics–a review of research and manufacturing. *Int. J. Pharm.*, 494, 2, 554–67, 2015 Oct 30.
20. Içten, E., Giridhar, A., Taylor, L.S., Nagy, Z.K., Reklaitis, G.V., Dropwise additive manufacturing of pharmaceutical products for melt-based dosage forms. *J. Pharm. Sci.*, 104, 5, 1641–9, 2015 May 1.
21. Alomari, M., Mohamed, F.H., Basit, A.W., Gaisford, S., Personalised dosing: Printing a dose of one's own medicine. *Int. J. Pharm.*, 494, 2, 568–77, 2015 Oct 30.
22. Lamichhane, S., Bashyal, S., Keum, T., Noh, G., Seo, J.E., Bastola, R., Choi, J., Sohn, D.H., Lee, S., Complex formulations, simple techniques: Can 3D printing technology be the Midas touch in pharmaceutical industry? *Asian J. Pharm. Sci.*, 14, 5, 465–79, 2019 Sep 1.
23. Acosta-Vélez, G.F. and Wu, B.M., 3D pharming: Direct printing of personalized pharmaceutical tablets. *Polym. Sci.*, 2, 1, 11, 2016.
24. Vadodaria, S. and Mills, T., Jetting-based 3D printing of edible materials. *Food Hydrocolloids*, 106, 105857, 2020 Sep 1.
25. Kollamaram, G., Faucher, A., Croker, D.M., Walker, G.M., Valvejet technology for the production of a personalised fixed dose combination of ramipril and glimepiride: An investigative study on the stability of ramipril. *Pharm. Res.*, 35, 1–5, 2018 Sep.
26. Kollamaram, G., Hopkins, S.C., Glowacki, B.A., Croker, D.M., Walker, G.M., Inkjet printing of paracetamol and indomethacin using electromagnetic technology: Rheological compatibility and polymorphic selectivity. *Eur. J. Pharm. Sci.*, 115, 248–57, 2018 Mar 30.
27. Ehtezazi, T., Dempster, N.M., Martin, G.D., Hoath, S.D., Hutchings, I.M., Development of high-throughput glass inkjet devices for pharmaceutical applications. *J. Pharm. Sci.*, 103, 11, 3733–42, 2014 Nov 1.
28. Clark, E.A., Alexander, M.R., Irvine, D.J., Roberts, C.J., Wallace, M.J., Sharpe, S., Yoo, J., Hague, R.J., Tuck, C.J., Wildman, R.D., 3D printing of

tablets using inkjet with UV photoinitiation. *Int. J. Pharm.*, 529, 1-2, 523–30, 2017 Aug 30.
29. Musazzi, U.M., Khalid, G.M., Selmin, F., Minghetti, P., Cilurzo, F., Trends in the production methods of orodispersible films. *Int. J. Pharm.*, 576, 118963, 2020 Feb 25.
30. Thabet, Y., Lunter, D., Breitkreutz, J., Continuous inkjet printing of enalapril maleate onto orodispersible film formulations. *Int. J. Pharm.*, 546, 1-2, 180–7, 2018 Jul 30.
31. Vakili, H., Nyman, J.O., Genina, N., Preis, M., Sandler, N., Application of a colorimetric technique in quality control for printed pediatric orodispersible drug delivery systems containing propranolol hydrochloride. *Int. J. Pharm.*, 511, 1, 606–18, 2016 Sep 10.
32. Alomari, M., Vuddanda, P.R., Trenfield, S.J., Dodoo, C.C., Velaga, S., Basit, A.W., Gaisford, S., Printing T3 and T4 oral drug combinations as a novel strategy for hypothyroidism. *Int. J. Pharm.*, 549, 1-2, 363–9, 2018 Oct 5.
33. Eleftheriadis, G.K., Katsiotis, C.S., Andreadis, D.A., Tzetzis, D., Ritzoulis, C., Bouropoulos, N., Kanellopoulou, D., Andriotis, E.G., Tsibouklis, J., Fatouros, D.G., Inkjet printing of a thermolabile model drug onto FDM-printed substrates: Formulation and evaluation. *Drug Dev. Ind. Pharm.*, 46, 8, 1253–64, 2020 Aug 2.
34. Palo, M., Kogermann, K., Laidmae, I., Meos, A., Preis, M., Heinamaki, J., Sandler, N., Development of oromucosal dosage forms by combining electrospinning and inkjet printing. *Mol. Pharmaceutics*, 14, 3, 808–20, 2017 Mar 6.
35. Iftimi, L.D., Edinger, M., Bar-Shalom, D., Rantanen, J., Genina, N., Edible solid foams as porous substrates for inkjet-printable pharmaceuticals. *Eur. J. Pharm. Biopharm.*, 136, 38–47, 2019 Mar 1.
36. Montenegro-Nicolini, M., Reyes, P.E., Jara, M.O., Vuddanda, P.R., Neira-Carrillo, A., Butto, N., Velaga, S., Morales, J.O., The effect of inkjet printing over polymeric films as potential buccal biologics delivery systems. *AAPS PharmSciTech*, 19, 3376–87, 2018 Nov.
37. Montenegro-Nicolini, M., Miranda, V., Morales, J.O., Inkjet printing of proteins: An experimental approach. *AAPS J.*, 19, 234–43, 2017 Jan.
38. Arshad, M.S., Shahzad, A., Abbas, N., AlAsiri, A., Hussain, A., Kucuk, I., Chang, M.W., Bukhari, N.I., Ahmad, Z., Preparation and characterization of indomethacin loaded films by piezoelectric inkjet printing: A personalized medication approach. *Pharm. Dev. Technol.*, 25, 2, 197–205, 2020 Feb 7.
39. Pere, C.P., Economidou, S.N., Lall, G., Ziraud, C., Boateng, J.S., Alexander, B.D., Lamprou, D.A., Douroumis, D., 3D printed microneedles for insulin skin delivery. *Int. J. Pharm.*, 544, 2, 425–32, 2018 Jun 15.
40. Boehm, R.D., Miller, P.R., Daniels, J., Stafslien, S., Narayan, R.J., Inkjet printing for pharmaceutical applications. *Mater. Today*, 17, 5, 247–52, 2014 Jun 1.
41. Boehm, R.D., Daniels, J., Stafslien, S., Nasir, A., Lefebvre, J., Narayan, R.J., Polyglycolic acid microneedles modified with inkjet-deposited antifungal coatings. *Biointerphases*, 10, 1, 011004, 2015 Mar 2.

42. Içten, E., Purohit, H.S., Wallace, C., Giridhar, A., Taylor, L.S., Nagy, Z.K., Reklaitis, G.V., Dropwise additive manufacturing of pharmaceutical products for amorphous and self emulsifying drug delivery systems. *Int. J. Pharm.*, 524, 1-2, 424–32, 2017 May 30.
43. Clark, E.A., Alexander, M.R., Irvine, D.J., Roberts, C.J., Wallace, M.J., Yoo, J., Wildman, R.D., Making tablets for delivery of poorly soluble drugs using photoinitiated 3D inkjet printing. *Int. J. Pharm.*, 578, 118805, 2020 Mar 30.
44. Cader, H.K., Rance, G.A., Alexander, M.R., Gonçalves, A.D., Roberts, C.J., Tuck, C.J., Wildman, R.D., Water-based 3D inkjet printing of an oral pharmaceutical dosage form. *Int. J. Pharm.*, 564, 359–68, 2019 Jun 10.
45. Stirling, F., Naydich, A., Bramante, J., Barocio, R., Certo, M., Wellington, H., Redfield, E., O'Keefe, S., Gao, S., Cusolito, A., Way, J., Synthetic cassettes for pH-mediated sensing, counting, and containment. *Cell Rep.*, 30, 9, 3139–48, 2020 Mar 3.
46. Wickström, H., Hilgert, E., Nyman, J.O., Desai, D., ŞenKaraman, D., De Beer, T., Sandler, N., Rosenholm, J.M., Inkjet printing of drug-loaded mesoporous silica nanoparticles—A platform for drug development. *Molecules*, 22, 11, 2020, 2017 Nov 21.
47. Lee, K.J., Kang, A., Delfino, J.J., West, T.G., Chetty, D., Monkhouse, D.C., Yoo, J., Evaluation of critical formulation factors in the development of a rapidly dispersing captopril oral dosage form. *Drug Dev. Ind. Pharm.*, 29, 9, 967–79, 2003 Jan 1.
48. Tian, P., Yang, F., Yu, L.P., Lin, M.M., Lin, W., Lin, Q.F., Lv, Z.F., Huang, S.Y., Chen, Y.Z., Applications of excipients in the field of 3D printed pharmaceuticals. *Drug Dev. Ind. Pharm.*, 45, 6, 905–13, 2019 Jun 3.
49. Infanger, S., Haemmerli, A., Iliev, S., Baier, A., Stoyanov, E., Quodbach, J., Powder bed 3D-printing of highly loaded drug delivery devices with hydroxypropyl cellulose as solid binder. *Int. J. Pharm.*, 555, 198–206, 2019 Jan 30.
50. Wilts, E.M., Ma, D., Bai, Y., Williams, C.B., Long, T.E., Comparison of linear and 4-arm star poly (vinyl pyrrolidone) for aqueous binder jetting additive manufacturing of personalized dosage tablets. *ACS Appl. Mater. Interfaces*, 11, 27, 23938–47, 2019 Jun 6.
51. Katstra, W.E., Palazzolo, R.D., Rowe, C.W., Giritlioglu, B., Teung, P., Cima, M.J., Oral dosage forms fabricated by Three Dimensional Printing™. *J. Control. Release*, 66, 1, 1–9, 2000 May 3.
52. Wang, C.C., Tejwani, M.R., Roach, W.J., Kay, J.L., Yoo, J., Surprenant, H.L., Monkhouse, D.C., Pryor, T.J., Development of near zero-order release dosage forms using three-dimensional printing (3-DP™) technology. *Drug Dev. Ind. Pharm.*, 32, 3, 367–76, 2006 Jan 1.
53. Yu, D.G., Branford-White, C., Ma, Z.H., Zhu, L.M., Li, X.Y., Yang, X.L., Novel drug delivery devices for providing linear release profiles fabricated by 3DP. *Int. J. Pharm.*, 370, 1-2, 160–6, 2009 Mar 31.

54. Shi, K., Tan, D.K., Nokhodchi, A., Maniruzzaman, M., Drop-on-powder 3D printing of tablets with an anti-cancer drug, 5-fluorouracil. *Pharmaceutics*, 11, 4, 150, 2019 Apr 1.
55. Sen, K., Manchanda, A., Mehta, T., Ma, A.W., Chaudhuri, B., Formulation design for inkjet-based 3D printed tablets. *Int. J. Pharm.*, 584, 119430, 2020 Jun 30.
56. Awad, A., Trenfield, S.J., Gaisford, S., Basit, A.W., 3D printed medicines: A new branch of digital healthcare. *Int. J. Pharm.*, 548, 1, 586–96, 2018 Sep 5.
57. Shaqour, B., Samaro, A., Verleije, B., Beyers, K., Vervaet, C., Cos, P., Production of drug delivery systems using fused filament fabrication: A systematic review. *Pharmaceutics*, 12, 6, 517, 2020 Jun 5.
58. Araújo, M.R., Sa-Barreto, L.L., Gratieri, T., Gelfuso, G.M., Cunha-Filho, M., The digital pharmacies era: How 3D printing technology using fused deposition modeling can become a reality. *Pharmaceutics*, 11, 3, 128, 2019 Mar 19.
59. Charoo, N.A., Barakh Ali, S.F., Mohamed, E.M., Kuttolamadom, M.A., Ozkan, T., Khan, M.A., Rahman, Z., Selective laser sintering 3D printing–an overview of the technology and pharmaceutical applications. *Drug Dev. Ind. Pharm.*, 46, 6, 869–77, 2020 Jun 2.
60. Charoo, N.A., Barakh Ali, S.F., Mohamed, E.M., Kuttolamadom, M.A., Ozkan, T., Khan, M.A., Rahman, Z., Selective laser sintering 3D printing–an overview of the technology and pharmaceutical applications. *Drug Dev. Ind. Pharm.*, 46, 6, 869–77, 2020 Jun 2.
61. Azad, M.A., Olawuni, D., Kimbell, G., Badruddoza, A.Z., Hossain, M.S., Sultana, T., Polymers for extrusion-based 3D printing of pharmaceuticals: A holistic materials–process perspective. *Pharmaceutics*, 12, 2, 124, 2020 Feb 3.
62. Pietrzak, K., Isreb, A., Alhnan, M.A., A flexible-dose dispenser for immediate and extended release 3D printed tablets. *Eur. J. Pharm. Biopharm.*, 96, 380–7, 2015 Oct 1.
63. Keerthi, M.L., Kiran, R.S., Rao, V.U., Sannapu, A., Dutt, A.G., Krishna, K.S., Evaluation aspects: A review multi unit dosage forms. *Int. J. Pharm.*, 28, 40, 214–21, 2014.
64. Gültekin, H.E., Tort, S., Acartürk, F., An effective technology for the development of immediate release solid dosage forms containing low-dose drug: Fused deposition modeling 3D printing. *Pharm. Res.*, 36, 1–3, 2019 Sep.
65. Khaled, S.A., Alexander, M.R., Irvine, D.J., Wildman, R.D., Wallace, M.J., Sharpe, S., Yoo, J., Roberts, C.J., Extrusion 3D printing of paracetamol tablets from a single formulation with tunable release profiles through control of tablet geometry. *AAPS PharmSciTech*, 19, 3403–13, 2018 Nov.
66. Martinez, P.R., Goyanes, A., Basit, A.W., Gaisford, S., Influence of geometry on the drug release profiles of stereolithographic (SLA) 3D-printed tablets. *AAPS PharmSciTech*, 19, 3355–61, 2018 Nov.
67. Kyobula, M., Adedeji, A., Alexander, M.R., Saleh, E., Wildman, R., Ashcroft, I., Gellert, P.R., Roberts, C.J., 3D inkjet printing of tablets exploiting bespoke

complex geometries for controlled and tuneable drug release. *J. Control. Release*, 261, 207–15, 2017 Sep 10.

68. Sheridan, G.K., Wdowicz, A., Pickering, M., Watters, O., Halley, P., O'Sullivan, N.C., Mooney, C., O'Connell, D.J., O'Connor, J.J., Murphy, K.J., CX3CL1 is up-regulated in the rat hippocampus during memory-associated synaptic plasticity. *Front. Cell. Neurosci.*, 8, 233, 2014 Aug 12.
69. Khaled, S.A., Burley, J.C., Alexander, M.R., Yang, J., Roberts, C.J., 3D printing of five-in-one dose combination polypill with defined immediate and sustained release profiles. *J. Control. Release*, 217, 308–14, 2015 Nov 10.
70. Pereira, B.C., Isreb, A., Isreb, M., Forbes, R.T., Oga, E.F., Alhnan, M.A., Additive manufacturing of a Point-of-Care "Polypill:" Fabrication of concept capsules of complex geometry with bespoke release against cardiovascular disease. *Adv. Healthcare Mater.*, 9, 13, 2000236, 2020 Jul.
71. Preis, M. and Öblom, H., 3D-printed drugs for children—Are we ready yet? *AAPS PharmSciTech*, 18, 303–8, 2017 Feb.
72. vanRiet-Nales, D.A., de Neef, B.J., Schobben, A.F., Ferreira, J.A., Egberts, T.C., Rademaker, C.M., Acceptability of different oral formulations in infants and preschool children. *Arch. Dis. Child.*, 98, 9, 725–31, 2013 Sep 1.
73. Öblom, H., Sjöholm, E., Rautamo, M., Sandler, N., Towards printed pediatric medicines in hospital pharmacies: Comparison of 2D and 3D-printed orodispersible warfarin films with conventional oral powders in unit dose sachets. *Pharmaceutics*, 11, 7, 334, 2019 Jul 14.
74. Goyanes, A., Madla, C.M., Umerji, A., Piñeiro, G.D., Montero, J.M., Diaz, M.J., Barcia, M.G., Taherali, F., Sánchez-Pintos, P., Couce, M.L., Gaisford, S., Automated therapy preparation of isoleucine formulations using 3D printing for the treatment of MSUD: First single-centre, prospective, crossover study in patients. *Int. J. Pharm.*, 567, 118497, 2019 Aug 15.
75. Karavasili, C., Gkaragkounis, A., Moschakis, T., Ritzoulis, C., Fatouros, D.G., Pediatric-friendly chocolate-based dosage forms for the oral administration of both hydrophilic and lipophilic drugs fabricated with extrusion-based 3D printing. *Eur. J. Pharm. Sci.*, 147, 105291, 2020 Apr 30.
76. Boateng, J., Drug delivery innovations to address global health challenges for pediatric and geriatric populations (through improvements in patient compliance). *J. Pharm. Sci.*, 106, 11, 3188–98, 2017 Nov 1.
77. Fastø, M.M., Genina, N., Kaae, S., KälvemarkSporrong, S., Perceptions, preferences and acceptability of patient designed 3D printed medicine by polypharmacy patients: A pilot study. *Int. J. Clin. Pharm.*, 41, 5, 1290–8, 2019 Oct.
78. Awad, A., Yao, A., Trenfield, S.J., Goyanes, A., Gaisford, S., Basit, A.W., 3D printed tablets (printlets) with braille and moon patterns for visually impaired patients. *Pharmaceutics*, 12, 2, 172, 2020 Feb.
79. Goyanes, A., Scarpa, M., Kamlow, M., Gaisford, S., Basit, A.W., Orlu, M., Patient acceptability of 3D printed medicines. *Int. J. Pharm.*, 530, 1-2, 71–8, 2017 Sep 15.

80. Gioumouxouzis, C.I., Karavasili, C., Fatouros, D.G., Recent advances in pharmaceutical dosage forms and devices using additive manufacturing technologies. *Drug Discov. Today*, 24, 2, 636–43, 2019 Feb 1.
81. Trenfield, S.J., Goyanes, A., Telford, R., Wilsdon, D., Rowland, M., Gaisford, S., Basit, A.W., 3D printed drug products: Non-destructive dose verification using a rapid point-and-shoot approach. *Int. J. Pharm.*, 549, 1-2, 283–92, 2018 Oct 5.
82. Guidance, F.D., *Technical considerations for additive manufactured medical devices*, Food and Drug Administration, New Hampshire, NH, USA, 2017.

9

3D Printing Techniques in a Medical Setting

Abstract

One of the most pressing problems in modern medicine is the lack of available organ donors for transplant procedures. Traditional procedures always carry the risk of difficulties, additional injuries, and a scarcity of donors. These problems may be amenable to resolution using three-dimensional (3D)-printing technology, which might be used to print out replacement tissues and organs as well as to print out individualized tissue engineering scaffolds, repair tissue abnormalities *in situ* with cells, and so on. Besides a perfect anatomical match with the patient's injured tissue, 3D-printed organs and implants can also feature designed material microstructures and cell groupings that spur cell proliferation and differentiation. Hence, the needed tissue restoration can be accomplished with the help of these implants, and the issue of a lack of donors may one day be resolved. This chapter discusses various kinds of biomedical materials, summarizes pertinent research and recent breakthroughs on four levels, and examines current concerns and research challenges associated with 3D-printing materials and *in vitro* extracellular matrix construction for medicinal use.

Keywords: 3D printing, organ donors, xeno-transplantation, implantation, artificial organ transplantation, computed tomography, MRI scan, surgical therapy analysis, customizable fabrication

9.1 Introduction

The utilization of existing procedures, such as autotransplantation, xenotransplantation, and the implantation of artificial mechanical organs, still has issues, and lesions and deformities that necessitate tissue or organ transplantation continue to be pressing problems in clinical medicine [1]. Although auto-transplantation can have a beneficial outcome, it does so at the expense of the antilogous health system and may result in several problems and secondary injuries. Immunological rejection and antiviral infection are risks

---

Rishabha Malviya and Rishav Sharma. 3D Printing in Healthcare: Novel Applications, (167–186)

associated with xeno-transplantation, and the availability of source donors is limited. Artificial organ transplantation has proven effective in the clinic and has improved patients' quality of life. Human bionic tissue or organs can be generated on demand using three-dimensional (3D)-printing techniques, which would be expected to eliminate problems that have repeatedly hampered traditional techniques. Additive manufacturing, which encompasses 3D printing, works on the notion of layered manufacture or the overlapping of materials in subsequent phases. The technique facilitates the rapid production of components of any complicated shapes by precisely accumulating components using the design from a CAD model or computed tomography scan under computer control [2, 3]. Medical advances, implant materials, and cell printing have all benefited greatly from the recent surge in the 3D-printing market as a result of 3D printers' decreased production costs and better printing speed and precision. It is possible to print immediately at the problem site, build customized scaffolds rapidly, and print organ models using CT or MRI scan data. The potential to build synthetic tissue or organs with 3D-printing technology presents fresh approaches to the problem of a lack of donors. There are currently four primary research emphases on the subject of 3D printing in medicine: printing of tissues and organs [4–6], manufacturing of dysfunctional organ models for use in preoperative planning and surgical therapy analysis [3], customizable fabrication of permanent non-bioactive implants [2], and fabrication of locally bioactive and biodegradable scaffolds [3], and so on. Significant scientific progress and applications have been made in these disciplines, although they are still distant from being widely used in clinical settings due to several critical technological and fundamental scientific hurdles that need to be answered. Transplantation of organs and tissues from deceased or living donors is a modern remedy to organ failure caused by trauma, congenital abnormalities, advanced age, etc. (Figure 9.1). Due to the scarcity of organ donors, however, only a lucky handful receive transplants. Additionally, organ transplant operations are so costly that they are unaffordable for most people. The scarcity of tissue-matching donors is another hurdle in the way of the widespread use of transplant surgery.

9.2 Medical 3D Printing on Four Different Levels

9.2.1 Organ Models for Preoperative Diagnosis and Treatment Evaluation

Clinical therapy and medical education benefit greatly from the use of high-fidelity physical organ models. Time and money are wasted in

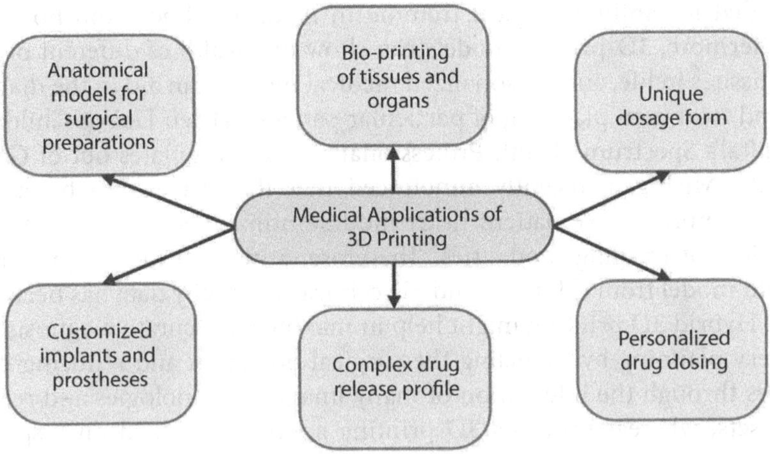

Figure 9.1 Different medical applications of 3D-printing technology.

traditional manufacturing procedures like casting and forging that do not take into account the patients' unique anatomy [7]. As no tools are required for 3D printing, it can produce unique medical models quickly and cheaply. As their name implies, 3D-printed organ models are largely used to aid in surgical analysis and preoperative training. Personal, complicated 3D-printed medical models have the potential to improve communication between medical professionals and engineers as well as aid in the preoperative and operative phases of surgical procedures. Medical models and *in vitro* equipment can be used for a variety of purposes without worrying about biocompatibility, such as postoperative planning, prosthetic design, testing standards, etc. By combining HeLa cells with gelatin/alginate/fibrinogen hydrogels, researchers in China and the United States have created *in vitro* models of cervical cancer [8]. High-resolution 3D imaging of the tumor microenvironment has now become possible. HeLa cells, which seem flat and elongated on 2D tissue culture plates, adopt a spheroidal shape in the 3D hydrogel, in which they exhibit a smooth surface and abundant cell–cell interactions. Unlike 2D planar cultures, models in 3D structures can provide insight into tumor cell qualities, assisting researchers and physicians in recognizing tumor cell proliferation, differentiation, and metastasis. Using computed tomography (CT) and planar laser scanning on authentic human anatomical specimens, researchers at Australia's Monash University 3D-printed a human anatomical model out of a gypsum-like powder or plastic. High-resolution 3D-printed anatomical models, comprising limbs, chest, abdomen, head, and neck, are provided for anthropological training in medical schools and hospitals. Furthermore, 3D-printed models can show the health of different organs and tissues in life, and personalized medical models can aid in the diagnosis and treatment planning of particular patients. Helen DeVos Children's Hospital's Spectrum Health Professionals, which originates out of Grand Rapids, Michigan, recently announced that they have 3D-fabricated a more comprehensive patient heart module utilizing synthetic data from a variety of imaging modalities. Therefore, a method for 3D printing a hybrid model from CT scans and 3D echocardiography data has been created. Hybrid 3D printing might help in making an accurate diagnosis and surgery planning by modeling the surgical operation and reducing difficulties through the integration of many imaging technologies and related data sets, whereas previous 3D printing approaches relied on a specific imaging modality. In terms of size and longevity, 3D-printed models are far superior to their plastinated counterparts. Tissue groups can be represented by different colors or materials. Challenges remain, however, and these include a lack of multi-materials that closely resemble the organ or tissue in question, a longer printing time, and a lower printing resolution [9]. Moreover, additional costs and 3D data collection accompanied these models. Development of materials with varying tactile elasticities, colors, and compositions to mimic the look of real tissues and organs and allow humans to acquire tactile sensations from models [10] could substantially enhance the efficacy of 3D-printed models.

9.2.2 Permanent Non-Bioactive Implants

Biomaterials which are not as susceptible to breakdown post-surgery are ideal for use in long-term medical implants, which are utilized by dentists and orthopedics. When compared to the time-consuming and error-prone process of making implants using conventional machining technologies, 3D printing allows for the rapid, precise, and customized fabrication of even the most complex implants. Traditional metallic implants seem to be more flexible than bone; consequently, stress-shielding events may readily occur during conventional bone treatments, putting bone integrity at risk. When 3D printing is combined with topology optimization, the resulting implant is lightweight and has a stiffness that can be fine-tuned [11]. The approach is additionally extremely compatible with standard digital measuring instruments, which makes it appropriate for data conversion and docking in space. A joint prosthesis was developed by Zhang *et al.* [12] based on the osseous architecture of excised proximal tibial osteosarcomas. The vast majority of patients in that study had full recoveries of their motor abilities with minor problems; nevertheless, long-term functional outcomes need more research. The results of neoadjuvant chemotherapy and limb-salvage procedures for patients with osteosarcoma of the proximal tibia or proximal tibiofibular joint using custom joint prosthesis reconstruction have been encouraging. Galasso *et al.* [13] fixed a custom distal femur modular prosthesis in a 20-year-old with stage IIB osteosarcoma. The patient's knee range of motion improved from zero to 110 after 10 months, and she was able to support her full body weight without pain or assistance. Although 3D printing of permanent implants has already been highly advanced, the current study centers on these three considerations. Considering the advanced state of the art in 3D printing of permanent implants, the present investigation centers on three primary areas: As a first topic, designers discuss how to make medical materials more effective—for instance, Winder *et al.* [14] simplified the technique by directly fabricating titanium (Ti) cranial implants from stereolithographic resin and detailed how cutting-edge technology is being used to produce implants with mechanical qualities that are a close match for bone. Take the case of the titanium hip implant that German company SLM Solutions made using the selective laser melting (SLM) technique for a patient in Australia. The lightweight and strong implant worked well with human tissue [15]. The third section provides an overview of how surface alterations can be used to increase biocompatibility and decrease the risk of infection in already mature medicinal materials. Bone morphogenetic protein-2 (BMP-2) was attached to hydroxyapatite (HA)-coated porous Ti using gelatin. They were able to successfully prepare an osteoinductive composite material consisting of porous 3D Ti. At 24 weeks, the porous Ti was packed with new bone, demonstrating its success in encouraging rapid bone healing. Hydrogel coatings can be applied to alloy scaffolds using a variety of components, not just HA. Biphasic scaffolds of Ti/type 1 collagen and Ti-Ta/type 1 collagen were constructed by Sing *et al.* [16] using SLM in combination with collagen infiltration. Bone regeneration and vascularization are aided by collagen, which promotes cell differentiation and development, and the scaffold provides essential mechanical strength. Another advantage of surface modification is that it prevents germs from sticking to the surface and forming a persistent biofilm that can then lead to infection. Infections caused by planktonic bacteria are more amenable to human defenses and conventional antibiotics, while biofilms have proven to be more resilient. Reducing the likelihood of implant infection requires preventing bacteria from initially attaching to reduce the likelihood of biofilm formation [17]. Current studies suggest that managing and preventing the bacterial adherence of implants can be achieved through modifying the antibacterial qualities of the implant surface, achieved mostly by chemical alteration of biomaterials through twitter-ionization, and distinctive surface nano-topography or architecture. Sanchez *et al.* [18] used direct-write assembly to design and manufacture zwitterionic HA with antiadhesive capabilities against bacteria and biocompatibility *in vitro*. In comparison to unaltered HA, bacterial adherence is reduced by more than 90%, attributed to the efficient interaction of these zwitterionic couples on the HA surface, and HA retains its *in vitro* biological compatibility throughout the testing. To avoid biofilm development, Izquierdo-Barba *et al.* [19] reported that a Ti6Al4V alloy plated with Ti nanomaterials using the encountering angle deposition process employing magnetron sputtering has a high nanocolumnar density and displays substantially hindered bacterial adhesion. New avenues are opened up by these strategies for 3D-printed permanent implants that are bacterial adhesion-free to fulfill medical needs.

9.3 Fabricating Local Bioactive and Biodegradable Scaffolds

Tissue and organ fabrication can proceed through two unique routes, depending on whether or not cells are continuously manipulated throughout development. The first approach is tissue engineering, typically called indirect cell assembly, because it includes assembling cells in a 3D scaffold. Scaffolds made from biocompatible materials, growth factors, and physical variables may be utilized alone or in conjunction with living cells to mimic the microarchitecture of biological tissues [20, 21]. Direct cell assembly is an alternative technique that includes fusing cells and materials together. A bionic element that makes up the extracellular matrix, also known as biodegradable scaffolds, has a vital function to play although they have limited usefulness and rapid degradation. 3D printing offers more powerful morphological and thermodynamic property control than traditional scaffold-fabrication methods, and it may be used to create complex structures with both tiny holes and macroscopic morphologies. Biocompatible and biodegradable scaffolds which respond favorably with human tissue after implantation can promote regeneration. Hydrogels are a unique kind of substance that functions with bionic properties that mirror those of the extracellular matrix but with highly 3D network structures; they may accelerate tissue regeneration and repair by accelerating cell migration and proliferation. Hydrogels are attractive biomaterials because of their potential for repairing and rebuilding soft tissues and organs; more and more scientists are realizing this and using hydrogels as transporters for transplantation cells and to facilitate preventing the immediate release of growth factors [22]. Researchers devote a lot of time to find ways to boost or speed up vascularization during tissue regeneration since it is a significant bottleneck. In order to stimulate the development of new blood arteries, a group of investigators [23] has developed a novel concept that refers to a hybrid scaffold made of alternating multiple layers of thin transparent membranes and filament weaves. By using direct-write assemblage inside a photocurable gel reservoir, 3D biomimetic microvascular networks may be created [24]. The procedure refines the 3D scaffolds' layer-by-layer pattern while broadening the scope of network creation. It is possible and useful to print 3D scaffolds *in situ* to aid in the regeneration of large areas of damaged tissue. Printing fibrin/collagen hydrogel, for instance, is possible by depositing thrombin from atomizing nozzles simultaneously on top of the fibroblast layer [25]. In the study, *in situ* skin printing was employed to successfully re-epithelialize the big wound, demonstrating its potential for usage in urgent wound care.

9.4 Characteristics of Scaffolds

The medical uses of 3D-printed customized scaffolds can be used to treat a wide range of illnesses, even those that vary from patient to patient. In order to function properly, these scaffolds require that they possess specific bio-physicochemical properties, architectural traits, mechanical capacities, etc. [26]. Scaffolds, which can be either two- or three-dimensional in shape, are used in both *in vitro* and *in vivo* regenerative settings as impermanent substrates to support and direct tissue growth. In recent years, scaffolds with the stated goal of controlling specific elements of tissue development have emerged.

9.4.1 Indirect Cell Assembly

Using a process of indirect cell assembly, cells are introduced onto porous gel scaffolds. Depending on the primary technique used to produce the scaffold, rapid fabrication methods with high water content, great biological compatibility, and controlled biodegradation [27] may be classified as extrusion-based, inkjet-based, or laser-assisted bioprinting. For bioprinting with extrusion, a computer-controlled extruder is combined with a robotic fluid-dispensing equipment. Ozbolat and Hospodiuk [28] developed a deposition process which involved the synchronized development of cylindrical filaments seeded using cells to build 3D custom-shaped structures.

Continuous inkjet bioprinting and drop-on-demand inkjet bioprinting are two types of inkjet-based bioprinting that provide substantial benefits in terms of simplicity of use and speed due to their capacity to carefully manage the deposition of cells and biomaterials. Ejecting droplets of bio-ink onto a receptive substrate is achieved by the application of the principles of fluid mechanics, gravity, and air pressure [29]. Microvalve-based bioprinting is a form of drop-on-demand printing, like inkjet-based bioprinting [30], but it is a more durable technology for high-throughput printing. Significant cellular viabilities and throughput rates are possible with the bioprinting technique, despite the method's low printing resolution. Laser-assisted bioprinting typically involves applying a light coating of laser-absorbing material to the substrate, followed by a hydrogel-like biomaterial with a thicker layer in which cells are embedded. When laser pulses are focused into the laser-absorbing layer, localized evaporation of the layer occurs, producing a high-pressure vapor bubble. Biomaterials are propelled by the vapor pressure within the bubble and captured as a droplet on the collecting slide [31]. Positive outcomes from cell experiments and surgical implants using individualized cell-loaded scaffolds prepared with different methods have been achieved due to the rewards of instantaneous printing of intricate structures allowed through the combination of CT images, CAD/computer-aided technology, customized biomimetic structural design, and the gel/cell hybrid processes.

9.4.2 Direct Cell Assembly

It is the process of forming 3D scaffolds out of cells and gel. When cells are seeded directly into 3D-printed scaffolds, however, the inoculation rate is low and the cell dispersion area increases dramatically [32, 33]. Researchers have found that encapsulating a cell/gel mixture within scaffolds constructed of another type of gel is an effective way to tackle these issues while still reaping the benefits of 3D scaffolds' superior mechanical strength and ability to conform to arbitrary geometries. The use of hydrogels in the technique demonstrates their potential function in homogenous encapsulation and cell adhesion. Both hematoxylin and eosin staining and safranin O staining reveal numerous, regularly spaced cells with lacuna that aggregate into islands of cartilage tissue. Combining the rigidity of the collagen gel with the unique mechanical characteristics of the rapid-prototyping poly(lactic-co-glycolic acid) scaffolding provides an optimal 3D growing environment for chondrocytes, which permits consistent and effective implantation into scaffolds. The surface of the material was covered in spindle cells, and the innermost layer, composed of round cells arranged in layers, developed into cartilage lacunae. Most of the densely packed cells were fully developed, while the randomly spread cells were mostly spherical and full of lacunae. Island cartilage tissue was encouraged as the cartilage matrix developed in the biomaterials' pores. Even after the scaffolds had fully disintegrated, the pores were still visible. Human embryonic kidney (HEK) cells were encapsulated in a type 1 rat-tail collagen solution by Hong *et al.* [34]. It was subsequently gelled onto the printed poly(ethylene glycol) (PEG)–sodium alginate–nanoclay network's interconnecting pores. After 7 days in culture, the majority of the seeded cells were still alive, proving that the nanoclay-containing hydrogels are biocompatible and well suited for long-term cell growth.

Making cells that are alive and gels using 3D printing creates living cells. To imitate the bionic arrangement of the extracellular matrix or scaffolding, *in vitro*, either cells or a mix of cells and gel must be enclosed within 3D scaffolds. There is always a chance that further harm will be done by implanting a scaffold into an affected area. Hydrogel encapsulation of cells has been an important step towards the realization of *in situ* repair *in vivo*, allowing researchers to control cell growth and dispersion in three dimensions at the same time. Poly(ethylene glycol)-diacrylate (PEG-DA) and alginate were used by Hockaday *et al.* [35] for generating porcine aortic valve interstitial cells (PAVICs). Almost 80% of the PAVIC cells remained viable on the scaffolds for 21 days. Researchers may be able to rapidly fabricate anatomically diverse valve circuits for cell transplantation using this method. Xue *et al.* [36] mixed human dental pulp cells with alginate/gelatin gel for use in a bioprinter to make scaffolds of varied sizes and forms. The density of the cells was manageable, and they attached strongly to the 3D matrix. The study laid the groundwork for bioprinting technology, which could provide a new approach to tooth regeneration and has additional uses in dental tissue engineering. Hydrogels can be printed at the wound site for *in situ* repair, which means that complexly damaged portions do not need to be replaced but rather repaired. It opens up new avenues for research into minimally invasive repair techniques. Repairs to cartilage and bone *in situ* have been accomplished with materials incorporating alginate hydrogel and a novel demineralized bone matrix composition. There was a little amount of surface defect at the repair sites [37], within the clinically acceptable error range. Changing the materials used and the types of cells used for seeding opens up the possibility of using the technique in disciplines outside of orthopedics, such as minimally invasive and individualized facial reconstruction. Significant advancements were also made in cell/gel *in situ* printing by Cui *et al.* [38]. Using poly(ethylene glycol) methacrylate and human articular chondrocytes as bio-ink, they built *in situ* prints in cartilage lesions and cured them with ultraviolet (UV) radiation. After printing, the gel scaffolds contained cells evenly, and those cells were able to maintain a high level of vitality while being spread across the gel. Based on the investigation, it appears that the printed hydrogel is a viable material for anatomic cartilage engineering, as its compressive modulus is within the range of properties of natural human articular cartilage. Even though *in vitro* tissue printing requires external environmental cues like UV light, temperature, and calcium availability to initiate a phase change after deposition, *in situ* bioprinting eliminates the requirement. However, *in situ*, bioprinting places a higher premium on careful path planning and deformation. Because of the nature of printing within a wound, chemical alteration and surface nanotopography are not possible through surface treatment. As a result, researchers need to give *in situ* bioprinting implants additional consideration to avoid bacterial adherence.

9.5 Enhancing the Mechanical Properties of Scaffolds

Personalized scaffolds and engineered cartilage substitutes should maintain structural stability and integrity and have a mechanical strength that matches the subchondral bone as well as adjacent cartilage of the implantation location to provide immediate and long-term load-bearing [39]. As a result of their weaknesses in mechanical characteristics such as quick shrinking, brittleness, and poor mechanical qualities, gel materials are often crosslinked to improve their mechanical properties [40]. Thermal crosslinking, ionic crosslinking, and pH crosslinking are three examples of such methods. Potentially harmful crosslinkers can be avoided through the introduction of alternative functional groups during crosslinking [41]. Wu *et al.* [42] showed that utilizing polyvinyl alcohol (PVA) as a thermo-crosslinking agent improved the mechanical features associated with 3D-printed biologically active glass scaffolds including a hierarchical pore organization, including properly organized microporosity in a wide range of geometrical forms.

9.6 Directly Printing Tissue and Organs

Growth factors only stimulate the development and differentiation of surface cells, and despite the fact that typical tissue engineering includes encapsulating cells within disintegrating scaffolds, there is no guarantee that cells will be appropriately transplanted into inner scaffolds. Research into cell and growth factor direct-printing has accelerated substantially because of its potential application in the manufacture of tissues and organs. Thomas Boland, a professor at Clemson University in the United States, is credited with proposing the idea of "cell and organ printing" in the year 2000, marking the beginning of modern 3D bioprinting. Printing with "biological ink" which includes seed cells, growth agents, and nutritional components allows for the subsequent growing of tissues as well as organs with physiological activity. The most difficult component of printing tissues or organs involves modeling the intricate blood flow system of an organ. This is why there has been so much research and development into blood vessel printing. In 2009 [43], the American firm Ganovo employed 3D printing to develop vascular prosthesis. Using a 3D-printing method and a combination of agarose as support and cells, researchers from the University of Michigan and the Southern California University of Health Sciences created a vascular network smaller than 3 mm in size [44].

9.7 Biomedical Material in 3D Printing

Numerous types of biomedical materials have been used in 3D printing to render long-lasting implants or matrix substrates. These materials range from hard metals (Ti) to soft hydrogels and elastomeric polymers like PDMS to thermoplastic polymers like polystyrene and PLGA.

9.8 Medical Metal Materials

Stainless steel, cobalt–chromium alloy, titanium alloy, and tantalum alloy are commonly used in the medical industry to prepare long-term implants. These metal alloys are biocompatible to an acceptable level for use in medicine. The use of 3D-printed biomedical metals has advantages over more conventional implants. Implants made from 3D-printed metal typically have finer grains, which improves their mechanical function [45]. Furthermore, printed components can be assured of a high degree of purity because of the tightly managed printing conditions. Implants with mechanical properties comparable to bone or teeth may now be created because of the simplified layout complexity of 3D-printed customized items. It is usual practice of modifying the surface of porous metal implants by electrolytic deposition, chemical modification, or alkali-heat preparation in order to boost their biological activity. Heat treatment is a key component of the value chain for metal 3D printing since it allows for the simultaneous modification of biocompatibility and mechanical qualities. With the right heat treatment technique and conditions, the Ti6Al4V surfaces produced by SLM are hydrophilic, rougher, and more uniform. The modulus and hardness of the surface were determined [46] through a statistical analysis of the surface features. Tantalum (Ta) can be used as a stabilizing element in Ti to further decrease the elastic modulus, thus minimizing the negative impact of stress shielding. Ti–Ta bulks manufactured using SLM have superior strength to Ti6Al4V while having a lower elastic modulus. Even more convincingly, Song *et al.* [47] used a regression analysis approach to demonstrate that laser-manufactured porous Ti–Ta cellular lattice structures are technically feasible. The Ti–Ta alloy lattice structures' dimensional accuracy and mechanical qualities are significantly impacted by the process conditions. Ni–Ti alloys, which have superelasticity from memory, can be processed with SLM technology without losing their useful qualities, according to researchers [48]. Special Ni–Ti unit cells have a prolonged fatigue life and compression characteristics that are at par with cerebral and trabecular bone. Because of its corrosion resistance and Young's modulus that is remarkably close to that of natural bone Mg (thus eliminating the stress-shielding effect), magnesium also shows tremendous potential as an implantation material. The mineral magnesium (Mg) is crucial for bone cell growth and differentiation.

9.9 Medical Polymer Materials

Medical models and biodegradable scaffolds are typically made from polymer materials, such as natural biomaterials or synthetic biomaterials. Among the natural polymeric materials employed in medicine, chitosan, collagen, and fibrin are the most prominent. Due to their elasticity and deformability, these polymers have a relatively low mechanical strength, but they are very compatible, encourage cell adhesion and growth, and help keep cell shapes intact. Shape, relative cellular mass, and degradation time are all variables that may be controlled in synthetic polymer materials, including polylactic acid, polyvinyl alcohol, and polycaprolactone [49, 50]. Cell loss and uneven distribution occur because polymer surfaces do not have the right "recognition spots" for cell adherence. Polymers can be useful in printing processes and medical implants if their mechanical performance, fluidity, and surface roughness are improved. More sophisticated capabilities were built into polymers by Yue *et al.* [51]. 3D-printed implants were shown to kill germs on contact without harming human cells when antimicrobial composite resins were prepared. These implants have the potential to one day replace standard dental fillings. Antimicrobial polymers may be 3D-printed, and the process can be easily adapted for usage in other fields besides medicine, such as food storage, water treatment, and toy production.

9.10 Medical Ceramic Materials

Artificial joints and dental implants made from ceramic materials (mostly HA and TCP) are commonly employed due to their superior biocompatibility, osteoconductivity, and stability in terms of physicochemical properties [52]. Their malleability in both shape and size, plus the fact that they can be easily dyed during 3D printing, makes them ideal dental materials. Rapid prototyping technologies such as selective laser sintering and selective laser melting are well suited to the ceramic substance HA, which is also a vital mineral that makes up bone and tooth tissue. Orthopedic and maxillofacial applications will soon have access to new resorbable ceramic biocomposites created by the European Union's project RESTORATION. The discomfort of joint replacement surgery can be considerably reduced by using 3D-printed joint prostheses made specifically for each patient. In comparison to metals and polymers, the tensile strength and pore morphologies of ceramic may be influenced by their unique consolidation approach and the presence of readily apparent remaining strains upon sintering. Powder layer deposition, laser–powder interaction, and so on are all important factors in the SLM or SLS process, which contribute to completely dense ceramic [53]. Cells *in vitro* will also be evaluated for the toxicity of residual binders. Further study of totally thick ceramics should concentrate on improving their biomechanical properties, printing resolution, biocompatibility, and sustained drug release [54]. For this reason, implants often combine several biomaterials to perform a variety of tasks, as each of the aforementioned types of biomaterials has its own set of advantages and limitations when used in clinical settings [55]. Whenever the 3D printing materials move forward, they will become increasingly useful in the medical field. A lot of people are enthusiastic about shape-memory materials which are also referred to as smart materials. When receiving a certain external stimulation, reversible SMMs can undergo a predetermined change in shape or characteristics [56]. Implanting a personalized device that can alter the shape in response to environmental cues like temperature, pressure, or magnetic fields allows doctors to better treat patients with larger tissue problems. As a result, biomedical applications of

3D-printed smart materials hold enormous promise for the development of less invasive forms of treatment.

9.11 Limitations

As an emerging and fast-growing multidisciplinary subject at the intersection of material science, biology, and clinical research, 3D printing's potential medical applications hold great promise to help address the critical shortage of organ donors. Although direct printing of cells is possible now, much more work needs to be done before *in vitro* engineering of tissue can be achieved [57]. Due to its multifaceted nature, the extracellular matrix (ECM) is notoriously challenging to replicate *in vitro*. Conventional methods, particularly mostly those that incorporate stacking cell-seeded hydrogels, fail to solve the issues of cellular feeding and oxygen transport. Not enough cells are currently available for use with bigger scaffolds. Cells in the preprophase, as opposed to those attached to the scaffold surface, are starved of nutrition. Cells can maintain themselves in a state of disequilibrium in 3D space [58, 59]. Other challenges including cell survival, growth and development, distinctiveness, or fusion, must be addressed and overcome for printed scaffolds, connective tissue, and organs to progress further. There are also material constraints to consider. The elastic modulus of several commonly used metals for permanent implants is high, which might cause a mismatch between the implant and the bone. Most printable biodegradable scaffolds are constructed from natural polymers with high biologic compatibility but poor mechanical properties. Although 3D printing was initially utilized in engineering, it continues to demand a wide spectrum of knowledge despite the recent rapid developments in the field. Partially slowing the advancement of technology for medical use is the fact that, at present, medical and engineering researchers have relatively distinct research domains and structural frameworks. Problems with cell induction and other ethical concerns must be taken seriously. Therefore, it will take time for attempts to adopt 3D printing for medical purposes [59–61].

9.12 Conclusions and Future Directions

The advent of 3D-printing technology has permitted for enormous strides to be made in the medical field, particularly in the creation of transplant models and permanent implants. Scientists have successfully used several techniques to improve biodegradable scaffolds' mechanical properties. Researchers both at home and abroad have begun looking into the feasibility of printing blood vessels utilizing printed tissue and organs, even if the instantaneous printing of tissues and organs is still in its infancy. Metals, polymers, and ceramics all make up the spectrum of medical biomaterials used in 3D printing, with the integration of numerous materials being the norm for achieving complicated functionality in printed components. Even though 3D printing is currently a reality in clinical applications, the materials and the ability to build ECM *in vitro* are still constrained by the current state of 3D-printing technology. Until progress is made, printed bioactive tissues and organs will not be ready for clinical use. These issues will be resolved in the future so that 3D printing can be used effectively in tissue engineering. The goals of the chapter include the creation of standardized guidelines for 3D-printed scaffolds, the improvement of market oversight to produce optimal implants for clinical use, the development of new equipment to ensure the scaffolds' superior dimensional stability and permeability, and the creation of a 3D printing framework to facilitate communication between hospitals, companies, and research institutes. 3D-printed tissue engineering scaffolds are expected to see increased use as a result of these developments.

References

1. Wolfe, R.A., Roys, E.C., Merion, R.M., Trends in organ donation and transplantation in the United States, 1999-2008. *Am. J. Transplant.*, 10, 4, 961–72, 2010 Apr 1.
2. Wan, Q., Liu, H., Ye, S., Ye, Q., Confirmed transmission of bacterial or fungal infection to kidney transplant recipients from donated after cardiac death (DCD) donors in China: A single-center analysis. *Med. Sci. Monit.: Int. Med. J. Exp. Clin. Res.*, 23, 3770, 2017.
3. Butscher, A., Bohner, M., Doebelin, N., Hofmann, S., Müller, R., New depowdering-friendly designs for three-dimensional printing of calcium phosphate bone substitutes. *Actabiomaterialia*, 9, 11, 9149–58, 2013 Nov 1.
4. Saunders, R.E., Gough, J.E., Derby, B., Delivery of human fibroblast cells by piezoelectric drop-on-demand inkjet printing. *Biomaterials*, 29, 2, 193–203, 2008 Jan 1.
5. Xu, T., Zhao, W., Zhu, J.M., Albanna, M.Z., Yoo, J.J., Atala, A., Complex heterogeneous tissue constructs containing multiple cell types prepared by inkjet printing technology. *Biomaterials*, 34, 1, 130–9, 2013 Jan 1.
6. Derby, B., Printing and prototyping of tissues and scaffolds. *Science*, 338, 6109, 921–6, 2012 Nov 16.

7. Wang, K., Ho, C.C., Zhang, C., Wang, B., A review on the 3D printing of functional structures for medical phantoms and regenerated tissue and organ applications. *Engineering*, 3, 5, 653–62, 2017 Oct 1.
8. Zhao, Y., Yao, R., Ouyang, L., Ding, H., Zhang, T., Zhang, K., Cheng, S., Sun, W., Three-dimensional printing of Hela cells for cervical tumor model *in vitro*. *Biofabrication*, 6, 3, 035001, 2014 Apr 11.
9. Yap, Y.L., Tan, Y.S., Tan, H.K., Peh, Z.K., Low, X.Y., Yeong, W.Y., Tan, C.S., Laude, A., 3D printed bio-models for medical applications. *Rapid Prototyp. J.*, 23, 227–235, 2017 Mar 20.
10. Mogali, S.R., Yeong, W.Y., Tan, H.K., Tan, G.J., Abrahams, P.H., Zary, N., Low-Beer, N., Ferenczi, M.A., Evaluation by medical students of the educational value of multi-material and multi-colored three-dimensional printed models of the upper limb for anatomical education. *Anat. Sci. Educ.*, 11, 1, 54–64, 2018 Jan.
11. Al-Tamimi, A.A., Fernandes, P.R., Peach, C., Cooper, G., Diver, C., Bartolo, P.J., Metallic bone fixation implants: A novel design approach for reducing the stress shielding phenomenon. *Virtual Phys. Prototyp.*, 12, 2, 141–51, 2017 Apr 3.
12. Zhang, Y., Yang, Z., Li, X., Chen, Y., Zhang, S., Du, M., Li, J., Custom prosthetic reconstruction for proximal tibial osteosarcoma with proximal tibiofibular joint involved. *Surg. Oncol.*, 17, 2, 87–95, 2008 Aug 1.
13. Galasso, O., Mariconda, M., Brando, A., Iannò, B., Disassembly of a distal femur modular prosthesis after tumor resection. *J. Arthroplasty*, 25, 2, 334–e5, 2010 Feb 1.
14. Winder, J., Cooke, R.S., Gray, J., Fannin, T., Fegan, T., Medical rapid prototyping and 3D CT in the manufacture of custom made cranial titanium plates. *J. Med. Eng. Technol.*, 23, 1, 26–8, 1999 Jan 1.
15. Bian, W.G., Lei, P., Liang, F.H., Bone, X.H., Morphogenetic protein-2 and gel complex on hydroxyapatite-coated porous titanium to repair defects of distalfemur in rabbits. *Chin. J. Orthop. Trauma*, 9, 6, 550–4, 2007.
16. Sing, S.L., Wang, S., Agarwala, S., Wiria, F.E., Ha, T.M., Yeong, W.Y., Fabrication of titanium based biphasic scaffold using selective laser melting and collagen immersion. *Int. J. Bioprinting*, 3, 1, 65–71, 2017.
17. Sanchez Salcedo, S., Colilla, M., Izquierdo-Barba, I., ValletRegí, M., Preventing bacterial adhesion on scaffolds for bone tissue engineering. *Int. J. Bioprinting*, 12, 52, 2017.
18. Sanchez-Salcedo, S., Colilla, M., Izquierdo-Barba, I., Vallet-Regí, M., Design and preparation of biocompatible zwitterionic hydroxyapatite. *J. Mater. Chem. B*, 1, 11, 1595–606, 2013.
19. Izquierdo-Barba, I., García-Martín, J.M., Álvarez, R., Palmero, A., Esteban, J., Pérez-Jorge, C., Arcos, D., Vallet-Regí, M., Nanocolumnar coatings with selective behavior towards osteoblast and Staphylococcus aureus proliferation. *Actabiomaterialia*, 15, 20–8, 2015 Mar 15.

20. Langer, R. and Vacanti, J.P., Tissue engineering. *Science*, 260, 5110, 920–6, 1993.
21. Li, S., Qian, T., Wang, X., Liu, J., Gu, X., Noncoding RNAs and their potential therapeutic applications in tissue engineering. *Engineering*, 3, 1, 3–15, 2017 Feb 1.
22. Billiet, T., Vandenhaute, M., Schelfhout, J., Van Vlierberghe, S., Dubruel, P., A review of trends and limitations in hydrogel-rapid prototyping for tissue engineering. *Biomaterials*, 33, 26, 6020–41, 2012 Sep 1.
23. An, J., Teoh, J.E., Suntornnond, R., Chua, C.K., Design and 3D printing of scaffolds and tissues. *Engineering*, 1, 2, 261–8, 2015 Jun 1.
24. Mosadegh, B., Xiong, G., Dunham, S., Min, J.K., Current progress in 3D printing for cardiovascular tissue engineering. *Biomed. Mater.*, 10, 3, 034002, 2015 Mar 16.
25. Ng, W.L., Wang, S., Yeong, W.Y., Naing, M.W., Skin bioprinting: Impending reality or fantasy? *Trends Biotechnol.*, 34, 9, 689–99, 2016 Sep 1.
26. Hutmacher, D.W., Scaffolds in tissue engineering bone and cartilage. *Biomaterials*, 21, 24, 2529–43, 2000 Dec 15.
27. Pan, T. and Cao, X., Progress in the development of hydrogel-rapid prototyping for tissue engineering. *Mater. Chin.*, 34, 3, 236–45, 2015.
28. Ozbolat, I.T. and Hospodiuk, M., Current advances and future perspectives in extrusion-based bioprinting. *Biomaterials*, 76, 321–43, 2016 Jan 1.
29. Gudapati, H., Dey, M., Ozbolat, I., A comprehensive review on droplet-based bioprinting: Past, present and future. *Biomaterials*, 102, 20–42, 2016 Sep 1.
30. Koch, L., Brandt, O., Deiwick, A., Chichkov, B., Laser-assisted bioprinting at different wavelengths and pulse durations with a metal dynamic release layer: A parametric study. *Int. J. Bioprinting*, 3, 1, 42–53, 2017.
31. Fedorovich, N.E., Schuurman, W., Wijnberg, H.M., Prins, H.J., Van Weeren, P.R., Malda, J., Alblas, J., Dhert, W.J., Biofabrication of osteochondral tissue equivalents by printing topologically defined, cell-laden hydrogel scaffolds. *Tissue Eng. Part C: Methods*, 18, 1, 33–44, 2012 Jan 1.
32. Martin, I., Wendt, D., Heberer, M., The role of bioreactors in tissue engineering. *Trends Biotechnol.*, 22, 2, 80–6, 2004 Feb 1.
33. Stephens, J.S., Cooper, J.A., Phelan Jr., F.R., Dunkers, J.P., Perfusion flow bioreactor for 3D *in situ* imaging: Investigating cell/biomaterials interactions. *Biotechnol. Bioeng.*, 97, 4, 952–61, 2007 Jul 1.
34. Hong, S., Sycks, D., Chan, H.F., Lin, S., Lopez, G.P., Guilak, F., Leong, K.W., Zhao, X., 3D printing of highly stretchable and tough hydrogels into complex, cellularized structures. *Adv. Mater.*, 27, 27, 4035–40, 2015 Jul.
35. Hockaday, L.A., Kang, K.H., Colangelo, N.W., Cheung, P.Y., Duan, B., Malone, E., Wu, J., Girardi, L.N., Bonassar, L.J., Lipson, H., Chu, C.C., Rapid 3D printing of anatomically accurate and mechanically heterogeneous aortic valve hydrogel scaffolds. *Biofabrication*, 4, 3, 035005, 2012 Aug 23.

36. Xue, S.H., Wang, Y., Zhao, Y., Zhang, T., Lin, F., Sun, W. *et al.*, Preliminary study on three dimensional bioprinting of human dental pulp cells. *Sci. Tech. Eng.*, 12, 17, 4103–7, 2012.
37. Cohen, D.L., Lipton, J.I., Bonassar, L.J., Lipson, H., Additive manufacturing for *in situ* repair of osteochondral defects. *Biofabrication*, 2, 3, 035004, 2010 Sep 8.
38. Cui, X., Breitenkamp, K., Finn, M.G., Lotz, M., D'Lima, D.D., Direct human cartilage repair using three-dimensional bioprinting technology. *Tissue Eng. Part A*, 18, 11-12, 1304–12, 2012 Jun 1.
39. Liu, Y., Zhou, G., Cao, Y., Recent progress in cartilage tissue engineering—Our experience and future directions. *Engineering*, 3, 1, 28–35, 2017 Feb 1.
40. Gratson, G.M., Xu, M., Lewis, J.A., Direct writing of three-dimensional webs. *Nature*, 428, 6981, 386, 2004 Mar 25.
41. Ivirico, J.L., Bhattacharjee, M., Kuyinu, E., Nair, L.S., Laurencin, C.T., Regenerative engineering for knee osteoarthritis treatment: Biomaterials and cell-based technologies. *Engineering*, 3, 1, 16–27, 2017 Feb 1.
42. Wu, C., Luo, Y., Cuniberti, G., Xiao, Y., Gelinsky, M., Three-dimensional printing of hierarchical and tough mesoporous bioactive glass scaffolds with a controllable pore architecture, excellent mechanical strength and mineralization ability. *Actabiomaterialia*, 7, 6, 2644–50, 2011 Jun 1.
43. Lian, Q., Li, D.C., Chen, C., Zhang, W.J., Liu, Y.X., He, J.K., Jin, Z.M., Tissue-Engineered soft tissue oriented manufacturing technologies and additive manufacturing. *Chin. J. Tissue Eng. Res.*, 18, 8, 1263, 2014 Feb 19.
44. Mironov, V., Kasyanov, V., Markwald, R.R., Organ printing: From bioprinter to organ biofabrication line. *Curr. Opin. Biotechnol.*, 22, 5, 667–73, 2011 Oct 1.
45. Yang, Y., Wang, K., Gu, X., Leong, K.W., Biophysical regulation of cell behavior—Cross talk between substrate stiffness and nanotopography. *Engineering*, 3, 1, 36–54, 2017 Feb 1.
46. Fischer, M., Joguet, D., Robin, G., Peltier, L., Laheurte, P., *In situ* elaboration of a binary Ti–26Nb alloy by selective laser melting of elemental titanium and niobium mixed powders. *Mater. Sci. Eng.: C*, 62, 852–9, 2016 May 1.
47. Song, C., Study on digital and direct manufacturing of customized implant based on selective laser melting [dissertation], South China University of Technology, Guangzhou, 2014.
48. Speirs, M., Van Hooreweder, B., Van Humbeeck, J., Kruth, J.P., Fatigue behaviour of NiTi shape memory alloy scaffolds produced by SLM, a unit cell design comparison. *J. Mech. Behav. Biomed. Mater.*, 70, 53–9, 2017 Jun 1.
49. Yang, Y., Wu, P., Lin, X., Liu, Y., Bian, H., Zhou, Y., Gao, C., Shuai, C., System development, formability quality and microstructure evolution of selective laser-melted magnesium. *Virtual Phys. Prototyp.*, 11, 3, 173–81, 2016 Jul 2.
50. Xu, T., Binder, K.W., Albanna, M.Z., Dice, D., Zhao, W., Yoo, J.J., Atala, A., Hybrid printing of mechanically and biologically improved constructs for

cartilage tissue engineering applications. *Biofabrication*, 5, 1, 015001, 2012 Nov 21.

51. Yue, J., Zhao, P., Gerasimov, J.Y., van de Lagemaat, M., Grotenhuis, A., Rustema-Abbing, M., van der Mei, H.C., Busscher, H.J., Herrmann, A., Ren, Y., 3D-printable antimicrobial composite resins. *Adv. Funct. Mater.*, 25, 43, 6756–67, 2015 Nov.
52. Pistone, A., Iannazzo, D., Espro, C., Galvagno, S., Tampieri, A., Montesi, M., Panseri, S., Sandri, M., Tethering of Gly-Arg-Gly-Asp-Ser-Pro-Lys peptides on Mg-doped hydroxyapatite. *Engineering*, 3, 1, 55–9, 2017 Feb 1.
53. Sing, S.L., Yeong, W.Y., Wiria, F.E., Tay, B.Y., Zhao, Z., Zhao, L., Tian, Z., Yang, S., Direct selective laser sintering and melting of ceramics: A review. *Rapid Prototyp. J.*, 23, 3, 611–23, 2017 Apr 18.
54. Trombetta, R., Inzana, J.A., Schwarz, E.M., Kates, S.L., Awad, H.A., 3D printing of calcium phosphate ceramics for bone tissue engineering and drug delivery. *Ann. Biomed. Eng.*, 45, 23–44, 2017 Jan.
55. Zhang, G., Li, J., Li, J., Zhou, X., Xie, J., Wang, A., Selective laser melting molding of individualized femur implant: Design, process, optimization. *J. Bionic Eng.*, 18, 128–37, 2021 Jan.
56. Lee, A.Y., An, J., Chua, C.K., Two-way 4D printing: A review on the reversibility of 3D-printed shape memory materials. *Engineering*, 3, 5, 663–74, 2017 Oct 1.
57. Quan, W., 3D-printed alginate/hydroxyapatite hydrogel in combination of Atsttrin to repair bone defects (Doctoral dissertation, dissertation], Zhejiang University, Hangzhou, 2023.
58. Yongnian, Y.A., Shengjie, L.I., Zhuo, X.I., Xiaohong, W.A., Ting, Z.H., Renji, Z.H., Fabrication technology of tissue engineering scaffold based on rapid prototyping. *J. Mech. Eng.*, 46, 5, 93–8, 2010 Mar 5.
59. McGuigan, A.P. and Sefton, M.V., Design criteria for a modular tissue-engineered construct. *Tissue Eng.*, 13, 5, 1079–89, 2007 May 1.
60. Chai, G., Zhang, Y., Liu, Q.H., Ma, S.X., Hu, Q.X., Cui, L., Cao, Y.L., A pilot study of three dimensional printing of human bone marrow stem cells (hBMSCs). *Shanghai Kou Qiang Yi Xue= Shanghai J. Stomatol.*, 19, 1, 77–80, 2010 Feb 1.
61. Mironov, V., Drake, C., Wen, X., Research project: Charleston bioengineered kidney project. *Biotechnol. J.: Healthc. Nutrition Technol.*, 1, 9, 903–5, 2006 Sep.

10

3D Printing in Hospital Administration and Management

Abstract
Three-dimensional (3D) printing is becoming increasingly commonplace in healthcare facilities, and the sophistication of the models and tools that can be produced with it is expanding. While the expansion is certainly promising, it also increases the chance of mistakes and lowers the quality of the end product for patients. It is more important than ever to have a solid quality management system (QMS) in place to help detect and prevent errors, lessen the impact of those that do occur, and improve the overall quality of the product given to patients. Without knowing whether or not the traditional care methods are helping or hurting, continuing to repeat them is counterproductive to patient care. Measuring, refining, and improving the process-level repetitive operations inside 3D printing leads to high-quality results in the same way that it does in any other industry. The authors discuss the trials and tribulations they encountered in implementing a QMS into their 3D-printing operations. They describe problems that arose and how they were fixed as well as how they have worked to increase uniformity, streamline communication, and repeat past triumphs. They clearly explain the importance of collaboration between healthcare professionals, regulatory bodies, and established manufacturers in achieving the ultimate aim of patient safety and satisfaction.

Keywords: 3D printing, patient-specific anatomic models, hospital 3D printing, quality management system

10.1 Introduction

The use of enhanced medical imaging data for the 3D printing of patient-specific anatomic models is spreading across all types of clinical settings. Many medical facilities have begun in-house 3D-printing services as a result of this motivation. Patient-specific anatomic models have multiple applications in the fields of surgery, medical training, and basic science [1–4]. Moreover, 3D-printed surgical cutting guides and implants

Rishabha Malviya and Rishav Sharma. 3D Printing in Healthcare: Novel Applications, (187–204)

customized for each patient are becoming increasingly prevalent, which can aid in the replication of preplanned osteotomy cuts and ultimately enhance surgical precision and patient outcomes [5]. Hospital 3D printing processes were initially transferred inside the device manufacturing area [6, 7] in the wake of the COVID-19 epidemic in March 2020. It facilitated the development of face shields, face masks, and accessories to fulfill the demand. There will be more people who can benefit from 3D printing in medicine because of its recent surge in popularity, yet it raises the stakes for implementing thorough quality controls to protect against medical mistakes and side effects. It presents the problem of how to assure the quality of 3D-printed models or medical devices and also the patient's safety in the face of an enormous explosion. 3D-printed models and gadgets customized for individual patients need to be both accurate and safe to be of any use. One of the six goals for improving US healthcare as listed by the National Academy of Medicine in "Crossing the Quality Chasm" [8, 9] is maintaining safe healthcare environments for all patients and reducing damage. Care that is not only risk-free but also effective, quick, efficient, fairly distributed, and patient-centered is what the World Health Organization (WHO) calls "quality" [10]. Incorporating patient safety and quality management systems (QMSs) can help hospitals and doctors maintain compliance with these regulations [11–13]. Radiologists, as imaging and anatomy specialists, play a crucial role in ensuring the accuracy of medical imaging data. Therefore, it stands to reason that they would be the ones to pioneer the establishment of sound procedures and benchmarks for producing 3D-printed models that are both precise and of sufficient quality to be used as patient-specific casts [14–17]. Incorporating 3D-printing safety into radiology departments' safety and quality programs has the potential to enhance patient experiences, reduce healthcare costs, build healthy communities, strengthen confidence and fulfillment in healthcare systems, or develop a genuine methodical approach [18, 19]. The author includes his personal experiences with 3D printing at the Veterans Affairs Puget Sound Health Care System and highlights the significance of both safety and quality in hospital-based 3D-printing projects. Designers discuss the importance of using checklists and SOPs to ensure uniformity, and the need for open lines of communication, thorough documentation, and in-depth training is stressed. Lastly, the researchers elaborate on the developing regulatory concerns for 3D-printed models in healthcare. To help individuals who are thinking about or have recently begun a 3D-printing program in a hospital, the study will provide an overview of the field.

10.2 Role of 3D Printing in Medicine

The medical applications of 3D printing are extensive. In the first place, it is a technique for making complicated 3D imaging datasets more accessible to a wider audience. It can improve communication among patients and doctors as well as between members of the care team (such as nurses and physicians during surgery). Another study found that patients who had a far better understanding of their malignancies and treatment plans were provided with a 3D-printed representation of their anatomy before urologic surgery [20]. Preprocedural management is aided by 3D printing because the operator can view the process in advance, perform any required alterations, and prepare for any potential issues [20, 21]. Pre-selecting the size of a device or implant used in a treatment using a 3D model can cut down on time spent in the operating room and the risk of complications [22]. Patient-specific surgical cutting and drill guides are just one example of how 3D printing is revolutionizing the medical device industry. The scaffolding has also been used for other applications that make use of its special properties, such as prosthetic knees, knee replacement cages, and patient-specific implantation for bone replacement in the chest wall [23–26]. People who underwent lumbar interbody fusion and were administered with 3D-printed titanium cages coupled with a bone graft substitute indicated high levels of satisfaction and successful fusion [27]. Patients are receiving more individualized treatment because of the proliferation of 3D printing in the medical field, which is being utilized for everything from communication and visualization to pre-procedural planning and the production of medical devices. Figure 10.1 illustrates the utilization of 3D oral pharmaceutical dosage form properties for fused deposition modeling.

10.3 What Can Go Wrong

To ensure the continued viability and efficacy of their products, makers of medical gear implement quality assurance (QA) procedures. The fact remains, though, that gadgets might break for a variety of reasons. The FDA authorized a class I recall of a patient-specific 3D-printed orthopedic cutting guide in April 2013 [28] because of the significant possibility of negative effects. These disposable cutting guides were designed to help orthopedic surgeons make precise incisions when implanting knee replacement components, allowing for a more individualized surgical procedure. The 3D-printed aids were created with the use of imaging data

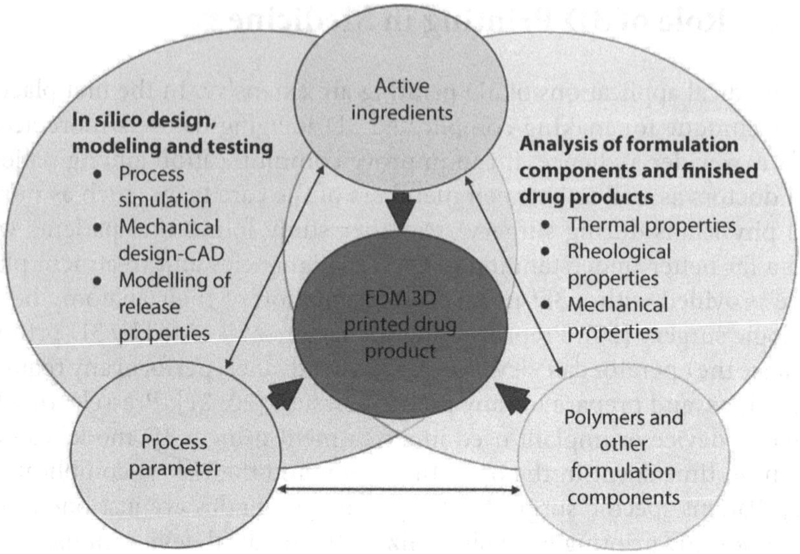

Figure 10.1 Characterizing the properties of 3D oral pharmaceutical dosage forms for use in fused deposition modeling.

from each patient. According to field reports, 3D-printed cutting guides might not always result in incisions and misalignment (such as depth and angle) that have been comparable with the surgeon's plan. Joint instability, reduced mobility, fractures, the need for additional surgery, and persistent discomfort all resulted from excessively deep and wide bone resections. Other 3D-printed patient-matched cutting guidelines have been associated with issues with misalignment and navigation problems that shift the surgical component outside the allowed range of alignment, leading to tragic consequences [28, 29]. Patient-specific preoperative planning models generated by hospitals can be inappropriate, which can cause harm. The severity of harm is usually proportional to the model's intended use. Poor outcomes from ill-fitting devices, e.g., vascular stents, and prosthetic valves can require modifications and additional device installation, and, in the worst case, it can cause harm and death [30, 31]. If wrong, anatomical models used by surgeons to visualize a patient's anatomy can affect them. It is because it may tempt surgeons to utilize a less-than-ideal technique or provide the appearance of a higher or reduced risk of problems. Patient injury and altered operation outcomes [32] could be avoided with effective quality and safety controls, as indicated by these examples of mistakes produced by the use of 3D-printed patient-specific models [33].

10.4 Techniques for 3D Printing in Clinical Settings

In conventional manufacturing facilities, QMSs and quality controls serve as the framework for ensuring that goods are consistent and of high quality. The same guidelines apply to the growing trend of 3D printing at the point of care. Clinical care and laboratory services QA are already commonplace in hospitals. A well-implemented quality management system is essential for guaranteeing that a 3D-printed model accurately represents a patient's anatomical structure. Using a QMS, you may lessen the likelihood of making mistakes or having something go wrong by eliminating the causes of such outcomes or adding safeguards to detect and address mistakes as soon as they happen. A QMS can be used to implement concepts and processes that can be applied to any endeavor, including the many forms of 3D printing that a hospital may perform. Nonetheless, 3D printing of patient anatomy models in a clinical setting is common and serves as a case study in the chapter. The processes involved in creating a 3D-printed model utilizing data from medical imaging have been extensively described [2, 14]. Next, the investigator looks at some concrete instances of issues and possibilities related to quality in the context of 3D-printing anatomical models tailored to individual patients. The treatment of chronic diseases is more challenging than the treatment of any other disease process, yet the management of all diseases is a considerable burden. Drug treatment for these conditions is generally required over the years, and patients must be closely monitored throughout their treatment. Although patient compliance and medication adherence are crucial for therapeutic efficacy, they may be hampered by noncompliance or nonadherence, respectively, which, in turn, may lead to adjustments in doses and dose-related side effects. However, 3D-printed tailored medicines may be a silver bullet for these issues, drastically lowering the need for dosing errors, treatment monitoring, and frequent follow-ups with healthcare practitioners. Figure 10.2 shows how 3D-printed medicines can be used in the treatment of chronic disorders.

10.5 Design Input and Output

The 3D printing organization should address the model's anticipated usage with the ordering provider before printing anatomical models [34]. Is the tool for use in preoperative planning or informing postoperative care? It may reduce the required level of accuracy. What weight do you give to the significance of hue and the rigidity or pliability of the material? If the model

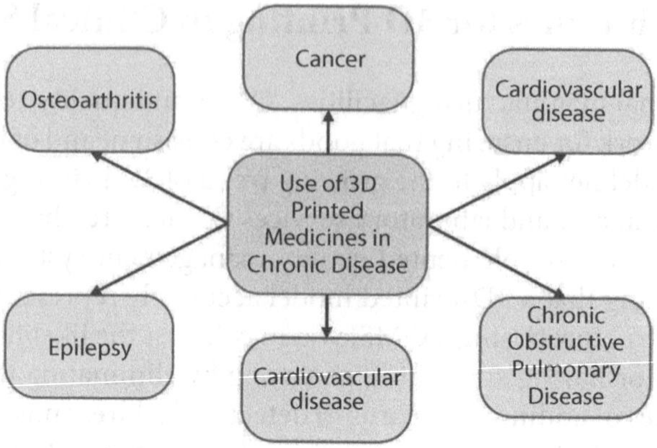

Figure 10.2 3D-printed medicine for the management of chronic diseases.

is going to be used to reshape a medical device or as a surgical guide, then a few more things need to be taken into account. The model's final application drives the design process. A 3D-printed model of the patient's tumor may be recommended to aid in surgical planning, which may require (a) printing a tangible 3D visualization of the tumor with surrounding tissue and (b) showcasing major blood vessels and the nerve. The best way to accomplish this is through interaction with the medical staff; a survey can serve as a useful tool for facilitating the dialogue and guaranteeing that all pertinent information is captured. Validation and verification of designs are techniques used to increase confidence so that the final product will satisfy the user. The official definition of design verification is "the process of determining, via inspection and the presentation of objective evidence," whether or not the requirements for a design have been met. As stated by [31, 35, 36], design validation is the process of acquiring and analyzing objective evidence of a device's specifications' conformity with user wants and planned uses. Customers' needs are the starting point for each product, including 3D-printed medical models. Is there anything missing that the user absolutely must have to finish their mission? To fully convey the need as design inputs, it may take more than one session. It could simply be a routine inquiry that comes in multiple times daily. Technical and logistical constraints, such as the need for connector bars in blood vessel models to ensure that they do not collapse when printing, are also considered during the design process. The device's tolerances are also a crucial requirement for its design. Tolerance refers to the allowable range of dimensions for a gadget or 3D-printed product without compromising its functionality [37]. Device tolerances are determined by design inputs and consider the effects that small changes could have on failure probability and user safety [38].

The kidney, tumor, arteries, veins, and the collecting system might all be shown in different colors, and the model might have a tolerance of ± 1 mm if it is meant to represent a renal tumor. More flexibility and precision may be needed in a prototype for transcatheter aortic valve replacement (TAVR). Tolerances in the submillimeter range are common in the design of surgical cutting guides, which are used to ensure a smooth, accurate cut against a bone. The facility may be unable to produce the part of the equipment or process used to create it that cannot achieve the required precision. After determining design inputs, the development company produces device specs and other descriptive materials (design outputs). The clinical staff or other appropriate individuals can review the digital model to ensure that it is up to snuff and provide feedback on how it can be enhanced for better visualization. The engineering team can check whether or not the supports are adequate for printing the blood vessels using computational methods. The design has been verified and is now ready for production because its outcomes are consistent with its inputs. Even though it may seem like a simple process, it is important to complete the verification and document it to prevent important details from being missed due to poor communication and to give designs for devices and models that can be continuously improved. After the part has been manufactured and the design verification processes have been completed, the device must be tested to ensure that it functions as intended (the customer's requirements). Design validation is the process of checking that a design is correct. The 3D-printed anatomical model appears to be a good fit for its intended use. For this reason, it is important that the cutaway parts be easily removable and reassembled in case the model does not adequately suit the need and further adjustments are required. Although each model must be tailored to the individual patient, the elements common to many operations can be compiled into a standard operating procedure (SOP). The user and the device's intended purpose are kept in the foreground by verifying (that our design meets our expectations) and validating the design iteratively throughout the development process. This kind of production is utilized by manufacturers across many different sectors; thus, it is crucial to include it in a hospital's quality management system tailored for 3D printing [31, 39].

10.6 Production Process and QA

There are many people involved in the 3D-printing process, and mistakes can easily be made and compounded. Part of the QMS involves being aware of certain types of mistakes and learning to spot and prevent them.

10.7 Image Acquisition

The first step in successfully printing a 3D model is selecting the most appropriate imaging method and procedure for that model's application. Due to its excellent spatial accuracy and clarity, computed tomography (CT) is utilized to develop 3D models of bones, whereas ECG-gated pictures are preferred for cardiac models due to their reduced motion and capacity to print structures at the suitable cardiac phase [2, 40, 41]. It is also crucial to gather high-quality, artifact-free volumetric imaging data. The accuracy of a 3D-printed device is often determined by the imaging technique and acquisition methodology used. Traditional CT scans and MRI scans employ thicker layers than the typical 0.05 to 0.1 mm used by 3D printers. Hence, the quality and accuracy of the printed model are directly related to the resolution of the image data. Many 3D-printing guides advise collecting data with a section thickness of less than 1 mm to prevent stair-step artifacts [15, 42, 43]. Errors and artifacts in the original image data, such as motion artifacts or metal streak artifacts [2, 44], can be transferred to the 3D-printed object. When re-examining a sample is not an option, artifacts can be eliminated either in advance through the use of imaging techniques or in post-processing by the modification of reconstruction parameters and the application of appropriate artifact reduction and correction algorithms [2]. Characterizing imaging acquisition methods and post-acquisition image processing techniques ensures that each set of operations has a known and repeatable fidelity, hence reducing the likelihood of imaging errors. Also, only accredited employees using only accredited scanners should ever gather datasets. Accreditation bodies like the American College of Radiology demand stringent quality assurance (QA) standards from individual departments, and as part of the process, regular performance tests are conducted to assess factors including picture quality and noise [15].

10.8 Segmentation

It is a technique for differentiating a specific part of a picture from its background (such as a tumor, heart valve, vascular system, or spinal column). Differences in a 3D-printed model can arise from a lack of understanding of the advantages and disadvantages of various segmentation methods [37, 41, 45]. Segmentation errors can multiply those from the picture acquisition phase [15]. Users at our facility need to have adequate training in software, processes, and anatomy because of the potential for error during segmentation due to structural segmentation, weak contrast, and interpretation in multi-stage analyses (such as mistaking a complex kidney cyst for a tumor). An integral aspect of any quality assurance program is a radiologist-supervised clinician validation step. Automated segmentation software has the potential to save time and improve uniformity, but it also carries the risk of introducing errors. Examples of CT artifacts that might be problematic for automatic segmentation methods include noise and excessive beam hardening [42, 46]. A model may not include or accurately depict abnormal anatomy if it falls outside the range of the algorithm's input data. Nonetheless, developments in machine learning methods are leading to more accurate automatic segmentation [47]. To develop optimal measures for risk reduction, it is vital to comprehend the conditions imposed by the autonomous segmentation process. The 3D-printable object is determined by a blended surface file that is generated as a product of the segmentation process. The stereolithography (STL) file format dominates the surface modeling world, and its usage of triangles to describe surface geometry characteristics is widespread. Other methods of collecting surface geometry and incorporating other object information like color, texture, or printer-specific settings are possible with the help of various file types (such as VRML, X3D, and Wavefront OBJ). Metadata such as the patient's name, the author of the file, copyright information, and the time and date the file was created may also be included. Using a more recent file type could potentially enhance the amount of information stored within the file, but it could also necessitate more checks to ensure compatibility with all software and 3D-printing equipment. The defaults of files need to be harmonized—for instance, it is important to carefully select the number of triangles used to represent the model based on the requirements of the application [15, 49]. A 3D-printed skull model should include at least 600,000 triangles. In contrast, a larger number may be necessary for anatomic models with a lot of moving parts (such as hearts and blood vessels). If there are not enough triangles, the object's surface might be altered [48].

10.9 Printing the Model

Vat photopolymerization, powder bed fusion, material jetting, selective laser sintering, and selective laser melting are utilized to make healthcare models. Fast printing, precise printing, and the ability to print on a variety of materials are just some of the advantages of the various printing methods currently available. All are susceptible to particular types of mistakes, which can be limited or eliminated with sufficient quality assurance procedures [48–51]. That is why it is important to adhere to a procedure tailored to the individual model and printing method being used. Many potential threats to print quality can be addressed and mitigated with a properly prepared file.

10.10 Validation and Verification of Processes

In addition, the production processes themselves are the focus of two essential quality assurance activities: process verification and validation. They consist of the aforementioned quality assurance techniques and output metrics. Direct measurements of device features are taken during process verification activities to prove compliance with standards. It may require taking precise measurements of each component, such as the length of a feature's curve or the distance between two key points [35, 37]. Checking for surface flaws or cracks may also be included. Destructive testing, which is used to establish mechanical strength, precludes post-production measurement or verification of several crucial properties. The method should then be validated to show that it is reliable enough to produce devices that fulfill the required standards. Investigators have determined that assessments (verification) are not required for crucial design features during production if the approach meets the crucial device's features for short development and testing batches and runs reliably and consistently [52, 53]. For this reason, designers double-check every model here at our university, even though their geometry-based features are generally sufficient. Our 3D-printing engineering team performs the verification procedure, which consists of a checklist of key properties for each model type and anatomical location. It involves taking measurements of certain model features to check their dimensions, checking labels to make sure information like the model's serial number and orientation can be read, and making sure that the physical model looks the same as it does in the files. A report is written up with the data and stored electronically. Any mistakes are recorded, prompting a CAPA review to figure out what went wrong.

10.11 Collaboration Between Medical Professionals

The term "point-of-care manufacturing" is being used more and more often to characterize 3D-printing operations in hospitals. The growing popularity of this word reflects the increasing interconnectedness of the medical and industrial sectors, which presents new possibilities and difficulties. Medical equipment manufacturers are subject to FDA regulations, while hospitals are regulated by the Joint Commission and other governing bodies [38]. In the future, hospitals may be classified as either of these types, depending on the kind of goods they produce via point-of-care manufacturing processes. A full quality management system for point-of-care 3D printing is expected to incorporate features from both the medical and manufacturing fields. One pillar of a 3D-printing quality program will be the use of preexisting quality controls and QA standards from various healthcare departments [54]. Another will be clinical supervision and knowledge, and a third will probably be processes borrowed from more conventional manufacturers. While hospitals are used to complying with the accreditation criteria set by organizations like the Joint Commission, they have traditionally found that many of the regulatory standards imposed on traditional manufacturers are beyond their purview. As the fields of medicine and manufacturing become more intertwined, it becomes more vital to be familiar with QMS standards such as ISO 9001 and ISO 13485 [55, 56]. The International Organization for Standardization (ISO) and ASTM International (originally the American Society for Testing and Materials) are just two examples of standards organizations that publish supplementary guidelines for quality assurance, performance standards, and operational processes [57].

10.12 Unique Obstacles and Regulatory Issues

The Food and Drug Administration must have focused a substantial amount of time and money on investigating the impact of 3D printing on the engineering and manufacturing of medical devices, and it has established appropriate guidelines for the entire industry [31, 38]. The FDA has recently sponsored seminars and town halls to collect comments on possible regulatory regimes for point-of-care manufacturing [58]. By having an open dialogue, we have helped spread certain key concepts for 3D printing at the point of care and improved the capacity of existing point-of-care 3D-printing facilities to meet the demands of quality assurance. Facilities should first think about how 3D-printed equipment will be used and whether or not that use comes with any concerns to the patient. Next, they need to think about what their facility is capable of doing, taking into account things like how familiar they are with various devices and models and how well they have been able to prove their claims of quality and reliability. Finally, they should think about the added value that using a 3D-printed part will bring to the patient. It can be compared to the device's natural dangers and the factory's ability to reliably create it. It is the scenario with some surgical equipment. Specified devices provide an unacceptable risk to the patient if they are not created in a controlled environment [58], while others offer benefits to the patient with low risk but exceeding the capabilities of a point-of-care setting.

10.13 Conclusion

Several hospital organizations' engagement in 3D printing shows that the technology has the potential to advance medical care. As more and more hospitals adopt and implement the technology, the healthcare and manufacturing industries will increasingly collaborate. The need for manufacturing-style quality controls, though, increases as the healthcare facility's aim to develop patient-matched simulations increases as well as pushes the potential of the technology. Hence, QA strategies from many fields within medicine and the medical device sector must be integrated. Patient care will remain the basis of the new approach to healthcare provision, which will also facilitate cooperation between industry and healthcare organizations. These advancements will have long-term positive effects on patients because of the priority placed on safety and quality.

References

1. Chepelev, L., Hodgdon, T., Gupta, A., Wang, A., Torres, C., Krishna, S., Akyuz, E., Mitsouras, D., Sheikh, A., Medical 3D printing for vascular interventions and surgical oncology: A primer for the 2016 radiological society of North America (RSNA) hands-on course in 3D printing. *3D Print. Med.*, 2, 1–7, 2016 Dec.
2. Matsumoto, J.S., Morris, J.M., Foley, T.A., Williamson, E.E., Leng, S., McGee, K.P., Kuhlmann, J.L., Nesberg, L.E., Vrtiska, T.J., Three-dimensional physical modeling: Applications and experience at Mayo Clinic. *Radiographics*, 35, 7, 1989–2006, 2015 Nov.
3. McAllister, P., Watson, M., Burke, E., A cost-effective, in-house, positioning and cutting guide system for orthognathic surgery. *J. Maxillofac. Oral. Surg.*, 17, 112–4, 2018 Mar.
4. Lin, H.H., Lonic, D., Lo, L.J., 3D printing in orthognathic surgery– a literature review. *J. Formos. Med. Assoc.*, 117, 7, 547–58, 2018 Jul 1.
5. Tel, A., Costa, F., Sembronio, S., Lazzarotto, A., Robiony, M., All-in-one surgical guide: A new method for cranial vault resection and reconstruction. *J. Cranio-Maxillofac. Surg.*, 46, 6, 967–73, 2018 Jun 1.

6. Sapoval, M., Gaultier, A.L., Del Giudice, C., Pellerin, O., Kassis-Chikhani, N., Lemarteleur, V., Fouquet, V., Tapie, L., Morenton, P., Tavitian, B., Attal, J.P., 3D-printed face protective shield in interventional radiology: Evaluation of an immediate solution in the era of COVID-19 pandemic. *Diagn. Interv. Imaging*, 101, 6, 413–5, 2020 Jun 1.
7. Tino, R., Moore, R., Antoline, S., Ravi, P., Wake, N., Ionita, C.N., Morris, J.M., Decker, S.J., Sheikh, A., Rybicki, F.J., Chepelev, L.L., COVID-19 and the role of 3D printing in medicine. *3D Print. Med.*, 6, 1, 1–8, 2020 Dec.
8. Abujudeh, H., Kaewlai, R., Shaqdan, K., Bruno, M.A., Key principles in quality and safety in radiology. *Am. J. Roentgenol.*, 208, 3, W101–9, 2017 Mar.
9. Kohn, L.T., Corrigan, J.M., Donaldson, M.S., Institute of Medicine Committee on Quality of Health Care in America, *To err is human: Building a safer health system*, National Academies Press, Washington (DC), USA, 2000.
10. World Health Organization, *The world health report 2006: Working together for health*, World Health Organization, Geneva, Switzerland, 2006 Mar 23.
11. Bastawrous, S., Wu, L., Strzelecki, B., Levin, D.B., Li, J.S., Coburn, J., Ripley, B., Establishing quality and safety in hospital-based 3D printing programs: Patient-first approach. *Radiographics*, 41, 4, 1208–29, 2021 Jul.
12. Siewert, B., Hochman, M., Eisenberg, R.L., Swedeen, S., Brook, O.R., Acing The joint commission regulatory visit: Running an effective and compliant safety program. *Radiographics*, 38, 6, 1744–60, 2018 Oct.
13. Johnson, C.D., Krecke, K.N., Miranda, R., Roberts, C.C., Denham, C., Developing a radiology quality and safety program: A primer. *Radiographics*, 29, 4, 951–9, 2009 Jul.
14. Christensen, A. and Rybicki, F.J., Maintaining safety and efficacy for 3D printing in medicine. *3D Print. Med.*, 3, 1, 1–0, 2017 Mar.
15. Leng, S., McGee, K., Morris, J., Alexander, A., Kuhlmann, J., Vrieze, T., McCollough, C.H., Matsumoto, J., Anatomic modeling using 3D printing: Quality assurance and optimization. *3D Print. Med.*, 3, 1–4, 2017 Mar.
16. Morrison, R.J., Kashlan, K.N., Flanangan, C.L., Wright, J.K., Green, G.E., Hollister, S.J., Weatherwax, K.J., Regulatory considerations in the design and manufacturing of implantable 3D-printed medical devices. *Clin. Transl. Sci.*, 8, 5, 594–600, 2015 Oct.
17. Chepelev, L., Wake, N., Ryan, J., Althobaity, W., Gupta, A., Arribas, E., Santiago, L., Ballard, D.H., Wang, K.C., Weadock, W., Ionita, C.N., Radiological Society of North America (RSNA) 3D printing Special Interest Group (SIG): Guidelines for medical 3D printing and appropriateness for clinical scenarios. *3D Print. Med.*, 4, 1, 1–38, 2018 Dec.
18. Kohn, L.T., Committee on Quality of Health Care in America, *To err is human: Building a safer health system*, National Academic Press, Washington (DC), USA, 2000.
19. Kruskal, J.B., Eisenberg, R., Sosna, J., Yam, C.S., Kruskal, J.D., Boiselle, P.M., Quality improvement in radiology: Basic principles and tools required to achieve success. *Radiographics*, 31, 6, 1499–509, 2011 Oct.

20. Wake, N., Rosenkrantz, A.B., Huang, R., Park, K.U., Wysock, J.S., Taneja, S.S., Huang, W.C., Sodickson, D.K., Chandarana, H., Patient-specific 3D printed and augmented reality kidney and prostate cancer models: Impact on patient education. *3D Print. Med.*, 5, 1–8, 2019 Dec.
21. Conti, M., Marconi, S., Muscogiuri, G., Guglielmo, M., Baggiano, A., Italiano, G., Mancini, M.E., Auricchio, F., Andreini, D., Rabbat, M.G., Guaricci, A.I., Left atrial appendage closure guided by 3D computed tomography printing technology: A case control study. *J. Cardiovasc. Comput. Tomogr.*, 13, 6, 336–9, 2019 Nov 1.
22. Li, Y., Li, L., Ma, Y., Zhang, K., Li, G., Lu, B., Lu, C., Chen, C., Wang, L., Wang, H., Cui, X., 3D-printed titanium cage with PVA-vancomycin coating prevents surgical site infections (SSIs). *Macromol. Biosci.*, 20, 3, 1900394, 2020 Mar.
23. Prakash, M., Ong, Q., Lo, C., Macemon, J.B., El Gamel, A., Rib cage stabilisation with 3D-printed polyethylene sternal prosthesis post-sternotomy mediastinitis. *Heart Lung Circ.*, 29, 10, 1561–5, 2020 Oct 1.
24. Sporer, S., MacLean, L., Burger, A., Moric, M., Evaluation of a 3D-printed total knee arthroplasty using radiostereometric analysis: Assessment of highly porous biological fixation of the tibial baseplate and metal-backed patellar component. *Bone Joint J.*, 101, 7_Supple_C, 40–7, 2019 Jul.
25. Wen, X., Gao, S., Feng, J., Li, S., Gao, R., Zhang, G., Chest-wall reconstruction with a customized titanium-alloy prosthesis fabricated by 3D printing and rapid prototyping. *J. Cardiothorac. Surg.*, 13, 1–7, 2018 Dec.
26. Mokawem, M., Katzouraki, G., Harman, C.L., Lee, R., Lumbar interbody fusion rates with 3D-printed lamellar titanium cages using a silicate-substituted calcium phosphate bone graft. *J. Clin. Neurosci.*, 68, 134–9, 2019 Oct 1.
27. Beck, J.M. and Jacobson, M.D., 3D printing: What could happen to products liability when users (and everyone else in between) become manufacturers. *Minn. J.L. Sci. & Tech.*, 18, 143, 2017.
28. Klatt, B.A., Goyal, N., Austin, M.S., Hozack, W.J., Custom-fit total knee arthroplasty (OtisKnee) results in malalignment. *J. Arthroplasty*, 23, 1, 26–9, 2008 Jan 1.
29. Odeh, M., Levin, D., Inziello, J., Lobo Fenoglietto, F., Mathur, M., Hermsen, J., Stubbs, J., Ripley, B., Methods for verification of 3D printed anatomic model accuracy using cardiac models as an example. *3D Print. Med.*, 5, 1, 1–2, 2019 Dec.
30. Christensen, A. and Wake, N., Regulatory perspectives for 3D printing in hospitals, in: *3D Printing for the Radiologist*, vol. 1, pp. 109–16, 2022 Jan.
31. Brook, O.R., Kruskal, J.B., Eisenberg, R.L., Larson, D.B., Root cause analysis: Learning from adverse safety events. *Radiographics*, 35, 6, 1655–67, 2015 Oct.

32. Thornton, E., Brook, O.R., Mendiratta-Lala, M., Hallett, D.T., Kruskal, J.B., Application of failure mode and effect analysis in a radiology department. *Radiographics*, 31, 1, 281–93, 2011 Jan.
33. Mitsouras, D., Liacouras, P., Imanzadeh, A., Giannopoulos, A.A., Cai, T., Kumamaru, K.K., George, E., Wake, N., Caterson, E.J., Pomahac, B., Ho, V.B., Medical 3D printing for the radiologist. *Radiographics*, 35, 7, 1965–88, 2015 Nov.
34. Chen, Y.L., Two-level process validation approach for medical devices. *J. Med. Eng. Technol.*, 43, 2, 139–49, 2019 Feb 17.
35. Coburn, J.C. and Grant, G.T., FDA regulatory pathways and technical considerations for the 3D printing of medical models and devices, in: *3D Printing in Medicine: A Practical Guide for Medical Professionals*, pp. 97–111, 2017.
36. George, E., Liacouras, P., Rybicki, F.J., Mitsouras, D., Measuring and establishing the accuracy and reproducibility of 3D printed medical models. *Radiographics*, 37, 5, 1424–50, 2017 Sep.
37. Braian, M., Jimbo, R., Wennerberg, A., Production tolerance of additive manufactured polymeric objects for clinical applications. *Dent. Mater.*, 32, 7, 853–61, 2016 Jul 1.
38. Di Prima, M., Coburn, J., Hwang, D., Kelly, J., Khairuzzaman, A., Ricles, L., Additively manufactured medical products–the FDA perspective. *3D Print. Med.*, 2, 1–6, 2016 Dec.
39. Shaheen, E., Sun, Y., Jacobs, R., Politis, C., Three-dimensional printed final occlusal splint for orthognathic surgery: Design and validation. *Int. J. Oral. Maxillofac. Surg.*, 46, 1, 67–71, 2017 Jan 1.
40. Levin, D., Mackensen, G.B., Reisman, M., McCabe, J.M., Dvir, D., Ripley, B., 3D printing applications for transcatheter aortic valve replacement. *Curr. Cardiol. Rep.*, 22, 1–9, 2020 Apr.
41. Huotilainen, E., Jaanimets, R., Valášek, J., Marcián, P., Salmi, M., Tuomi, J., Mäkitie, A., Wolff, J., Inaccuracies in additive manufactured medical skull models caused by the DICOM to STL conversion process. *J. Craniomaxillofac. Surg.*, 42, 5, e259–65, 2014 Jul 1.
42. Bastawrous, S., Wake, N., Levin, D., Ripley, B., Principles of three-dimensional printing and clinical applications within the abdomen and pelvis. *Abdom. Radiol.*, 43, 2809–22, 2018 Oct.
43. Huotilainen, E., Paloheimo, M., Salmi, M., Paloheimo, K.S., Björkstrand, R., Tuomi, J., Markkola, A., Mäkitie, A., Imaging requirements for medical applications of additive manufacturing. *Acta Radiol.*, 55, 1, 78–85, 2014 Feb.

44. Winder, J. and Bibb, R., Medical rapid prototyping technologies: State of the art and current limitations for application in oral and maxillofacial surgery. *J. Oral. Maxillofac. Surg.*, 63, 7, 1006–15, 2005 Jul 1.
45. Fourie, Z., Damstra, J., Schepers, R.H., Gerrits, P.O., Ren, Y., Segmentation process significantly influences the accuracy of 3D surface models derived from cone beam computed tomography. *Eur. J. Radiol.*, 81, 4, e524–30, 2012 Apr 1.
46. Ripley, B., Levin, D., Kelil, T., Hermsen, J.L., Kim, S., Maki, J.H., Wilson, G.J., 3D printing from MRI data: Harnessing strengths and minimizing weaknesses. *J. Magn. Reson. Imaging*, 45, 3, 635–45, 2017 Mar.
47. Guo, K., Zou, D., Chen, X., 3D mesh labeling via deep convolutional neural networks. *ACM Trans. Graphics (TOG)*, 35, 1, 1–2, 2015 Dec 29.
48. Sheikh, A., Chepelev, L., Christensen, A.M., Mitsouras, D., Schwarz, B.A., Rybicki, F.J., Beginning and developing a radiology-based in-hospital 3D printing lab, in: *3D Printing in Medicine: A Practical Guide for Medical Professionals*, pp. 35–41, 2017.
49. Rahman, Z., Barakh Ali, S.F., Ozkan, T., Charoo, N.A., Reddy, I.K., Khan, M.A., Additive manufacturing with 3D printing: Progress from bench to bedside. *AAPS J.*, 20, 1–4, 2018 Nov.
50. Rojek, I., Mikołajewski, D., Dostatni, E., Kopowski, J., Specificity of 3D printing and AI-based optimization of medical devices using the example of a group of exoskeletons. *Appl. Sci.*, 13, 2, 1060, 2023 Jan.
51. Tagliaferri, V., Trovalusci, F., Guarino, S., Venettacci, S., Environmental and economic analysis of FDM, SLS and MJF additive manufacturing technologies. *Materials*, 12, 24, 4161, 2019 Dec 11.
52. Broder, J.C., Cameron, S.F., Korn, W.T., Baccei, S.J., Creating a radiology quality and safety program: Principles and pitfalls. *Radiographics*, 38, 6, 1786–98, 2018 Oct.
53. Manghani, K., Quality assurance: Importance of systems and standard operating procedures. *Perspect. Clin. Res.*, 2, 1, 34, 2011 Jan.
54. Bastawrous, S., Wu, L., Strzelecki, B., Levin, D.B., Li, J.S., Coburn, J., Ripley, B., Establishing quality and safety in hospital-based 3D printing programs: Patient-first approach. *Radiographics*, 41, 4, 1208–29, 2021 Jul.
55. International Organization for Standardization, Quality management systems: Requirements, International Organization for Standardization, 2008.
56. Bos, G., ISO 13485: 2003/2016—Medical devices—Quality management systems—Requirements for regulatory purposes, in: *Handbook of Medical Device Regulatory Affairs in Asia*, pp. 153–174, Jenny Stanford Publishing, Dubai, U.A.E., 2018 Mar 28.

57. Beitler, B.G., Abraham, P.F., Glennon, A.R., Tommasini, S.M., Lattanza, L.L., Morris, J.M., Wiznia, D.H., Interpretation of regulatory factors for 3D printing at hospitals and medical centers, or at the point of care. *3D Print. Med.*, 8, 1, 7, 2022 Feb 1.
58. Rath, S.N. and Sankar, S., 3D printers for surgical practice, in: *3D Printing in Medicine*, pp. 127–147, Woodhead Publishing, Cambridge, United Kingdom, 2023 Jan 1.

11

Emerging Applications of 3D Printing in Plastic Surgery

Abstract
Preoperative planning in plastic and reconstructive surgery relies heavily on modern imaging tools. Unfortunately, the capabilities of 2D workstations restrict the use of conventional modalities such as 3D reconstructions. Printing three-dimensional objects layer by layer from a computer-aided design (CAD) was traditionally the purview of industry. Medical imaging is being employed to guide the 3D printing of models that clinicians can handle and manipulate to better understand the anatomical relationship between different body parts. Researchers are able to produce 3D models employing a variety of 3D-printing methods, including stereolithography, multijet modeling, selective laser sintering, binder jet approach, and fused deposition modeling. There is debate among medical professionals as to whether or not the benefits outweigh the costs of continuing to utilize the technique. While several important patents related to 3D printing have expired over the past decade, the price and footprint of these machines have shrunk dramatically. Advances in diagnostic imaging and accessible 3D software have made it possible to build anatomical structures and implants in 3D on a computer without resorting to outsourcing. These innovations hold a great deal of potential for bringing 3D printing to the bedside for usage in a variety of healthcare settings. Here the investigator takes a look at the many ways in which 3D printing is currently being utilized in plastic surgery, from improving the aesthetic outcomes of craniofacial implant surgery to making facial transplantation templates. Designers also address how 3D printing may help in preoperative planning, the development of intraoperative guidance aids, the teaching of patients and surgical trainees, and the development of patient-specific prostheses, all of which can be done in the comfort of an organizational setting.

Keywords: 3D printing, plastic surgery, computer-aided design, preoperative planning, education, urology

Rishabha Malviya and Rishav Sharma. 3D Printing in Healthcare: Novel Applications, (205–228)

11.1 Introduction

Preoperative planning in plastic surgery now routinely incorporates the use of state-of-the-art medical imaging technology. More precise and reputable preoperative choice of the donor site, flap, perforators, and optimal method of dissection [1–3] has been possible with the advent of computed tomography angiography and it has been reported to improve clinical results. In order to better prepare for surgery, recent developments in 3D and 4D CTA [4, 5] have enabled an improved comprehension of the perforator arteries, vasculature area, and dynamical flow characteristics. Unfortunately, the capabilities of contemporary imaging methods are restricted by the constraints of a two-dimensional display, such as a computer monitor. A 3D-printed haptic model can instead help the surgeon and patient better grasp the anatomy and process, leading to more precise surgical planning. Clinicians interested in making use of the benefits of 3D printing have historically had to outsource the process due to the technological complications of 3D software and the high cost of early 3D printers. Recent developments in 3D printing have allowed it to move from the R&D lab to the clinical "bedside," and researchers discuss how they could make it a widespread application in plastic surgery. Patients with severe physical and mental health issues often suffer from tissue and organ damage or deformity as a result of illness, injury, tumors, or congenital anomalies. Although plastic surgeons have long sought solutions to the challenge of restoring and cosmetically improving patients' tissues and organs, these solutions have frequently been limited by the limitations of conventional surgical techniques. In clinical surgical therapy, the aesthetic demands of particular patients often necessitate the development of implants with distinctive forms. Conventional biomaterials (e.g., growth, silicone, etc.) are capable of causing complications such as encapsulating information infection and bleeding after surgery, typically falling short of meeting the particular needs for high precision. Although autologous tissue transplantation has many potential benefits, it also comes with risks, including injury to the donor site and increased surgical difficulty [5]. However, with the advancements in 3D-bioprinting technology, custom grafts may be designed for each patient, thus improving the accuracy and efficacy. It significantly lessens the difficulty, risk, and time required for cosmetic surgery. Customized, individual grafts are now feasible due to advancements in 3D-bioprinting technology, which have resulted in the growth of several bio-inks and printing processes. When compared to traditional biomaterials, those printed from a patient's seed cells offer

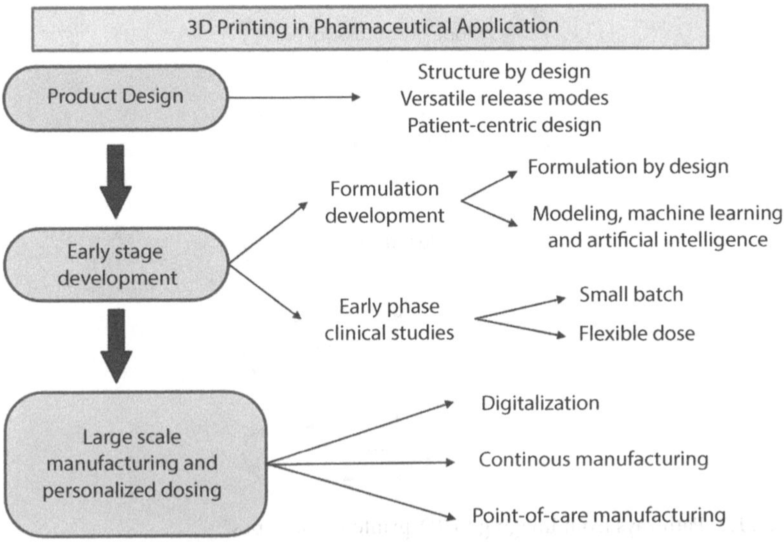

Figure 11.1 Pharmaceutical 3D printing.

increased biocompatibility and decreased immunogenicity. In addition, discomfort and inflammation, which can arise from the donor area being manipulated surgically, are avoided during autologous transplantation [6–12]. Intraoperative bioprinting is just one example of a cutting-edge printing technology that has led to revolutionary concepts in plastic surgery [13]. Figure 11.1 provides an analysis of 3D printing's potential in the medical field.

11.2 3D Printing

In 3D printing, also known as fast prototyping or additive manufacturing, a product is built from a computer-aided design by adding consecutive layers of material, as demonstrated in Figure 11.2 [6]. In comparison to traditional production techniques like injection molding, three-dimensional printing has brought in a new era of inventive freedom by facilitating the rapid production of unique objects with intricate geometries [11]. Three-dimensional printing (or "3D printing") has several benefits, one of the most important being the speed and low cost with which an idea may be turned into a finished object. It reduces production costs [12] by eliminating unnecessary steps including product development, assembly lines, delivery, and storage of parts and by employing less expensive materials

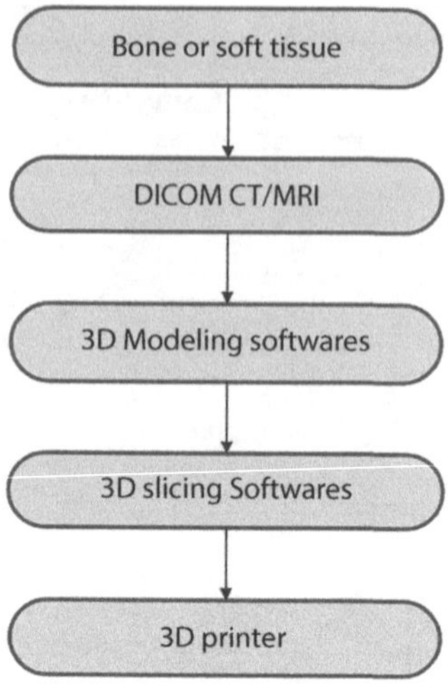

Figure 11.2 Pathways from imaging to 3D-printed prototypes.

and labor. Industrial designers have been using 3D printing for decades, but the technology has only recently been adopted for use in medicine [14]. The 3D-printer makers' proprietary software transforms these files into print-ready data slices. Although many different 3D-printing technologies have been created for use in the commercial sector, relatively few have been explored for possible use in the medical sector. A few examples are selective laser sintering (SLS), binder jetting, fused deposition modeling (FDM), multijet modeling (MJM), and stereolithography (SLA). Researchers explore each of these to assess how they have been used in practice and where they have room to grow, covering everything from hard-to-reach bone to more supple soft tissues.

11.3 3D Printing in Medicine

Over the past decade or two, scientists have shown that 3D printing may be put to use in a variety of surgical specialties. Tactile feedback from 3D-printed haptic models in the clinical setting allows for the simulation of complicated anatomical movements, such as temporomandibular joint articulation, that would otherwise be impossible to duplicate in software [15]. Surgeons can have a better understanding of the spatial relationship between anatomical features due to these aids [16]. It may lead to less time spent in surgery, less time spent with the patient under general anesthesia, less time spent with the wound exposed, and less blood loss during the procedure [17–22].

11.4 Preoperative Planning

Preoperatively, 3D-printed models had been encountered to be useful in determining the course of excision of bony lesions in orthopedic surgery [29–34], prefabricated components of bony attachment plates in maxillofacial surgery [22–28], craniofacial geographical area reconstruction [22–28], skull base reconstructed images, and cervical spine reconstruction [22–28] in neurosurgery. Congenital heart defects and tracheobronchial variation in cardiac hepatectomy and liver transplantation can be effectively treated by general surgery [35–37]. The urologists frequently perform a partial nephrectomy when treating renal tumors [38]. Reconstructing frontal sinus deficits is a common procedure in otolaryngology [39–43].

11.5 Intraoperative Guidance

Surgery specialties as diverse as maxillofacial [44–49], neurosurgery [50], orthopedic [51], hand [52], and general [53] have profited from customized surgical templates and real-time intraoperative guidance devices made possible by 3D software.

11.5.1 Education

Medical students and residents alike can benefit from 3D-printed haptic models [54–63] when it comes to patient education and surgical training.

11.5.2 Customized Prosthesis

However, 3D printing has made it simple and fast to produce one-of-a-kind implantation. Researchers have developed individualized implants for a variety of anatomical sites, including the mandible in maxillofacial surgery [64–66], the cranium in cranioplasty in neurosurgery [67, 68], the hip in orthopedic surgery [69, 70], and the airway in pediatric cardiothoracic surgery for cases of challenging tracheobronchomalacia.

11.5.3 Allied Health

Hearing aid production is another area where 3D printing has had a major effect on the healthcare system; at present, 99% of all hearing aids sold worldwide are 3D-printed [71, 72]. Also, 3D printing has aided in the following areas of medicine: forensics [73], anatomy [74], podiatry [75], dentistry [76–78], the pharmaceutical industry [79, 80], the production of patient-specific 3D-printed medication, and regenerative medicine [81, 82].

11.6 Bioprinting for Plastic Surgery Applications

Repairing and reconstructing damaged or malformed human tissues and organs as well as reshaping the normally developed human body, using surgical means to improve aesthetics and restore function, is known as plastic surgery. When it comes to plastic surgery, the spectrum of organ tissues that can be repaired or rebuilt is extensive. The standard for plastic surgeons is continually being raised because of the risks of infection, discomfort, and deformity when using grafts (both autologous and allogeneic) as well as the dangers of destroying the donor location during surgery. The ability to print a wide range of physiologically natural cells, a matrix of extracellular particles, cell proliferation factors, and environmentally friendly polymer supporting components allows for the generation of individualized and custom-tailored surgical implants based on patient requirements, such as *in situ* printing, immediately on the patient's affected region to promote wound healing. The advent of these tools allows for the practice of accurate medicine, which has greatly streamlined surgery and eradicated postoperative problems [83, 84]. Key areas of plastic surgery that have benefited from 3D bioprinting research include surgical procedures for mending and regenerating skin, ears, noses, breasts, and the jawbone and facial bones.

11.6.1 Skin Wounds

Substantial skin tissue abnormalities that cannot be healed by the immune system on their own might be the result of severe burns, diabetic ulcers, malignancies, and other causes. Autologous epidermal grafting or autologous flap (bone flap) grafting is a therapeutic therapy for skin defects; however, it differs depending on the kind of lesion. Traditional methods of treatment do not come without their share of challenges, however [85, 86]. Plastic surgeons now have access to innovative tools credited to the 3D bioprinting of skin tissue products for the treatment of skin problems and stimulation of skin regeneration. Because of its high biocompatibility and quick cure time, GelMA finds extensive application in skin tissue engineering. A novel bio-ink composed of GelMA and COL combined with tyrosinase was proposed for application in skin development by Y Shi *et al.* [87]. In addition, Lin *et al.* [88] demonstrated that Si-GelMa, created by adding Si into GelMA, degrades more slowly and boosts human dermal fibroblast activity without lowering its printability point. The healing properties of GelMA hydrogel comprising vascular endothelial growth factor mimic peptide were confirmed in animal tests by Jang *et al.* [89]. As a biomaterial, CHO incorporates great promise for application in skin regeneration. The relevance of CHO in rejuvenation of the skin was proven by Intini and colleagues [90] by *in vitro* tests of its biophysical compatibility, cytocompatibility, and neurotoxicity to fibroblasts from human beings and keratin-forming cells. Additional evidence for the beneficial physicochemical properties of CHO materials for skin tissue engineering comes from the work of Sandri *et al.* [91], who successfully experimentally created a CHO/glycosaminoglycan-based bioscaffold for the healing of severe skin wounds by first cross-linking the CHO scaffolds with non-toxic genipin and then heparinizing them. According to research on their physicochemical properties and wound healing activities, SDF-1 therapeutic stents have been proven to enhance neovascularization in local wounds and encourage the repair of local skin tissue [92]. The clinical challenge of full-thickness skin regeneration is far from solved. To make a bioactive 3D sponge, Dong *et al.* [93] re-cross-linked pig SIS with a polyethylene glycol that possessed succinimidyl glutarate terminal branches. If accurate, that would be a brilliant solution to the problem. After 21 days of SIS–PEG treatment, separated epidermal and dermal cells formed rebuilt skin with regrown hair [93]. The concept of minimum functional skin units autologous skin was introduced by Peng Chang as an additional contribution, which consists of a fully functioning skin unit embedded in a full-thickness skin microstructure. When compared to bioscaffolds loaded with single seed cells, MFU-laden bioscaffolds had a more potent healing potential [94]. Deficiencies in graft-host anastomosis, induced angiogenesis, and vascular architecture are only a few of the difficulties associated with tissue-engineered permanent skin replacements. The micropillars of homogenous strontium silicate were manufactured by Ma's team and included in biomaterial inks to serve as a stable cell-inducing agent for angiogenesis. Bioprinting bionic multicellular systems serve as functional skin replacements [95]. In addition, human Wharton's jelly mesenchymal stem cell endothelial cells were transplanted into the dermal defect wound of SD mice using a biological scaffold. The research investigation demonstrated that the transplantation cells' ability to trigger and speed up the development of vascular and skin reconstitution was boosted by the multiscale multilayered development of macroporous filamentous protein scaffolds containing nanofibrous microstructures [96]. More cells were able to infiltrate the area, more COL was deposited, and more growth factors were expressed. Autologous epithelial grafting is currently being used clinically to treat patients with burns that affect more than 60% of their bodies. However, the medicinal advantages of autologous epithelial grafting for dermal tissues that have been shown to have ruptured in severe burns are limited. A 3D bioprinter was used by Roshangar *et al.* [97] to inject adipose-derived stem cells into a 3D gel scaffold. Hematoxylin–eosin staining and scanning electron microscopy were used to evaluate 3D scaffolds for morphology and cell adhesion qualities, and methylthiazolyl diphenyl tetrazolium bromide analysis was used to calculate cell viability. The use of 3D gel scaffolds, with or without the addition of ADSC, has been shown to hasten wound contraction and healing in an experimental model of whole-layer burns in rats. Nevertheless, epithelialization occurred earlier in rats treated with gel scaffolds made with bio-ink loaded with ADSC [98]. Healing of serious skin lesions may be the subject of future studies using 3D-bioprinting technology paired with stem cells.

11.7 3D Printing in Plastic and Reconstructive Surgery

Preoperative preparation, intraoperative supervision and guidelines, and the development of 3D-printed haptic models might be used in a variety of ways in plastic and reconstructive surgery, including the creation of custom prostheses for individual patients.

11.8 Preoperative Planning: Soft Tissue Mapping

When significant soft tissue defects need to be repaired following trauma or oncologic resection, perforator flap surgery is frequently used. CTA has changed preoperative planning in reconstructive surgery by helping surgeons select the best donor location, flap, and perforator for a free flap transfer [99], hence increasing the success rate of flap transfers and bettering the clinical results overall [100]. More clinical insight can be gained via visual and tactile evaluation of 3D models, complementing the information provided by CTA. Researchers recently published a study detailing the process of creating a "reverse" model of an ankle lesion to plan a perforator flap-based reconstruction [101]. Regular CTA was performed on both the recipient's lower extremities and the donor's forearms, Osirix was used to convert the DICOM data to a CAD file. Using Magics software (Materialise NV), a "reverse" model reflecting the wound defect is constructed by digitally subtracting the normal contralateral ankle from the problematic side of the 3D image. Free open-source software like Osirix and 3D Slicer also allow for the mirroring function to be accomplished. That way, the surgeon could plan ahead of time on how big a free flap would need to be to cover the deformity. The Cube 2 printer (3D Systems) was used to create both the normal and abnormal ankle models in PLA filaments. Perforator flap repair of a sacral wound defect after oncologic excision is another area where we have recently demonstrated that a 3D-printed model can be helpful in the design process [102]. To do the same for the sacral CTA data acquired before surgery, we turned to Osirix to create a computer-aided design drawing. Owing to the limitations of the Cube 2 printer (its maximum construction dimensions are 16 cm), the 3D image of the sacral defect had to be reduced in size before it could be printed. The haptic model maintained its validity in depicting the defect's form, extent, and relationship to neighboring anatomical components. The volume of soft tissues can be evaluated with the help of 3D printing. At present, surgeons use either 2D photography or 3D scanning technologies such as VECTRA (Canfield Imaging Systems, Fairfield, NJ, USA) [103] for volumetric analysis, which is a crucial part of breast reconstruction surgery. The inability to take into account the underlying chest wall asymmetry, which may wrongly lead to an asymmetrical appearance despite equal breast parenchymal volumes, is a major drawback of 3D photography techniques like VECTRA. In addition, patients need to stand with their backs against a wall for the scans to be accurate, which can be difficult for those with kyphosis or scoliosis. A 3D-printed replica of a patient's breasts after a mastectomy was used for preoperative planning, according to a recent article [104]. An actual copy, however, reduced in size to accommodate the printer's construction chamber, allowed doctors to visualize the variation in breast shape and volume. To further quantify the breast parenchymal volume differential, researchers used Osirix's segmentation tool.

11.9 Preoperative Planning: Vascular Mapping

In order to better understand the perforator vessels and how they connect to surrounding tissues, CTA has become standard practice as a preoperative assessment before perforator flap surgery [105, 106]. In a recent cadaver study, Gillis and Morris [107] reported how they used a binder jet 3D printer (ProJet x60 series, 3D Systems) to produce a replica of the perforators of the internal mammary artery and adjacent ribs. The surgeons were still able to instinctively interpret the replica's vascular architecture when it was shrunk to fit the printer's size. Strangely, the DIEA perforators could not be 3D-printed using the existing method. As the resolution of the CTA's DICOM data is 0.625 mm, the Cube 2 printer's resolution is 0.200 mm, and the average diameter of a DIEA perforator is between 1 and 1.4 mm [108], the discrepancy is probably due to a restriction in the 3D modeling program, 3D Slicer. Future avoidance of the issue may be possible through the use of free supplemental software features, such as those offered by the Vascular Modeling Toolkit for the use with 3D Slicer. VMTK is intended to particularly segment vascular structures. They are still in their infancy on the technological scale, making them tricky to work with unless you have extensive experience in computer engineering. When technology in the area improves, designers should anticipate an equally improved user experience.

11.10 Preoperative Planning: Bony Mapping

Plastic and reconstructive surgery can also benefit from 3D printing to treat forearm, wrist, and hand bone pathologies. For medical applications of 3D printing, CT scans have proven to be the most reliable imaging modality. As bones are so easily distinguished, 3D printing techniques for bony structures have become standard in several types of surgery, including maxillofacial [109–111], neuro, and orthopedic [112–116]. A 3D-printed replica of the first carpometacarpal joint that had been subluxated was created by our study group while employing Osirix and a Cube 2 printer. Understanding the first metacarpal's anatomical relationship to the trapezium can be done intuitively. This was enabled by the model's multi-perspective visualization and tactile feedback. The data assisted in formulating the most effective strategy for reduction.

11.11 Intraoperative Guidance

Customized surgical templates and tools that aid in directing the surgeon during surgery have been made possible by the widespread availability of 3D printing. In maxillofacial surgery, 3D printing has been shown to be useful for things like patient-specific orthognathic templates used to guide osteotomy and a device to lessen the effects of a mandibular fracture [117, 118]. The use of a drill template helps in the surgical treatment of multi-layered cervical spine instability [120] and the use of screw fixation guidance device during spinal neurosurgery [119]. Fuller *et al.* showed how 3D printing may be used to expedite the creation of custom implants for use in plastic and reconstructive surgery and development of a bespoke bone reduction clamp design for hand fractures, in contrast to the time-consuming and potentially discouraging techniques typically used [120]. The FDM prototypes' 3D printing was outsourced for USD 75 and took between 3 days and a week to arrive. Direct metal laser sintering, an additive manufacturing approach, was used to create the metal final design at a cost of US$1,200 within a turnaround period of 2 days. Researchers formally recognized that using 3D software for prototyping is not straightforward for practitioners with only minimal computer expertise. The whole cost was more than what one would spend for stock hardware. However, assuming that 3D-printing technology progresses and 3D printing is done "in-house," this disparity may quickly disappear.

11.12 Surgical Training

A plastic surgeon's skill and the goals of a surgical education program depend on his or her in-depth familiarity with the anatomy of the human body and the spatial relationships between its many parts. In the course of conventional medical education, a future surgeon can gather procedural experiences by dissecting the gradual acquiring of surgical skills through monitoring of human cadavers while studying medicine in college and working with seasoned surgeons throughout residency expertise. Embossing fluids containing formalin is becoming increasingly unpopular due to the rising costs to maintain them as well as cultural and societal challenges and safety concerns [121, 122], such that human cadavers are disappearing from the anatomical instruction curriculum. In addition, working under an experienced surgeon as an assistant is a good way to learn some practical knowledge, but there is no substitute for being an operator itself. Anatomical models created on a 3D printer can serve as a haptic visualisation tool and a surgical simulator. In addition, trainee surgeons may prepare for probable intraoperative difficulties and postoperative results using 3D-printed haptic models that imitate complicated, patient-specific conditions. Clinical results and complication rates may both benefit from a surgeon's ability to acquire new skills over time. Neurosurgeons [123,

124], thoracic surgeons [125–127], urologists [128], and general surgeons are only a few of the researchers who have shown that 3D printing is useful in surgical education. One of the main obstacles, however, is the lack of ingredients that mimic the biomechanical properties and permeability of human tissue, allowing for photorealistic color printing. New materials for 3D printing will allow for more convincing reproductions of human anatomy in the future [129].

11.13 Patient Education

An essential component of obtaining informed consent is the doctor–patient consultation, and 3D-printed replicas can help both parties better comprehend the desired surgery, its potential outcomes, and any issues that may arise. Patients who lack a medical background typically struggle to make sense of conventional CT or MRI studies. To precisely mimic the results of cosmetic treatment on a computer screen, plastic surgeons have recently begun using 3D scanning technologies, such as VECTRA (Canfield Imaging Systems) [130]. On the other hand, research shows that a 3D haptic model's visual and tactile feedback is more effective than 2D or 3D imaging techniques at conveying an awareness of anatomical features [131].

11.14 Patient-Specific Prosthesis

The adaptability of 3D printing potentially lower the cost and increase the accessibility of patient-specific prostheses, which is crucial as personalzsed medicine gains ground in the medical field. It has been shown that custom-made implants are more likely to successfully restore both function and aesthetics than standard implants [132, 133]. Sterilization of common 3D-printing materials can be accomplished with common chemicals, including techniques for employing glutaraldehyde that has been approved by the Food and Drug Administration as well as steam and gas [134] for intraoperative use. Researchers have reported 3D-printed nose [135], ear [136], eye, face [137, 138], and hand [139] prostheses in the past decade. Another example is the "Ear and Nose Library" established by an Italian research team led by De Crescenzio and Ciocca, which includes CAD files of 3D-photographed ears and noses of average college students. Whenever constructing a prosthesis for a patient with a disease affecting both ears or the entire nose, physicians can choose which is the most acceptable CAD file from the database [140]. This is due to the fact that clinicians can avoid the problem altogether by not copying the normal contralateral side. Standard breast implants in plastic surgery come in a range of volumes but just a few distinct silhouettes. Hence, 3D-printed breast implants that are tailored to the patient's unique chest wall anatomy and aesthetic goals may provide superior aesthetic results.

It has been widely reported [136] that the aesthetic quality of 3D-printed custom prostheses is significantly higher than that of wax-based handcrafted prostheses. Improved clinical results, including shorter surgical times, less anesthetic use, and fewer chances of problems like infection, are possible because tailored implants eliminate the need for intraoperative modification and adjustment required by standard implants. Most custom implants are made utilizing high-priced 3D-printing methods like MJM and SLS [141], which is a big downside. However, the manufacturing cycle gets prolonged and the cost is increased [139], whereas low-cost FDM 3D printers have been employed to make negative molds for silicone or wax-based casts. It is large because, as of right now, the only FDM filament options are ABS and PLA, both of which are too rigid to be used in the fabrication of soft tissue prosthetics. The investigator anticipates, however, that, in the not-too-distant future, we will be able to immediately construct a custom-made prosthesis at a reasonable price as 3D-printing research and development continues to expand dramatically and as new materials become available for FDM.

11.15 Conclusion

Plastic surgeons have discovered that image-guided 3D-printed haptic models are an invaluable adjunct to 3D imaging modalities in preoperative planning, the development of postoperative guidance tools, education and training of patients and surgical learners, and the advancement of patient-specific implants over the past decade. Due to the initial high cost of machines and the technical difficulty of 3D software, medical 3D printing was first unattainable. The considerable decline in price and exponential growth of the 3D printing industry can be directly attributed to the expiration of several key patents. At the end of the day, researchers think that the increasing prevalence of 3D printing has an opportunity to make such technologies an integral part of the plastic surgeon's clinical bedside toolkit.

References

1. Rozen, W.M., Anavekar, N.S., Ashton, M.W., Stella, D.L., Grinsell, D., Bloom, R.J., Taylor, G.I., Does the preoperative imaging of perforators with CT angiography improve operative outcomes in breast reconstruction? *Microsurgery: Official Journal of the International Microsurgical Society and the European Federation of Societies for Microsurgery*, 28, 7, 516–23, 2008.
2. Rozen, W.M., Ashton, M.W., Grinsell, D., Stella, D.L., Phillips, T.J., Taylor, G.I., Establishing the case for CT angiography in the preoperative imaging of abdominal wall perforators. *Microsurgery: Official Journal of the International Microsurgical Society and the European Federation of Societies for Microsurgery*, 28, 5, 306–13, 2008.
3. Rozen, W.M., Ashton, M.W., Stella, D.L., Phillips, T.J., Grinsell, D., Taylor, G.I., The accuracy of computed tomographic angiography for mapping the perforators of the deep inferior epigastric artery: A blinded, prospective cohort study. *Plast. Reconstr. Surg.*, 122, 4, 1003–9, 2008 Oct 1.
4. Colohan, S., Wong, C., Lakhiani, C., Cheng, A., Maia, M., Arbique, G., Saint-Cyr, M., The free descending branch muscle-sparing latissimus dorsi flap: Vascular anatomy and clinical applications. *Plast. Reconstr. Surg.*, 130, 6, 776e–87e, 2012 Dec 1.
5. Nie, J.Y., Lu, L.J., Gong, X., Li, Q., Nie, J.J., Delineating the vascular territory (perforasome) of a perforator in the lower extremity of the rabbit with four-dimensional computed tomographic angiography. *Plast. Reconstr. Surg.*, 131, 3, 565–71, 2013 Mar 1.
6. Gerstle, T.L., Ibrahim, A.M., Kim, P.S., Lee, B.T., Lin, S.J., A plastic surgery application in evolution: Three-dimensional printing. *Plast. Reconstr. Surg.*, 133, 2, 446–51, 2014 Feb 1.
7. Hunter-Smith, D.J., Chae, M.P., Rozen, W., Image-guided 3D-printing and haptic modeling in plastic surgery, in: *Imaging in Plastic Surgery*, pp. 811–822, CRC Press, Boca Raton, Florida, 2015.
8. Goiato, M.C., Santos, M.R., Pesqueira, A.A., Moreno, A., dos Santos, D.M., Haddad, M.F., Prototyping for surgical and prosthetic treatment. *J. Craniofac. Surg.*, 22, 3, 914–7, 2011 May 1.
9. Levy, G.N., Schindel, R., Kruth, J.P., Rapid manufacturing and rapid tooling with layer manufacturing (LM) technologies, state of the art and future perspectives. *CIRP Ann.*, 52, 2, 589–609, 2003 Jan 1.
10. Sealy, W., Additive manufacturing as a disruptive technology: How to avoid the pitfall. *Am. J. Eng. Technol. Res.*, 11, 10, 91–92, 2012.
11. Hoy, M.B., 3D printing: Making things at the library. *Med. Ref. Serv. Q.*, 32, 1, 93–9, 2013 Jan 1.
12. Srinivasan, V. and Bassan, J., 3D printing and the future of manufacturing, in: *CSC Leading Edge Forum 2012*, vol. 7, Computer Sciences Corporation, Tysons, VA, USA, p. 36.

13. Schubert, C., van Langeveld, M.C., Donoso, L.A., Innovations in 3D printing: A 3D overview from optics to organs. *Br. J. Ophthalmol.*, 98, 2, 159–61, 2014 Feb.
14. Au, A.K., Huynh, W., Horowitz, L.F., Folch, A., 3D-printed microfluidics. *Angew. Chem. Int. Ed.*, 55, 12, 3862–81, 2016 Mar 14.
15. Chen, Y., Niu, F., Yu, B., Liu, J., Wang, M., Gui, L., Three-dimensional preoperative design of distraction osteogenesis for hemifacial microsomia. *J. Craniofac. Surg.*, 25, 1, 184–8, 2014 Jan 1.
16. Way, T.P. and Barner, K.E., Automatic visual to tactile translation. i. human factors, access methods and image manipulation. *IEEE Trans. Rehabil. Eng.*, 5, 1, 81–94, 1997 Mar.
17. D'Urso, P.S., Barker, T.M., Earwaker, W.J., Bruce, L.J., Atkinson, R.L., Lanigan, M.W., Arvier, J.F., Effeney, D.J., Stereolithographic biomodelling in cranio-maxillofacial surgery: A prospective trial. *J. Cranio-maxillofac. Surg.*, 27, 1, 30–7, 1999 Feb 1.
18. Guarino, J., Tennyson, S., McCain, G., Bond, L., Shea, K., King, H., Rapid prototyping technology for surgeries of the pediatric spine and pelvis: Benefits analysis. *J. Pediatr. Orthop.*, 27, 8, 955–60, 2007 Dec 1.
19. Liu, Y.F., Xu, L.W., Zhu, H.Y., Liu, S.S., Technical procedures for template-guided surgery for mandibular reconstruction based on digital design and manufacturing. *Biomed. Eng. Online*, 13, 1–5, 2014 Dec.
20. Tsai, M.J. and Wu, C.T., Study of mandible reconstruction using a fibula flap with application of additive manufacturing technology. *Biomed. Eng. Online*, 13, 1–5, 2014 Dec.
21. Lim, C.G., Campbell, D.I., Clucas, D.M., Rapid prototyping technology in orbital floor reconstruction: Application in three patients. *Craniomaxillofac. Trauma Reconstr.*, 7, 2, 143–6, 2014 Jun.
22. Engel, M., Hoffmann, J., Castrillon-Oberndorfer, G., Freudlsperger, C., The value of three-dimensional printing modelling for surgical correction of orbital hypertelorism. *Oral. Maxillofac. Surg.*, 19, 91–5, 2015 Mar.
23. Azuma, M., Yanagawa, T., Ishibashi–Kanno, N., Uchida, F., Ito, T., Yamagata, K., Hasegawa, S., Sasaki, K., Adachi, K., Tabuchi, K., Sekido, M., Mandibular reconstruction using plates prebent to fit rapid prototyping 3-dimensional printing models ameliorates contour deformity. *Head Face Med.*, 10, 1, 1–8, 2014 Dec.
24. Jeong, H.S., Park, K.J., Kil, K.M., Chong, S., Eun, H.J., Lee, T.S., Lee, J.P., Minimally invasive plate osteosynthesis using 3D printing for shaft fractures of clavicles. *Arch. Orthop. Trauma Surg.*, 134, 1551–5, 2014 Nov.
25. Tam, M.D., Laycock, S.D., Bell, D., Chojnowski, A., 3-D printout of a DICOM file to aid surgical planning in a 6 year old patient with a large scapular osteochondroma complicating congenital diaphyseal aclasia. *J. Radiol. Case Rep.*, 6, 1, 31, 2012 Jan.
26. Schmauss, D., Haeberle, S., Hagl, C., Sodian, R., Three-dimensional printing in cardiac surgery and interventional cardiology: A single-centre experience. *Eur. J. Cardio-Thorac. Surg.*, 47, 6, 1044–52, 2015 Jun 1.

27. Witschey, W.R., Pouch, A.M., McGarvey, J.R., Ikeuchi, K., Contijoch, F., Levack, M.M., Yushkevick, P.A., Sehgal, C.M., Jackson, B.M., Gorman, R.C., Gorman III, J.H., Three-dimensional ultrasound-derived physical mitral valve modeling. *Ann. Thorac. Surg.*, 98, 2, 691–4, 2014 Aug 1.
28. Schmauss, D., Gerber, N., Sodian, R., Three-dimensional printing of models for surgical planning in patients with primary cardiac tumors. *J. Thorac. Cardiovasc. Surg.*, 145, 5, 1407–8, 2013 May 1.
29. Nakata, M., Sawada, S., Yamashita, M., Saeki, H., Kurita, A., Takashima, S., Tanemoto, K., Surgical treatments for multiple primary adenocarcinoma of the lung. *Ann. Thorac. Surg.*, 78, 4, 1194–9, 2004 Oct 1.
30. Sodian, R., Weber, S., Markert, M., Loeff, M., Lueth, T., Weis, F.C., Daebritz, S., Malec, E., Schmitz, C., Reichart, B., Pediatric cardiac transplantation: Three-dimensional printing of anatomic models for surgical planning of heart transplantation in patients with univentricular heart. *J. Thorac. Cardiovasc. Surg.*, 136, 4, 1098–9, 2008 Oct 1.
31. Vickers, N.J., Animal communication: When i'm calling you, will you answer too? *Curr. Biol.*, 27, 14, R713–5, 2017 Jul 24.
32. Markert, M., Weber, S., Lueth, T.C., A beating heart model 3D printed from specific patient data, in: *2007 29th Annual International Conference of the IEEE Engineering in Medicine and Biology Society*, 2007 Aug 22, IEEE, pp. 4472–4475.
33. Nakada, T., Akiba, T., Inagaki, T., Morikawa, T., Thoracoscopic anatomical subsegmentectomy of the right S2b+ S3 using a 3D printing model with rapid prototyping. *Interact. Cardiovasc. Thorac. Surg.*, 19, 4, 696–8, 2014 Oct 1.
34. Akiba, T., Inagaki, T., Nakada, T., Three-dimensional printing model of anomalous bronchi before surgery. *Ann. Thorac. Cardiovasc. Surg.*, 20, Supplement, 659–62, 2014.
35. Tam, M.D., Laycock, S.D., Brown, J.R., Jakeways, M., 3D printing of an aortic aneurysm to facilitate decision making and device selection for endovascular aneurysm repair in complex neck anatomy. *J. Endovasc. Ther.*, 20, 6, 863–7, 2013 Dec.
36. Håkansson, A., Rantatalo, M., Wanhainen, A., Hansen, T., Patient specific biomodel of the whole aorta: The importance of calcified plaque removal. *Vasa*, 40, 6, 453–9, 2011.
37. Sodian, R., Schmauss, D., Schmitz, C., Bigdeli, A., Haeberle, S., Schmoeckel, M., Markert, M., Lueth, T., Freudenthal, F., Reichart, B., Kozlik-Feldmann, R., 3-dimensional printing of models to create custom-made devices for coil embolization of an anastomotic leak after aortic arch replacement. *Ann. Thorac. Surg.*, 88, 3, 974–8, 2009 Sep 1.
38. Vickers, N.J., Animal communication: When i'm calling you, will you answer too? *Curr. Biol.*, 27, 14, R713–5, 2017 Jul 24.

39. Daniel, M., Watson, J., Hoskison, E., Sama, A., Frontal sinus models and onlay templates in osteoplastic flap surgery. *J. Laryngol. Otol.*, 125, 1, 82–5, 2011 Jan.
40. Suzuki, M., Ogawa, Y., Kawano, A., Hagiwara, A., Yamaguchi, H., Ono, H., Rapid prototyping of temporal bone for surgical training and medical education. *Acta Otolaryngol.*, 124, 4, 400–2, 2004 May 1.
41. Igami, T., Nakamura, Y., Hirose, T., Ebata, T., Yokoyama, Y., Sugawara, G., Mizuno, T., Mori, K., Nagino, M., Application of a three-dimensional print of a liver in hepatectomy for small tumors invisible by intraoperative ultrasonography: Preliminary experience. *World J. Surg.*, 38, 3163–6, 2014 Dec.
42. Ikegami, T. and Maehara, Y., 3D printing of the liver in living donor liver transplantation. *Nat. Rev. Gastroenterol. Hepatol.*, 10, 12, 697–8, 2013 Dec.
43. Zein, N.N., Hanouneh, I.A., Bishop, P.D., Samaan, M., Eghtesad, B., Quintini, C., Miller, C., Yerian, L., Klatte, R., Three-dimensional print of a liver for preoperative planning in living donor liver transplantation. *Liver Transplant.*, 19, 12, 1304–10, 2013 Dec.
44. Kang, S.H., Kim, M.K., Kim, B.C., Lee, S.H., Orthognathic Y-splint: A CAD/CAM-engineered maxillary repositioning wafer assembly. *Br. J. Oral. Maxillofac. Surg.*, 52, 7, 667–9, 2014 Sep 1.
45. Adolphs, N., Liu, W., Keeve, E., Hoffmeister, B., RapidSplint: Virtual splint generation for orthognathic surgery–results of a pilot series. *Comput. Aided Surg.*, 19, 1-3, 20–8, 2014 Jan 1.
46. Cousley, R.R. and Turner, M.J., Digital model planning and computerized fabrication of orthognathic surgery wafers. *J. Orthod.*, 41, 1, 38–45, 2014 Mar 1.
47. Davies, D., Jindal-Snape, D., Digby, R., Howe, A., Collier, C., Hay, P., The roles and development needs of teachers to promote creativity: A systematic review of literature. *Teach. Teach. Educ.*, 41, 34–41, 2014 Jul 1.
48. Rogers, S.N., Harvey-Woodworth, C.N., Hare, J., Leong, P., Lowe, D., Patients' perception of the financial impact of head and neck cancer and the relationship to health related quality of life. *Br. J. Oral. Maxillofac. Surg.*, 50, 5, 410–6, 2012 Jul 1.
49. Wang, C.C., Kok, S.H., Hou, L.T., Yang, P.J., Lee, J.J., Cheng, S.J., Kuo, R.C., Chang, H.H., Ectopic mandibular third molar in the ramus region: Report of a case and literature review. *Oral. Surg. Oral. Med. Oral. Pathol. Oral. Radiol. Endod.*, 105, 2, 155–61, 2008 Feb 1.
50. Burrows, P.E. and Mason, K.P., Percutaneous treatment of low flow vascular malformations. *J. Vasc. Interv. Radiol.*, 15, 5, 431–45, 2004 May 1.
51. Spottiswoode, B.S., Van den Heever, D.J., Chang, Y., Engelhardt, S., Du Plessis, S., Nicolls, F., Hartzenberg, H.B., Gretschel, A., Preoperative three-dimensional model creation of magnetic resonance brain images as a tool to assist neurosurgical planning. *Stereotact. Funct. Neurosurg.*, 91, 3, 162–9, 2013.

52. Fuller, S.M., Butz, D.R., Vevang, C.B., Makhlouf, M.V., Application of 3-dimensional printing in hand surgery for production of a novel bone reduction clamp. *J. Handb. Surg.*, 39, 9, 1840–5, 2014 Sep 1.
53. Rankin, T.M., Giovinco, N.A., Cucher, D.J., Watts, G., Hurwitz, B., Armstrong, D.G., Three-dimensional printing surgical instruments: Are we there yet? *J. Surg. Res.*, 189, 2, 193–7, 2014 Jun 15.
54. Waran, V., Narayanan, V., Karuppiah, R., Owen, S.L., Aziz, T., Utility of multi-material 3D printers in creating models with pathological entities to enhance the training experience of neurosurgeons. *J. Neurosurg.*, 120, 2, 489–92, 2014 Feb 1.
55. Abla, A.A. and Lawton, M.T., Three-dimensional hollow intracranial aneurysm models and their potential role for teaching, simulation, and training. *World Neurosurg.*, 83, 35–6, 2015.
56. Mashiko, T., Otani, K., Kawano, R., Konno, T., Kaneko, N., Ito, Y., Watanabe, E., Development of three-dimensional hollow elastic model for cerebral aneurysm clipping simulation enabling rapid and low cost prototyping. *World Neurosurg.*, 83, 351–61, 2015.
57. Wurm, G., Tomancok, B., Pogady, P., Holl, K., Trenkler, J., Cerebrovascular stereolithographic biomodeling for aneurysm surgery. *J. Neurosurg.*, 100, 1, 139–45, 2004 Jan 1.
58. Wurm, G., Lehner, M., Tomancok, B., Kleiser, R., Nussbaumer, K., Cerebrovascular biomodeling for aneurysm surgery: Simulation-based training by means of rapid prototyping technologies. *Surg. Innov.*, 18, 3, 294–306, 2011 Sep.
59. Waran, V., Narayanan, V., Karuppiah, R., Thambynayagam, H.C., Muthusamy, K.A., Rahman, Z.A., Kirollos, R.W., Neurosurgical endoscopic training via a realistic 3-dimensional model with pathology. *Simul. Healthc.*, 10, 1, 43–8, 2015 Feb 1.
60. Costello, J.P., Olivieri, L.J., Su, L., Krieger, A., Alfares, F., Thabit, O., Marshall, M.B., Yoo, S.J., Kim, P.C., Jonas, R.A., Nath, D.S., Incorporating three-dimensional printing into a simulation-based congenital heart disease and critical care training curriculum for resident physicians. *Congenit. Heart Dis.*, 10, 2, 185–90, 2015 Mar.
61. Biglino, G., Verschueren, P., Zegels, R., Taylor, A.M., Schievano, S., Rapid prototyping compliant arterial phantoms for *in-vitro* studies and device testing. *J. Cardiovasc. Magn. Reson.*, 15, 1–7, 2013 Dec.
62. Bustamante, S., Bose, S., Bishop, P., Klatte, R., Norris, F., Novel application of rapid prototyping for simulation of bronchoscopic anatomy. *J. Cardiothorac. Vasc. Anesth.*, 28, 4, 1122–5, 2014 Aug 1.
63. Laali, K.K., Greves, W.J., Correa-Smits, S.J., Zwarycz, A.T., Bunge, S.D., Borosky, G.L., Manna, A., Paulus, A., Chanan-Khan, A., Novel fluorinated curcuminoids and their pyrazole and isoxazole derivatives: Synthesis, structural studies, Computational/Docking and *in-vitro* bioassay. *J. Fluor. Chem.*, 206, 82–98, 2018 Feb 1.

64. Li, J., Hsu, Y., Luo, E., Khadka, A., Hu, J., Computer-aided design and manufacturing and rapid prototyped nanoscale hydroxyapatite/polyamide (n-HA/PA) construction for condylar defect caused by mandibular angle ostectomy. *Aesthetic Plast. Surg.*, 35, 636–40, 2011 Aug.
65. Vickers, N.J., Animal communication: When i'm calling you, will you answer too? *Curr. Biol.*, 27, 14, R713–5, 2017 Jul 24.
66. Saijo, H., Igawa, K., Kanno, Y., Mori, Y., Kondo, K., Shimizu, K., Suzuki, S., Chikazu, D., Iino, M., Anzai, M., Sasaki, N., Maxillofacial reconstruction using custom-made artificial bones fabricated by inkjet printing technology. *J. Artif. Organs*, 12, 200–5, 2009 Sep.
67. Vickers, N.J., Animal communication: When i'm calling you, will you answer too? *Curr. Biol.*, 27, 14, R713–5, 2017 Jul 24.
68. D'Urso, P.S., Effeney, D.J., Earwaker, W.J., Barker, T.M., Redmond, M.J., Thompson, R.G., Tomlinson, F.H., Custom cranioplasty using stereolithography and acrylic. *Br. J. Plast. Surg.*, 53, 3, 200–4, 2000 Apr 1.
69. Bicanic, G., Barbaric, K., Bohacek, I., Aljinovic, A., Delimar, D., Current concept in dysplastic hip arthroplasty: Techniques for acetabular and femoral reconstruction. *World J. Orthop.*, 5, 4, 412, 2014 Sep 9.
70. Koulouvaris, P., Stafylas, K., Sculco, T., Xenakis, T., Distal femoral shortening in total hip arthroplasty for complex primary hip reconstruction. A new surgical technique. *J. Arthroplasty*, 23, 7, 992–8, 2008 Oct 1.
71. Zopf, D.A., Hollister, S.J., Nelson, M.E., Ohye, R.G., Green, G.E., Bioresorbable airway splint created with a three-dimensional printer. *New Engl. J. Med.*, 368, 21, 2043–5, 2013 May 23.
72. Reeves, P., Additive manufacturing & 3D printing medical & healthcare: A new industrial perspective. *The 3D Printing & Additive Manufacturing People*, 2014.
73. Woźniak, K., Rzepecka-Woźniak, E., Moskała, A., Pohl, J., Latacz, K., Dybała, B., Weapon identification using antemortem computed tomography with virtual 3D and rapid prototype modeling—A report in a case of blunt force head injury. *Forensic Sci. Int.*, 222, 1-3, e29–32, 2012 Oct 10.
74. Vaccarezza, M. and Papa, V., 3D printing: A valuable resource in human anatomy education. *Anat. Sci. Int.*, 90, 1, 64–5, 2015 Jan.
75. Giovinco, N.A., Dunn, S.P., Dowling, L., Smith, C., Trowell, L., Ruch, J.A., Armstrong, D.G., A novel combination of printed 3-dimensional anatomic templates and computer-assisted surgical simulation for virtual preoperative planning in Charcot foot reconstruction. *J. Foot Ankle Surg.*, 51, 3, 387–93, 2012 May 1.
76. Yun, P.Y., The application of three-dimensional printing techniques in the fi eld of oral and maxillofacial surgery. *J. Korean Assoc. Oral. Maxillofac. Surg.*, 41, 4, 169, 2015 Aug.
77. Vickers, N.J., Animal communication: When i'm calling you, will you answer too? *Curr. Biol.*, 27, 14, R713–5, 2017 Jul 24.

78. Flügge, T.V., Nelson, K., Schmelzeisen, R., Metzger, M.C., Three-dimensional plotting and printing of an implant drilling guide: Simplifying guided implant surgery. *J. Oral. Maxillofac. Surg.*, 71, 8, 1340–6, 2013 Aug 1.
79. Goyanes, A., Buanz, A.B., Hatton, G.B., Gaisford, S., Basit, A.W., 3D printing of modified-release aminosalicylate (4-ASA and 5-ASA) tablets. *Eur. J. Pharm. Biopharm.*, 89, 157–62, 2015 Jan 1.
80. Skowyra, J., Pietrzak, K., Alhnan, M.A., Fabrication of extended-release patient-tailored prednisolone tablets via fused deposition modelling (FDM) 3D printing. *Eur. J. Pharm. Sci.*, 68, 11–7, 2015 Feb 20.
81. Lueders, C., Jastram, B., Hetzer, R., Schwandt, H., Rapid manufacturing techniques for the tissue engineering of human heart valves. *Eur. J. Cardiothorac. Surg.*, 46, 4, 593–601, 2014 Oct 1.
82. Chang, J.W., Park, S.A., Park, J.K., Choi, J.W., Kim, Y.S., Shin, Y.S., Kim, C.H., Tissue-engineered tracheal reconstruction using three-dimensionally printed artificial tracheal graft: Preliminary report. *Artif. Organs*, 38, 6, E95–105, 2014 Jun.
83. Jovic, T.H., Combellack, E.J., Jessop, Z.M., Whitaker, I.S., 3D Bioprinting and the future of surgery. *Front. Surg.*, 7, 609836, 2020 Nov 27.
84. Ozbolat, I.T., Moncal, K.K., Gudapati, H., Evaluation of bioprinter technologies. *Addit. Manuf.*, 13, 179–200, 2017 Jan 1.
85. Lei, L., Wang, X., Zhu, Y., Su, W., Lv, Q., Li, D., Antimicrobial hydrogel microspheres for protein capture and wound healing. *Mater. Des.*, 215, 110478, 2022 Mar 1.
86. Lei, L., Zhu, Y., Qin, X., Chai, S., Liu, G., Su, W., Lv, Q., Li, D., Magnetic biohybrid microspheres for protein purification and chronic wound healing in diabetic mice. *Chem. Eng. J.*, 425, 130671, 2021 Dec 1.
87. Shi, Y., Xing, T.L., Zhang, H.B., Yin, R.X., Yang, S.M., Wei, J., Zhang, W.J., Tyrosinase-doped bioink for 3D bioprinting of living skin constructs. *Biomed. Mater.*, 13, 3, 035008, 2018 Mar 6.
88. Lin, F.S., Lee, J.J., Lee, A.K., Ho, C.C., Liu, Y.T., Shie, M.Y., Calcium silicate-activated gelatin methacrylate hydrogel for accelerating human dermal fibroblast proliferation and differentiation. *Polymers*, 13, 1, 70, 2020 Dec 27.
89. Jang, M.J., Bae, S.K., Jung, Y.S., Kim, J.C., Kim, J.S., Park, S.K., Suh, J.S., Yi, S.J., Ahn, S.H., Lim, J.O., Enhanced wound healing using a 3D printed VEGF-mimicking peptide incorporated hydrogel patch in a pig model. *Biomed. Mater.*, 16, 4, 045013, 2021 Apr 9.
90. Intini, C., Elviri, L., Cabral, J., Mros, S., Bergonzi, C., Bianchera, A., Flammini, L., Govoni, P., Barocelli, E., Bettini, R., McConnell, M., 3D-printed chitosan-based scaffolds: An *in vitro* study of human skin cell growth and an *in-vivo* wound healing evaluation in experimental diabetes in rats. *Carbohydr. Polym.*, 199, 593–602, 2018 Nov 1.

91. Sandri, G., Rossi, S., Bonferoni, M.C., Miele, D., Faccendini, A., Del Favero, E., Di Cola, E., Cornaglia, A.I., Boselli, C., Luxbacher, T., Malavasi, L., Chitosan/glycosaminoglycan scaffolds for skin reparation. *Carbohydr. Polym.*, 220, 219–27, 2019 Sep 15.
92. Yao, C.H., Chen, K.Y., Cheng, M.H., Chen, Y.S., Huang, C.H., Effect of genipin crosslinked chitosan scaffolds containing SDF-1 on wound healing in a rat model. *Mater. Sci. Eng.: C*, 109, 110368, 2020 Apr 1.
93. Dong, Y., Liu, Z., Qi, F., Jin, L., Zhang, L., Zhu, N., Polyethylene-glycol-ornamented small intestinal submucosa biosponge for skin tissue engineering. *ACS Biomater. Sci. Eng.*, 5, 5, 2457–65, 2019 Apr 9.
94. Chang, P., Li, S., Sun, Q., Guo, K., Wang, H., Li, S., Zhang, L., Xie, Y., Zheng, X., Liu, Y., Large full-thickness wounded skin regeneration using 3D-printed elastic scaffold with minimal functional unit of skin. *J. Tissue Eng.*, 13, 20417314211063022, 2022 Jan.
95. Ma, J., Qin, C., Wu, J., Zhang, H., Zhuang, H., Zhang, M., Zhang, Z., Ma, L., Wang, X., Ma, B., Chang, J., 3D printing of strontium silicate microcylinder-containing multicellular biomaterial inks for vascularized skin regeneration. *Adv. Healthc. Mater.*, 10, 16, 2100523, 2021 Aug.
96. Li, X., You, R., Zhang, Q., Yan, S., Luo, Z., Qu, J., Li, M., Engineering vascularized dermal grafts by integrating a biomimetic scaffold and Wharton's jelly MSC-derived endothelial cells. *J. Mater. Chem. B*, 9, 32, 6466–79, 2021.
97. Roshangar, L., Rad, J.S., Kheirjou, R., Khosroshahi, A.F., Using 3D-bioprinting scaffold loaded with adipose-derived stem cells to burns wound healing. *J. Tissue Eng. Regen. Med.*, 15, 6, 546–55, 2021 Jun.
98. Chen, P., Miao, Y., Zhang, F., Fan, Z., Huang, J., Mao, X., Chen, J., Hu, Z., Wang, J., Tissue engineering ECM-enriched controllable vascularized human microtissue for hair regenerative medicine using a biomimetic developmental approach. *J. Adv. Res.*, 38, 77–89, 2022 May 1.
99. Vickers, N.J., Animal communication: When i'm calling you, will you answer too? *Curr. Biol.*, 27, 14, R713–5, 2017 Jul 24.
100. Allison, J.D. and Cardé, R.T., *Pheromone communication in moths: Evolution, behavior, and application*, Univ of California Press, California, USA, 2016 Oct 25.
101. Chae, M.P., Lin, F., Spychal, R.T., Hunter-Smith, D.J., Rozen, W.M., 3D-printed haptic "reverse" models for preoperative planning in soft tissue reconstruction: A case report. *Microsurgery*, 35, 2, 148–53, 2015 Feb.
102. Garcia-Tutor, E., Romeo, M., Chae, M.P., Hunter-Smith, D.J., Rozen, W.M., 3D volumetric modeling and microvascular reconstruction of irradiated lumbosacral defects after oncologic resection. *Front. Surg.*, 3, 66, 2016 Dec 13.
103. Donfrancesco, A., Montemurro, P., Hedén, P., Three-dimensional simulated images in breast augmentation surgery: An investigation of patients'

satisfaction and the correlation between prediction and actual outcome. *Plast. Reconstr. Surg.*, 132, 4, 810–22, 2013 Oct 1.
104. Chae, M.P., Hunter-Smith, D.J., Spychal, R.T., Rozen, W.M., 3D volumetric analysis for planning breast reconstructive surgery. *Breast Cancer Res. Treat.*, 146, 457–60, 2014 Jul.
105. Fedorov, A., Beichel, R., Kalpathy-Cramer, J., Finet, J., Fillion-Robin, S.P., Jennings, D., Bauer, C., Fennessy, F., Sonka, M., Buatti, J., Miller, J.V., Pieper, S., Aylward, S.R., Kikinis, R., 3D slicer as an image computing platform for the quantitative imaging network. *Magn. Reson. Imaging*, 30, 1323–41, 2012.
106. Rozen, W.M. and Ashton, M.W., Modifying techniques in deep inferior epigastric artery perforator flap harvest with the use of preoperative imaging. *ANZ J. Surg.*, 79, 9, 598–603, 2009 Sep.
107. Gillis, J.A. and Morris, S.F., Three-dimensional printing of perforator vascular anatomy. *Plast. Reconstr. Surg.*, 133, 1, 80e–2e, 2014 Jan 1.
108. Rozen, W.M., Ashton, M.W., Le Roux, C.M., Pan, W.R., Corlett, R.J., The perforator angiosome: A new concept in the design of deep inferior epigastric artery perforator flaps for breast reconstruction. *Microsurgery: Official Journal of the International Microsurgical Society and the European Federation of Societies for Microsurgery*, 30, 1, 1–7, 2010 Jan.
109. Lee, J.W., Fang, J.J., Chang, L.R., Yu, C.K., Mandibular defect reconstruction with the help of mirror imaging coupled with laser stereolithographic modeling technique. *J. Formos. Med. Assoc.*, 106, 3, 244–50, 2007 Jan 1.
110. Cao, D., Yu, Z., Chai, G., Liu, J., Mu, X., Application of EH compound artificial bone material combined with computerized three-dimensional reconstruction in craniomaxillofacial surgery. *J. Craniofac. Surg.*, 21, 2, 440–3, 2010 Mar 1.
111. Katsuragi, Y., Kayano, S., Akazawa, S., Nagamatsu, S., Koizumi, T., Matsui, T., Onitsuka, T., Yurikusa, T., Huang, W.C., Nakagawa, M., Mandible reconstruction using the calcium-sulphate three-dimensional model and rubber stick: A new method,'mould technique', for more accurate, efficient and simplified fabrication. *J. Plast. Reconstr. Aesthet. Surg.*, 64, 5, 614–22, 2011 May 1.
112. Hsieh, M.K., Chen, A.C., Cheng, C.Y., Chou, Y.C., Chan, Y.S., Hsu, K.Y., Repositioning osteotomy for intra-articular malunion of distal radius with radiocarpal and/or distal radioulnar joint subluxation. *J. Trauma Acute Care Surg.*, 69, 2, 418–22, 2010 Aug 1.
113. Gan, Y., Xu, D., Lu, S., Ding, J., Novel patient-specific navigational template for total knee arthroplasty. *Comput. Aided Surg.*, 16, 6, 288–97, 2011 Nov 1.
114. Kunz, M., Ma, B., Rudan, J.F., Ellis, R.E., Pichora, D.R., Image-guided distal radius osteotomy using patient-specific instrument guides. *J. Handb. Surg.*, 38, 8, 1618–24, 2013 Aug 1.
115. Kataoka, T., Oka, K., Miyake, J., Omori, S., Tanaka, H., Murase, T., 3-Dimensional prebent plate fixation in corrective osteotomy of malunited

upper extremity fractures using a real-sized plastic bone model prepared by preoperative computer simulation. *J. Handb. Surg.*, 38, 5, 909–19, 2013 May 1.

116. Minns, R.J., Bibb, R., Banks, R., Sutton, R.A., The use of a reconstructed three-dimensional solid model from CT to aid the surgical management of a total knee arthroplasty: A case study. *Med. Eng. Phys.*, 25, 6, 523–6, 2003 Jul 1.
117. Fuller, S.M., Butz, D.R., Vevang, C.B., Makhlouf, M.V., Application of 3-dimensional printing in hand surgery for production of a novel bone reduction clamp. *J. Handb. Surg.*, 39, 9, 1840–5, 2014 Sep 1.
118. Switzer, N.J. and Karmali, S., The sleeve gastrectomy and how and why it can fail. *Surgery: Curr. Res.*, 4, 3, 2014.
119. Sugawara, T., Higashiyama, N., Kaneyama, S., Takabatake, M., Watanabe, N., Uchida, F., Sumi, M., Mizoi, K., Multistep pedicle screw insertion procedure with patient-specific lamina fit-and-lock templates for the thoracic spine. *J. Neurosurg.: Spine*, 19, 2, 185–90, 2013 Aug 1.
120. Fuller, S.M., Butz, D.R., Vevang, C.B., Makhlouf, M.V., Application of 3-dimensional printing in hand surgery for production of a novel bone reduction clamp. *J. Handb. Surg.*, 39, 9, 1840–5, 2014 Sep 1.
121. Vaccarezza, M. and Papa, V., 3D printing: A valuable resource in human anatomy education. *Anat. Sci. Int.*, 90, 1, 64–5, 2015 Jan.
122. Lambrecht, J.T., Berndt, D.C., Schumacher, R., Zehnder, M., Generation of three-dimensional prototype models based on cone beam computed tomography. *Int. J. Comput. Assist. Radiol. Surg.*, 4, 175–80, 2009 Mar.
123. Kimura, T., Morita, A., Nishimura, K., Aiyama, H., Itoh, H., Fukaya, S., Sora, S., Ochiai, C., Simulation of and training for cerebral aneurysm clipping with 3-dimensional models. *Neurosurgery*, 65, 4, 719–26, 2009 Oct 1.
124. Chueh, J.Y., Wakhloo, A.K., Gounis, M.J., Neurovascular modeling: Small-batch manufacturing of silicone vascular replicas. *Am. J. Neuroradiol.*, 30, 6, 1159–64, 2009 Jun 1.
125. Allison, J.D. and Cardé, R.T., *Pheromone communication in moths: Evolution, behavior, and application*, Univ of California Press, California, USA, 2016 Oct 25.
126. Kalejs, M. and Segesser, L.K., Rapid prototyping of compliant human aortic roots for assessment of valved stents. *Interact. Cardiovasc. Thorac. Surg.*, 8, 2, 182–6, 2009 Feb 1.
127. Armillotta, A., Bonhoeffer, P., Dubini, G., Ferragina, S., Migliavacca, F., Sala, G., Schievano, S., Use of rapid prototyping models in the planning of percutaneous pulmonary valved stent implantation. *Proc. Inst. Mech. Eng., Part H: J. Eng. Med.*, 221, 4, 407–16, 2007 Apr 1.
128. Bruyere, F., Leroux, C., Brunereau, L., Lermusiaux, P., Rapid prototyping model for percutaneous nephrolithotomy training. *J. Endourol.*, 22, 1, 91–6, 2008 Jan 1.
129. Yamazaki M., Takayama T., Fujita A., *et al.*, 3D printed kidney model could be an important educational tool for residents. *Asian J. Endosc. Surg.*, 16, 2, 197–202, 2023. doi:10.1111/ases.13136.

130. Overschmidt, B., Qureshi, A.A., Parikh, R.P., Yan, Y., Tenenbaum, M.M., Myckatyn, T.M., A prospective evaluation of three-dimensional image simulation: Patient-reported outcomes and mammometrics in primary breast augmentation. *Plast. Reconstr. Surg.*, 142, 2, 133e–44e, 2018 Aug 1.
131. Burrows, P.E. and Mason, K.P., Percutaneous treatment of low flow vascular malformations. *J. Vasc. Interv. Radiol.*, 15, 5, 431–45, 2004 May 1.
132. Chan, Y.C., Qing, K.X., Cheng, S.W., Custom-made fenestrated stent grafts to preserve accessory renal arteries in patients with abdominal aortic aneurysms. *Acta Chir. Belg.*, 114, 3, 183–8, 2014 Jan 1.
133. Hourfar, J., Kanavakis, G., Goellner, P., Ludwig, B., Fully customized placement of orthodontic miniplates: A novel clinical technique. *Head Face Med.*, 10, 1–7, 2014 Dec.
134. Lee, S.J., Lee, H.P., Tse, K.M., Cheong, E.C., Lim, S.P., Computer-aided design and rapid prototyping–assisted contouring of costal cartilage graft for facial reconstructive surgery. *Craniomaxillofac. Trauma Reconstr.*, 5, 2, 75–81, 2012 Jun.
135. Wu, G., Zhou, B., Bi, Y., Zhao, Y., Selective laser sintering technology for customized fabrication of facial prostheses. *J. Prosthet. Dent.*, 100, 1, 56–60, 2008 Jul 1.
136. De Crescenzio, F., Fantini, M., Ciocca, L., Persiani, F., Scotti, R., Design and manufacturing of ear prosthesis by means of rapid prototyping technology. *Proc. Inst. Mech. Eng. Part H: J. Eng. Med.*, 225, 3, 296–302, 2011 Mar 1.
137. Ciocca, L. and Scotti, R., Oculo-facial rehabilitation after facial cancer removal: Updated CAD/CAM procedures. A pilot study. *Prosthet. Orthot. Int.*, 38, 6, 505–9, 2014 Dec.
138. Xie, P., Hu, Z., Zhang, X., Li, X., Gao, Z., Yuan, D., Liu, Q., Application of 3-dimensional printing technology to construct an eye model for fundus viewing study. *PLoS One*, 9, 11, e109373, 2014 Nov 13.
139. Tsuji, M., Noguchi, N., Ihara, K., Yamashita, Y., Shikimori, M., Goto, M., Fabrication of a maxillofacial prosthesis using a computer-aided design and manufacturing system. *J. Prosthodont.: Implant, Esthetic and Reconstructive Dentistry*, 13, 3, 179–83, 2004 Sep.
140. Fantini, M., De Crescenzio, F., Ciocca, L., Design and rapid manufacturing of anatomical prosthesis for facial rehabilitation. *Int. J. Interact. Des. Manuf. (IJIDeM)*, 7, 51–62, 2013 Feb.
141. Laurentis, K.J. and Mavroidis, C., Mechanical design of a shape memory alloy actuated prosthetic hand. *Technol. Health Care*, 10, 2, 91–106, 2002 Jan 1.

12

Safety, Efficacy, and Point-of-Care for 3D Printing in Healthcare

Abstract
More and more hospitals, clinics, and other medical institutions are seriously considering adopting or expanding their 3D-printing capabilities as the technology continues to find more and more uses in the medical field. Recent developments in 3D-printing technology have been welcomed by medical professionals as a strong instrument to aid in the delivery of high-quality patient care with an eye toward sustainability. There is great promise for the use of 3D printing at the point of care (POC) in a hospital or clinic, but its widespread implementation will require careful thought and planning. The authors lay out the foundational ideas and factors to consider while establishing the infrastructure to support 3D printing in a healthcare setting. Creating a digital workflow and contemplating the potential future use of electronic health records are all part of the process. So, too, is developing a business case for doing so. The authors elaborate on the quality and regulatory concerns of medical 3D printing and emphasize the supported applications and benefits of the technology. The supplied data is aimed to serve as a guide for radiology departments interested in learning more about POC 3D printing and perhaps incorporating it into routine clinical practice.

Keywords: 3D printing, point-of-care, medicine, transcatheter aortic valve replacement, patient-specific planning

12.1 Introduction

Customized treatment plans for each unique patient are at the heart of personalized medicine, which replaces the standard "one size fits all" approach. Selecting the most appropriate medication for each unique patient at the most optimal time is the ultimate objective of customized medicine. There has been a rise in the application of 3D-printing technology to the delivery of tailored medication in the medical field as a result of recent technological advancements [1–4]. 3D-printed models obtained from CT and MRI

Rishabha Malviya and Rishav Sharma. 3D Printing in Healthcare: Novel Applications, (229–248)

datasets do. To more accurately view the tumor's localization about the breast, the skin, the nipple, and the surrounding muscles during surgery, surgeons can use a 3D-printed model of the patient's breast [5]. A 3D-printed simulation might be helpful in a variety of circumstances, including the patient's bedside or the operating table. A patient-specific (or patient-matched or patient-derived) model is a 3D-printed replica of an individual patient's anatomy that would be generated using the patient's imaging data. In the medical field, 3D printing is particularly frequently employed to produce anatomic models for preoperative planning and visualization of complex anatomy, in addition to its use in patient instruction as well as the creation of personalized medical devices. Also, 3D printing can be used to make custom orthotics and prostheses [6, 7], surgical guides and implants [8, 9], and educational and simulation models. The American Society for Testing and Materials (ASTM International) has published standards outlining seven separate 3D-printing methods [9–13]. Material jetting, material extrusion, binder jetting, vat photopolymerization, and powder bed fusion are used in medicine. Directed energy deposition and sheet lamination, the last two types of 3D printing, are employed in the medical field less frequently. There has been a significant increase in interest in learning about using 3D printing to directly assist patients at the point of care (POC). Sometimes, a healthcare facility, like a hospital, will include a 3D printer for use at the point of care. According to the minimal raw product specifications of 3D printing, models can be produced "just in time" (with a short turnaround period) and with minimal costs. While sending patient-specific models to a 3D printing service can be expensive, hospitals can save money by doing the printing themselves [14]. Because of the in-house rather than outsourced nature of the manufacturing, a quality management system and other measures of organization and process are necessary [15, 16]. As the usage of 3D printing in medicine continues to expand, more and more medical facilities are installing 3D printers in their radiology departments. It takes a series of stages in a specific order for a 3D printer to create a replica of an organ or a body part that is both [1]. From just three in 2010, the number of US hospitals having point-of-care 3D-printing capability rose to 99 in 2016 [17]. In keeping with the trend, the Veterans Health Administration (VHA) of the United States will have 60 3D printers by the year 2020, up from three in 2017 [15, 18]. The purpose of this chapter is to discuss the pros and downsides of implementing a point-of-care (3D printing) program in a hospital setting. Researchers also analyze the technological workflow, quality management, regulatory environment, and regulatory requirements that must be in place to ensure the safety and efficacy of 3D printing in the medical area. The attention of the medical community would continue to be pushed by investigators toward 3D-printing technologies, progressing from localized, centralized systems to global, pervasive ones.

12.2 The Call for Standardization and Guidelines

The investigators are aware that many open questions persist despite the aforementioned clarity. Given the field's rapid expansion, addressing these is crucial as well. The first inquiry is whether it is preferable to receive models from an external vendor or to work with in-house 3D-printing capabilities, such as those found in hospitals. Researchers think there should not be a difference. The reasoning is that, to ensure the highest level of safety and effectiveness, both groups of experts should adhere to the same criteria. The use of 3D printing in medicine by both researchers and clinicians highlights the need for strict criteria to ensure that "patient-first" interests are prioritized as the field develops. Members of the relatively tiny community that engages in medical 3D printing today have very high-quality standards, and as a result, the field has mostly focused on niche applications. The metrics for model reproducibility have been published, and commercial vendors often employ proprietary methods designed to maximize a model's usefulness in the medical field [19]. The sheer number of users in a community tends to amplify the effects of identified areas where quality can be compromised as the community expands in size. The problem will be exacerbated if people make and use technologies that have not been thoroughly tested by scientists and regulators. As a result of many of the ideas discussed here, the authors conclude that 3D-printing technologies should be standardized across healthcare facilities [20]. By creating uniform guidelines, the investigator can ensure the highest level of patient safety. It would also aid in ensuring that hospitals are operating by FDA regulations and best practices. Two sets of rules are also desperately needed. The first set consists of technical specifications for groups I, II, and III models that are suitable for both doctors and patients. The second group is made up of clinical guidelines that explain when 3D printing is and is not a good idea in various clinical settings, much to the current American College of Radiology Appropriateness Criteria®.

12.3 Applications and Benefits of Medical 3D Printing

Medical, dental, and surgical groups are progressively accumulating archives of peer-reviewed studies that demonstrate the advantages of medical 3D printing. In certain healthcare settings, a patient-specific, outcome-improving, patient-specific strategy made possible by 3D-printed models of the patient's anatomy is possible and has the potential to significantly improve individual patient outcomes. Here, the researchers begin by elaborating on the advantages and uses of 3D printing in hospitals. Using 3D-printed models has been demonstrated to improve orthopedic surgery in several ways, including faster operating times, less blood loss during the procedure, and less need for intraoperative fluoroscopy [21–23]. The success of technology for 3D printing in patient-specific planning for a transcatheter aortic valve replacement [24, 25] and operational processes to treat congenital heart disease and blockage of the left atrial appendage [26, 27] could be due to differences in anatomical characteristics among patients. Neurosurgeons could save time as well as enhance accuracy when addressing children with complex neurovascular disorders due to 3D-printed models that appropriately reflect the shape and dimensions of cerebral infarction [27–29]. Patients suffering from gastrointestinal, hepatobiliary, and abdominal problems can benefit from kidney and liver 3D prints, which are among the most commonly produced abdominal organs. It has been shown that the preoperative use of 3D models can aid patients undergoing laparoscopic liver resection by providing a more accurate visual assessment of the tumor's position than 2D scans alone [30, 31]. Renal tumor therapy simulation and preoperative planning benefit greatly from the usage of 3D-printed models. According to a review of past research [32], 3D-printed renal models fabricated from MRI data impacted preoperative decision-making and the surgical strategy employed during nephrectomy planning. Preoperative planning for the excision of colon and rectal cancer has benefited from the use of 3D-printed models of solid organs [33, 34]. Furthermore, it has been determined that visualizations of complicated anatomic features, such as the central mesenteric arteries and the pelvis, were equally useful. Utilizing patient-specific 3D models has been additionally proven to enhance communications, knowledge, and interaction in treatment planning among patients and medical teams [35]. Wake *et al.* [36] utilized 3D-printed simulations of kidney and prostate cancers to better explain the conditions and the therapeutic options available to treat them than equivalent 3D computer models. So, what does that mean for a radiology lab? The aforementioned studies only represent a fraction of the growing body of research demonstrating the usefulness of 3D printing in healthcare. Collaborative efforts exhibiting 3D printing's potential for expansion and success stories were led by professional and academic groups in radiography. The Radiological Society of North America's 3D Printing Special Interest Group [20] is putting great effort to design helpful guidelines for the secure development of 3D-printed models and to improve clinical possibilities [37]. The RSNA and the RSNA 3D Printing Special Interest Group have released practical and detailed instructions for creating 3D-printed models for a variety of cardiovascular and thoracic procedures, including those involving congenital heart disease, vascular treatments, and thoracic surgery [38–40]. For adults with heart disease as well as abdominal, hepatobiliary, and gastrointestinal diseases, evidence-based appropriateness guidelines for medical 3D printing are also available [41, 42]. Radiologists are in a prime position to lead the medical industry in adopting 3D printing because the 3D models are based on the images that they evaluate daily. The Radiological Society of North America (RSNA) and the American College of Radiology (ACR) have together launched a 3D-printing clinical data registry to collect information on POC 3D printing's appropriate use and clinical decision-making [43]. Three-dimensional printing, also known as additive manufacturing, builds a 3D object layer by layer from feedstock material like thermoplastic polymer. Rapid prototyping with 3D printing is used in many fields. Fused deposition modeling (FDM) is the most prevalent 3D printing method, which starts with thermoplastic filaments and extrudes them in layers above their melting point to build a 3D object. HME can make these filaments. HME can make a homogenous solid dispersion of two or more pharmaceutical excipient polymers and even include a thermostable drug in the filament composition, which is impossible with other methods. HME 3D-printing filament development can increase drug bioavailability, solubility, and release time. The latter is important for 3D-printing medical implants. To ensure good quality and efficacy with reduced batch-to-batch fluctuation of pharmaceutical products, continuous manufacturing has become more popular in recent years. Figure 12.1 shows examples of the use of hot-melt extrusion combined with fused deposition modeling (FDM) 3D printing for individualized dosage administration.

12.4 Deciding to Become a POC Manufacturer

Several considerations are needed before beginning an in-house POC 3D-printing operation. Patients and their healthcare teams can benefit greatly from advanced technology, but it is time-consuming and expensive to set up and maintain. According to a white paper on POC manufacturing [15] published by the Society of Manufacturing Engineers (SME), the top three obstacles to the expansion of POC 3D-printing centers are the availability of financial resources, the regulatory framework, and the need

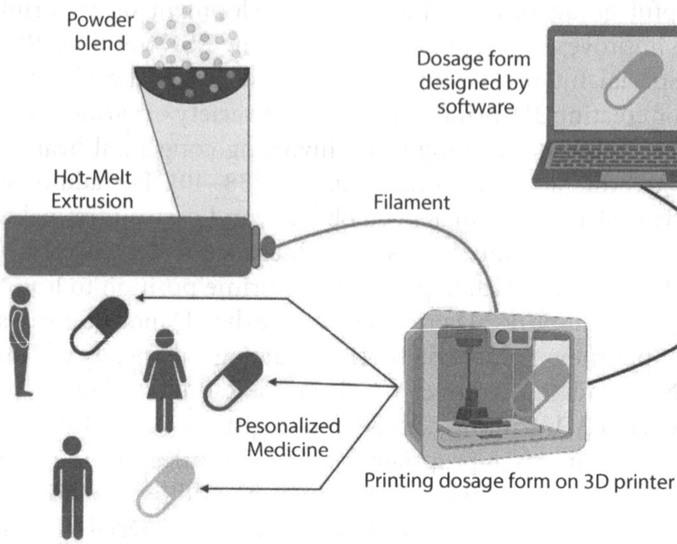

Figure 12.1 Applications of hot-melt extrusion coupled with fused deposition modeling 3D printing for individualized dosage administration of drugs.

for compensation for patients. To fully comprehend the unique obstacles and resources at each healthcare facility, it is important to perform a thorough assessment of needs and to create a budget. Costs that are classified as "fixed" do not fluctuate based on the volume of activity and are typically included in proposals with a longer time horizon. Consumables and the time spent by experts like engineers and technicians are examples of variable expenses [43, 44], which fluctuate with changes in production volume and activity. Although 3D printing has decreased in price, it still requires a considerable time and money commitment to get started. Initial investment start-up expenditures can include things like a $10,000–$30,000 tiny printer, basic supplies, inexpensive software, free or reduced-rate labor, and free or reduced-rate rent. Building up a fully operational lab with expert personnel, FDA-approved 3D-printing software, and cutting-edge equipment can cost hundreds of thousands of dollars [45]. Material jetting printers on the industrial level can cost a few hundred thousand dollars; however, desktop material extrusion machines (such as a fused deposition modeling printer) could be acquired for a few thousand dollars [46]. Moreover, post-processing software, specialized personnel, and software licensing expenses (up to $15,000 annually) [46, 47] should also be taken into account. The price of the models varies based on their size, intricacy, materials, and intended function. Metals used in powder bed fusion, for instance, can cost anywhere from $300 to $600 per kilogram. Depending on the required postprocessing stages, it can add up to an approximate cost of $2,000 to $4,000 per model. The pros and downsides of both in-house and outsourced 3D printing should be weighed throughout the evaluation of potential solutions [48]. The presence of prerequisites such as a suitable location, knowledgeable staff, and a clinical need should be taken into account as a first step. In addition to determining whether the seeking departments have the necessary facilities and buildings, staffing demands, financing, and possibilities for development and interaction with in-house specialists [49]. Decisions about the use of 3D-printing technology at the point of care must take into account the needs of both patients and healthcare practitioners. To make the most informed investment in 3D-printing technology, it is important to first determine what models, features, and materials would be required. POC 3D printing would be simpler to put into operation as most hospitals' radiological departments already generate the high-definition picture data needed for it. Some of these divisions might even have pre-existing 3D-printing methods, along with state-of-the-art visualization software for the post-processing and segmenting of images.

12.5 Obtaining 3D-Printing Management Support

The approval of the institution's higher-ups is necessary for a POC 3D-printing service to be implemented successfully. An economic case scenario may be required before the technology is invested in by healthcare leadership. The business case needs to show how the budgeted initial outlay, ongoing maintenance, and ROI all relate to one another. Investigators have found that (a) improved patient outcomes, (b) reduced costs and/or avoided costs, (c) increased patient access to care, and (d) new therapeutic innovations all contribute to a positive return on investment. The medical applications of 3D printing hold great promise. Indications of high-quality care include decreased radiation exposure due to shorter fluoroscopic examinations, lower doses of intravenous contrast material used in interventional procedures, and enhanced surgical outcomes [50, 51]. There are several quantitative clinical outcomes [42, 52–55] connected with the implementation of 3D-printed models before surgical procedures, such as the prevention of high-risk operations and the reduction of less invasive treatments. These models are made of materials that react similarly to actual tissue and provide tactile feedback. Recent research [24, 56] shows that high-fidelity instructional simulation can motivate previously inactive students to take an active role in their education. After a model is built using a 3D-printing method, it can be reproduced as needed to serve as a consistent training aid for surgeries; in turn, this may boost students' self-assurance and their overall surgical training experience. The possibility of financial savings or avoidance thanks to 3D printing is also a major factor in the technology's widespread adoption in formal settings. Studies have demonstrated that using 3D-printed models during surgery can reduce the length of the operation, the total cost, the risk of complications, the surgeon's anxiety, and the patient's blood loss [47, 53, 57]. An investigation by Ballard *et al.* [58] shows that using patient-specific oromaxillofacial and orthopedic implementations of 3D-printed anatomic models, surgical cutting guides, and implants can minimize the number and cost of invasive surgeries. Customizable and potentially cheaper than commercially available alternatives, 3D-printed imaging phantoms can be used to test the efficacy of a new imaging method or to prepare for image-guided treatments [59]. When compared to buying devices from a third-party manufacturer, making devices in-house that are tailored to each patient can be more cost-effective. Recent research [57] on patients with severe midfacial trauma found that using in-house 3D-printed models rather than industry-produced models reduced both costs and turnaround times. In 2019, 3D printing class III current procedural terminology procedures will be successfully implemented [60], and there is a potential possibility of reimbursement mechanisms. Category III codes are meant to be used temporarily and describe new technologies that have not yet received the level of peer review required for category I codes and hence are not always covered by insurance. These codes may eventually become category I code when more clinical data becomes available and more research is done on 3D printing. With the use of data collected and tracked by the RSNA and ACR's 3D-printing clinical data registry [57, 58], the movement toward category I code may be smoothed. Although the use of 3D-printed models can improve the results of some medical procedures, innovation remains in its development; further studies are required as well to confirm its effectiveness in the hospital [47, 61].

12.6 Setting Up a Platform to Assist POC 3D Printing

12.6.1 Training and Staff

The extensive use of 3D printing in hospitals is still in its infancy; hence, there are no tried-and-true ways to formally teach employees. To ensure that all employees are on the same page, facilities might incorporate SOPs and job instructions into the training curriculum [62, 63]. The workflows for different types of 3D anatomic models are outlined in SOPs, and work instructions provide specifics for everything from initial model conception to handoff to the clinical staff. Every hospital POC center needs a 3D-printing technician to run the machines, update the software, and finish processing the models printed there. Anybody with technical and problem-solving skills is also required to coordinate with the asking supplier, assess the item for quality, and determine the most efficient means of transforming the raw materials into the final good. The person usually comes from an engineering (mechanical, electrical, etc.) background. Depending on the complexity of the models, designers may also require segmentation experts and design engineers able to generate the digital 3D model. Radiologists or other imaging professionals offer or monitor presurgical planning models, which require anatomic, and segmentation skills. An expert in computer-aided design (CAD) software is essential for the production of gadgets. The radiologist is an essential component of the 3D printing team since he or she is involved in the workflow, ensures that the imaging data is accurate, and checks the model's accuracy after printing [64].

12.6.2 Facility Requirements: Area, Building, and Power

The infrastructure and safety requirements for establishing a 3D-printing laboratory can vary widely between different types of medical facilities. Low-end 3D printers do not break the bank and do not have unusual space or power needs. Desktop printers with a "plug and play" design take up minimal room and may be used immediately. Some examples are vat photopolymerization technology (such as stereolithographic) printers and desktop material extrusion printers, while others are digital light processing printers. The space and facility needs, however, quickly grow when postprocessing activities to ready the delivery model are taken into account. Desktop stereolithographic and digital light processing printer-produced components, for instance, frequently call for post-curing with ultraviolet radiation and/or heat as well as an isopropyl alcohol wash. Isopropyl alcohol must be kept in fireproof containers. An additional fume hood may be required due to the presence of isopropyl alcohol bath vapors [65]. Several types of post-processing equipment, such as high-powered lasers and industrial-strength thermal ovens, can be quite power-hungry and may require separate circuits. More room may be needed than was initially anticipated when trying to find suitable spots to house equipment for various postprocessing stages [66, 67]. More space and supporting machinery are required for larger machines. Space constraints and the necessity for ancillary equipment that are integral to the printing process provide a problem for efficient workspace design in healthcare facilities when using production-level printers. The space requirements of powder bed fusion and directed energy deposition technology printers may be too great for the majority of medical facilities' 3D-printing laboratories and X-ray departments. Before relocating or acquiring equipment, it is helpful to have a chat with the hospital's facilities personnel, and the close collaboration should continue throughout the laboratory's installation and maintenance [68]. The sort of technology utilized also affects other factors to think about, such as potential occupational dangers—for instance, powder-based 3D printers generate a lot of dust during post-processing and may need to be isolated from other machines to prevent the contamination of raw materials and damage to delicate equipment used for other types of printing. Those working in these regions are required to take the usual precautions for occupational safety, such as wearing a protective gear.

12.6.3 Sterilization

Sterilization is essential to prevent infection when using 3D-printed models or guides in clinical settings where they may come into contact with patient tissues (such as intraoperative applications) [69]. Sterilizable materials are necessary for model construction if they are to have any practical use. Sterilization can be achieved by a variety of means, such as autoclave steam sterilization, exposure to ethylene oxide gas, plasma generated from hydrogen peroxide gas, or gamma radiation. Steam autoclaving is the most common method of sterilization in hospitals, while gamma radiation using cobalt 60 necessitates sending models elsewhere. Members of the 3D-printing team at every given institution need to be well versed in the various sterilizing methods in use there as well as the validation of these methods and how they could affect the model's or part's material properties after printing.

12.6.4 Quality Management System

For the successful implementation and ongoing operation of a 3D-printing program, a solid quality management framework is essential but must be tailored to the specific needs of the facility and the types of products it produces. Managing quality is much more than just a set of rules and regulations; it is a way of thinking that the whole team needs to buy into to guarantee the reliability and usefulness of their 3D-printed models. The Quality System Regulation (21 CFR part 820) is legislation governing the production, distribution, storage, and consumption of food and medications in the United States [62]. Standards for equipment, purchasing, materials, manufacturing, and facilities are all part of a comprehensive quality management system that also includes design and process validation. In addition to dealing with defective items and preventing future issues, the quality management system also addresses acceptance operations (such as double-checking the printed part or model to ensure that it is correct). The chapter will just provide an overview review of the most significant ideas involved in 3D-printing quality control as the researcher has recently detailed the many components of such a system [16]. The gathering of imaging data is the first step in the quality control process for patient-specific devices, making radiologists an important component of any 3D-printing quality management system. As stated in [68], quality imagery is crucial since it paves the way for reliable 3D models. The most effective imaging protocols for 3D printing make use of high signal intensity (in the case of MRI) and high contrast (in the case of CT) to bring out and distinguish anatomical structures for segmentation, and they use a thin section thickness for CT (submillimeter section thickness is recommended) to improve the details for reconstruction. Multiphase contrast-enhanced computed tomography and magnetic resonance imaging (MRI) could be viable options, depending on the circumstances and the specifications of the model. Imaging segmentation and computer-aided planning process necessitate an in-depth knowledge of the model's intended application to be carried out successfully throughout the design phase [69].

12.6.5 Regulatory Considerations

The Joint Commission is responsible for regulating and certifying health services, while the Center for Devices and Radiological Health of the Food and Drug Administration regulates medical device manufacturers (CDRH). The FDA has released information [70–72] summarizing the many functions and regulatory bodies implicated in the clearance of 3D-printed medical devices, in addition to the technical considerations and guidelines. Where does the manufacturing plant begin and the hospital end is a difficult question to answer when making POCs. There are a lot of sophisticated aspects to answer that fall outside the focus of the investigation. To help POC operators visualize the regulatory approval needed for carrying out numerous 3D printing activities, the FDA has developed a conceptual risk-based framework for POC manufacturing, identified as scenarios A–E [73]. The scenarios were designed with 3D printing in mind for the proof-of-concept stage [67] and are based on the idea of risk management. Regularly, the FDA consults with leaders in clinical practice, industry, and other interested parties to determine the best applications for 3D printing [70]. The Recommendations for Medical 3D Printing was established by the RSNA 3D Printing Special Interest Group [20] to assist in the increasing application of 3D printing in healthcare settings. Parameters for practice, as well as suggestions and criteria for clinical appropriateness, are all covered in these rules [74].

12.7 Powder-Based Binding Method

The pharmaceutical industry is especially interested in powder-based rapid prototyping because it has many similarities to existing manufacturing processes and could provide a more efficient long-term printing solution [75]. Spraying a binder or medication solution with extra excipients in tiny droplets from an X–Y print head (in two-dimensional fashions) over a powder bed on a built platform is how multilayer 3D printing items are made. Then, when each successive layer is built, it is moved downward along the Z-axis. Adhesion or welding could be used to join the layers in a fluid solution or suspension (Figure 12.2). After the 3D printing process

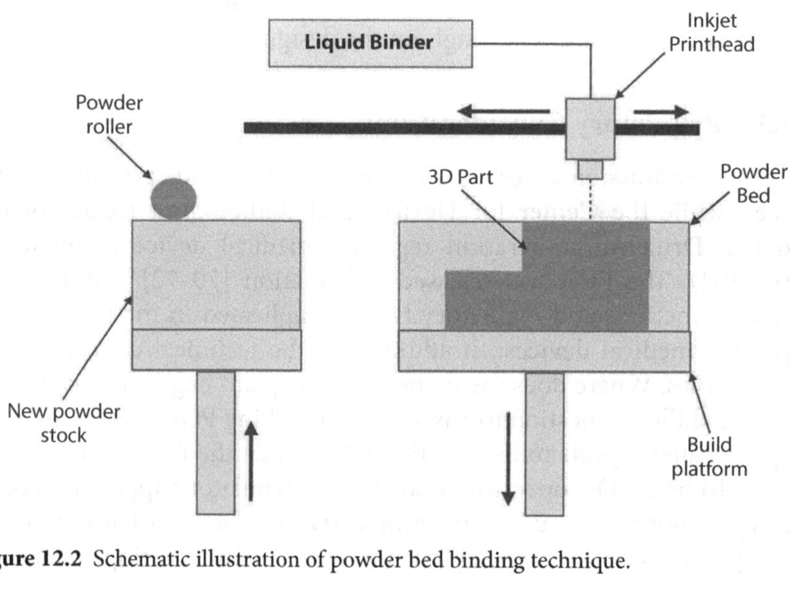

Figure 12.2 Schematic illustration of powder bed binding technique.

is complete, any excess solvent or unbound powder must be washed away (post-printing phase). Pharmaceutical ingredients may be printed quickly and reliably with powder bed 3D printing. In addition, the production cost of 3D-printed goods is greatly reduced without sacrificing quality. The technique has considerable promise for producing regulated and quick-release medication formulations, multilayer tablets with various and precise active ingredients, and high-dose formulations of medicinal substances. Because of these benefits, the method has found widespread use in the pharmaceutical industry [76]. Choosing the right binder and concentration may ensure that 3D pharmaceuticals maintain their structural integrity. The quality of the 3D prints can also be affected by other factors, such as the powder's particle size.

12.8 Conclusion

Medical 3D printing is developing, allowing the creation of patient-specific anatomic models. 3D printing in POC facilities is varied but likely to grow. Bioprinting and tailored medicine dosing are prospects of 3D printing, with multidisciplinary research already underway. 3D printing at the POC poses challenges, but it offers several patient-centered benefits. Radiologists lead the technological revolution that transforms medical imaging from 3D virtual projections to tactile 3D models. Besides its limitations, POC 3D printing may have benefits for patient care in hospitals that utilize it. As 3D printing is becoming more prevalent and evidence accumulates, the radiologist will be in a unique position to make contributions to multidisciplinary patient care and support both medical and surgical professionals beyond image interpretation. 3D-printing technology can help radiologists lead new areas and improve healthcare.

References

1. Mitsouras, D., Liacouras, P., Imanzadeh, A., Giannopoulos, A.A., Cai, T., Kumamaru, K.K., George, E., Wake, N., Caterson, E.J., Pomahac, B., Ho, V.B., Medical 3D printing for the radiologist. *Radiographics*, 35, 7, 1965–88, 2015 Nov.
2. Matsumoto, J.S., Morris, J.M., Foley, T.A., Williamson, E.E., Leng, S., McGee, K.P., Kuhlmann, J.L., Nesberg, L.E., Vrtiska, T.J., Three-dimensional physical modeling: Applications and experience at Mayo Clinic. *Radiographics*, 35, 7, 1989–2006, 2015 Nov.

3. Mitsouras, D., Liacouras, P.C., Wake, N., Rybicki, F.J., RadioGraphics update: Medical 3D printing for the radiologist. *Radiographics*, 40, 4, E21–3, 2020 Jul.
4. Talanki, V.R., Peng, Q., Shamir, S.B., Baete, S.H., Duong, T.Q., Wake, N., Three-dimensional printed anatomic models derived from magnetic resonance imaging data: Current state and image acquisition recommendations for appropriate clinical scenarios. *J. Magn. Reson. Imaging*, 55, 4, 1060–81, 2022 Apr.
5. Galstyan, A., Bunker, M.J., Lobo, F., Sims, R., Inziello, J., Stubbs, J., Mukhtar, R., Kelil, T., Applications of 3D printing in breast cancer management. *3D Print. Med.*, 7, 1, 1–0, 2021 Dec.
6. Dall'Ava, L., Hothi, H., Henckel, J., Di Laura, A., Shearing, P., Hart, A., Comparative analysis of current 3D printed acetabular titanium implants. *3D Print. Med.*, 5, 1–0, 2019 Dec.
7. Manero, A., Smith, P., Sparkman, J., Dombrowski, M., Courbin, D., Kester, A., Womack, I., Chi, A., Implementation of 3D printing technology in the field of prosthetics: Past, present, and future. *Int. J. Environ. Res. Public Health*, 16, 9, 1641, 2019 May.
8. Marconi, S., Pugliese, L., Botti, M., Peri, A., Cavazzi, E., Latteri, S., Auricchio, F., Pietrabissa, A., Value of 3D printing for the comprehension of surgical anatomy. *Surg. Endosc.*, 31, 4102–10, 2017 Oct.
9. Alexander, A.E., Wake, N., Chepelev, L., Brantner, P., Ryan, J., Wang, K.C., A guideline for 3D printing terminology in biomedical research utilizing ISO/ASTM standards. *3D Print. Med.*, 7, 1–6, 2021 Dec.
10. Huang, Y. and Leu, M.C., Frontiers of additive manufacturing research and education.
11. Mani, M., Lyons, K.W., Gupta, S.K., Sustainability characterization for additive manufacturing. *J. Res. Natl. Inst. Stand. Technol.*, 119, 419, 2014.
12. Mitsouras, D., George, E., Rybicki, F.J., Quality and safety of 3D-printed medical models, in: *3D Printing in Medicine: A Practical Guide for Medical Professionals*, pp. 113–23, 2017.
13. Shahrubudin, N., Lee, T.C., Ramlan, R.J., An overview on 3D printing technology: Technological, materials, and applications. *Proc. Manuf.*, 35, 1286–96, 2019 Jan 1.
14. Olivieri, L.J., Su, L., Hynes, C.F., Krieger, A., Alfares, F.A., Ramakrishnan, K., Zurakowski, D., Marshall, M.B., Kim, P.C., Jonas, R.A., Nath, D.S., "Just-in-time" simulation training using 3-D printed cardiac models after congenital cardiac surgery. *World J. Pediatr. Congenit. Heart Surg.*, 7, 2, 164–8, 2016 Mar.
15. Hodgdon, T., Danrad, R., Patel, M.J., Smith, S.E., Richardson, M.L., Ballard, D.H., Ali, S., Trace, A.P., DeBenedectis, C.M., Zygmont, M.E., Lenchik, L., Logistics of three-dimensional printing: Primer for radiologists. *Acad. Radiol.*, 25, 1, 40–51, 2018 Jan 1.
16. Bastawrous, S., Wu, L., Strzelecki, B., Levin, D.B., Li, J.S., Coburn, J., Ripley, B., Establishing quality and safety in hospital-based 3D printing programs: Patient-first approach. *Radiographics*, 41, 4, 1208–29, 2021 Jul.

17. Ludwig, P.E., Huff, T.J., Zuniga, J.M., The potential role of bioengineering and three-dimensional printing in curing global corneal blindness. *J. Tissue Eng.*, 9, 2041731418769863, 2018 Apr 11.
18. Jamróz, W., Szafraniec, J., Kurek, M., Jachowicz, R., 3D printing in pharmaceutical and medical applications–recent achievements and challenges. *Pharm. Res.*, 35, 1–22, 2018 Sep.
19. Christensen, A. and Rybicki, F.J., Maintaining safety and efficacy for 3D printing in medicine. *3D Print. Med.*, 3, 1, 1–0, 2017 Mar.
20. Bastawrous, S., Wu, L., Strzelecki, B., Levin, D.B., Li, J.S., Coburn, J., Ripley, B., Establishing quality and safety in hospital-based 3D printing programs: Patient-first approach. *Radiographics*, 41, 4, 1208–29, 2021 Jul.
21. Cherkasskiy, L., Caffrey, J.P., Szewczyk, A.F., Cory, E., Bomar, J.D., Farnsworth, C.L., Jeffords, M., Wenger, D.R., Sah, R.L., Upasani, V.V., Patient-specific 3D models aid planning for triplane proximal femoral osteotomy in slipped capital femoral epiphysis. *J. Child. Orthop.*, 11, 2, 147–53, 2017 Apr.
22. Morgan, C., Khatri, C., Hanna, S.A., Ashrafian, H., Sarraf, K.M., Use of three-dimensional printing in preoperative planning in orthopaedic trauma surgery: A systematic review and meta-analysis. *World J. Orthop.*, 11, 1, 57, 2020 Jan 1.
23. Punyaratabandhu, T., Liacouras, P.C., Pairojboriboon, S., Using 3D models in orthopedic oncology: Presenting personalized advantages in surgical planning and intraoperative outcomes. *3D Print. Med.*, 4, 1, 1–3, 2018 Dec.
24. Giannopoulos, A.A., Mitsouras, D., Yoo, S.J., Liu, P.P., Chatzizisis, Y.S., Rybicki, F.J., Applications of 3D printing in cardiovascular diseases. *Nat. Rev. Cardiol.*, 13, 12, 701–18, 2016 Dec.
25. Ripley, B., Kelil, T., Cheezum, M.K., Goncalves, A., Di Carli, M.F., Rybicki, F.J., Steigner, M., Mitsouras, D., Blankstein, R., 3D printing based on cardiac CT assists anatomic visualization prior to transcatheter aortic valve replacement. *J. Cardiovasc. Comput. Tomogr.*, 10, 1, 28–36, 2016 Jan 1.
26. Li, H., Shu, M., Wang, X., Song, Z., Application of 3D printing technology to left atrial appendage occlusion. *Int. J. Cardiol.*, 231, 258–63, 2017 Mar 15.
27. Valverde, I., Gomez-Ciriza, G., Hussain, T., Suarez-Mejias, C., Velasco-Forte, M.N., Byrne, N., Ordoñez, A., Gonzalez-Calle, A., Anderson, D., Hazekamp, M.G., Roest, A.A., Three-dimensional printed models for surgical planning of complex congenital heart defects: An international multicentre study. *Eur. J. Cardio-Thorac. Surg.*, 52, 6, 1139–48, 2017 Dec 1.
28. Weinstock, P., Prabhu, S.P., Flynn, K., Orbach, D.B., Smith, E., Optimizing cerebrovascular surgical and endovascular procedures in children via personalized 3D printing. *J. Neurosurg.: Pediatr.*, 16, 5, 584–9, 2015 Nov 1.
29. Pietrabissa, A., Marconi, S., Negrello, E., Mauri, V., Peri, A., Pugliese, L., Marone, E.M., Auricchio, F., An overview on 3D printing for abdominal surgery. *Surg. Endosc.*, 34, 1–3, 2020 Jan.
30. Witowski, J., Budzyński, A., Grochowska, A., Ballard, D.H., Major, P., Rubinkiewicz, M., Złahoda-Huzior, A., Popiela, T.J., Wierdak, M., Pędziwiatr,

M., Decision-making based on 3D printed models in laparoscopic liver resections with intraoperative ultrasound: A prospective observational study. *Eur. Radiol.*, 30, 1306–12, 2020 Mar.

31. Witowski, J.S., Pędziwiatr, M., Major, P., Budzyński, A., Cost-effective, personalized, 3D-printed liver model for preoperative planning before laparoscopic liver hemihepatectomy for colorectal cancer metastases. *Int. J. Comput. Assist. Radiol. Surg.*, 12, 2047–54, 2017 Dec.
32. Wake, N., Rude, T., Kang, S.K., Stifelman, M.D., Borin, J.F., Sodickson, D.K., Huang, W.C., Chandarana, H., 3D printed renal cancer models derived from MRI data: Application in pre-surgical planning. *Abdom. Radiol.*, 42, 1501–9, 2017 May.
33. Hamabe, A. and Ito, M., A three-dimensional pelvic model made with a three-dimensional printer: Applications for laparoscopic surgery to treat rectal cancer. *Tech. Coloproctol.*, 21, 383–7, 2017 May.
34. Luzon, J.A., Andersen, B.T., Stimec, B.V., Fasel, J.H., Bakka, A.O., Kazaryan, A.M., Ignjatovic, D., Implementation of 3D printed superior mesenteric vascular models for surgical planning and/or navigation in right colectomy with extended D3 mesenterectomy: Comparison of virtual and physical models to the anatomy found at surgery. *Surg. Endosc.*, 33, 567–75, 2019 Feb 15.
35. Biglino, G., Capelli, C., Wray, J., Schievano, S., Leaver, L.K., Khambadkone, S., Giardini, A., Derrick, G., Jones, A., Taylor, A.M., 3D-manufactured patient-specific models of congenital heart defects for communication in clinical practice: Feasibility and acceptability. *BMJ Open*, 5, 4, e007165, 2015 Apr 1.
36. Wake, N., Alexander, A.E., Christensen, A.M., Liacouras, P.C., Schickel, M., Pietila, T., Matsumoto, J., Creating patient-specific anatomical models for 3D printing and AR/VR: A supplement for the 2018 Radiological Society of North America (RSNA) hands-on course. *3D Print. Med.*, 5, 1, 1–0, 2019 Dec.
37. Chepelev, L., Wake, N., Ryan, J., Althobaity, W., Gupta, A., Arribas, E., Santiago, L., Ballard, D.H., Wang, K.C., Weadock, W., Ionita, C.N., Radiological Society of North America (RSNA) 3D printing Special Interest Group (SIG): Guidelines for medical 3D printing and appropriateness for clinical scenarios. *3D Print. Med.*, 4, 1, 1–38, 2018 Dec.
38. Chepelev, L., Hodgdon, T., Gupta, A., Wang, A., Torres, C., Krishna, S., Akyuz, E., Mitsouras, D., Sheikh, A., Medical 3D printing for vascular interventions and surgical oncology: A primer for the 2016 radiological society of North America (RSNA) hands-on course in 3D printing. *3D Print. Med.*, 2, 1–7, 2016 Dec.
39. Chepelev, L., Souza, C., Althobaity, W., Miguel, O., Krishna, S., Akyuz, E., Hodgdon, T., Torres, C., Wake, N., Alexander, A., George, E., Preoperative planning and tracheal stent design in thoracic surgery: A primer for the 2017 Radiological Society of North America (RSNA) hands-on course in 3D printing. *3D Print. Med.*, 3, 1–26, 2017 Mar.

40. Giannopoulos, A.A., Chepelev, L., Sheikh, A., Wang, A., Dang, W., Akyuz, E., Hong, C., Wake, N., Pietila, T., Dydynski, P.B., Mitsouras, D., 3D printed ventricular septal defect patch: A primer for the 2015 Radiological Society of North America (RSNA) hands-on course in 3D printing. *3D Print. Med.*, 1, 1, 1–20, 2015 Dec.
41. Ali, A., Ballard, D.H., Althobaity, W., Christensen, A., Geritano, M., Ho, M., Liacouras, P., Matsumoto, J., Morris, J., Ryan, J., Shorti, R., Clinical situations for which 3D printing is considered an appropriate representation or extension of data contained in a medical imaging examination: Adult cardiac conditions. *3D Print. Med.*, 6, 1–9, 2020 Dec.
42. Ballard, D.H., Wake, N., Witowski, J., Rybicki, F.J., Sheikh, A., Radiological Society of North America (RSNA) 3D Printing Special Interest Group (SIG) clinical situations for which 3D printing is considered an appropriate representation or extension of data contained in a medical imaging examination: Abdominal, hepatobiliary, and gastrointestinal conditions. *3D Print. Med.*, 6, 1, 1–7, 2020 Dec.
43. Bastawrous, S., Wu, L., Liacouras, P.C., Levin, D.B., Ahmed, M.T., Strzelecki, B., Amendola, M.F., Lee, J.T., Coburn, J., Ripley, B., Establishing 3D printing at the point of care: Basic principles and tools for success. *Radiographics*, 42, 2, 451–68, 2022 Mar.
44. Roberts, R.R., Frutos, P.W., Ciavarella, G.G., Gussow, L.M., Mensah, E.K., Kampe, L.M., Straus, H.E., Joseph, G., Rydman, R.J., Distribution of variable vs fixed costs of hospital care. *JAMA*, 281, 7, 644–9, 1999 Feb 17.
45. Stefanowicz, E. and O'Connell, B., Hospital 3D printing: Part 2–a clear path to value capture.
46. Farooqi, K.M., Cooper, C., Chelliah, A., Saeed, O., Chai, P.J., Jambawalikar, S.R., Lipson, H., Bacha, E.A., Einstein, A.J., Jorde, U.P., 3D printing and heart failure: The present and the future. *JACC: Heart Fail.*, 7, 2, 132–42, 2019 Feb.
47. Daoud, G.E., Pezzutti, D.L., Dolatowski, C.J., Carrau, R.L., Pancake, M., Herderick, E., VanKoevering, K.K., Establishing a point-of-care additive manufacturing workflow for clinical use. *J. Mater. Res.*, 6, 1–20, 2021 Jul.
48. Chen, X., Liu, X., Childs, P., Brandon, N., Wu, B., A low cost desktop electrochemical metal 3D printer. *Adv. Mater. Technol.*, 2, 10, 1700148, 2017 Oct.
49. Sheikh, A., Chepelev, L., Christensen, A.M., Mitsouras, D., Schwarz, B.A., Rybicki, F.J., Beginning and developing a radiology-based in-hospital 3D printing lab, in: *3D Printing in Medicine: A Practical Guide For Medical Professionals*, pp. 35–41, 2017.
50. Ghazi, A., Melnyk, R., Farooq, S., Bell, A., Holler, T., Saba, P., Joseph, J., Validity of a patient-specific percutaneous nephrolithotomy (PCNL) simulated surgical rehearsal platform: Impact on patient and surgical outcomes. *World J. Urol.*, 40, 3, 627–37, 2022 Mar.
51. Obasare, E., Mainigi, S.K., Morris, D.L., Slipczuk, L., Goykhman, I., Friend, E., Ziccardi, M.R., Pressman, G.S., CT based 3D printing is superior to transesophageal echocardiography for pre-procedure planning in left atrial

appendage device closure. *Int. J. Cardiovasc. Imaging*, 34, 821–31, 2018 May.

52. Li, Q., Chen, X., Lin, B., Ma, Y., Liao, J.X., Zheng, Q., Three-dimensional technology assisted trabecular metal cup and augments positioning in revision total hip arthroplasty with complex acetabular defects. *J. Orthop. Surg. Res.*, 14, 1–9, 2019 Dec.
53. Lupulescu, C. and Sun, Z., A systematic review of the clinical value and applications of three-dimensional printing in renal surgery. *J. Clin. Med.*, 8, 7, 990, 2019 Jul 8.
54. van Doremalen, R.F., van der Linde, R.A., Kootstra, J.J., van Helden, S.H., Hekman, E.E., Can 3D-printing avoid discomfort-related implant removal in midshaft clavicle fractures? A four-year follow-up. *Arch. Orthop. Trauma Surg.*, 141, 1899–907, 2021 Nov.
55. Hermsen, J.L., Burke, T.M., Seslar, S.P., Owens, D.S., Ripley, B.A., Mokadam, N.A., Verrier, E.D., Scan, plan, print, practice, perform: Development and use of a patient-specific 3-dimensional printed model in adult cardiac surgery. *J. Thorac. Cardiovasc. Surg.*, 153, 1, 132–40, 2017 Jan 1.
56. Ganguli, A., Pagan-Diaz, G.J., Grant, L., Cvetkovic, C., Bramlet, M., Vozenilek, J., Kesavadas, T., Bashir, R., 3D printing for preoperative planning and surgical training: A review. *Biomed. Microdevices*, 20, 1–24, 2018 Sep.
57. Lor, L.S., Massary, D.A., Chung, S.A., Brown, P.J., Runyan, C.M., Cost analysis for in-house versus industry-printed skull models for acute midfacial fractures. *Plast. Reconstr. Surg. Glob. Open*, 8, 5, 1–6, 2020 May.
58. Ballard, D.H., Mills, P., Duszak Jr, R., Weisman, J.A., Rybicki, F.J., Woodard, P.K., Medical 3D printing cost-savings in orthopedic and maxillofacial surgery: Cost analysis of operating room time saved with 3D printed anatomic models and surgical guides. *Acad. Radiol.*, 27, 8, 1103–13, 2020 Aug 1.
59. Mitsouras, D., Lee, T.C., Liacouras, P., Ionita, C.N., Pietilla, T., Maier, S.E., Mulkern, R.V., Three-dimensional printing of MRI-visible phantoms and MR image-guided therapy simulation. *Magn. Reson. Med.*, 77, 2, 613–22, 2017 Feb.
60. Transmittal, M., Update of the Hospital Outpatient Prospective Payment System (OPPS), July 2009, Published 06-23-09; 1760.
61. Diment, L.E., Thompson, M.S., Bergmann, J.H., Clinical efficacy and effectiveness of 3D printing: A systematic review. *BMJ Open*, 7, 12, e016891, 2017 Dec 1.
62. Ménard, T., Barros, A., Ganter, C., Clinical quality considerations when using next-generation sequencing (NGS) in clinical drug development. *Ther. Innovation Regul. Sci.*, 55, 5, 1066–74, 2021 Sep.
63. Tino, R., Moore, R., Antoline, S., Ravi, P., Wake, N., Ionita, C.N., Morris, J.M., Decker, S.J., Sheikh, A., Rybicki, F.J., Chepelev, L.L., COVID-19 and the role of 3D printing in medicine. *3D Print. Med.*, 6, 1, 1–8, 2020 Dec.

64. George, E., Liacouras, P., Rybicki, F.J., Mitsouras, D., Measuring and establishing the accuracy and reproducibility of 3D printed medical models. *Radiographics*, 37, 5, 1424–50, 2017 Sep.
65. Chan, F.L., Hon, C.Y., Tarlo, S.M., Rajaram, N., House, R., Emissions and health risks from the use of 3D printers in an occupational setting. *J. Toxicol. Environ. Health, Part A*, 83, 7, 279–87, 2020 Apr 2.
66. Bastawrous, S., Wu, L., Liacouras, P.C., Levin, D.B., Ahmed, M.T., Strzelecki, B., Amendola, M.F., Lee, J.T., Coburn, J., Ripley, B., Establishing 3D printing at the point of care: Basic principles and tools for success. *Radiographics*, 42, 2, 451–68, 2022 Mar.
67. Christensen, A. and Rybicki, F.J., Maintaining safety and efficacy for 3D printing in medicine. *3D Print. Med.*, 3, 1, 1–0, 2017 Mar.
68. Leng, S., McGee, K., Morris, J., Alexander, A., Kuhlmann, J., Vrieze, T., McCollough, C.H., Matsumoto, J., Anatomic modeling using 3D printing: Quality assurance and optimization. *3D Print. Med.*, 3, 1–4, 2017 Mar.
69. Shea, G.K., Wu, K.L., Li, I.W., Leung, M.F., Ko, A.L., Tse, L., Pang, S.S., Kwan, K.Y., Wong, T.M., Leung, F.K., Fang, C.X., A review of the manufacturing process and infection rate of 3D-printed models and guides sterilized by hydrogen peroxide plasma and utilized intra-operatively. *3D Print. Med.*, 6, 1, 1–1, 2020 Dec.
70. Ripley, B., Levin, D., Kelil, T., Hermsen, J.L., Kim, S., Maki, J.H., Wilson, G.J., 3D printing from MRI data: Harnessing strengths and minimizing weaknesses. *J. Magn. Reson. Imaging*, 45, 3, 635–45, 2017 Mar.
71. Bastawrous, S., Wu, L., Liacouras, P.C., Levin, D.B., Ahmed, M.T., Strzelecki, B., Amendola, M.F., Lee, J.T., Coburn, J., Ripley, B., Establishing 3D printing at the point of care: Basic principles and tools for success. *Radiographics*, 42, 2, 451–68, 2022 Mar.
72. Di Prima, M., Coburn, J., Hwang, D., Kelly, J., Khairuzzaman, A., Ricles, L., Additively manufactured medical products–the FDA perspective. *3D Print. Med.*, 2, 1–6, 2016 Dec.
73. Rai, K. and Pradhan, U.U., Empowering advances in medical devices with 3D-printing technology, in: *3D Printing Technology and its Diverse Applications*, pp. 155–188, Apple Academic Press, Florida, USA, 2021 Dec 22.
74. Food US. Drug Administration, https://www. fda. gov/newsevents/newsroom/pressannouncements/ucm473971. htm. (accessed on February 2023).
75. Daly, R., Harrington, T.S., Martin, G.D., Hutchings, I.M., Inkjet printing for pharmaceutics–a review of research and manufacturing. *Int. J. Pharm.*, 494, 2, 554–67, 2015 Oct 30.
76. Infanger, S., Haemmerli, A., Iliev, S., Baier, A., Stoyanov, E., Quodbach, J., Powder bed 3D-printing of highly loaded drug delivery devices with hydroxypropyl cellulose as solid binder. *Int. J. Pharm.*, 555, 198–206, 2019 Jan 30.

13

3D Printing in Robotic Urosurgery

Abstract
The use of 3D printing in urology has been the subject of a rapidly expanding corpus of research during the past 5 years. Progress in exciting new fields of study has been made possible by incentives including work-hour restrictions and patient-safety programs, as well as by innovations in biomaterials and quick printing techniques. However, difficulties with its wide usage comprise high prices, unfamiliarity with the technical processes required, as well as absence of potential applications. The investigation of the concept for 3D printing in urological practice depends on robotic surgery to enhance pre-operative planning, update surgeon training, and better educate patients. Models of the prostate are frequently used in the preparation for nerve-sparing surgeries. Early research has shown enough realism and educational effectiveness to warrant continuing the project. Further investigation has shown enhanced surgeon assurance, surgical efficiency, and enhanced patient outcomes, with high levels of patient satisfaction among the highlights. Standard desktop 3D printers now make it possible to produce realistic, precise models in a matter of hours at a price that would not break the bank. Most typically, 3D printing has been utilized to create anatomical replicas of sick organs to replace the haptic feedback that is lost during robotic surgeries. Urologists are rapidly expanding and continuously improving in adaptive mode, and thus the benefits to patients were expected to exceed the diminishing drawbacks, indicating that subsequent transformation in surgical education, robotics techniques, and individualized therapy may occur simultaneously.

Keywords: 3D printing, surgical education, robotic urology, stereolithography, digital imaging

13.1 Introduction

In 1983, Charles Hull pioneered stereolithography, a technique for 3D printing that uses ultraviolet light to cure and fuse photopolymer resins. Early users included specialists in orthopedics and maxillofacial surgery [1, 2]. Urology has been a "hot spot" of progress in robotic surgery educational

Rishabha Malviya and Rishav Sharma. 3D Printing in Healthcare: Novel Applications, (249–262)

programs because of the convergence of advancements in minimally invasive procedures as well as the shift toward simulation-based training over the past decade. Among the numerous uses for robotics in hospitals around the world are the advancement of informed consent procedures, the enrichment of resident education, and the optimization of preoperative robotic surgery planning. Developing dynamic technology beyond the fabrication of basic visual aids and providing an interactive platform with the authenticity required to complete an operation in its entirety require constant innovation and the pursuit of new frontiers. Printing a 3D object from a series of 2D images, as in 3D printing, is characterized as an additive manufacturing technique in comparison with conventional sequential and substitutive methods of production. Digital Imaging and Communications in Medicine (DICOM) image files of high quality are the gold standards for medical imaging, and MRIs, CTs, and other axial imaging modalities are preferred wherever possible. To make a digital 3D model, these DICOM files must be transformed into a CAD code, such as standard tessellation language. The slicer is the central piece of software in 3D printing; it takes the CAD model as input and uses it as a blueprint to produce a set of G-codes that the printer can use to fabricate the 3D object [3]. With the use of postprocessing tools, models may be fine-tuned for highly accurate and reproducible reconstructions, and new software developments have made it possible to encode extra data points like color and texture into the file formats. Prototyping of new pieces of machinery may be done quickly with the help of 3D printing, and medical imaging can be used to create life-like models of a patient's anatomy. With its growing list of applications, 3D printing technology has emerged as a fertile ground for medical innovation, yet does it mean that it is a useful supplement to urological practice? Here, the investigator provides a condensed systematic review of the literature on 3D printing in urology, discussing its potential advantages and the research gaps that prevent us from fully realizing those potential benefits. Following the principles defined in the Preferred Reporting Items for Systematic Reviews and Meta-Analyses (PRISMA) statement, investigators systematically appraise works published until December 2019. In total, 67 of the 117 articles found are included, focusing on the most important aspects of the field, such as the application of patient-specific models to the tasks of patient education, surgical planning, and surgical training. Bioprinting graft tissues was another ground-breaking use case, along with printed surgical equipment and guidelines tailored to each patient. Further studies are needed to indicate that 3D printing can measurably improve patients' lives, that it can lead to better surgical outcomes consistently, or that it can lead to simulations that are more realistic and more effective

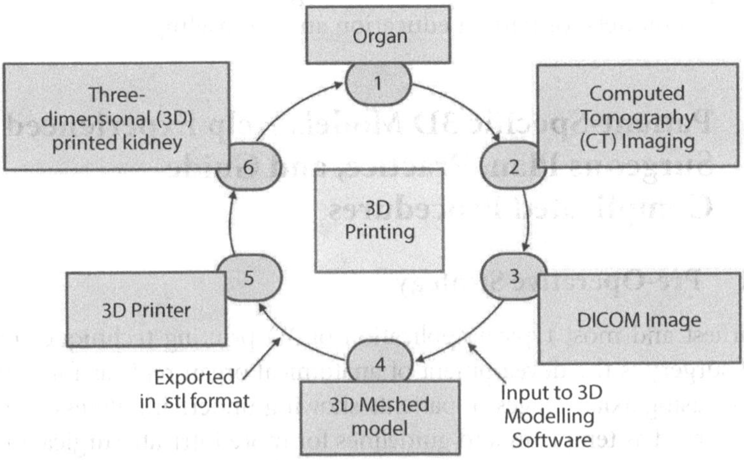

Figure 13.1 The procedures involved in the patient-specific three-dimensional (3D) printing process for a kidney model.

than the currently available tools for training surgeons. Although research into the uses of 3D printing in urology is still in its infancy, the technology's indisputable importance as a resource and its potential for fostering collaborative design make it an exciting prospect with promising future developments. Despite these developments, nonresectable resins remain the preferred material for 3D-printing surgical education models [4]. The procedure that leads to the development of a patient-specific kidney model using three-dimensional (3D) printing is depicted in Figure 13.1.

13.2 Potential Urological Applications

Innovative technology must be demonstrated to be both practical and accurate before it can be widely adopted. It was initially hoped that a 3D-printed model would help urologists better comprehend kidney cancers [5]. Many studies are highlighting the use of 3D technology to build simulation platforms for the hands-on learning of trainees or the performance of practicing surgeons [6]. While it is happening, many other studies have shown how useful these materials can be as patient and medical student surgical educational tools. To further understand these programs, consider them in the following contexts:

1. Patient-specific 3D models for planning, practicing, and guiding difficult procedures for surgeons
2. 3D models for patient education and counseling

13.3 Patient-Specific 3D Models Help Experienced Surgeons Plan, Practice, and Guide Complicated Procedures

13.3.1 Pre-Operative Strategy

The earliest and most typical application of 3D printing techniques in the area of surgery is the development of anatomical organ replicas for surgical purposes using axial images of patients showing underlying illnesses. These models served as templates and guidelines for more intricate surgical operations before surgery [7]. Such models increase decision-making and surgeon confidence in describing the surgical challenge and recognizing the specialized and anatomical components of the treatment, which may improve operative outputs like shorter procedure times and reduced blood loss. Seeing the 3D models and realizing that they might provide the tactile/haptic input that is lost during robotic procedures [8, 9] have been shown to influence the surgical approach of as much as 30–50% of surgeons, according to other research [10]. The majority of urological studies (over 55.8%) identified surgical planning as a primary outcome of the investigation [11], with kidney disease surgery becoming the top priority of most of the investigations and prostate cancer treatments being the secondary focus. With the increasing use of enhanced, thin-slice axial imaging in the diagnosis of suspected renal cell carcinoma, and the challenge of the technique due to complex renal hilar anatomy, uncertainty in tumor invasion depth, as well as the uncertainty of renal ischemic damage, however, 3D printing is a good transition for the preoperative planning of a nephron-sparing surgery. The study reviews not just publications from the field of robotic surgery but also a laparoscopic publication with noteworthy methodology, outcomes, or conclusions. Face validity (as measured by evaluations of realism) and content validity (as measured by ratings of instructional efficiency) were both established for 3D-printed renal tumor models used in preoperative planning for tumor excision by Zhang *et al.*, 2016. (on a scale of 1–10). Simulations were accorded high grades for their accuracy in showing the size of an excised tumor, its value in surgical planning and training, and its overall efficiency [12]. However, Zhang *et al.* were unable to clarify how 3D-printed models can be used in surgical planning or to address any particular questions that may have emerged. Wake *et al.*

[7] investigated these concerns and showed how the use of 3D models might influence preoperative planning decisions, including the type of nephrectomy to be performed, the surgical approach taken, whether or not clamping will be performed, and whether or not the collecting system would be repaired. The MRIs were analyzed independently by three seasoned urologists, and then the MRIs and 3D-printed models of 10 patients with complicated kidney carcinoma were compared (nephelometry score of 6–10). During each session, the participants filled out a questionnaire and evaluated their surgical strategy with and without the 3D model. The strategy included (1) whether to perform a partial or radical nephrectomy, (2) whether to use an open or robotic approach, (3) whether to perform a transperitoneal or retroperitoneal approach, and (4) whether to use clamping. Decisions about whether to use a transperitoneal or retroperitoneal approach, as well as hilar clamping, were the most frequently altered in the pre-operative planning stage (30–50%). While the authors acknowledged that it was technically possible to create 3D models from MRI data, they also noted that doing so was both time-consuming (with an average of 7 h for image post-processing and 10 h for printing) and expensive (at around $1,000 for each case of kidney tumor). After that, they filled out a questionnaire that includes subjective questions about the 3D-printed models' correctness and utility. Both surgical planning (scoring 7–9/10) and anatomical correctness (scoring 10/10) were successful. The urologists, including the actual surgeons and the assistants, were quite pleased with the printed models [10–12]. Shin *et al.* [13] observed that combining MRI with 3D models should help localize tumors identified with multi-parametric MRI and their linkages to neurovascular bundles and the prostate capsule [13]. With the method, the surgeon was able to make fine-tuned adjustments to the operation and a nerve-sparing technique without sacrificing their oncological efficacy. To execute and plan nerve-sparing prostatectomies, it is necessary to use 3D-printed models to understand the spatial relationships of the NVB, as stated by Chandak *et al.* [14]. The physicians observed that interfacing with 3D-printed models during the robotic treatment brought back the haptic feedback that is typically lost in robotic surgery. As a consequence, the surgeon was able to spare more nerve tissue or remove more of the NVBs around the detectable tumors, improving both the results and the satisfaction of the patients. The role of 3D printing in preoperative planning for renal transplantation has not been thoroughly researched [15].

13.3.2 Surgical Training

Conventional 3D printing technologies cannot generate the high-resolution model with tissue-like characteristics needed for hands-on surgical simulations and postoperative case rehearsal. It is due to the unavailability of printing polymers with the necessary characteristics to accurately simulate human tissue. As an added complication, it is difficult to form polymers already accessible into the printing material that can be easily altered to replicate the qualities of human tissue. Polymer casting was used in conjunction with 3D printing to produce models made of silicone, wax, and/or hydrogels, allowing them to circumvent these restrictions [16]. These materials can mimic the mechanical properties of biological tissues. Although much of the published work employing a production approach has focused on laparoscopic surgery, it is starting to change [17, 18]. The computer model and patient had similar mean resection time (6:58 vs. 8:22 min, $P = 0.162$) and tumor volume (38.88 vs. 38.50 vs. 41.79 mm^3, $P = 0.98$). The authors contend to show the study's significance in evaluating whether RAPN is possible within a reasonable overall ischemia period and whether the procedure should be performed at all. Ghazi *et al.* created a unique kidney model that includes five lesions to simulate the vascular repercussions in von Hippel–Lindau (VHL) syndrome patients. To determine if a RAPN is possible in an ischemia setting, these models were put through their paces in mock surgeries [19]. The model's predictive power and capacity to enable repeated simulations with the kidney perfused to explore various tactics for resecting the tumors (including resecting two of the smaller tumors off clamp before causing warm ischemia) and contributed to the surgery's success, according to the investigators. The platform went above and beyond von Rundstedt's easily manufactured, life-like silicone models by modeling not only the kidney's texture, structure, and perfusion but also the perinephric fat, colon, and muscles as well as blood arteries to simulate bleeding after tumor excision. The seven models were made out of a surgically resectable resin (agarose gel solution), which was used to generate sponge-like renal parenchyma, tumor, vascular structures, collecting system components, and the proximal ureter, all having their unique texture and coloration such that they may be easily distinguished [20]. To prepare for RAPN, a simulation was run on the da Vinci system.

13.4 Surgical Training Using 3D Generic Technique Models

The production of simulation-based teaching models is a pressing use of 3D printing in the field of surgical education. With ACGME work hour constraints, the high cost of operating room time, and a greater focus on patient safety, it is crucial that inexperienced surgeons, especially trainees, receive training outside of the operating room [21]. Learners can perfect their psychomotor, technical, and judgmental abilities in a risk-free environment with the use of simulators [22]. Newcomers to the field of urology might benefit from the versatility offered by 3D printing by practicing on both typical models used for assessment and on unusual problems and anatomical variants that they might not encounter otherwise [23]. The technical skills required for laparoscopic and endoscopic procedures can be learned with the help of 3D-printed models [24, 25]. While there is currently just a small body of research demonstrating the benefits of 3D models for training in urological robotic procedures, it is quickly changing. The effectiveness of a 3D-printed hybrid simulation model for robotic-assisted kidney transplantation was reported by Uwechue *et al.* [26], which featured a 3D-printed moulage in contrast to vessels retrieved from deceased donors. The artificial pelvic system consisted of a 3D-printed model of a human pelvis, a kidney without blood vessels, and a platform to keep the kidney in the correct position during surgery. Vascular anastomoses were done by two robotic surgeons utilizing 6.0 prolene sutures to connect the cadaveric iliac arteries to the 3D-printed renal vessels. The average time spent performing an anastomosis on a vessel was 20 min. Intravascular saline injection with a hypodermic needle was used to assess vascular anastomotic patency. The simulations showed that the anastomoses were highly patent and leak-resistant. The model's goal was to provide a time-based and reproducible framework for improving vascular anastomosis training for surgeons, hence facilitating more a objective evaluation of their abilities. The next phase in the development of minimally invasive surgery (MIS) was called robot-assisted minimally invasive surgery (RAMIS). It was the next step because it provided an enhanced vision system, more accurate and intuitive instrument control, and an ergonomic master console. The da Vinci Surgical System, manufactured by Intuitive Surgical Inc. in Sunnyvale, California, is a teleoperated, master–slave-type surgical robot. It has proven to be the most successful RAMIS system to date. Around the year 1971, the National Aeronautics and Space Administration (NASA) came up with the fundamental idea for a remote-controlled telesurgical system. The system was supposed to be used for distant surgeries, with the slave robot located on the spaceship, but the proposal was scrapped. In the instance of the da Vinci Surgical System, the surgeon can perform surgery while seated at an ergonomic master console. From the position, he has access to master arms that can be intuitively operated. The surgeon can use pedals to handle unique surgical devices, such as a clutch as well as the endoscopic arm. As a result, the surgeon is the only person who can operate the camera during the procedure. A motion mechanism known as the "remote center of motion" (RCM), which can guarantee patient safety, is located at the patient side of the da Vinci system. The motion mechanism allows the remotely controlled slave arms, which are located at the patient side of the da Vinci system, to perform minimally invasive interventions. The assistant crew operates at the patient side of the da Vinci system, where they are in a position to assist the operating surgeon and provide support for the intervention—for example, the assistant crew can change the surgical instruments while the procedure is being performed. The images captured by the 3D endoscopic camera located on the slave side are transmitted to the screens located in the master console. As a result, the surgeon can observe a 3D representation of the surgical site. On the patient side of the da Vinci system, the motion of the surgeon can be re-scaled, which can give more accurate motion. However, the concept of remote surgery was first conceived to do operations at great distances; however, for the time being, an aspect of the procedure is not included in clinical practice. The da Vinci Surgical System does not do any kind of automation or decision-making, nor does it provide decision support. The only extremely low-level automation that is present in the da Vinci system is tremor and sudden motion filtering. It is crucial to emphasize it, as it goes against the label "robot". Researchers have discovered that the da Vinci system has a very steep learning curve [5, 6]. Consequently, even though RAMIS can lessen the mental workload of the surgeon, as demonstrated by studies, RAMIS is still a difficult operation to perform, not only physically but also mentally due to the constant conditions of communication, teamwork, leadership, decision-making, and workload. Figure 13.2 gives an overview on how 3D printing is used in surgical education for robotic urology operations.

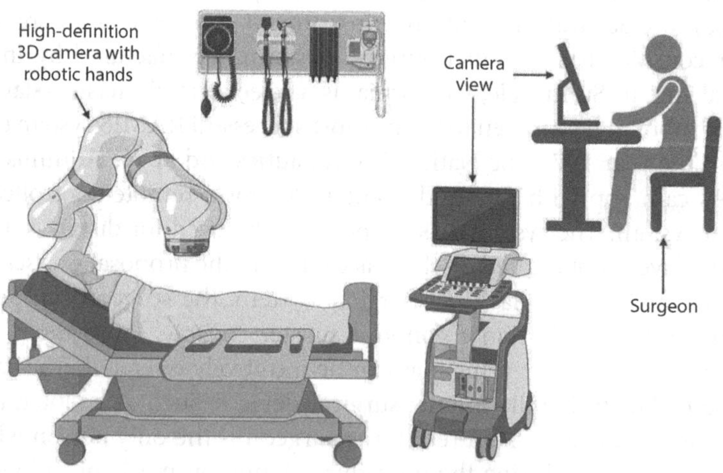

Figure 13.2 3D-printed models are used to teach surgeons about robotic urology.

13.5 Patient Education and Counseling

Patients should be given sufficient time to ask questions and get answers before any operations are performed. It is important from both a practical and an ethical standpoint as it is expected that doctors will engage in good faith shared decision-making with their patients. Pictorial pictures, diagrams, and 2D imaging, which are used in the current surgical counseling/planning technique, are poor in portraying patient-specific subtleties, posing a conceptual problem [27]. When both the patient and the surgeon can examine an exact 3D replica of the patient's organs, they gain a more complete picture of the patient's condition and can make more educated decisions about the treatment plan, including the procedure's goals, potential benefits and risks, and alternative approaches. Positive effects of using 3D models for patient education have been found in both qualitative and quantitative assessments. Virtually rendered 3D-printed models were put to the test by Porpiglia *et al.* before live robot-assisted prostatectomy for prostate cancer and nephron-sparing procedures [28]. To test the reliability and validity of the survey's face and content, administrators used a custom-made questionnaire with free-form questions and a Likert scale with 10 possible responses. When asked how they felt about the surgeon's use of the technique, 18 out of 18 patients gave positive responses (average score of 9.0). The patients and their families with complicated renal malignancies planned for RAPN verbally reported a better comprehension of size, location, and surgical intervention after viewing their 3D-printed renal models [28]. A further study by the same group showed that patients who were shown 3D-printed representations of their kidneys and pathologies before RAPN had a greater grasp of the material and were more satisfied with the procedure [29]. Standardized survey scores showed that patients who were taught about the kidney's physiology and anatomy utilizing MRI and CT scans had a deeper comprehension of these topics than those who had been taught using CT images alone. The patients' knowledge of kidney anatomy, physiology, tumor features, and surgical process all increased by at least 16 percentage points after viewing their 3D kidney model and, in some cases, by as much as 44 percentage points. The patients were more pleased with their surgical experience, in general, once they had insight into their condition and the rationale behind the procedure [30]. Finally, Zhang *et al.* stated that the patients gave their models an average grade of 9.0 on a scale from 0 to 10, where 0 is not useful and 10 is outstanding. The study noted that it can help patients who know little about their disease because of their low health literacy levels [31]. A person's health decision-making skills are greatly enhanced when they have access to and an understanding of the health resources they require. It has been demonstrated that health literacy is a key component of healthcare quality and that patients with higher health literacy levels have better outcomes. It is expected that 3D-printed models could benefit patients in better understanding their medical issues, contributing to more informed treatment decisions and informed consent.

13.6 Conclusion

Patients, medical students, and even seasoned surgeons are finding 3D modeling to be a fresh, fascinating, and useful tool. Its specialized uses in urology have been extensively researched in the previous 5 years, and the results have been encouraging. Its greatest utility as a teaching tool is in helping surgical residents and fellows hone their skills in a risk-free setting. Because of its usefulness in pre-operative planning, robotic partial nephrectomies and radical prostatectomies have benefited greatly. The procedure is improved, precious operating time is saved, and the surgeon's confidence is boosted. Last but not least, it has been warmly welcomed by patients and educators alike as a modality that may greatly enhance their understanding of anatomy, the intricacies of surgical diseases, and the techniques on offer. The current research suffers from the same problems that plague other innovative applications, namely, a lack of level-one evidence and inadequate sample sizes with limited follow-up. The shortage of technological standardization (covering file formats, software, and accessibility), as well as the absence of control groups, and the diverse variety of cost estimates make it hard to evaluate previous research. Notwithstanding these caveats, the device has gained widespread acceptance, with some surgeons experiencing an intangible cognitive benefit. To accurately assess the practical advantages of technology and to measure its added value, randomized prospective studies are necessary. Several obstacles are preventing the technique from becoming commonplace in urological surgery, but answers are being developed all the time. The price tag is a major consideration, and it is affected by factors including the type of materials and method used, the accessibility of design programs, and the availability of a 3D printer. Additional problems include the lack of regulatory policies and problems with biocompatibility with 3D-printing materials. The ramifications of 3D printing in healthcare are currently being discussed in consultation with some regulatory agencies. Using 3D printing to solve problems in urology is a promising field. It could be the next big thing in surgical training, education, and simulation. 3D-printing files/databases may, one day, replace traditional 2D images in medical textbooks. Augmented reality and telesurgery/telementoring have made it possible to acquire remote guidance from an experienced surgeon and examine live images on wearable screens. Research suggests operating in a paradigm-shifting period, in which the possibilities for innovation in robotic education by employing 3D-printing technology appear to be limitless.

References

1. Martelli, N., Serrano, C., van den Brink, H., Pineau, J., Prognon, P., Borget, I., El Batti, S., Advantages and disadvantages of 3-dimensional printing in surgery: A systematic review. *Surgery*, 159, 6, 1485–500, 2016 Jun 1.
2. Auricchio, F. and Marconi, S., 3D printing: Clinical applications in orthopaedics and traumatology. *EFORT Open Rev.*, 1, 5, 121, 2016 May.
3. Parikh, N. and Sharma, P., Three-dimensional printing in urology: History, current applications, and future directions. *Urology*, 121, 3–10, 2018 Nov 1.
4. Malik, H.H., Darwood, A.R., Shaunak, S., Kulatilake, P., Abdulrahman, A., Mulki, O., Baskaradas, A., Three-dimensional printing in surgery: A review of current surgical applications. *J. Surg. Res.*, 199, 2, 512–22, 2015 Dec 1.
5. Silberstein, J.L., Maddox, M.M., Dorsey, P., Feibus, A., Thomas, R., Lee, B.R., Physical models of renal malignancies using standard cross-sectional imaging and 3-dimensional printers: A pilot study. *Urology*, 84, 2, 268–73, 2014 Aug 1.
6. Silberstein, J.L., Maddox, M.M., Dorsey, P., Feibus, A., Thomas, R., Lee, B.R., Physical models of renal malignancies using standard cross-sectional imaging and 3-dimensional printers: A pilot study. *Urology*, 84, 2, 268–73, 2014 Aug 1.
7. Wake, N., Rude, T., Kang, S.K., Stifelman, M.D., Borin, J.F., Sodickson, D.K., Huang, W.C., Chandarana, H., 3D printed renal cancer models derived from MRI data: Application in pre-surgical planning. *Abdom. Radiol.*, 42, 1501–9, 2017 May.
8. Chandak, P., Byrne, N., Lynch, H., Allen, C., Rottenberg, G., Chandra, A., Raison, N., Ahmed, H.U., Kasivisvanathan, V., Elhage, O., Dasgupta, P., 3D printing in robotic assisted radical prostatectomy-an IDEAL Phase 2a study. *BJU Int.*, 122, 360–361, 2018 Mar 6.
9. Westerman, M.E., Matsumoto, J.M., Morris, J.M., Leibovich, B.C., Three-dimensional printing for renal cancer and surgical planning. *Eur. Urol. Focus*, 2, 6, 574–6, 2016 Dec 15.
10. Porpiglia, F., Bertolo, R., Checcucci, E., Amparore, D., Autorino, R., Dasgupta, P., Wiklund, P., Tewari, A., Liatsikos, E., Fiori, C., ESUT Research Group, Development and validation of 3D printed virtual models for robot-assisted

radical prostatectomy and partial nephrectomy: Urologists' and patients' perception. *World J. Urol.*, 36, 201–7, 2018 Feb.

11. Cacciamani, G.E., Okhunov, Z., Meneses, A.D., Rodriguez-Socarras, M.E., Rivas, J.G., Porpiglia, F., Liatsikos, E., Veneziano, D., Impact of three-dimensional printing in urology: State of the art and future perspectives. A systematic review by ESUT-YAUWP Group. *Eur. Urol.*, 76, 2, 209–21, 2019 Aug 1.
12. Zhang, Y., Ge, H.W., Li, N.C., Yu, C.F., Guo, H.F., Jin, S.H., Liu, J.S., Na, Y.Q., Evaluation of three-dimensional printing for laparoscopic partial nephrectomy of renal tumors: A preliminary report. *World J. Urol.*, 34, 533–7, 2016 Apr.
13. Shin, T., Ukimura, O., Gill, I.S., Three-dimensional printed model of prostate anatomy and targeted biopsy-proven index tumor to facilitate nerve-sparing prostatectomy. *Eur. Urol.*, 69, 2, 377, 2016 Feb.
14. Chandak, P., Byrne, N., Lynch, H., Allen, C., Rottenberg, G., Chandra, A., Raison, N., Ahmed, H.U., Kasivisvanathan, V., Elhage, O., Dasgupta, P., 3D printing in robotic assisted radical prostatectomy-an IDEAL Phase 2a study. *BJU Int.*, 360–361, 2018 Mar 6.
15. Hameed, A.M., Yao, J., Allen, R.D., Hawthorne, W.J., Pleass, H.C., Lau, H., The evolution of kidney transplantation surgery into the robotic era and its prospects for obese recipients. *Transplantation*, 102, 10, 1650–65, 2018 Oct 1.
16. Smektala, T., Gołab, A., Królikowski, M., Słojewski, M., Low cost silicone renal replicas for surgical training. Technical note. *Arch. Esp. Urol.*, 69, 7, 434–6, 2016.
17. Kusaka, M., Sugimoto, M., Fukami, N., Sasaki, H., Takenaka, M., Anraku, T., Ito, T., Kenmochi, T., Shiroki, R., Hoshinaga, K., Initial experience with a tailor-made simulation and navigation program using a 3-D printer model of kidney transplantation surgery. *Transplant. Proc.*, 47, 3, 596–599, 2015 Apr 1. Elsevier.
18. Golab, A., Smektala, T., Kaczmarek, K., Stamirowski, R., Hrab, M., Slojewski, M., Laparoscopic partial nephrectomy supported by training involving personalized silicone replica poured in three-dimensional printed casting mold. *J. Laparoendosc. Adv. Surg. Tech.*, 27, 4, 420–2, 2017 Apr 1.
19. Ghazi, A.E. and Teplitz, B.A., Role of 3D printing in surgical education for robotic urology procedures. *Transl. Androl. Urol.*, 9, 2, 931, 2020 Apr.
20. Maddox, M.M., Feibus, A., Liu, J., Wang, J., Thomas, R., Silberstein, J.L., 3D-printed soft-tissue physical models of renal malignancies for individualized surgical simulation: A feasibility study. *J. Robot. Surg.*, 12, 27–33, 2018 Mar.
21. Reznick, R.K. and MacRae, H., Teaching surgical skills—Changes in the wind. *N. Engl. J. Med.*, 355, 25, 2664–9, 2006 Dec 21.
22. Badash, I., Burtt, K., Solorzano, C.A., Carey, J.N., Innovations in surgery simulation: A review of past, current and future techniques. *Ann. Transl. Med.*, 4, 23, 1–10, 2016 Dec.

23. Cacciamani, G.E., Okhunov, Z., Meneses, A.D., Rodriguez-Socarras, M.E., Rivas, J.G., Porpiglia, F., Liatsikos, E., Veneziano, D., Impact of three-dimensional printing in urology: State of the art and future perspectives. A systematic review by ESUT-YAUWP Group. *Eur. Urol.*, 76, 2, 209–21, 2019 Aug 1.
24. Parikh, N. and Sharma, P., Three-dimensional printing in urology: History, current applications, and future directions. *Urology*, 121, 3–10, 2018 Nov 1.
25. Malik, H.H., Darwood, A.R., Shaunak, S., Kulatilake, P., Abdulrahman, A., Mulki, O., Baskaradas, A., Three-dimensional printing in surgery: A review of current surgical applications. *J. Surg. Res.*, 199, 2, 512–22, 2015 Dec 1.
26. Uwechue, R., Gogalniceanu, P., Kessaris, N., Byrne, N., Chandak, P., Olsburgh, J., Ahmed, K., Mamode, N., Loukopoulos, I., A novel 3D-printed hybrid simulation model for robotic-assisted kidney transplantation (RAKT). *J. Rob. Surg.*, 12, 541–4, 2018 Sep.
27. Ghazi, A., Stone, J., Candela, B., Richards, M., Joseph, J., Simulated inanimate model for physical learning experience (simple) for robotic partial nephrectomy using a 3d printed kidney model. *J. Urol.*, 193, 4, e778, 2015 Apr 1.
28. Porpiglia, F., Bertolo, R., Checcucci, E., Amparore, D., Autorino, R., Dasgupta, P., Wiklund, P., Tewari, A., Liatsikos, E., Fiori, C., ESUT Research Group, Development and validation of 3D printed virtual models for robot-assisted radical prostatectomy and partial nephrectomy: Urologists' and patients' perception. *World J. Urol.*, 36, 201–7, 2018 Feb.
29. Silberstein, J.L., Maddox, M.M., Dorsey, P., Feibus, A., Thomas, R., Lee, B.R., Physical models of renal malignancies using standard cross-sectional imaging and 3-dimensional printers: A pilot study. *Urology*, 84, 2, 268–73, 2014 Aug 1.
30. Knoedler, M., Feibus, A.H., Lange, A., Maddox, M.M., Ledet, E., Thomas, R., Silberstein, J.L., Individualized physical 3-dimensional kidney tumor models constructed from 3-dimensional printers result in improved trainee anatomic understanding. *Urology*, 85, 6, 1257–62, 2015 Jun 1.
31. Zhang, Y., Ge, H.W., Li, N.C., Yu, C.F., Guo, H.F., Jin, S.H., Liu, J.S., Na, Y.Q., Evaluation of three-dimensional printing for laparoscopic partial nephrectomy of renal tumors: A preliminary report. *World J. Urol.*, 34, 533–7, 2016 Apr.

14

3D Printing in Ophthalmology

Abstract

Over three decades have passed since the introduction of 3D printing. Nonetheless, its use in healthcare is becoming increasingly widespread, particularly in recent years, to address problems associated with drug delivery and clinical practice. The low-cost method employs biocompatible materials to create model implants for the study of human anatomy and illness, with applications ranging from organ transplants and surgical planning to the production of cutting-edge drug delivery systems. More individualized care is possible with the help of 3D-printed medical implants and gadgets. Recent developments in 3D bioprinting have opened up innovative therapeutic avenues in ophthalmology that can be utilized to treat individuals suffering from a variety of eye disorders. The goal of this chapter is to introduce readers to the benefits and potential uses of 3D printing in the treatment of various corneal, retinal, lid, and orbital disorders.

Keywords: 3D printing, cornea, laser beam machining, ophthalmology, eye illness, corneal disease, AM technology

14.1 Introduction

Adding material in successive layers yields the final result in additive manufacturing (AM), also known as three-dimensional (3D) printing. Recent developments in 3D printing have made it possible to explore new technologies, materials, and applications [1–5]. The medical field is one of the most prominent examples of the diverse uses for 3D printing [6, 7]. Medical instruments, pharmaceuticals, diagnostics, orthopedics, medication delivery, cardiology, dentistry, pandemic preparedness, general surgery, spinal surgery, maxillofacial surgery, neurosurgery, and cardiac surgery are only a few of the procedures mentioned in the literature as using 3D printing. Ophthalmology and eyecare have long benefitted from 3D printing; however, with the development of high-resolution pico- to micrometer-scale 3D printers, the innovation has taken on new significance. The most typical

Rishabha Malviya and Rishav Sharma. 3D Printing in Healthcare: Novel Applications, (263–278)

applications are in the ophthalmic industry, including the production of implantable prostheses and surgical tools for the eye and surrounding tissues. Moreover, it can be employed for pre-operative surgical planning, simulations, training, and teaching [8, 9]. The ability to tailor treatments to individual patients is a key benefit of AM [10]. The benefit is mirrored in the procedure for making a 3D-printed medical gadget. The process commences with a CT or MRI scan of the patient's intended organ to acquire images of the organ in question. Finally, the 3D model is 3D-printer-ready after being optimized for printing [11]. Important printing parameters include those that might affect cell survival, materials, API, and printability, such as printing speed, nozzle size, material, and temperature [12]. The quality and biocompatibility of printed goods can be improved with careful consideration of all printing parameters. Hence, AM is favored in the production of ophthalmic, dental, and orthopedic devices due to its ability to create individualized treatment plans. Treatment options for many eye problems may soon look very different from the possible applications of 3DP. The significant shortage of donor corneas can be alleviated by the development of 3D cornea [13]. Due to its ability to tailor a design to each patient's specifications, AM technology can also deliver a more satisfactory anatomical match. Subtractive manufacturing techniques including high-speed multi-axis computer numerical control (CNC) machining and laser beam machining (LBM) have been widely used in the production of ocular implants in the past [14]. Typically, they cause the patient's anatomy and mechanical qualities to become rigid. With AM technology, it is possible to make a product with the ideal combination of physical properties that customers have been requesting [15]. In addition, we may tailor the printing methods to the needs of both doctors and patients by selecting biocompatible materials. 3D-printed implants have several advantages over those made using more conventional methods of production. The self-expanding capacity of a 3DP tracheobronchial stent, for instance, can aid patients with a collapsed bronchus in taking deep, cleansing breaths [16]. Patients with fetal craniofacial malformations can also benefit from the AM technology's precision in reconstructing their missing facial structures [17]. As a replacement for traditional medical treatment, 3DP's effective drug delivery technology has potential in the field of ophthalmology. Because of AM's adaptability and personalization, it is possible to make glaucoma and cataract implants from a patient's particular biomaterials. Patients who experience complications following ophthalmic surgeries or negative reactions to medications may benefit from 3DP in the future, even though there are still many obstacles to overcome in terms of selecting biocompatible materials and ensuring their printability using various 3DP

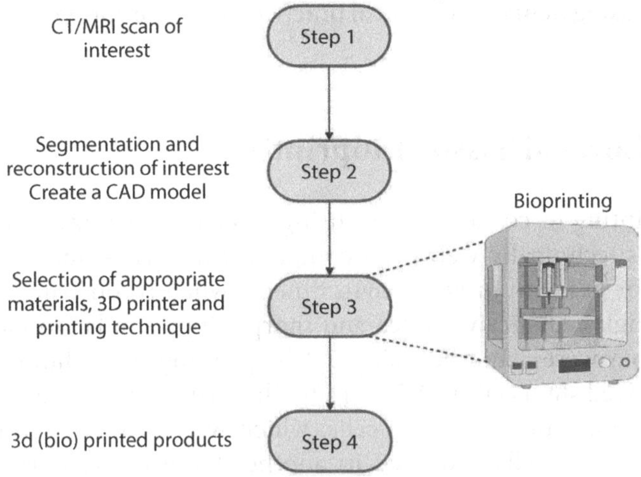

Figure 14.1 Procedure for 3D printing and bioprinting.

techniques. This chapter explores how cutting-edge AM technology has been implemented in several subspecialties of ophthalmology and offers a glimpse of the benefits that 3DP can bring. The authors hope that the survey of 3DP in eye care would serve as a springboard for anyone interested in using AM technology for their pursuits. The ability to tailor treatments to individual patients is a key benefit of additive manufacturing. The benefit is mirrored in the procedure for making a 3D-printed medical gadget. First, a CT or MRI scan is performed to obtain images of the organ of interest within the patient's body. After capturing these photos, a computer-aided design (CAD) program is used to segment the desired tissue and create a 3D model (Figure 14.1).

14.2 External Eye Illness and Corneal Disease

The cornea, the clear outermost layer of the eye, transmits and bends light. Millions of people throughout the world are affected by corneal blindness caused by bacterial infections. Self-renewing epithelial stem cells can be seen in the corneal limbus [18]. Patients with extensive damage to their limbal tissues typically require a corneal transplant to restore their naturally regenerating epithelium. When the limbus is injured, the corneal stroma is often affected as well, and conventional transplantation can help with that, too. Nevertheless, there is a lack of corneal donors, and the transplanted corneas cannot self-renew indefinitely. As a result, there is an ever-increasing demand in clinical practice for a superior option to corneal donors.

14.3 Corneal Tissue Bioprinting

3D bioprinting of corneal tissues using biomaterials mixed with human proteins is technically viable. Biocompatible materials must be carefully selected for usage in *in vitro* environments when reconstructing corneal tissues. High cell survival rates and morphology similar to natural corneal stroma were achieved using 3D bioprinting using human adipose tissue-derived stem cells (hASCs) [19]. The structure and biological functions of limbal epithelial stem cells, which were produced from human embryonic stem cells and used in another bioprinting, were similar to those of the corneal epithelium. The interaction of hASC-containing 3DP stroma with a porcine cornea showed preliminary immunogenicity to integrate into host tissue. Laser-assisted bioprinting (LaBP) can produce significant medical devices that match practically any stem cell. Therefore, the biological and functional properties of these stem cells are preserved in the LaBP prints. It is required that the artificial corneas mimic the exact curvature and collagen lamellar architecture of the natural cornea. The curved corneal surface was manufactured by Li *et al.* [20] using a plastic contact lens mold, into which corneal epithelial cells were inserted *in vitro*. In 2018, Isaacson *et al.* used pneumatic 3D extrusion bioprinting to create 3D bioprinted corneas [21]. The 3D models were made with the use of topographic data collected from the corneas of adult humans. In the research, the scientists examined the effects of combining collagen and alginate, two bio-inks with a relatively low viscosity. Models printed with collagen-1 bio-ink that also included alginate proved to be mechanically more sound. The viability of incorporated corneal keratocytes was found to be high after printing, and it stayed at that level for 7 days after cell integration. Hence, the preservation of highly viable keratocytes suggests that collagen and alginate bio-ink composites can be employed to make 3D corneas. As was previously established, the cornea relies on the precise arrangement of collagen fibrils to create the clear layer necessary for refraction and vision. The transparency of the cornea is affected by the collagen lattice structure of the stroma [22]. Despite the use of cutting-edge methods like magnets and electrospinning, the replicated corneas still have poor transparency. Three-dimensional printing can be utilized to make shear-induced fibers. Collagen fibers are unique from collagen fibrils and can modify corneal keratocytes [22–24]; therefore, thin collagen fibrils generated from decellularized corneal tissues are favorable. Using atelocollagen fibrils in place of collagen fibers, Kim *et al.* looked into the implications of controlled shear stress [25]. Researchers found that collagen fibrils and cell behaviors responded differently to varying shear loads. Changing the bio-ink's viscosity, the flow velocity, and the nozzle's internal diameter is an effective way to generate shear stress. In addition, biological processes like apoptosis might be impacted by shear stress during the printing procedure. Shear stress was generated in differentiated keratocytes using a nozzle of three different sizes. After 28 days, different cellular morphologies manifested themselves in the printed samples. The results showed that keratocyte expression was highest in the 25G and 30G shear pressure groups. Some corneal injury was also seen in the 30G group. The 25G group had samples cultivated *in vitro* and *in vivo* for a total of 28 days. Cells in the 25G group were more aligned, the keratocytes were more active, and more type-I collagen was released. Because 3DP allows for the application of shear stress, collagen fibrils can be oriented to closely resemble those of a human cornea in its natural state [21]. For correcting vision, contact lenses were first developed in the 1800s. It was a major step forward in contact lens technology when hydrogel soft lenses were available. Manufacturers of contact lenses have spent a lot of time looking for biocompatible materials that are oxygen permeable and have strong mechanical qualities and have driven much of the development of the lenses themselves. There are a lot of procedures in the production of contact lenses, and the design options are limited. Three-dimensional printing (3DP) can be used to make a wide variety of contact lenses, including "smart" lenses that can diagnose and treat eye disorders. In most cases, the digital light printing (DLP) method is chosen over the fused deposition modeling (FDM) method for light-curing-based polymerization 3DP due to DLP's superior printing resolution [22]. Asiga DentaClear Resin is extensively used in the dental industry and may be printed using DLP to generate corrective contact lenses. "Smart" contact lenses can be made by utilizing DLP 3D-printed contact lenses, toward which nanopatterns have already been incorporated using direct laser interference patterning (DLIP). With the help of these high-tech lenses, doctors can track their patients' eye health over time. A thin polyvinyl chloride (PVC) plastic film on 3DP contact lenses allows for light transmission of roughly 90%; however, it would be fascinating to compare the mechanical, physical, and chemical features of these innovative lenses to those of conventional contact lenses [23]. As an added benefit, AM allows for the creation of contact lenses that are specifically designed for each patient's eye structure and medical history.

14.4 Drug Delivery

The conjunctiva is an area of the eye where a medication patch printed with a hydrogel-based formulation can aid in the efficient release of the medicine without causing any vision impairment or uncomfortable blinking. Lyophilized ocular patches that may generate new dosages and be adjusted for individual patients were proposed by Tagami *et al.* [24]. The antibiotic levofloxacin was packaged in the transdermal patches. The hydrogel-based bio-ink used to print the 3DP drug-releasing patch included the medication alongside hydroxypropyl methylcellulose (HPMC), mannitol, and xylitol. A freeze-drying procedure was used in the making of the formulation. HPMC, mannitol, and xylitol at various concentrations were also evaluated and compared. A patch's printability may be affected by the bio-ink's viscosity, which was, in turn, determined by the biomaterials' composition. These lyophilized ocular patches were also evaluated on a range of physical features, including their ability to absorb water, their antibacterial efficacy, and their rate of drug release. The bio-ink's thickness was significantly influenced by the ratio of mannitol to xylitol in the formulation. Because xylitol, like sorbitol, is extremely soluble in water, products based on it can absorb liquids quickly. Moreover, in *in vitro* assays, the combination of these patches and levofloxacin was able to effectively combat the presence of germs. Notably, the patches can be loaded with a wide variety of pharmacologically active substances and adjusted to release individualized amounts for distinct patients. These eye patches are capable of delivering a comprehensive variety of medications, including eye drops for patients receiving cataract surgery and mini-tablets for the therapy of the inferior conjunctival fornix. To create an ocular patch unique to each patient, it is possible to leverage the drug release patch's materials' chemical and physical properties. When used following glaucoma or cataract surgery, the biocompatible drug-releasing patch can help reduce the frequency with which patients need eye drops.

14.5 Glaucoma

The number of persons with glaucoma is expected to rise to 112 million by 2040 from the 76 million it presently affects [25]. Glaucoma is an eye condition that is characterized by optic nerve damage resulting from elevated intraocular pressure; it is cured by reducing the intraocular pressure (IOP) with medications, lasers, or surgeries [26]. Reducing IOP by slowing or speeding up the outflow of aqueous humor from the eye is one strategy for slowing or stopping the progression of glaucoma.

14.6 Drug-Eluting Implants

Anti-glaucoma eye solutions, used to treat the disease by lowering the intraocular pressure, are commonly used in treatment. For glaucoma patients who have trouble taking their anti-glaucoma pills regularly, drug-eluting implants provide a new option for treatment. It is encouraging to know that glaucoma can be treated using ocular implants that incorporate effective drug delivery systems. The drug-eluting implants must be safe and well-tolerated by patients. Conventional medication implants now available have drawbacks, such as a short time for drug release and a high concentration of active medicinal ingredients. Drugs administered by these implantable devices can have systemic effects since they go via the bloodstream to every part of the body, yet 3DP is highly adaptable and can be used to create highly individualized eyewear [27]. Mohamdeen *et al.* established a contact lens infusion method for the beta-blocker timolol maleate that permitted the sustained release of the medicine for 7 days [28]. Such implantable contact lenses are fabricated using hot-melt extrusion and fusion deposition modeling. The combination of ethylene vinyl acetate, poly(lactic acid), and timolol maleate with a weight-to-weight ratio of 84:15:1 (wt-to-wt) was shown to be extremely stable and exhibited superior thermal stability. Moreover, the scientists highlighted the best printing characteristics, including low print speed and small nozzle diameter, to obtain excellent resolution and a smooth surface [28]. The drug-eluting implant shows promise, but its slow diffusion of the polymer mixture limits its potential to sustainably release the drug.

14.7 Minimally Invasive Glaucoma Surgery Devices

Projection micro-stereolithography (PuSL) is another 3DP technique that has been utilized to create glaucoma treatment devices. PuSL combines the advantages of DLP and SLA technologies. The drainage of aqueous humor from the eyes of glaucoma patients has been significantly improved by the growth in the number of minimally invasive glaucoma surgery (MIGS) gadgets in the last decade. iStent, Hydrus, and XEN are just a few of the technologies currently available on the market; these all remove aqueous humor, albeit in their unique ways [28]. The patients' health requirements determine whether minimally invasive implants are better suited to them. Regrettably, fibrotic encapsulation undermines the efficacy of all of these treatments in the short run. The need for precision during surgery poses additional difficulties for minimally invasive technologies. With the help of AM, surgeons can create a custom device that enhances the quality of their operations. The 3D-printing technology provides a wide range of options for making complex surgical devices. It takes only a few minutes to put together and only a few seconds to use a 3D-printed cable to guide a steerable tool for minimally invasive surgery [29]. Ergonomic handgrip, responsive steering controls, and maximum efficiency when grasping tissues are all made possible by the design. Because of the design of the tool, surgeons may perform their work with greater ease and less restriction on their wrists. AM's solutions are adaptable to the needs of individual patients and surgeons through the adjustment of the gripper handle. In addition, 3D-printed devices for minimally invasive surgery can be adapted simply to different specialties. The clinical management of IOP in glaucoma requires vigilant monitoring of aqueous humor drainage from the eye. The anterior chamber can be modeled in 3D, allowing doctors to evaluate the drainage mechanism of aqueous humor and gain insight into the unique physiology of each patient with glaucoma. The outflow of aqueous humor can be modeled with the use of a 3D-printed anterior chamber [30]. Verification of the apparatus reveals the outflow velocity, pressure, and dispersion. It can also aid doctors in determining the best course of treatment for glaucoma patients by shedding light on how their IOP fluctuates over time.

14.7.1 Retina

The retina is a multilayered, sophisticated tissue that detects and transduces light information as electrical impulses to the brain. Rods and cones are two types of photoreceptors that perform phototransduction. A monolayer named retinal pigment epithelium (RPE) protects the retina from the choroid. The RPE is crucial to photoreceptor health because of the growth hormones it supplies and the nutrients it helps transport and phagocytose [31–33]. Diseases like AMD and retinitis pigmentosa are caused by damage to the retina, which can happen at any age (RP). Deterioration of the RPE is the underlying cause of many disorders. Thus, the diseased eye can be treated with retinal regeneration methods. To achieve normal function, it is essential to preserve the retina's cellular and layer organization. Scaffold techniques were first used, but they did not work as well as the human retina. The complexity of the retina, which is essential to its function, can be generated in 3DP. Patients can have devices made just for them using 3DP technology. The patients' eye geometries can be collected with CT technology and then utilized in a 3D CAD model. The features of the medical appliance designed specifically for the patient can be extracted from the 3D model. Pappas *et al.* [34] have shown that CT scans and 3DP may be used to create a bespoke macular buckle for a patient with extreme myopia. Biocompatible materials are used in the creation of the macular buckle, which is customized to each patient's eye. The macular buckle's novel design will facilitate its implantation by ocular surgeons and eliminate the need for additional manipulations before, during, and after the procedure. In addition, 3DP has been used effectively in the creation of RPE and retinal photoreceptors (Y79). To simulate Bruch's membrane, human retinal pigment epithelium (ARPE-19) cells were printed onto a very thin membrane. There is a small layer of connective tissue called Bruch's membrane between both the retina and the choroid, and RPE cells attach to the membrane. The growth of ARPE-19 cells was followed by the creation of a stable monolayer. Thus, the ARPE-19 cells sown on the ultrathin membrane stood in for Bruch's membrane and the RPE. Onto the monolayer, we printed photoreceptor (Y79) bio-ink. Cell viability was not affected by placing the printed retinas in the culture. The bio-ink was shown to be porous using scanning electron microscopy (SEM), creating an ideal setting for the development of new photoreceptors. In addition, Masaeli *et al.* described the inkjet bioprinting of a functional model of the retina [33]. The researchers started by creating a Bruch's membrane out of a thin layer of gelatin methacryloyl (GelMA), which they then used to model the retina's microenvironment. Thereafter, Bruch's membrane was printed using RPE cells. They showed that the proteins produced by the RPE cells were structurally comparable to those found in the RPE layer of the eye *in vivo*. In addition, pig eye photoreceptors were deposited onto the RPE monolayer after being separated and differentiated, thus recreating the structure of the retina's various cell layers. Bioprinting was successful in producing properly positioned photoreceptors 3 days later. Clinical applications of functioning retinal bioprinted structures were first demonstrated by Masaeli *et al.* [33], who demonstrated for the first time that printed RPE and photoreceptors generated important transcription factors. Figure 14.2 provides an overview of the eye's anatomy as well as the corresponding 3D-printed therapies.

14.7.2 Lids and Orbit

The bones around the orbit can shatter or buckle owing to blunt force trauma, and that is what causes orbital fractures. The restoration of the

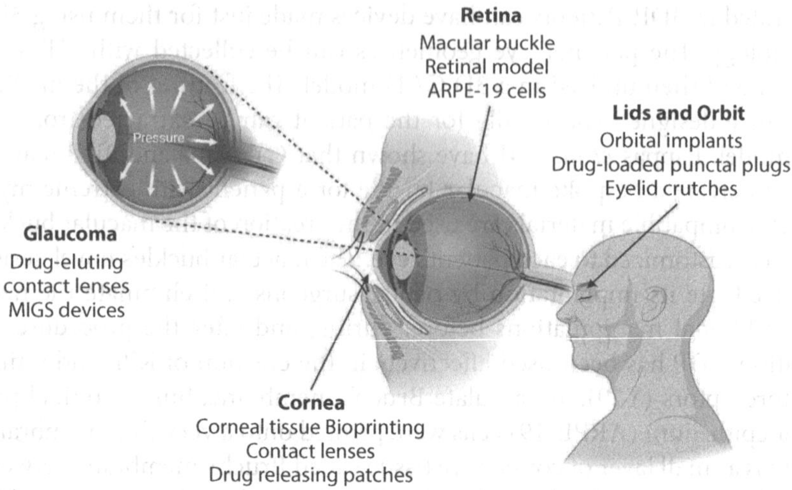

Figure 14.2 Anatomy of the eye and the associated 3D-printed therapies.

orbital wall is difficult, even with modern surgical procedures, because the improper placement of implants can cause enophthalmos and other vision impairments. To this day, craniofacial surgeons are challenged by the complex 3D concavo-convex shape of the orbit. Patients also have varying orbital diameters and shapes. For a successful orbital wall reconstruction, it is essential to accurately restore the intraorbital volume because even a small change in orbital volume might cause enophthalmos (the posterior relocation of the eye). To make titanium-Medpor mesh implants for surgical usage, researchers manipulated CT images and used simulated RP models. A total of 104 participants all had orbital fractures caused by a blowout on one side. The implants were designed using a mirrored image of the uninjured side, which was projected onto the damaged side using the RP model made before surgery. CT scans were collected after the implants were placed in the orbital wall successfully. No statistically significant difference was seen between the pre- and post-operative orbital volumes of intact and damaged patients. In addition, no cases of enophthalmos or any other problems were reported among patients. Hence, advanced digital methods such as rapid prototyping modeling can help find ways around the obstacles encountered when trying to recreate the orbital wall. The implants can be shaped to the precise specifications of each patient using the RP models, which allows for more efficient and less time-consuming surgical procedures [34].

14.8 Regulatory Considerations

Despite the promising future of 3DP applications in medicine, the legal rules of 3DP technology for pharmaceutical products are not yet finalized. The 3DP medicine Spritam was approved by the FDA in 2015; however, the agency did not publish application advice for 3DP until 2017 [35]. The Food and Drug Administration has not released any official guidelines for 3D printing [36]. It is a stumbling block on the path to the widespread use of 3D-printed medical devices and a bottleneck in the process of taking 3DP items from the lab to the clinic. Thus, it is impossible to specify liability for litigation over the security concerns of 3DP devices. However, regulatory agencies have just recently begun developing plans and assigning teams to start producing standard norms for 3DP [37]. Several national regulatory authorities have started considering how to regulate the unique medical uses of 3D printing in 2019, following in the footsteps of the Food and Drug Administration. These include the European Medicines Agency (EMA), the Medicines and Healthcare Products Regulatory Agency (MHRA), Health Canada, and the Therapeutic Goods Administration (TGA, Australia) [38]. The topic of providing comprehensive regulatory guidance to guarantee the safety and efficacy of 3D-printed medical equipment is still up for debate in 2022.

14.9 Expert Opinion and Future Directions

New treatments for many ocular illnesses have been inspired by the development of 3DP and its application in the healthcare sector. We have been able to use human stem cells in cornea stromal reconstruction. The 3DP cornea with the patient's stem cells can prevent the immunological rejection that commonly happens after corneal transplantation [39]. The viability of 3D printing implants depends on the materials and pigments used. A bio-ink made of alginate and collagen, for instance, was doable and produced functional 3D-printed corneas [39, 40]. Adjusting the bio-ink's physical qualities, such as its viscosity, influenced printability by inducing shear stress similar to that experienced by the natural human cornea [41]. Research into the potential of 3D bioprinting extends beyond corneal transplantation into the realm of retinal regeneration. In most complex human tissues, the retina can be recreated with 3D bioprinting. By employing inkjet printing, retinal cells from rats could be 3D-printed without harming their ability to divide and multiply [42]. Moreover, the glial cells' influence on neurite outgrowth in retinal ganglion cells was maintained. It demonstrates the viability of 3D bioprinting as a tool for regenerating human retinal tissue. More studies are needed to determine the vascular structure necessary for the full regeneration of retinal tissues. There are a variety of 3DP methods that can be used to successfully create ocular devices, each with its unique set of benefits. To print nanopatterns on contact lenses, for instance, DLP is the method of choice. Patients' eye health can be monitored with the help of an electronic photodetector using the 3DP method [43, 44]. Patients having drug-release implants will benefit from these 3DP contact lenses with photosensors because they will be able to monitor the local effects of the released drugs. These 3D-printable drug delivery implants are used by people with glaucoma and cataract, and they can be modified to fit each person's preferences. Changing the bio-ink's chemical composition allowed for variable dosing in hydrogel-based lyophilized eye patches containing the antibiotic [45, 46]. The adaptable 3DP has applications in the development of drug-eluting systems for the management of glaucoma. Nonetheless, drug implants are necessary to keep the drug release rate consistent and to ensure that the medication diffuses uniformly to the target area [47–49]. During eye excision procedures like enucleation and evisceration, artificial eyes or ocular prosthesis are required [50]. Time is a factor in the conventional production of artificial eyes. In contrast, 3D printing lets us quickly produce a mold of prosthetic eyes that are tailored to each patient based on their eyes' unique structure [51, 52]. While the fact that 3DP only allows us to manufacture plain eyeballs with few cosmetic ornaments at the moment, they have the potential to have attached photodetectors to produce artificial eyes that are functional [53].

14.10 Conclusions

3D-printing technology has allowed us to create customized medical supplies that were previously impossible to make. Dentistry and orthopedics are only two examples of how 3D printing's versatility and adaptability can improve treatment outcomes. The promising results of 3DP in ophthalmology stimulate medical professionals to continue developing cutting-edge care and gaining the patients' respect. It is undeniable that 3DP has the potential to give new solutions for a wide range of eye problems, but further research and development are required. The introduction of 3D bioprinting as a new technology in medicine represents a paradigm shift. The development of bio-inks for 3D printing holds promise for alleviating the scarcity of corneal donors and fostering more effective tissue regeneration.

Also, AM production can be made uniquely for each customer, which is credited to the ever-developing 3DP processes designed for ophthalmic devices and medication delivery systems. Given the difficulties inherent in 3D-printing biomedical components, the technology's potential applications in healthcare should be explored further. Although the current legislation for 3D printing in medicine is still being finalized, when it has been established, on-demand, patient-specific 3D-printed pharmaceutical treatments will be capable of contributing to the fulfillment of both pressing clinical needs and patient preferences.

References

1. Nadagouda, M.N., Rastogi, V., Ginn, M., A review on 3D printing techniques for medical applications. *Curr. Opin. Chem. Eng.*, 28, 152–7, 2020 Jun 1.
2. Bozkurt, Y. and Karayel, E., 3D printing technology; methods, biomedical applications, future opportunities and trends. *J. Mater. Res. Technol.*, 14, 1430–50, 2021 Sep 1.
3. Kumar, R., Kumar, M., Chohan, J.S., The role of additive manufacturing for biomedical applications: A critical review. *J. Manuf. Processes*, 64, 828–50, 2021 Apr 1.
4. Jadhav, A. and Jadhav, V.S., A review on 3D printing: An additive manufacturing technology. *Mater. Today: Proc.*, 62, 2094–9, 2022 Jan 1.
5. Praveena, B.A., Lokesh, N., Buradi, A., Santhosh, N., Praveena, B.L., Vignesh, R., A comprehensive review of emerging additive manufacturing (3D printing technology): Methods, materials, applications, challenges, trends and future potential. *Mater. Today: Proc.*, 52, 1309–13, 2022 Jan 1.
6. Sheoran, A.J., Kumar, H., Arora, P.K., Moona, G., Bio-medical applications of additive manufacturing: A review. *Proc. Manuf.*, 51, 663–70, 2020 Jan 1.
7. Al-Dulimi, Z., Wallis, M., Tan, D.K., Maniruzzaman, M., Nokhodchi, A., 3D printing technology as innovative solutions for biomedical applications. *Drug Discov. Today*, 26, 2, 360–83, 2020 Nov 16.
8. Yan, Q., Dong, H., Su, J., Han, J., Song, B., Wei, Q., Shi, Y., A review of 3D printing technology for medical applications. *Engineering*, 4, 5, 729–42, 2018 Oct 1.
9. Javaid, M. and Haleem, A., Additive manufacturing applications in medical cases: A literature based review. *Alexandria J. Med.*, 54, 4, 411–22, 2018.
10. Culmone, C., Smit, G., Breedveld, P., Additive manufacturing of medical instruments: A state-of-the-art review. *Addit. Manuf.*, 27, 461–73, 2019 May 1.
11. Varghese, R., Sood, P., Salvi, S., Karsiya, J., Kumar, D., 3D printing in the pharmaceutical sector: Advances and evidences. *Sens. Int.*, 25, 100177, 2022 Apr.

12. Yang, J., Cheng, Y., Gong, X., Yi, S., Li, C.W., Jiang, L., Yi, C., An integrative review on the applications of 3D printing in the field of *in vitro* diagnostics. *Chin. Chem. Lett.*, 33, 5, 2231–42, 2022 May 1.
13. Javaid, M. and Haleem, A., Current status and challenges of additive manufacturing in orthopaedics: An overview. *J. Clin. Orthop. Trauma*, 10, 2, 380–6, 2019 Mar 1.
14. Kumar, L., Haleem, A., Javaid, M., Impact of three dimensional printing in orthopedics. *Glob. Health J.*, 5, 4, 178–82, 2021 Dec 1.
15. Reddy, R.D. and Sharma, V., Additive manufacturing in drug delivery applications: A review. *Int. J. Pharm.*, 589, 119820, 2020 Nov 15.
16. Wang, J., Zhang, Y., Aghda, N.H., Pillai, A.R., Thakkar, R., Nokhodchi, A., Maniruzzaman, M., Emerging 3D printing technologies for drug delivery devices: Current status and future perspective. *Adv. Drug Deliv. Rev.*, 174, 294–316, 2021 Jul 1.
17. Lindquist, E.M., Gosnell, J.M., Khan, S.K., Byl, J.L., Zhou, W., Jiang, J., Vettukattil, J.J., 3D printing in cardiology: A review of applications and roles for advanced cardiac imaging. *Ann. 3D Print. Med.*, 4, 100034, 2021 Dec 1.
18. Bhargav, A., Sanjairaj, V., Rosa, V., Feng, L.W., Fuh, Y.H.J., Applications of additive manufacturing in dentistry: A review. *J. Biomed. Mater. Res. Part B: Appl. Biomater.*, 106, 5, 2058–64, 2018 Jul.
19. Vakharia, V.N., Khan, S., Marathe, K., Giannis, T., Webber, L., Choi, D., Printing in a pandemic: 3D printing solutions for healthcare during COVID-19. A Protocol for a PRISMA systematic review. *Ann. 3D Print. Med.*, 2, 100015, 2021 Jun 1.
20. Li, F., Carlsson, D., Lohmann, C., Suuronen, E., Vascotto, S., Kobuch, K., Sheardown, H., Munger, R., Nakamura, M., Griffith, M., Cellular and nerve regeneration within a biosynthetic extracellular matrix for corneal transplantation. *Proc. Natl. Acad. Sci.*, 100, 26, 15346–51, 2003 Dec 23.
21. Isaacson, A., Swioklo, S., Connon, C.J., 3D bioprinting of a corneal stroma equivalent. *Exp. Eye Res.*, 173, 188–93, 2018 Aug 1.
22. Tack, P., Victor, J., Gemmel, P., Annemans, L., 3D-printing techniques in a medical setting: A systematic literature review. *Biomed. Eng. Online*, 15, 1–21, 2016 Dec.
23. Huang, W. and Zhang, X., 3D printing: Print the future of ophthalmology. *Investig. Ophthalmol. Vis. Sci.*, 55, 8, 5380–1, 2014 Aug 1.
24. Tagami, T., Goto, E., Kida, R., Hirose, K., Noda, T., Ozeki, T., Lyophilized ophthalmologic patches as novel corneal drug formulations using a semi-solid extrusion 3D printer. *Int. J. Pharm.*, 617, 121448, 2022 Apr 5.
25. Kim, H., Park, M.N., Kim, J., Jang, J., Kim, H.K., Cho, D.W., Characterization of cornea-specific bioink: High transparency, improved *in vivo* safety. *J. Tissue Eng.*, 10, 2041731418823382, 2019 Jan.
26. Tham, Y.C., Li, X., Wong, T.Y., Quigley, H.A., Aung, T., Cheng, C.Y., Global prevalence of glaucoma and projections of glaucoma burden through 2040:

A systematic review and meta-analysis. *Ophthalmology*, 121, 11, 2081–90, 2014 Nov 1.
27. Sanghani, A., Kafetzis, K.N., Sato, Y., Elboraie, S., Fajardo-Sanchez, J., Harashima, H., Tagalakis, A.D., Yu-Wai-Man, C., Novel PEGylated lipid nanoparticles have a high encapsulation efficiency and effectively deliver MRTF-B siRNA in conjunctival fibroblasts. *Pharmaceutics*, 13, 3, 382, 2021 Mar 13.
28. Mohamdeen, Y.M., Tabriz, A.G., Tighsazzadeh, M., Nandi, U., Khalaj, R., Andreadis, I., Boateng, J.S., Douroumis, D., Development of 3D printed drug-eluting contact lenses. *J. Pharm. Pharmacol.*, 74, 10, 1467–76, 2022 Oct.
29. Pillunat, L.E., Erb, C., Jünemann, A.G., Kimmich, F., Micro-invasive glaucoma surgery (MIGS): A review of surgical procedures using stents. *Clin. Ophthalmol.*, 29, 1583–600, 2017 Aug.
30. Culmone, C., Lussenburg, K., Alkemade, J., Smit, G., Sakes, A., Breedveld, P., A fully 3D-printed steerable instrument for minimally invasive surgery. *Materials*, 14, 24, 7910, 2021 Dec 20.
31. Akkara, J.D. and Kuriakose, A., The magic of three-dimensional printing in ophthalmology. *Kerala J. Ophthalmol.*, 30, 3, 209–15, 2018 Sep 1.
32. Schubert, C., Van Langeveld, M.C., Donoso, L.A., Innovations in 3D printing: A 3D overview from optics to organs. *Br. J. Ophthalmol.*, 98, 2, 159–61, 2014 Feb 1.
33. Masaeli, E., Forster, V., Picaud, S., Karamali, F., Nasr-Esfahani, M.H., Marquette, C., Tissue engineering of retina through high resolution 3-dimensional inkjet bioprinting. *Biofabrication*, 12, 2, 025006, 2020 Jan 31.
34. Pappas, G., Vidakis, N., Petousis, M., Maniadi, A., Individualized ophthalmic exoplants by means of reverse engineering and 3D printing technologies for treating high myopia complications with macular buckles. *Biomimetics*, 5, 4, 54, 2020 Oct 22.
35. Fan, D., Li, Y., Wang, X., Zhu, T., Wang, Q., Cai, H., Li, W., Tian, Y., Liu, Z., Progressive 3D printing technology and its application in medical materials. *Front. Pharmacol.*, 11, 122, 2020 Mar 20.
36. Aimar, A., Palermo, A., Innocenti, B., The role of 3D printing in medical applications: A state of the art. *J. Healthcare Eng.*, 2019, 1–10, 2019 Mar 21.
37. Derakhshanfar, S., Mbeleck, R., Xu, K., Zhang, X., Zhong, W., Xing, M., 3D bioprinting for biomedical devices and tissue engineering: A review of recent trends and advances. *Bioact. Mater.*, 3, 2, 144–56, 2018 Jun 1.
38. Ji, S. and Guvendiren, M., Recent advances in bioink design for 3D bioprinting of tissues and organs. *Front. Bioeng. Biotechnol.*, 5, 23, 2017 Apr 5.
39. Tsui, J.K., Bell, S., da Cruz, L., Dick, A.D., Sagoo, M.S., Applications of three-dimensional printing in ophthalmology. *Surv. Ophthalmol.*, 67, 4, 1287–310, 2022 Jul 1.
40. Zein, N.N., Hanouneh, I.A., Bishop, P.D., Samaan, M., Eghtesad, B., Quintini, C., Miller, C., Yerian, L., Klatte, R., Three-dimensional print of a liver for preoperative planning in living donor liver transplantation. *Liver Transplant.*, 19, 12, 1304–10, 2013 Dec.

41. Qiu, K., Haghiashtiani, G., McAlpine, M.C., 3D printed organ models for surgical applications. *Annu. Rev. Anal. Chem.*, 11, 287–306, 2018 Jun 12.
42. Goyanes, A., Det-Amornrat, U., Wang, J., Basit, A.W., Gaisford, S., 3D scanning and 3D printing as innovative technologies for fabricating personalized topical drug delivery systems. *J. Control. Release*, 234, 41–8, 2016 Jul 28.
43. Konta, A.A., García-Piña, M., Serrano, D.R., Personalised 3D printed medicines: Which techniques and polymers are more successful? *Bioengineering*, 4, 4, 79, 2017 Sep 22.
44. Whitford, W.G. and Hoying, J.B., A bioink by any other name: Terms, concepts and constructions related to 3D bioprinting. *Future Sci. OA*, 2, 3, FSO133, 1–5.
45. Hospodiuk, M., Dey, M., Sosnoski, D., Ozbolat, I.T., The bioink: A comprehensive review on bioprintable materials. *Biotechnol. Adv.*, 35, 2, 217–39, 2017 Mar 1.
46. Zhang, Y.S. and Khademhosseini, A., Advances in engineering hydrogels. *Science*, 356, 6337, eaaf3627, 2017 May 5.
47. Ashammakhi, N., Ahadian, S., Xu, C., Montazerian, H., Ko, H., Nasiri, R., Barros, N., Khademhosseini, A., Bioinks and bioprinting technologies to make heterogeneous and biomimetic tissue constructs. *Mater. Today Bio.*, 1, 100008, 2019 Jan 1.
48. Zhang, B., Xue, Q., Li, J., Ma, L., Yao, Y., Ye, H., Cui, Z., Yang, H., 3D bioprinting for artificial cornea: Challenges and perspectives. *Med. Eng. Phys.*, 71, 68–78, 2019 Sep 1.
49. Davis, R., Singh, A., Jackson, M.J., Coelho, R.T., Prakash, D., Charalambous, C.P., Ahmed, W., da Silva, L.R., Lawrence, A.A., A comprehensive review on metallic implant biomaterials and their subtractive manufacturing. *Int. J. Adv. Manuf. Technol.*, 120, 3-4, 1473–530, 2022 May.
50. Zopf, D.A., Flanagan, C.L., Wheeler, M., Hollister, S.J., Green, G.E., Treatment of severe porcine tracheomalacia with a 3-dimensionally printed, bioresorbable, external airway splint. *JAMA Otolaryngol.-Head Neck Surg.*, 140, 1, 66–71, 2014 Jan 1.
51. VanKoevering, K.K., Morrison, R.J., Prabhu, S.P., Torres, M.F., Mychaliska, G.B., Treadwell, M.C., Hollister, S.J., Green, G.E., Antenatal three-dimensional printing of aberrant facial anatomy. *Pediatrics*, 136, 5, e1382–5, 2015 Nov.
52. Sun, T.T. and Lavker, R.M., Corneal epithelial stem cells: Past, present, and future. *J. Investig. Dermatol. Symp. Proc.*, 9, 3, 202–207, 2004 Sep 1. Elsevier.
53. Sorkio, A., Koch, L., Koivusalo, L., Deiwick, A., Miettinen, S., Chichkov, B., Skottman, H., Human stem cell based corneal tissue mimicking structures using laser-assisted 3D bioprinting and functional bioinks. *Biomaterials*, 171, 57–71, 2018 Jul 1.

Index

Printed in the USA/Agawam, MA
September 16, 2026

910661.083